Kahlil Joseph and the Audiovisual Atlantic

New Approaches to Sound, Music, and Media

Series Editors: Carol Vernallis, Holly Rogers, and Lisa Perrott

Forthcoming Titles:
Musical New Media by Nicola Dibben
David Bowie and the Transformation of Music Video by Lisa Perrott
Popular Music, Race, and Media since 9/11 by Nabeel Zuberi
Musicking TikTok: A Musical Ethnography from a Glocal Austrian Context by Juan Bermúdez
Aesthetic Amalgams and Political Pursuits: Intertextuality in Music Videos edited by Tomasz Dobrogoszcz, Agata Handley, and Tomasz Fisiak

Published Titles:
Transmedia Directors by Carol Vernallis, Holly Rogers, and Lisa Perrott
Dangerous Mediations by Áine Mangaoang
Resonant Matter by Lutz Koepnick
Cybermedia: Science, Sound, and Vision edited by Carol Vernallis, Holly Rogers, Jonathan Leal, and Selmin Kara
The Rhythm Image: Music Videos in Time by Steven Shaviro
YouTube and Music: Cyberculture and Everyday Life edited by Holly Rogers, Joana Freitas, and João Francisco Porfírio
More Than Illustrated Music: Aesthetics of Hybrid Media Between Pop, Art and Video edited by Elfi Vomberg and Kathrin Dreckmann
Remediating Sound: Repeatable Culture, YouTube and Music edited by Holly Rogers, Joana Freitas, and João Francisco Porfírio
David Bowie and the Art of Music Video by Lisa Perrott
Haunted Soundtracks: Audiovisual Cultures of Memory, Landscape and Sound edited by K.J. Donnelly and Aimee Mollaghan
Traveling Music Videos edited by Tomáš Jirsa and Mathias Bonde Korsgaard
Vincenzo Bellini on Stage and Screen, 1935–2020 edited by Emilio Sala, Graziella Seminara, and Emanuele Senici
Kahlil Joseph and the Audiovisual Atlantic: Music, Modernity, Transmedia Art by Joe Jackson

Praise for *Kahlil Joseph and the Audiovisual Atlantic*

This is a book that powerfully explores the creative work of Kahlil Joseph through an audiovisual Black Atlantic lens. This allows the writing to use a significant artistic figure to both decolonize our understanding of Blackness and Black identity, and to create a rhizomic map that newly and uniquely connects and articulates the threads of Black (art) history across time, space and cultural trajectories and legacies. The intervention, to show how sound is as essential as seeing, to demonstrate how audio carries identities on the images they are wedded to, is beautifully conceived, argued and illustrated. A pleasure and privilege to read, think and feel on.
Sean Redmond, Professor of Film and Television, Deakin University, Australia, and author of Liquid Space: Science Film and Television in the Digital Age *(Bloomsbury, 2017)*

Joe Jackson has succeeded in capturing the richness of Kahlil Joseph's multifaceted creative journey by situating it within the broader context of his time. He transforms it into an epic where interests and ideals collide. Definitely a thought-provoking text.
Karine Barclais, Founder, Pavillon Afriques at Cannes Film Festival – Marché du Film

Kahlil Joseph and the Audiovisual Atlantic understands that we live in a digital era where media businesses are becoming increasingly entangled. Written in an accessible style, the book offers promising new perspectives on the global film, music video and advertising industries. A useful read for producers and practitioners as well as university audiences who want to learn more about international production today.
Jean-Frédéric Garcia, Managing Director, The Location Guide

If you want to make sense of contemporary Black cultural production, this is a must-read book. A moving, revolutionary and multi-modal reading experience at the crossroads of Black cultural studies, race, and media studies. Joe Jackson offers the very first in-depth study of award-winning filmmaker Kahlil Joseph's subversive creative work with remarkable rigour, care and radical engagement, leading to the theorization of the *audiovisual Atlantic*. Words that become sound, images and feelings, which affectively challenge the 'white racial frame' in today's understandings of modernity.
Estrella Sendra, Lecturer in Culture, Media and Creative Industries Education (Events and Festivals), King's College London, UK

Kahlil Joseph and the Audiovisual Atlantic illuminates the transmedia and bold diasporic stylings of Kahlil Joseph's audio-visual artworks in all of their perplexing, and sometimes contradictory, glory. Jackson eruditely positions Kahlil's offerings at the nexus of Africa, America and Europe and at the intersection of art and capital in a way that holds a mirror up to the digitized neoliberal era we live in today. Jackson never loses site of the humanism and cultural pluralism that underpins Kahlil Joseph's films, music videos and commercials and in so doing, manages to foreground this same humanism and pluralism in his writing, making for an incredibly insightful read.

Michael W. Thomas, Lecturer in Film and Screen Studies, SOAS, University of London, UK, and author of Popular Ethiopian Cinema: Love and other Genres *(Bloomsbury, 2022)*

Kahlil Joseph and the Audiovisual Atlantic

Music, Modernity, Transmedia Art

Joe Jackson

Foreword by
Clive Chijioke Nwonka

BLOOMSBURY ACADEMIC
NEW YORK • LONDON • OXFORD • NEW DELHI • SYDNEY

BLOOMSBURY ACADEMIC
Bloomsbury Publishing Inc
1385 Broadway, New York, NY 10018, USA
50 Bedford Square, London, WC1B 3DP, UK
29 Earlsfort Terrace, Dublin 2, Ireland

BLOOMSBURY, BLOOMSBURY ACADEMIC and the Diana logo are trademarks of Bloomsbury Publishing Plc

First published in the United States of America 2024

Copyright © Joe Jackson, 2024

For legal purposes the Acknowledgements on p. xv constitute an extension of this copyright page.

Cover image by David Uzochukwu

All rights reserved. No part of this publication may be reproduced or transmitted in any form or by any means, electronic or mechanical, including photocopying, recording, or any information storage or retrieval system, without prior permission in writing from the publishers.

Bloomsbury Publishing Inc does not have any control over, or responsibility for, any third-party websites referred to or in this book. All internet addresses given in this book were correct at the time of going to press. The author and publisher regret any inconvenience caused if addresses have changed or sites have ceased to exist, but can accept no responsibility for any such changes.

A catalog record for this book is available from the Library of Congress.

ISBN: HB: 979-8-7651-0316-6
        PB: 979-8-7651-0315-9
        ePDF: 979-8-7651-0318-0
        eBook: 979-8-7651-0317-3

Series: New Approaches to Sound, Music, and Media

Typeset by Integra Software Services Pvt. Ltd.
Printed and bound in Great Britain

To find out more about our authors and books visit www.bloomsbury.com and sign up for our newsletters.

Parts of this book – which appeared in different formats in: *Black Camera; Contemporary African Screen Worlds*; and *Music, Sound, and the Moving Image* – have kindly been republished with permissions from Indiana University Press, Duke University Press and Liverpool University Press.

because of Caspar
remembering Benji, Hristo, Malcolm and Veselin

Contents

List of figures	xi
About the author	xiv
Acknowledgements	xv
Foreword	xvi

1 Introduction 1
   1.1 Kahlil Joseph, art and knowledge 1
   1.2 Formations and transformations: a family, career and intellectual biography 6
   1.3 Seeing and hearing the Black Atlantic: audiovisual art as counterculture of modernity 19
      1.3.1 Crossroads of cultural traffic 30
      1.3.2 Crossroads of capital 32
      1.3.3 Crossroads of aesthetics 35
   1.4 Book structure and chapter overview 44

2 The early works of Kahlil Joseph 49
   2.1 Merging scenes: from Los Angeleno rebels to contemporary jazz hip-hop 49
   2.2 Where lamb killers tread: resisting the slaughter in *Belhaven Meridian* (2010) 53
   2.3 Activating A-Free-Ka: rolling through the smoke in *Cheeba* (2010) 63
   2.4 Sleepless in Hollywood: material richness and spiritual longing in Chapters One and Two of *The Model* (2010) 71

3 Webs of expression 81
   3.1 Internet music videos and new forms of representation 81
   3.2 Of soul and capital: comparing Derek Pike and Kahlil Joseph's *I Need a Dollar* projects (2010) 87
   3.3 Fragments of a fever dream: piecing together Shabazz palaces in *Black Up* (2011) 97

4	Exhibiting resilience	107
	4.1 To popularize the underground: movements towards the community arts space	107
	4.2 Dancing through death realms and dreamscapes: sculpting in time, activating African cosmology in *Until the Quiet Comes* (2012)	111
	4.3 FlyLo at the All-Black rodeo: cowboys and angels in *Wildcat* (2013)	121
	4.4 Mad city's children: remembering kid Kendrick's Compton in *m.A.A.d.* (2014)	129
5	Sights and sounds across the sea	139
	5.1 Looking for Langstons: Black waves and British connections within a transatlantic paradigm	139
	5.2 Performance in the face of bigotry: processing prejudice, negotiating the *Video Girl* (2014)'s demons	144
	5.3 Digital spirits and platform limits: between Sampha's Morden and Freetown in *Process* (2017)	152
6	The contemporary Audiovisual Atlantic	161
	6.1 Intercontinental journeys and transmedia screen arts of the digital diasporas	161
	6.2 (Mis)Remembering Harlem's sounds and spaces: experiences of *Fly Paper* (2017) at 180 The Strand	166
	6.3 Digital media disruption as new audiovisual aesthetic: disruptive news and countercultural reportage in *BLKNWS* (2018–Present)	173
7	Conclusion(s) and crosscurrents	183
	7.1 Music as the muse: Africa's role in reinventing cinema	183
	7.2 Media matters: future pathways for filmmakers and musicians of the Audiovisual Atlantic	186

Bibliography	190
Mediography	219
Index	226

Figures

Chapter One

1.1 Director Kahlil Joseph and Assistant Curator at MOCA Lanka Tattersall attend MOCA's Leadership Circle and Members' Opening of 'Carl Andre: Sculpture as Place, 1958–2010' and 'Arthur Jafa: Love Is The Message, The Message Is Death' on 1 April 2017 in Los Angeles, California. Photo by Donato Sardella/Getty Images for MOCA — 2

1.2 Onye Anyanwu, artist Kahlil Joseph, MOCA Chief Curator Helen Molesworth and curator Susan Dackerman attend the 2015 MOCA Gala presented by Louis Vuitton at The Geffen Contemporary at MOCA on 30 May 2015 in Los Angeles, California. Photo by Stefanie Keenan/WireImage for the Museum of Contemporary Art, Los Angeles (MOCA) — 7

1.3 Kahlil Joseph, Jesse Williams and Charles D. King speak during the 2020 Sundance Film Festival – Digital Aerosol and the Re-Imaginarium: A Fireside Chat With Kahlil Joseph and Jesse Williams Panel at the Ray on 26 January 2020 in Park City, Utah. Photo by Morgan Lieberman/Getty Images — 14

1.4 *Until the Quiet Comes* (2012), Kahlil Joseph and Flying Lotus © Warp Records — 23

1.5 *Hub-Tones* (2018), Jenn Nkiru and Kamasi Washington © Young Turks — 43

Chapter Two

2.1 *Belhaven Meridian* (2010), Kahlil Joseph and Shabazz Palaces © What Matters Most — 59

2.2 *La Noire De …* (1966), Ousmane Sembène © Filmi Domirev and Les Actualités Françaises — 59

2.3 *Killer of Sheep* (1978), Charles Burnett © UCLA & Third World Newsreel — 61

2.4 *Belhaven Meridian* (2010), Kahlil Joseph and Shabazz Palaces © What Matters Most — 62

2.5 *Cheeba* (2010), Kahlil Joseph and Shafiq Husayn © Plug Research — 66

2.6 *Cheeba* (2010), Kahlil Joseph and Shafiq Husayn © Plug Research — 69

2.7 *Cheeba* (2010), Kahlil Joseph and Shafiq Husayn © Plug Research 70
2.8 *The Model – Chapter One: Marcello in Limbo* (2010), Kahlil Joseph, Seu Jorge and Almaz © What Matters Most 72
2.9 *The Model – Chapter Two: Oshun and the Dream* (2010), Kahlil Joseph, Seu Jorge and Almaz © What Matters Most 75

Chapter Three

3.1 *Bohemian Rhapsody* (1975), Bruce Gowers and Queen © Hollywood Records and Virgin EMI Records 83
3.2 *Here It Goes Again* (2006), Trish Sie and OK Go © Capitol & EMI 86
3.3 *I Need a Dollar [Nevada version]* (2010), © Derek Pike and Aloe Blacc © LRG/Lifted Research Group 88
3.4 *I Need a Dollar [Harlem version]* (2010), Kahlil Joseph and Aloe Blacc © What Matters Most 89
3.5 *I Need a Dollar [Nevada version]* (2010), © Derek Pike and Aloe Blacc © LRG/Lifted Research Group 94
3.6 *Black Up* (2011), Kahlil Joseph and Shabazz Palaces © What Matters Most 99
3.7 *Black Up* (2011), Kahlil Joseph and Shabazz Palaces © What Matters Most 99

Chapter Four

4.1 *Until the Quiet Comes* (2012), Kahlil Joseph and Flying Lotus © Warp Records 112
4.2 *Until the Quiet Comes* (2012), Kahlil Joseph and Flying Lotus © Warp Records 114
4.3 *Until the Quiet Comes* (2012), Kahlil Joseph and Flying Lotus © Warp Records 118
4.4 *Wildcat* (2013), Kahlil Joseph and Flying Lotus © What Matters Most and Brainfeeder 123
4.5 *The First World Festival of Negro Arts* (1968), William Greaves © Motion Picture and Television Service of the United States Information Agency 125
4.6 *m.A.A.d* (2014), Kahlil Joseph and Kendrick Lamar © Top Dawg Entertainment, Interscope Records and Aftermath Entertainment 130

Chapter Five

5.1	*She's Gotta Have It* (1986), Spike Lee © 40 Acres and a Mule Filmworks	140
5.2	*Handsworth Songs* (1986), Black Audio Film Collective © Black Audio Film Collective (Lina Paul)	143
5.3	*Video Girl* (2014), Kahlil Joseph and FKA twigs © Pulse Films	148
5.4	*Video Girl* (2014), Kahlil Joseph and FKA twigs © Pulse Films	148
5.5	*Video Girl* (2014), Kahlil Joseph and FKA twigs © Pulse Films	148
5.6	*Video Girl* (2014), Kahlil Joseph and FKA twigs © Pulse Films	148
5.7	*Process* (2017), Kahlil Joseph and Sampha © Pulse Films	154
5.8	*Process* (2017), Kahlil Joseph and Sampha © Pulse Films	158

Chapter Six

6.1	*Crazy Classic Life* (2018), Alan Ferguson and Janelle Monae © Wondaland	162
6.2	*Kaniama Show* (2019), Baloji © Africalia	164
6.3	Photo of public screening of *BLKNWS* (2018 to Present), Nina Sim © 2021	176

Chapter Seven

7.1	*Music Is My Mistress* (2017), Kahlil Joseph © KENZO	184
7.2	Kahlil Joseph speaks during the 2020 Sundance Film Festival – Digital Aerosol and the Re-Imaginarium: A Fireside Chat with Kahlil Joseph and Jesse Williams Panel at the Ray on 26 January 2020 in Park City, Utah. Photo by Morgan Lieberman/Getty Images	186
7.3	*Belhaven Meridian* (2010), Kahlil Joseph and Shabazz Palaces © What Matters Most	189
7.4	*Belhaven Meridian* (2010), Kahlil Joseph and Shabazz Palaces © What Matters Most	189

About the author

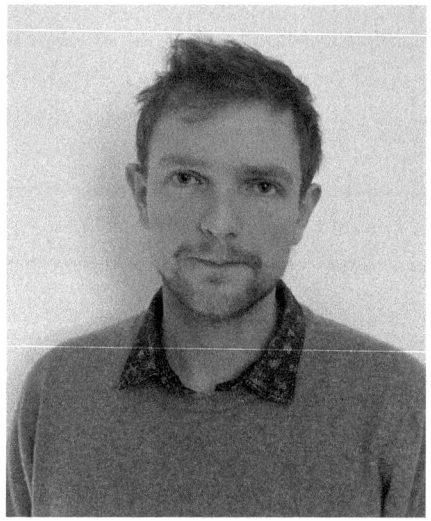

Joe Jackson is Lecturer in Communications & Media (Multimedia Production) at London College of Communication, University of the Arts London, UK. He studied at the School of Oriental and African Studies (PhD, MA) and University College London (BA). He is a member of the Screen Worlds collective, wrote about global media production as Web Editor for The Location Guide, and previously created educational resources at the Institution of Civil Engineers. This is his first book. He is a Fellow of the Higher Education Academy (FHEA). For more information about Joe's work, check out: www.josephowenjackson.com

Acknowledgements

Thank you to past and present colleagues, students, mentors and friends teaching, researching, building and creating across: London College of Communication (LCC) and the remaining art and design colleges which together constitute University of the Arts London (UAL); University College London (UCL), the School of Oriental and African Studies (SOAS) and the Bloomsbury cluster of universities; the European Research Council (ERC) and those who have contributed to the research project African Screen Worlds: Decolonising Film and Screen Studies over the years; the Institution of Civil Engineers (ICE); UoL Screen Studies Group (SSG); The Location Guide; The Blue School in Wells, Somerset; and far beyond. Most of the work on which this book is grounded was made possible by a three-year academic scholarship from SOAS Doctoral School, for which I am and always will be deeply grateful.

I must wholeheartedly thank: Holly, Carol and Lisa; Rachel and Tsitsi; Lindiwe and Caspar; Clive and Ash; Estrella, Mike, Nobunye, Añuli, Anna, Remi, Kate and Georgia; Gil, Grace, Hayden, Jake D, Jake PM, Jed, Jess, Lauren, Mark, Mikey G and Nath; Chris and the Mackintosh crew, Bracelli and Nina; Alex and Jack; the Davidsons (both sets), Mains and Saverys; the Tomlinhos; and Ilina, Issy, Ed, Mum, Dad and Wes. Without their collective patience, belief, support and encouragement, I would have not undertaken or completed this project. A big thanks to the editorial and production teams at Bloomsbury Academic for all their care and enthusiasm throughout the different stages of the publishing process.

I stand on the shoulders of so many giants: thank you to the artists and educators – and those restless souls that hover somewhere between both – who inspired this project.

Foreword

Clive Chijioke Nwonka

Associate Professor of Film, Culture and Society, University College London

In the continuously generative but complex encounter with Black visuality that remains in a protracted contestation against and through the ossified hegemony of white normativity to demand anti-Eurocentric looking practices and to express, and have acknowledged, Afrodiasporic artistic principles, there is an inherent politics of difference that guides our navigation through the intersections of Black life, visual identity, technology and capitalism. Much of the thinking behind my idea of a Black Neoliberal Aesthetic (2022), of which this book displays an interest in and which in turn finds a shared but asymmetrically evinced genealogy with this book in an indebtedness to Paul Gilroy's *The Black Atlantic* (1993), attempted to grapple with the social, cultural, political and aesthetic terms through which creative endeavours claim and possess an instinctive Black diasporic extensivity. In the work of the visual practitioner Kahlil Joseph, such an encounter, with the omnipresence of Blackness at the emotional and conceptual formation of a creative agenda that oscillates between a number of mediums and stylistic approaches, would naturally compel us to conclude that Joseph's aesthetic practice, à la the Black Atlantic, orchestrates a seamless, organic and horizontal textual, representational and spectatorial convergence between Black America, Africa, the Caribbean and Europe.

With this in mind, the book aims to situate Joseph's creative practices at the central point of an analytical nexus that attempts to draw the Black audio-visual analyses of Gilroy, Tina Campt, Stuart Hall and my own conceptual endeavours (that argue that capitalism's more hegemonic orchestration of popular Black visuality at the level of context produces a neoliberal affect at the level of text, despite their distinctive geographical epistemologies) into both a departing dialect and a corresponding synergy. However, the purpose of Jackson's intellectual engagement with the concept and his subsequent analytical investment in the application of this to the range of overlapping tensions across Joseph's audio-visual oeuvre cannot be determined in the simple, linear identification within Joseph's work of the instances in which an uncomplicated Black Neoliberal Aesthetic, applied either pejoratively as the index of the glacial accumulation of the production and products of Black culture by the economic, contextual and textual determinants of capitalism or the essentialist strategy of Black creatives in consolidating a space within the heavily contested field of cultural production in its most popular iterations as necessity within contemporary cultural hegemony as a war of position, reveals itself to undermine any claim to authenticity, realness, or the legitimate articulation and representation of local or transglobal Black identity. To accept this as such would be to neglect all that is distinctive in, and central to, the task of the multidimensional cultural analysis that has been historically undertaken in the more interrogative inflections of Black cultural studies and its dissection of the genealogies, industrial contexts and social circulation of Black visual culture, that certainly became the mandative interests of Hall, Spillers, Mercer, Gilroy, Snead and many others, and this book in many ways coalesces on the intellectual examples of these works to establish a stable analytical framework that can retain an interpretative value within the shifting meanings of audio-visual culture. Indeed, as we'll encounter in this book, as Joseph's creative outputs venture beyond the arenas afforded by digital technology and its attendant modes of distribution and into the more esoteric and socio-geographically marked exhibition spaces, there is a need to match in analytical rigour and flexibility the very hybridity and heterogeneity of not only Joseph's creative output but the relationships and points of interaction that are argued here to be a novel feature of an audio-visual oeuvre that is engaged in a generative, dynamic but tension-laden and translocational racial context.

In considering some of the thinking on the construction of Joseph's Afrodiasporic artworks offered here by Jackson, Joseph's work can be described as born from and circulating within an ecology of contesting aesthetes, of Black identification and recognition, where the bidirectional flow of its relationships across space, time, medium, identity and territory renders such a dynamic to aptly be termed as a certain cultural traffic. However, our engagement with this aesthetic conglomeration is one that should not be extracted of all interrogative and, at points, critical evaluation. This being that within Joseph's audio-visual work we encounter the very contradictions and paradoxes that display a fidelity to the equally cosmopolitan flows of neoliberalism that mark Joseph's creative practice as it osculates between the very public arena of Black popular culture and the private spaces of the exhibition rooms that his installation work occupies and becomes naturally embedded in the arcane, spectatorial and interpretative language forms of the gallery context. What comes to the foreground in our reading of what this book interprets as the collaborative nature of Joseph's audio-visual practice is what occurs and what is accrued and refracted back to us as it moves not just to the centrifugal instincts of the diffuse spectatorships of the Black Atlantic but equally to the orchestration of the capitalistic instincts of the extractive spectacularizing of racial difference that undoubtedly find a sometimes covert and sometimes conspicuous regulating position within the very fissures of the new audio-visual technologies and modes of consumption that have expanded, accentuated and expedited its permeation and consumption throughout the territories of the Black Atlantic and beyond. Equally, our interpretations of Joseph's multidimensional Black creative practice, as this book attempts, must emerge as cognizant of the intellectual and spiritual hazards of Black scholarly hagiography, where the fascination with the spectacle of racial difference in all its performativity and authenticity to be observed in the production of Black culture becomes superimposed and fixed onto an uncritical liberal aggrandizing of the textual representations of Black life, Black art forms and its both unified and at times singular circulation within any given social and critical juncture, particularly those that, in renovating Stuart Hall's instructive on the unguaranteed critical Black politics that is claimed in the essentializing of the Black subject, allow for neoliberalist market orthodoxies to fix Black identity and our attendant, disparate and convergent Afrodiasporic cultural and subcultural forms within a standardizing logic of an all-encompassing Black cultural value. As we are now coming into a more fuller understanding and appreciation of such neoliberal entanglements via the paradigms of cultural studies, Black studies, literature or their interdisciplinary meeting points, just as the cyclical junctures of race that inevitably accompany our most violent and damaging moments of anti-Blackness, the subsequent proliferation of celebratory Black works can result in our interrogation of the ethics of representation becoming overwhelmed by the sheer thrust of the dispersal of often institutionalized and compensatory notions of Black culture and cultural artefacts that, as we observed in the wake of George Floyd and the American Summer, can successfully conceal an undiminished racism within a temporary and reactive appreciation for Black audio, visual and literary excellence. With this in mind, and notwithstanding the myopia of such racial junctures, the study of Black visual culture and moving image remains as a fugitive scholarship that emerges from and is respondent to the tenors of race struggle within an academic industrial complex where the vital question of ethics, verticality, extraction, positionality, asymmetrical looking practices, power relations and racialized gazes cannot be simply theorized into insignificance via a recourse to the most unsophisticated, misinterpretative, simplified and permissible citational engagements with the readings of Black music and audio-visual culture as practised throughout the various disciplinary analyses of Gilroy's Black Atlantic, nor be assumed as immaterial in the postmodernist celebration of Black audio-visual cultures and practices as an uncomplicated site of racial and cultural conviviality, but actively worked through within the very practice of cultural criticism.

What is offered to us in *Kahlil Joseph and the Audiovisual Atlantic* is a book that is not simply concerned with the chronological tracing of Kahlil Joseph's various creative guises from film, video and music to art installation, but one that asks pertinent questions that The Black Neoliberal Aesthetic, in all its nascent theoretical provocations, opens up for further exploration. What aesthetic, economic and transcultural dialectics and cohabitations are to be found in the capaciousness of Black audio-visual cultures as it circulates across multiple Black geographies? What is it that we actually look for in the study of Black cultural production? How are its meaning and affects arrived at, and what is revealed to us when we consider the totality of its constitutive elements, which, in this book's example, are to be explored in what Jackson will argue is a body of work comprised of crossroads and Black Atlanticist meeting points that give the work the functions of an aesthetics of resistance? These questions naturally require answers that are beyond the ambit of any single intellectual endeavour, let alone one that is invested in the diverse creative outputs of a single visual practitioner. But this is also revealing of what is most generative about the ideas and readings proposed in this book. It is part of the continuum of the intellectual and non-intellectual study of Black cultural forms, Black cultural production and the corresponding investments from a multitude of positions, imperatives and meanings. That the neoliberal reconfiguration of the production, circulation and terms of Black culture is so heavily layered and multi-constituted, the parenthesis to my own conceptual exploration is that if, and if so how, are the products, artefacts and audio-visual practices of the Black creative imagination reliable and affirmative entry points into an examination, understanding and appreciation of Black life worlds? This remains defined by a contradiction and paradox that revels in the cohabitation of both the carnivalesque enthusiasm for the images of Black identity and anti-blackness in its specific but consenting curation of the most hegemonic image streams of Black identity. In this focused reading of Kahlil Joseph's creative oeuvre, Jackson offers a multi and intra disciplinary study that places his audio-visual works at the nexus of a theoretical synthesis of a number of creative optics. Indeed, what we'll find to be this book's primary interdisciplinary thesis – that we are unable to fully comprehend the heterogeneous and unstable nature of Joseph's visual outputs without the attendant understanding of the methodological possibilities, rather than the wholesale application onto a contemporary Afrodiasporic creative artefact, of Gilroy's *The Black Atlantic*, which in itself provides an intellectual framework where the very interpretative approaches to be found in this landmark text share a rhizomatic genealogy, trajectory and reach – speaks not just to the non-linearity of Joseph's practice, but to its very transience across the Black Atlantic's various points of interaction, connection and contention.

1

Introduction

1.1 Kahlil Joseph, art and knowledge

The camera focuses on Alice Smith singing. A jamming session nears its end, she holds the note for one last time: nothing else matters, for a few precious moments it feels impossible to see or hear anything else. *I Put a Spell on You* – originally written and composed by Jalacy 'Screaming Jay' Hawkins in 1957 – has been covered numerous times, perhaps most notably by musician and civil rights activist Nina Simone in 1965. Here, in a short film commissioned by the Tate Modern in London to coincide with its exhibition *Soul of a Nation: Art in the Age of Black Power*, the song is electrified with new meaning, drawing visual inspiration from Simone's politicized, proudly Afrocentric headscarves and kaftans as well as the black and white (predominantly Black) photography of Roy DeCarava, all the while playing with and reconfiguring a constellation of musical lineages from Hawkins to Smith by way of the pathbreaking High Priestess of Soul herself. These are the 'spellbinding' final moments of *Black Mary* (2017) – at once a short film, music video, installation piece and far more – that in turn exemplify the interdisciplinary, transcontinental energies underpinning the work of filmmaker Kahlil Joseph. What follows in this book is a deep exploration of the director's transmedia art, his sonic *and* visual influences and their relationship(s) to the Black Atlantic in its broadest sense, tracing movements back and forth Africa, America, Europe and the Caribbean or, in other words, the multidirectional ebbs and flows that dynamize what this book terms: the Audiovisual Atlantic.[1]

Kahlil Joseph – the professional name of Kahlil Davis – is a multi-award-winning African-American filmmaker, music video director and installation artist, as well as the recipient of a Special Jury Award at the Sundance Film Festival 2012, a John Simon

---

[1] The English word 'Africa' is loaded with diverse meanings and origins, stemming from the Berber signification for 'cave' (Geo 1903), the Phoenician word for 'dust' (Venter and Neuland 2005) and a Punic term for the indigenous population of Carthage (Cox 1988), as well as possessing the Greek meaning for 'without cold or fear' (Africanus 2010 [1550]) and the Latin signification for an area of Africa – possibly Libya – to the West of the Nile (Lewis 1879). Although I refer to 'Africa' in the continental sense, I also recognize that geographical areas, as well as discursive meanings, situated under the umbrella term 'Africa' have shifted and changed throughout history, and therefore address in detail moments of contestation surrounding the continent's physical and metaphysical identities when such tensions arise. On a similar note, while I refer to skin pigmentation when I use the lowercase 'b' for 'black' or 'blackness', I refer to metaphysical discourses which orbit around the cultures of black people when I capitalize 'Black', 'Blackness' or 'Black-Britishness'. The same applies for 'whiteness' and 'White'.

Guggenheim Memorial Foundation Fellowship in 2016, an Eye Art & Film Prize in 2020 and the Herb Alpert Award in Arts in 2021. He has collaborated across a range of media formats with musicians Alice Smith, Aloe Blacc, Beyoncé, FKA twigs, Flying Lotus, Kelsey Lu, Kendrick Lamar, Sampha, Seu Jorge and Shabazz Palaces, as well as the fashion labels KENZO and Vans, and telecommunications company 02, developing into one of – if not *the* – visual artist(s) of choice to accompany musicians (re)making Black popular music in the twenty-first century.

Joseph's audiovisual works frequently combine contemporary African-American and Black-British music with various visual references to continental African culture, citing Yoruba deities, Senegalese film masters and Bantu-Kongo cosmology while expressing the multi-layered experiences of contemporary African diasporas in a variety of contexts, settings and situations. When harnessing the transnational flows of Afrocentric musical lineages, Joseph forges a range of formal and informal relationships between the encoded messages of his audiovisual works, contemporary communication technologies through which his art is circulated (laptops, mobile phones, televisions, projections) and new spaces in which his art is consumed (living rooms, bedrooms, classrooms, parties, lectures, public discussions).

Joseph's collection of work frequently merges visual representations of transcontinental experiences with Afrodiasporic music's countercultural energies,

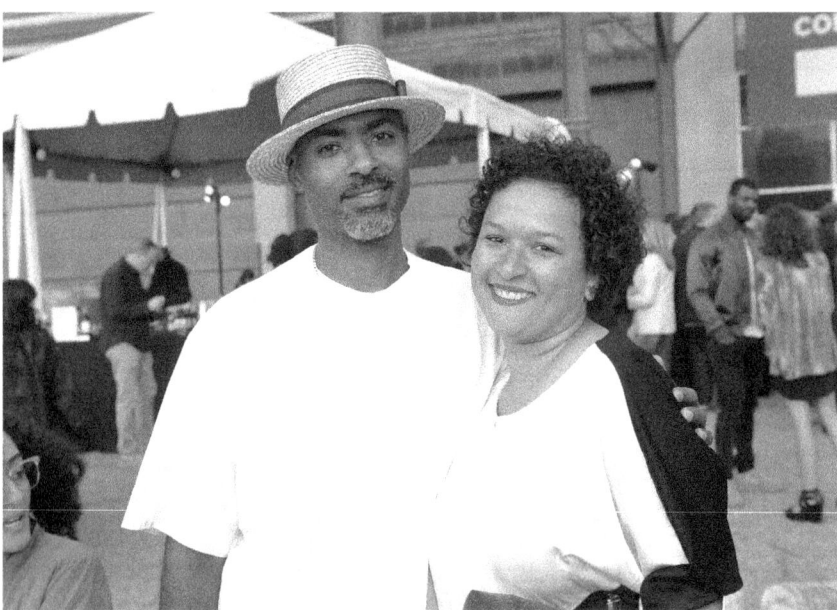

Figure 1.1 Director Kahlil Joseph and Assistant Curator at MOCA Lanka Tattersall attend MOCA's Leadership Circle and Members' Opening of 'Carl Andre: Sculpture as Place, 1958–2010' and 'Arthur Jafa: Love Is The Message, The Message Is Death' on 1 April 2017 in Los Angeles, California. Photo by Donato Sardella/Getty Images for MOCA.

thereby presenting alternative frameworks for contemporaneity that subvert the Eurocentricity and latent Whiteness underpinning modernity in the West. The situatedness of Joseph's works in 'traditional' settings for art (such as museums, galleries and cinemas) thus creates new opportunities for countercultural discourses, challenging the Eurocentric heritage of art gallery spectatorship and its relationship to Westernized distinctions between 'high' and 'low' culture. At the same time, Joseph's works create numerous paradoxes and tensions because these screen texts are products located within an economic world system of neoliberal capitalism. The content of his work often critiques this world system, at once presenting alternative ways of navigating the present moment yet also participating in – and thus sustaining – the dominant societal frameworks that it otherwise attempts to challenge.

In order to disentangle and scrutinize the tensions that arise as Joseph's works oscillate between cultural spheres on both local, regional and national levels, one must recognize that Joseph's screen texts operate as nodes within numerous theoretical networks concurrently, reflecting the present world system's complex network environment. Throughout this book, I tie together strands of Alexander Weheliye's sonic Afro-modernity (2005) and Tsitsi Ella Jaji's stereomodernism theories (2014) with the crossroads concepts from Harry J. Elam Jr and Kenneth Jackson's *Black Cultural Traffic* (2005) and Akinwumi Adesokan's *Postcolonial Artists and Global Aesthetics* (2011), forming dialogues between Weheliye and Jaji's ideas and Arthur Jafa's Black Visual Intonations (1992), Tina Campt's still-moving-images (2019), Clive Chijioke Nwonka's Black Neoliberal Aesthetic (2020) and Jenn Nkiru and Zara Julius's respective boundless/marketed time notions (2020). By generating conversations between a range of audial and visual theories that are shaped by Paul Gilroy's conceptualization of the Black Atlantic (1993), I examine the crossroads between cultural traffic, capital and aesthetics throughout Joseph's art. I scrutinize the director's work through overlaps of emergent music video and new media theories that emphasize hybridity – drawing from the perspectives of African film, music and media theorists as well as American and European voices where they are relevant – and thereby demonstrate how the transnational flows of Joseph's work bring contemporary Black Atlantic music into conversation with continental African filmmaking, arguing that such an interdisciplinary approach enriches the possibilities of their respective and, simultaneously, entwined branches of knowledge.

As Paul Gilroy's ground-breaking text *The Black Atlantic: Modernity and Double Consciousness* (1993) emphasizes, myriad forms of Afrocentric musical expression can move across geographical borders and communicate complex feelings beyond the limitations of language, capturing 'the reconciliation of art and life' if we think beyond neoliberal structures and dare to rescue music 'from its status as a mere commodity' (Gilroy 1993: 124). Throughout the book, I apply the disruptive audiocentric ideas underscoring Gilroy's *The Black Atlantic* to contemporary media forms generated by Kahlil Joseph and his peers alike, drawing from Carol Vernallis's argument that music and moving images may merge on an ontological level when sharing digital code (Vernallis in Vernallis, Rogers and Perrott 2020). My research thus seeks to challenge the latent formations of Whiteness and underlying Eurocentricity on which today's dominant theorizations of 'modernity' are grounded, offering an alternative framework for negotiating the dizzying contradictions and multidirectional, intercontinental transensory flows of our media-saturated present: namely, the Audiovisual Atlantic.

Although I am visibly identifiable as white and openly identify as British, this book draws heavily from academic theories across different continents, focuses on the flows of Joseph's art and Gilroy's ideas across Africa, America, Europe and the Caribbean, and is intrinsically shaped by my own subjective British experiences which are influenced by – yet not always directly connected to – these various parts of the world. While neat 'race-symmetrical' and 'race-matched' relationships between researchers and research topics can, in many situations, 'make productive contributions to research practices' by generating rich, meaningful conversations based on one's own lived experiences (Vass 2017: 137–8), Nicola Rollock observes that blindly adopting such an approach at all times, in all circumstances, risks compartmentalizing the complexities of human experience by moving towards the controversial direction of 'narrow, essentialist interpretation[s] or race' (Rollock 2013: 499). She argues that, in certain situations, we might glean far more valuable forms of knowledge by focusing 'on the political awareness of the researcher and their proactive engagement with notion[s] of whiteness and blackness' (ibid. 506), reminding white researchers who do choose to carry out race research that they bear 'a particular responsibility to critically reflect upon and demonstrate awareness of … the dynamics of race and their responses to it' (ibid.). Throughout this book, I have thus attempted to consider deeply questions relating to 'my own racial, ethnic, cultural and social position' both within and far beyond the narrow confinements of academia, striving to be 'explicitly cognisant of where and how knowledge is constructed' within educational environments while, at the same time, remembering 'the nature and importance of representation' outside such scholarly contexts (Ramdeo 2023).

In this sense – as will be discussed in further detail in the **Seeing and Hearing the Black Atlantic: Audiovisual Art as Counterculture of Modernity (1.3.1)** section – I have found the work of Obioma Nnaemeka particularly helpful when trying to navigate carefully my personal 'complicities and engagements … of and with whiteness' during various stages of writing and researching (Mirzoeff 2023: vii). Nnaemeka's conceptualization of 'nego-feminism' as an Afrocentric philosophy 'structured by cultural imperatives and modulated by ever-shifting local and global exigencies' offers ways to challenge the 'reification of a construct or framework' (Nnaemeka 2004: 378) such as 'the cultural unconscious of whiteness' and the ways that this all-consuming framework privileges 'white reality' over the experiences of others (Mirzoeff 2023: 4). While Stuart Hall reminds us of the dangers of ignoring and downplaying 'the difficult problems that arise from trying to live with difference' (Hall 1993a: 363), Nnaemeka argues that research perspectives underpinned by 'negotiation' and 'no ego' (Nnaemeka 2004: 360) allow us to better process 'the multiple perspectives *and challenges* rooted in heterogeneity' (my emphasis) (ibid. 378). In turn, a 'nego-feminist' approach has helped me develop and sustain a 'critically reflexive practice' when writing this book 'crucial to making the process of whiteness visible' where it might otherwise parade unseen and underexplored somewhere in the background (Rollock 2013: 507).

Since 'warding off or refusing to live with difference' does not subvert hegemonic discourses but in fact represents 'a retreat from modernity' and its accompanying complications deep into the dangerous realms of cultural ignorance (Hall 1993a: 375), it is useful to consider how a certain 'fruitfulness' that underpins 'encounters with difference' is made possible through 'creative interactions and collaborations' that connect different parts of the world together (Jaji 2018). In an attempt to counteract some of the hegemonized power structures that are imbedded within our higher education system – while, simultaneously, drawing inspiration from the dynamic, multi-layered spirits of creativity and negotiation that are exemplified by the likes of Joseph and Nnaemeka – I have tried to weave together and articulate my ideas in such a way that mirrors the winding, frequently uneven currents of the Atlantic Ocean. By crafting an accessible, free-flowing style of communication (influenced by interactions between different parts of the world yet liberated from the constraints of certain scholarly conventions) *Kahlil Joseph and the Audiovisual Atlantic: Music, Modernity, Transmedia Art* seeks to explore the manner in which the aesthetic styles of contemporary academic writing – across the humanities and far beyond – might echo and actively perform some of the interdisciplinary flows and transcontinental movements generated by the artfulness and sophistication underpinning their subject matter, thereby opening up scholarly explorations to new audiences within and beyond the academy and, in turn, offering alternative ways of disrupting today's institutionalized, predominantly hierarchized structures of knowledge production.

Beyond this book, after all, my research agendas tend to focus on the uneven and imbalanced ways in which arts and academia overlap and interact. I was first drawn to Kahlil Joseph's work via YouTube, seeking new music online and discovering his videos. When I started to engage with these screen texts more deeply, learning about their various cultural flows across numerous parts of the planet and consequently scrutinizing my own relationships to Whiteness and modernity in further depth, I then turned to academic literature for assistance. By processing Joseph's audiovisual work through Gilroy's transatlantic yet predominantly audiocentric paradigm, this book thus attempts to examine the moments where – beneath the intense flows of our volatile and complex mediasphere – one may extract certain hidden values from media products which extend beyond the marketplace, those precious yet delicate moments that point to something that surpasses the formulaic logic of the neoliberal world order, meriting civic worth on a more humanistic level. These hidden values – commonly cultural, emotional and personal – are abundant in Joseph's works, constantly reminding our communities black, white and beyond that the logic of the marketplace should serve humanity rather than vice versa. At the same time, however, such values are volatile, precarious and oftentimes contradictory, their fragility capturing the uneven relationships that manifest when human consumers and unfeeling processes of commodification collide.

In a manner akin to his media works' sophisticated hybridizations of film, music video and advertisement components, the (trans)formations that nuance Joseph's filmmaking career – as well as the fluctuations that (re-)shape his public persona as an interdisciplinary *and* cross-cultural audiovisual artist – are complex processes characterized by perpetual states of change, development and dynamism. *Kahlil Joseph and the Audiovisual Atlantic*, then, focuses on the ways in which the director's construction of his filmmaking persona works *in tandem* with his artworks to challenge fixed, monocentric or stable notions of identity and, in turn, resist universalizing understandings of human experience which might otherwise underpin constructions of modernity. In the next section, I offer a family, career and intellectual biography of Kahlil Joseph, outlining the formative moments that shape his artistic development while, at the same time, highlighting the contradictions that characterize Joseph's directorial persona as well as his filmic output.

1.2 Formations and transformations: a family, career and intellectual biography

Joseph was born in Seattle in 1981, and his immediate family members are mother Dr Faith Childs-Davis, father Keven Joseph Davis (7 October 1958 – 23 December 2011) and younger brother Noah Davis (3 June 1983 – 29 August 2015). Over three decades Dr Childs-Davis has held a variety of positions within the arts and education spheres, including Editor at Essence Magazine and Producer of the BRAVO Awards for Los Angeles County. Following completion of her Doctor of Education in Educational Leadership at the University of California, Los Angeles in 2013, she launched the Los Angeles office of the non-profit foundation Exploring the Arts and acted as its inaugural Director. However, before embarking on her wide-ranging career in cultural education and community leadership, she met Joseph's father Keven at Los Angeles's Loyola Marymount University. Keven Joseph Davis – the man to whom Kahlil Davis owes his professional filmmaking alias – earned a law degree from the University of California, Berkeley after graduating from Loyola Marymount, and eventually became a prominent sports and entertainment attorney. He represented tennis players Venus and Serena Williams – when they were seven and eight years old, roughly the same age as his sons – and would continue to do so throughout the sportswomen's respective careers.

When Venus Williams signed a contract with English-American footwear and clothing company Reebok on 21 December 2000, the five-year $40 million deal was the largest endorsement signed by any female athlete. Keven Joseph Davis had negotiated the contract, his close relationship with the Williams sisters and their father Richard Dove Williams Jr playing a key role in helping the sporting pair transition from their semi-professional statuses to the intensely competitive, and often hostile, environment of international sports stardom and its immense wealth (Krishnan 2012; Rhoden 2012). While Joseph recalls how he and Noah were 'excited for [our] dad being this small-town lawyer from Seattle doing this thing for these girls who were turning out to be supericonic' (Joseph, in conversation with Solway 2019), their father would continue to represent a range of high-profile clients as the brothers grew up, including musicians Wynton Marsalis, Ludacris, Sir Mix-A-Lot and P-Diddy. Although Keven

Joseph Davis may have been a 'small-town lawyer' during the early stages of his legal career, the boys experienced a comfortable, prosperous upbringing in Seattle, their supportive and hardworking parents fostering 'close-knit' ties with their sons (London 2020: 257).

In many ways the trajectory of Joseph's young adult life mirrors pathways taken by his parents and brother. Noah attended but did not graduate from New York City's Cooper Union School of Art, moving to Los Angeles before his studies were completed to work in the Museum of Contemporary Art's bookstore, trying to develop a name for himself as a painter (Alley-Barnes and Danzker 2016; Molesworth 2020). Joseph joined downtown Los Angeles's Loyola Marymount University – the institution where his parents met – to take classes in photography, art history and television. He aspired to become an artist yet – in the same vein as his older sibling – never graduated from university. Instead, Joseph immersed himself within the professional sphere of media production while peers completed their studies, developing relationships with a range of established filmmakers before he started to direct videos on his own. Initially, Joseph covered his expenses working as an assistant for a post-production house in Los Angeles. He then held an internship at the studio of installation artist Doug Aitken.

Aitken primarily studied magazine illustration at Pasadena's Art Centre College of Design in 1987 before moving into Fine Arts and graduating in 1991 (Spears 2011). His work encompasses a broad range of artistic practices – from photography,

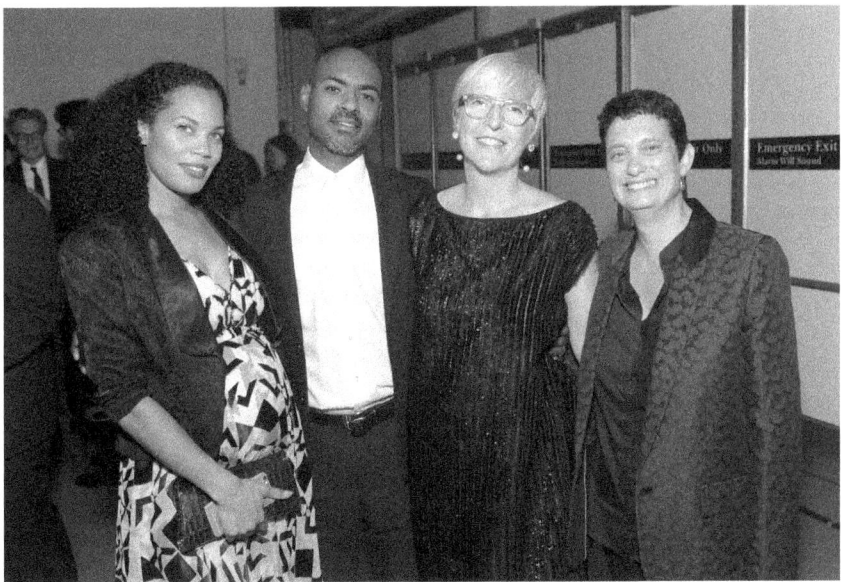

Figure 1.2 Onye Anyanwu, artist Kahlil Joseph, MOCA Chief Curator Helen Molesworth and curator Susan Dackerman attend the 2015 MOCA Gala presented by Louis Vuitton at The Geffen Contemporary at MOCA on 30 May 2015 in Los Angeles, California. Photo by Stefanie Keenan/WireImage for the Museum of Contemporary Art, Los Angeles (MOCA).

architecture and print media to single and multi-channel videos and live performances – and the interdisciplinary elements of his screen-based installations and their ambient soundscapes are traceable in Joseph's audiovisual combinations of music, moving images, dance and improvised performance. While Aitken has created music videos for Interpol and Fat Boy Slim, he frequently positions famous musicians at the heart of his own filmic and installation works in a manner akin to Joseph, working with Outkast's André 3000 in multiscreen sound-film experiment *Interiors* (2002) as well as the indie music bands Lichen and No Age for films *Migration* (2008) and *Black Mirror* (2011), respectively. Seu Jorge, who collaborated with Joseph for the two-part advertisement-cum-short film *The Model* (2010), partnered with Aitken alongside singer-songwriter Cat Power, busker Ryan Donowho and actors Donald Sutherland and Tilda Swinton to produce a large-scale projection piece screened on the outside walls of New York's Museum of Modern Art (Smith 2007; Michel 2007). The project, titled *Sleepwalkers* (2007), was filmed across the city's five boroughs with each cast member playing an urban worker negotiating the city at night, and the disruptive qualities of Aitken's transformation of the museum's imposing exterior walls into a public cinema screen echo Joseph's blurring of high and low art formats as his installation works are transformed into two-dimensional videos and disseminated online for widespread accessibility on Youtube and Vimeo.

After interning at Aitken's studio, Joseph joined the Directors Bureau – a commercial and music video production company where he spent the next five years of his career. As well as working within the vicinity of internationally acclaimed directors Sofia Coppola (whose brother Roman co-founded the Directors Bureau) and Wes Anderson, Joseph assisted photographer Melodie McDaniel. Her proclivity for 'integrating herself into subcultures' through resistance to rigidly choreographed photography shoots in favour of improvisation and street casting is partly mirrored by Joseph's own media works (Peltier 2020). From the respective groups of black cowboys featured in *Wildcat* (2013) and *m.A.A.d.* (2014) to the inclusion of non-specialist acting extras from the city of Freetown in *Process* (2017), Joseph frequently attempts to capture a variety of cultures from diverse and distinguishable contexts in ways that eschew formulaic representations or antagonistic clichés associated with his subjects.

However, the filmmaker's direct references to gun violence in *Until the Quiet Comes* (2012) – and, to a lesser extent, his indirect allusions to similar crimes in *Belhaven Meridian* (2010) – contradict McDaniel's approach to photography, her attempts to counteract the problematic visualizations which stereotype black people from different parts of the world. While one can trace in other dimensions of his oeuvre the influence of McDaniel's framing of Afrodiasporic experiences in a countercultural fashion, the contradictions of Joseph's artwork exemplify the paradoxes and complications of artistic expression under the conditions of neoliberal capitalism, the ways in which audiovisual art can at once subvert *and* support the Western biases that underpin the modern world order.

As well as assisting McDaniel, Joseph interned for the multiple award-winning filmmaker Terrence Malick during his time at the Directors Bureau. Since 1973 Malick has directed ten films, receiving the Golden Bear at the 49th Berlin International Film

Festival, the Palme d'Or at the 64th Cannes Film Festival and three Academy Award nominations. Malick studied at three higher education institutions in total: he learned about filmmaking alongside David Lynch and Paul Schrader in the inaugural class of the American Film Institute Conservatory, a private not-for-profit graduate film school in Los Angeles's Hollywood Hills, where he graduated in 1969 with a Master of Fine Arts qualification; he was a member of Harvard University's Phi Beta Kappa Society and in 1965 graduated summa cum laude with a bachelor's degree in Philosophy, and he began a doctorate as a Rhodes Scholar at Oxford University's Magdalen College but left prematurely, following a disagreement with supervisor Gilbert Ryle over his proposed research on Martin Heidegger, Søren Kierkegaard and Ludwig Wittgenstein. Although Malick taught phenomenology at MIT for a period and even produced an authoritative translation of Heidegger's *Vom Wesen des Grundes* [*The Essence of Reasons*] (1969), ultimately he abandoned a career in academia in favour of filmmaking (Sinnerbrink 2019).

Malick's films frequently present 'a conversation or debate between what he suggests is the dominant Western worldview and a competing perspective,' following a Heideggerian school of thought 'in identifying the Western worldview with the Enlightenment drive to systemize and conquer nature' and, in turn, challenging the West's 'default' position whereby art is both generated and consumed with heightened intensity and purpose (Baskin 2010). In doing so, the director's rejection of practices which are otherwise commonplace in mainstream cinemas throughout the world is on occasion criticized for being pretentious, overtly theoretical and void of entertainment (Collin 2017) or, in some cases, unable to strike a balance between formal experimentation and self-indulgence (Brody 2019). At the same time, Malick's rejection of Hollywood filmmaking conventions has inspired comparisons with the contemplative cinemas of Andrei Tarkovsky and Yasujirō Ozu, the stillness and deliberation of his camera signifying an attempt to capture aspects of nature as they 'simply are ... not moulded to a human purpose' (Critchley 2005: 147).

By applying Heidegger's critique of Western modes of thinking to his own audiovisual subversions of modernity's underlying Eurocentricity, Joseph recontextualizes Malick's philosophical cinema across his own collection of media works. Massimiliano Gioni thus suggests that Malick has taught Joseph 'to look at everyday life with a sense of cosmic awe', finding intensity and purpose in meandering shots of vast landscapes and wild spaces, the natural world uninterrupted by human activity (Gioni 2020). Developing this line of thought, one might argue that Joseph learned from his internship with Malick that the virtues of quietness exist both within *and* beyond the screen. Marc Furstenau and Leslie MacAvoy observe that Malick is 'notoriously silent about his films' because he believes they are 'capable of functioning without any subsequent comment on his part' (Furstenau and MacAvoy 2003), mirroring the ways in which Joseph is often described as 'notoriously tight-lipped' in an attempt to avoid consequently loading interpretations of his work with any particular bias (Kane 2017; O'Falt 2020). In this sense, Kahlil Davis's professional persona as Kahlil Joseph echoes Malick's careful curation of his own filmmaking identity, preferring coyness and reservation to emphatic declarations in the public sphere.

While Malick cultivates the image of an ex-philosopher turned enigmatic film practitioner, Joseph is a cryptic and at times paradoxical figure whose media artworks and career invite multidimensional levels of engagement and exploration. For example, although Joseph acknowledges that he greatly developed his filmmaking skills by 'editing stuff for other people' under Malick's stewardship (Joseph, in conversation with Dallas 2017: 145), he also concedes: 'I could tell I wasn't going to get very far in that space … It was very influential but very white' (Joseph, in conversation with Solway 2019). Joseph therefore highlights the problematic ways in which the industry's pre-existing social dynamics – which are rooted in the race-based disequilibria at the heart of global capitalism, the very same branches of Eurocentricity which Malick's films strive to critique – shape the contemporary experiences of aspiring black filmmakers, engendering disadvantages for people who are held back by, or do not directly profit from, this particular world system.

Joseph was raised by a family whose achievements include negotiating what was one of the most lucrative sports deals of all time – yet he faced an uncomfortable sensation that the quest for personal development would be limited within this particular environment as a result of the colour of his skin. Although the aforementioned video-making organization offered solid opportunities for Joseph's technical training and housed ample role models through Anderson, the Coppolas, Malick and McDaniel, the feeling that pathways for career progression were restricted by systemic barriers within this space – impeding his progress towards sole directorial duties and limiting his opportunities for development and self-expression – eventually caused Joseph to depart the Directors Bureau.

In search of autonomy as a filmmaker, Joseph commenced his independent career by collaborating with the Seattle-based rap group Shabazz Palaces. In two of his first projects as solo director, Joseph hybridized film and music video formats to promote the band's work through two audiovisual projects: *Belhaven Meridian* (2010) and *Black Up* (2011). While Joseph's later commissions for conglomerates KENZO, 02 and Apple Music and collaborations with high-profile 'superstar' musicians Beyoncé and Sampha were conducted with large financial backing, his early forays into filmmaking with Shabazz Palaces were built on modest budgets between $5,000 and $10,000. It is difficult for emerging filmmakers to gain access to large sums of project funding until they have proved themselves, and Joseph acknowledges that: 'no one really allowed [him] to do a proper big budget video' at this stage of his career (Joseph in conversation with Kane 2017).

Despite having access to a relatively modest budget, Joseph's early projects showed signs of promise that defied his monetary limitations. Arthur Jafa contends that the relationships between sound and moving images in Joseph's works explore 'continuities … [or] secret histories' that connect forms of Black music and Black visual cultures (Jafa, in conversation with Joseph 2017), and *Belhaven Meridian* and *Black Up* draw from classic film sources that hold relatively niche positions within the Anglo-American cultural psyche and its ensuant markets – specifically: Ousmane Sembène's *La Noire De …* (1966) and Charles Burnett's *Killer of Sheep* (1978) in *Belhaven Meridian*; Djibril

Diop Mambéty's *Touki Bouki* (1973) in *Black Up* – while generating favourable reviews from critics and gaining wide exposure.[2]

Although the films *Killer of Sheep*, *La Noire De ...* and *Touki Bouki* are exemplars of African and African-American cinema, these works are infrequently referenced in popular cultural outputs in the contemporary West – and, when they are cited, the outcome is often problematic. For example, Beyoncé and Jay-Z copied *Touki Bouki*'s film poster of motorcyclists Mory and Anta to promote their On the Run II World Tour, and Mati Diop – the Senegalese filmmaker, actor and niece of *Touki Bouki*'s late director Djibril Mambéty Diop – was 'a little troubled' by their actions because she felt whoever brought the image to Beyoncé and Jay-Z's attention was not especially 'concerned about what artistic and political story is behind it' (Diop, cited by Gilbey 2018).[3]

Joseph, in contrast, incorporates elements of *Killer of Sheep*, *La Noire De ...* and *Touki Bouki* into his collaborations with Shabazz Palaces in a manner that amplifies their outreach online to new audiences and, at the same time, respects and captures the subversive qualities of the original material: in *Belhaven Meridian*, blatant remediation of a key scene from *Killer of Sheep* is counterbalanced by an indirect reference to the symbolic mask in *La Noire De ...*, nuancing the media lineages between African and African-American filmmaking across film and music video forms; vivid shots of slaughtered animals across the rural Senegalese village Colobane in *Touki Bouki* and the industrial outskirts of Los Angeles's cityscape in *Killer of Sheep* are recontextualized in a Puerto Rican township by Joseph's short film-music video hybridization *Black Up*, illustrating how media arts across the Atlantic may merge and blur rigid boundaries between diverse cultural contexts. Joseph therefore markets Shabazz Palaces's music

---

[2] *Belhaven Meridian* has approximately 113,000 Youtube views and *Black Up*'s figures are in the region of 426,000. The *liquid blackness* project locates Shabazz Palaces alongside Kendrick Lamar, Flying Lotus and FKA Twigs, arguing that Joseph 'gained notoriety in the early 2010s for his beautifully-shot short films made in collaboration with some of the most respected, politically engaged and forward-thinking hip-hop artists of the moment' (*liquid blackness* 2016a), and one critic goes as far as suggesting that both projects are 'radical and wondrous cinematic gems' (Dallas 2017: 144).

[3] In the original film, cowherd Mory and student Anta are an ambitious couple who seek to escape their harsh existence in post-independence Senegal by fleeing to Paris, lured by the idealized notion of a new life in Europe free from the sensations of disenchantment and stagnation engendered by life in their hometown. However, when the time arrives for the pair to board the ferry to France, Anta is abandoned by her boyfriend and must travel alone. Mory – suddenly unable to extricate himself from his roots – searches wildly for his motorcycle, only to find it destroyed in an accident, the vehicle's broken Zebu horns mimicking the splintering of his dreams with Anta and their future in Europe. While the film poster of Mory and Anta riding the motorcycle with the Zebu horns still intact represents the bold yet fragile impulses motivating their journey across Senegal in search of a new, rewarding life, the promotional material for Beyoncé and Jay-Z's On the Run II tour copies *Touki Bouki*'s reworking of the Bonnie and Clyde dynamic to emphasize the strength of the couple's relationship. Beyoncé and Jay-Z's adaptation of the film's content controversially ignores how the lure of a new life in the West destroys Mory and Anta's relationship, thereby framing the image solely as an endorsement of the musicians' solidarity rather than acknowledging the original film's nuanced critique of power imbalances between Africa and the West. A similar incident occurred in 2021 when Beyoncé and Jay-Z posed in front of a never-before-seen Jean-Michel Basquiat painting as part of an advertising campaign for jewellery brand Tiffany & Co, raising concerns about how the late anti-capitalist graffiti artist would feel about the collaboration.

broadly while, simultaneously, broadcasting encoded messages about the overlaps between African and American film lineages across an array of geographical territories.

Various contradictory forces would continue to shape both the content and circulation of Joseph's art throughout his career. For example, the filmmaker's early works were released during a controversial period for African-American representation on screen, wherein two major Hollywood films about slavery from 2012 – Quentin Tarantino's *Django Unchained* and Steven Spielberg's *Lincoln* – were followed by another wave of US movies about American slavery: including Steve McQueen's Oscar-winning *12 Years a Slave* (2013), Lee Daniels's *The Butler* (2013), Thomas K. Philips's *The North Star* (2013), Jeroen Leinders's *Tula: The Revolt* (2013), Peter Cousens's *Freedom* (2014) and Nate Parker's *Birth of a Nation* (2016). While Donald Bogle speculates that many of the films from 2013 might not have 'the same draw' that inspired people to watch *Django Unchained* because slavery 'is not a subject that people rush out to see as a rule' and the film's violent revisionist history of the Antebellum South and the Old West 'told the story of slavery in a very unique way that hadn't been done before and probably won't be again', he also admits that it is 'difficult not to question the timing of these films and what it really means' in light of this slave narrative trend emerging during the presidency of Barack Obama, the United States' first black leader (Bogle cited by Samuels 2013).

It was during the second year of this spate of 'slave-master' films that Joseph's *Until the Quiet Comes* (2012) project with musician Flying Lotus won the Special Jury Prize for short film at the Sundance Film Festival, in certain ways counteracting the misleading representations of Afrodiasporic experiences circulated by the cinematic slave narratives. Duane Deterville argues that *Until the Quiet Comes* draws from Bantu-Kongo cosmology throughout its representation of two shootings in Los Angeles's Nickerson Garden projects (Deterville 2013). Joseph's provocative recontextualization of the Kalunga barrier – which, in Bantu-Kongo cosmology, separates the ancestral spirit world from our realm of the living – thus incorporates underexplored African traditions within broader popular discourses in the West. In doing so, the filmmaker offers a formula for cultural production which garners critical acclaim from a prestigious film festival and, at the same time, remains 'popular' or 'accessible' for broader audiences as an online media artefact generating over three million Youtube views.

The film's driving narrative force, however, stems from familiar imagery of a black man and boy killed as a result of gun violence, problematizing Joseph's otherwise 'progressive' unification of African spirituality with masculinized violence in the West through its representation of the controversial 'Black Neoliberal Aesthetic' (Nwonka 2020).[4] Although *Until the Quiet Comes* challenges global discourses which marginalize representations of Africa, the association of young black men with gun violence in turn counteracts such countercultural messages by circulating stereotypical formations of masculinity. The award-winning short film's contradictions, or, in other words, their

---

[4] I explore Clive Chijioke Nwonka's arguments in further depth in the **Crossroads of Aesthetics (1.3.3)** section.

production of the Black Neoliberal Aesthetic, therefore illustrate the paradoxical relationship between Joseph's filmic output and the imbalanced world order in which the filmmaker and his works are situated.

After winning an award at the Sundance Film Festival in 2013, Joseph claims that avoiding clichéd representations of African-American life became a fundamental preoccupation when arranging new projects. He recalls telling his team amid reading and writing film scripts: 'Pass on anything that feels stereotypical on any level in terms of the black male. Strip club, Compton, gangbangin', hip-hop, all that shit. Look for the other thing' (Joseph in conversation with Solway 2019). However, funding opportunities for projects and chances to collaborate with specific artists often appear suddenly and unexpectedly in the chaotic and unpredictable filmmaking and music industries; thus Joseph was drawn to Compton for his next large-scale project. Shortly after *Until the Quiet Comes*'s release – when the award from the Sundance Festival had validated Joseph's reputation as a filmmaker and started to generate more attention for his work – he received a call from the manager of West Coast rapper Kendrick Lamar, asking if the director was available to work on a new project focusing on the rapper's upbringing in Compton.

Joseph and Lamar's respective management teams had previously attempted to arrange a music video shoot that never materialized, yet at this particular moment Lamar had been asked to support Kanye West on his Yeezus tour. When directing music videos, Lamar often collaborates with his long-term friend Dave Free. The creative duo, known as The Little Homies, have filmed videos for the rapper's songs *Ignorance Is Bliss* (2010), *i* (2014) and *ELEMENT.* (2017). In this case, however, Lamar had never toured on such a large scale and needed a creative director whom he admired and trusted to produce visuals for on-stage usage in a short space of time.

Joseph, meanwhile, had never created moving images for a live music performance yet was eager to collaborate with the performer. After the release of his Grammy-nominated album *good kid, m.A.A.d city* (2012), Lamar was no longer 'another upstart lyricist trying to find his place in music' but one of the country's most important and far-reaching voices, uniting the hostility of the streets with the popular mainstream by producing 'rhymes in underground ciphers ... beside the biggest pop stars' (Moore 2020: 2 and 5). From the hours of footage that were provided by Kendrick's manager for the live-show project, Joseph's editor produced a three-minute video that included home footage shot by Lamar's uncle in 1990. Inspired by the editor's video and its inclusion of the family-based content,[5] Joseph in turn produced a rough-cut after nine months working with the footage. By this point in time, however, the rapper's tour had passed, leaving Lamar and his management group appreciative of Joseph's work yet unsure what to do with the project.

As Joseph's career as a filmmaker was starting to rapidly accelerate, his father's health had begun deteriorating. After frequent spells in hospital battling brain cancer, Keven Joseph Davis passed away aged fifty-four, two days before Christmas Day in

---

[5] The camcorder footage filmed by Lamar's uncle is timestamped 23 March 1992, roughly a month before the verdict was given for the Rodney King trial.

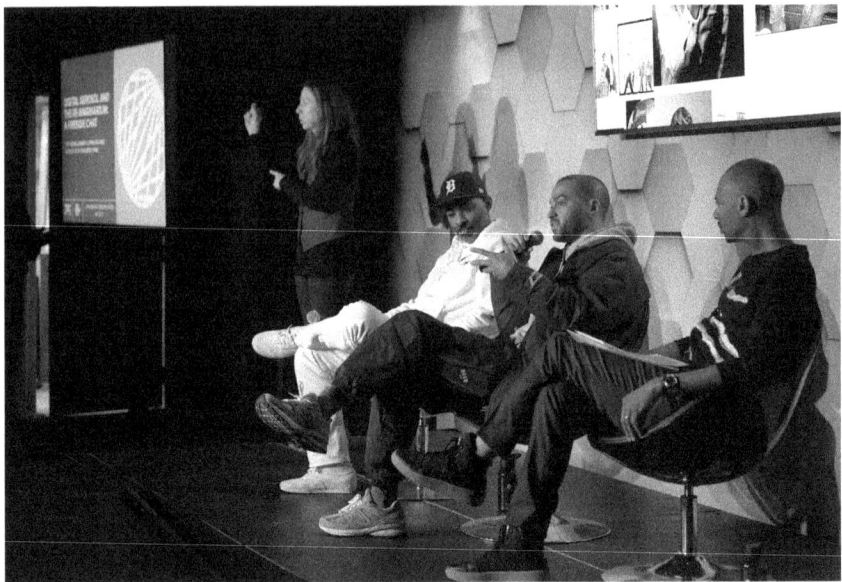

Figure 1.3 Kahlil Joseph, Jesse Williams and Charles D. King speak during the 2020 Sundance Film Festival – Digital Aerosol and the Re-Imaginarium: A Fireside Chat With Kahlil Joseph and Jesse Williams Panel at the Ray on 26 January 2020 in Park City, Utah. Photo by Morgan Lieberman/Getty Images.

2011. According to Dr Childs-Davis, her husband 'was meeting with clients, sending emails and trying to close a deal until he couldn't anymore' (Childs-Davis, cited by Krishnan 2012). On his deathbed, Keven Joseph Davis arranged with his sons that they would use their inheritance money to create 'a community platform for connection' (Solway 2019). Joseph and Noah thus co-founded the Underground Museum in 2012, a non-profit gallery located in Los Angeles's Arlington Heights area that – from 2012 to 2022 – promoted the work of black artists.

When Joseph was unsure about what to do with the Kendrick Lamar video, Noah suggested that his older brother finish the project and install it at the Underground Museum in a dual screen format. While initially sceptical because he regarded himself as a 'moving image guy' and had never visualized his work in such a context (Joseph in conversation with Solway 2019), Joseph heeded Noah's advice and 'all of a sudden ... [became] a fine artist' as the framing of his screen text in this particular manner shifted its meaning from a background music video to an art installation (Joseph cited by McDermon 2017). Noah was therefore the first curator to feature his brother's work in an exhibition context, a feat largely indebted to the advantageous position both brothers held as a result of their family's wealth.

In their later lives, the brothers' capacity to afford the costs connected to establishing and consequently co-running a professional gallery space in Los Angeles through their inheritance fund communicates the uneven relationships within our neoliberal, (post) colonial world system which give some members of society more practical means than others through which to support and influence their communities. Nevertheless, the Underground Museum actively attempted to remove the institutional barriers which commonly impede access to the arts. As well as creating a space which would serve as 'an incubator for artists, activists, and thinkers' (Davis in conversation with Solway 2017), Joseph and his brother Noah sought to improve the accessibility of contemporary art for the local communities of the predominantly Latino and African-American Arlington Heights neighbourhood where the gallery space was based, thereby using the financial and social capital generated over the years by their family to empower and support groups of American society who, in contrast, have been historically and remain marginalized by structures of social organization.

While Joseph, Noah and their mother were influential figures in establishing the Underground Museum, Noah's wife played a large role in shaping the museum's direction and continued to run the organization until its closure in 2022. Karon Davis is the daughter of Broadway actor and ballet dancer Ben Vereen, sharing a similarly privileged background to her husband and brother-in-law. She attended film school at the University of Southern California before meeting Noah in 2005 and marrying him in 2008. The pair were determined to enact Keven's vision for the Underground Museum yet initially struggled to do so. After unsuccessfully contacting various museums in the area to see if they would be willing to establish a partnership with the newly-founded establishment in Arlington Heights, the Chief Curator at the Museum of Contemporary Art agreed to rent a range of specialist artworks to the family's Underground Museum. Karon supported the terms of the loan scheme because:

> The conversations I was having at the UM I was not going to have at MOCA … So it's not a simple thing to say, 'OK, now we're going to open the doors, and black people are going to come in, and it's all going to be the same.' Those spaces were by, for, and about white people. So what does it mean to really shift your orientation and give away some of the authority? We didn't say, 'You guys play in our sandbox,' but rather, 'We give you control, and we'll let the artwork that is in our care be interpreted and used differently than we would interpret it.' My mantra with them all along has been, Don't get in their way.
>
> (Davis in conversation with Solway 2017)

The Underground Museum, therefore, represented an attempt to break down the traditional barriers which frame the institutionally white art gallery world, offering a physical location where ideas and plans are exchanged, as well as symbolizing the legacy of Joseph and Noah's family and their contributions to Afrodiasporic arts curation in Los Angeles.

The status of the museum as a safe communal space for the exploration of Blackness through contemporary artistic practices is emphasized by the fact that an array of key cultural figures such as the artist David Hammons, filmmaker Raoul Peck and musicians John Legend, Beyoncé and Solange Knowles organized and took part in events at the museum. Barry Jenkins participated in a screening and director's Q+A session for *Moonligh*t (2016) on the evening after the 2016 US Presidential Election. The filmmaker claims he was struck by 'what a diverse crowd it was – tons of black folks, people from the neighbourhood, white, Latino, Asian', and had an epiphanic moment during the session, declaring: 'This is America ... Nothing could replicate the feeling that we had that night. It was almost like group therapy, all of us just out there under the stars, witnessing this thing we'd made and using it to bring us together' (Jenkins, cited by Solway 2017).

In 2015, at the age of thirty-two, Noah passed away as a result of a rare type of soft tissue cancer – on the same day that the first MOCA-supported show opened at the Underground Museum. Noah's premature passing tragically occurred three years after Keven had fatally succumbed to brain cancer. Karon Davis continued to co-run the Underground Museum alongside Joseph, his mother Faith and his wife, the film producer Onye Anyanwu, until 2022. A public letter announced that running the museum had been 'an incredible journey' and 'also deeply painful' in the shadow of Noah's passing and an amalgamation of complex, deftly balanced scenarios further complicated by the Covid-19 pandemic and the grassroots movements for Black Lives. While emphasizing their commitment towards ensuring that Noah's family and the Underground Museum would at some point together 'flourish once again', the letter asked that the group behind the project be given 'the space and privacy needed to understand the future of the museum and to heal both individually and collectively,' shutting its doors until further notice (Davis 2022).

Joseph talks about his brother and father fondly in interviews but rareley reveals the specific mechanics of their familial relationships, citing Keven's passing as a key inspiration for the emotionally charged explorations of life and death between physical and noumenal plains in his award-winning film *Until the Quiet Comes* (Kane 2017), repeatedly pointing to his brother's artistic legacy in lieu of divulging the personal details shaping their connection (Joseph, in conversation with Dallas 2017).

In the same spirit of privacy nuancing his delicately controlled discussions of his paternal and brotherly relationships, Joseph seldom publicly discusses family life about his partner and their two children. Despite the fact that Joseph and Anyanwu have collaborated together on a range of media projects including *Video Girl* (2014), *Process* (2017) and *Lemonade* (2016), the pair are intensely private about their interlocking careers as well as the dynamics of their relationship. Reflecting on the aforementioned period that Joseph spent developing his editing skills while working on projects for other people in Texas, Barbara London draws parallels between Joseph and Malick's professionalism and their private lives as 'both keep a low profile yet are deeply engaged with the world' (London 2020: 258).

Joseph's awareness of and deep engagement with the decolonization of popular visual content affirms in part London's characterization of the filmmaker, echoing the manner in which Malick's Heideggerian cinema challenges the latent Eurocentricity on which modernity is grounded. However, Joseph's commitment to maintaining a level of privacy while interacting with the contemporary Afrodiasporic art trends and debates about its relationships to the mainstreams and margins of various global cultures could be explained by a variety of motivating forces – a simple disdain for ego-fashioning and celebrity fetishization in the mass media, or a tactical career move in a similar vein to Malick whereby public silence about one's own private life amplifies an artist's messages and in turn augments the focus of public attention afforded to such work.

Although Joseph seems to possess ample emotional and material support from his caring and affluent family, Paul Gilroy suggests:

> … in the critical thought of blacks in the West, social self-creation through labour is not the centre-piece of emancipatory hopes. For the descendants of slaves, work signifies only servitude, misery, and subordination. Artistic expression, expanded beyond recognition from the grudging gifts offered by the masters as a token substitute for freedom from bondage, therefore becomes the means towards both individual self-fashioning *and* communal liberation.
>
> (Gilroy 1993: 40 [my emphasis])

Using Gilroy's understanding of Afrodiasporic artistic expression as connected to the creation of one's personal identity as well as deeply rooted in the broader quest for humanity's emancipation from the enduring toxicities of racism and corrosive legacies of slavery, the relative silence of Joseph's public persona subtly suggests the artist is motivated by a combination of both individualized self-fashioning *and* a core belief in the promise and achievability of shared liberation for humanity through artistic expression and alternative ways of being. As well as accumulating the cultural capital associated with being a socially conscious artist publicly displaying liberal, progressive politics, Joseph's usage of his family inheritance to establish and sustain the Underground Museum demonstrates a desire for his public persona to become characterized by his support of collective knowledge-sharing, this emphatic act of self-fashioning linked to forging communal human relationships and valuing the exchange of information between people.

Paul Dallas notes that Joseph repeatedly acts as 'an independent filmmaker' and yet, as a result of the formal complexity of the director's artworks, he concedes that Joseph's films 'are rarely thought of in that context' (Dallas 2017: 145). The word 'independent' in the phrase 'independent cinema' is loaded with as many overlapping and contradictory significations as such terms as 'modernity', 'Africa' and 'Blackness', thereby complicating the potential framework(s) within which one may situate certain products of Joseph's artistic oeuvre. However, James Snead raises the important observation that: 'No filmmaker is *independent* in the way that, say, a poet is … [because] filmmaking, both capital- and labor-intensive, is the most *dependent* art form' (my emphasis) (Snead 1994: 125).[6] While most artforms are woven into the uneven oscillations of neoliberal capitalism's volatile, frequently unpredictable market environments, independent filmmaking is especially tied to the ability to remunerate the work of various different parties and departments, from actors and cinematographers to distributors and

---

[6] The What Matters Most collective, for example, are one of the independent film production companies with whom Kahlil Joseph partners most frequently, and the group have nurtured a reputation as 'a new generation of artists and filmmakers seeking to improve their respective crafts *through collaboration*' (my emphasis) (Hagle 2014).

salespeople. When positioned alongside the complicated situations that African diasporas have continuously negotiated ever since their original displacement(s) and consequent movements across various geographical borders, Afrodiasporic independent filmmaking is thus characterized by various complex and paradoxical histories, fluctuating from uninvested and neglected projects struggling to make any significant cultural impacts to popular bodies of work articulating some of the world's most important filmmaking voices.

Further complicating Joseph's status as an *independent* filmmaker is his tendency to *collaborate* with musicians, dancers and other artists, thus the malleability of his reputation means that Kahlil Davis's professional persona as Kahlil Joseph is itself 'a medium to be moulded and shaped across media' (Rogers in Vernallis, Rogers and Perrot 2020: 11). For example, Kahlil Joseph is attributed the role of director in the screen texts selected for discussion within this book, which in turn affects how the products are marketed, distributed and then consumed and decoded by recipients *in spite of* the involvement of myriad professionals from the film and music industries in shaping the final versions of these artworks. On a more personal level, Kahlil Davis comes across as an intensely private individual who occasionally surfaces from beneath the security of his professional alias, infrequently divulging cryptic information about his father, mother and brother in interviews and almost never speaking about his wife and children.

In one of the most revealing and intimate conversations about Noah and his body of work, Joseph is joined by Karon and the curator Helen Molesworth in celebration of his brother's life and work, offering rare insights into their personal relationships with Noah while emphasizing that everyone has 'a version of Noah that [they] walk around with' (Joseph in conversation with Molesworth and Davis 2020). Indeed, in an age of celebrity idolization and constant information exchange, one must note that Joseph similarly strives to cultivate a malleable, multidimensional status whereby large parts of his public persona are formed by projection on the part of his audiences (Dyer [1979] 1998; Redmond 2018). Although the director contributes to the construction of his working persona through aforementioned insinuations across interviews and public discussions, determining 'who' Kahlil Davis is and 'what' he stands for beneath his identity as Kahlil Joseph presents 'an interpretative gap' which necessitates critically engaging with his work (Rogers 2017: 19). As previously outlined, this book explores the ways in which the development of Joseph's filmmaking persona operates in conjunction with his art to subvert fixed or monocentric understandings of identity, challenging generalizing conceptualizations of human experience that might otherwise underpin prevalent formulations of modernity. And in order to extrapolate how these points of cross-cultural *and* interdisciplinary contact challenge the hegemonic discourses on which Western modernity is grounded, it is necessary to move away from restrictions imposed by rigid, land-bound formulations of (trans) national identity and instead head towards the sea – to the various 'crossroads' which lie at heart of the Atlantic Ocean – by way of the seminal theorist of Afrodiasporic arts and culture whose work shapes both *Black Cultural Traffic* and *Postcolonial Artists and Global Aesthetics*: Paul Gilroy.

1.3 Seeing and hearing the Black Atlantic: audiovisual art as counterculture of modernity

Although a large number of Joseph's productions take place in Los Angeles and involve collaborators based in the United States, his incorporation of cultural ideas and objects from Nigeria, Senegal and Sierra Leone into collaborations with both African-American and Black-British artists demonstrates a view of social formation processes that extends beyond the limitations imposed by rigid formations of the nation-state. Paul Gilroy's *The Black Atlantic: Modernity and Double Consciousness* (1993) offers a fundamental starting point for this project's discussions, constructing an appropriately borderless understanding of both continental *and* diasporic African identities that echoes the restless journeys of a ship sailing across the Atlantic Ocean. The vast, imposing space of the Atlantic – where millions of African people were ferried, transformed from humans to commodities through the barbaric practice of slavery[7] – is framed by Gilroy as a single unit that connects Africa, America, Europe and the Caribbean, thereby providing 'an explicitly transnational *and* intercultural perspective' through which to evaluate Black cultural expressions across the globe (my emphasis) (Gilroy 1993: 15).

While Gilroy's focus on mobility offers fruitful avenues through which to challenge 'nationalist or ethnically absolute approaches' to the construction of racial identities in the modern world, the Black Atlantic's emphasis on the disruptive or 'countercultural' properties of Black music is connected to the lineages of music and sound-imbued media from African-American, Black-British and continental African artists in which I attempt to situate the interdisciplinary works of Kahlil Joseph (ibid.). Western intellectual thought has 'averred that the origin of language in warmer, southern climes was connected to music and the natural inflections of the voice' ever since the essayist Jean-Jacques Rousseau first ruminated on the topic of sound, laying problematic groundwork for future theorizations of Eurocentric modernism wherein the global South 'is often derided for stubbornly failing to obey the (supposedly rational) logic of the state, that sine qua non of Western modernity' (Steingo and Sykes 2019: 1–2). For Gilroy, however, the 'power' of Black music exists in its ability to support transnational solidarity and develop Afrodiasporic struggles 'by communicating information, organising consciousness … testing out or deploying the forms of objectivity which are required by political agency, whether individual or collective, defensive or transformational' (Gilroy 1993: 36). In turn, Black musical expression plays an integral role in producing 'a distinctive counterculture of modernity' that transcends the limits

---

[7] It is estimated that 1.8 million people – more than 14 per cent of 12.5 million Africans who were forced to sail across the Middle Passage – never reached the Americas (Eltis and Richardson 2010). Memories of friends and family dying from disease and malnutrition at sea 'remained with those who survived to labour on plantations, normalizing a system of control rooted in violence and dehumanization, transforming free individuals with names into traumatized, numbered captives and, ultimately, into enslaved commodities' (Sluyter 2020: 4).

of both linguistic *and* geographical boundaries, positioning the racialized and uneven foundations on which modernity rests 'against the world as the racially subordinated would like it to be' (ibid).

While Gilroy firmly underlines the centrality of music for Black Atlantic expression's countercultural aims, throughout the years his arguments have grown increasingly less enthusiastic about the empowering potential of popular Black cultural forms that inhabit the various realms of visual communication. Gilroy connects the rising popularity of hip hop music videos to processes of 'iconization' whereby black performers (from musicians and athletes to actors and models) become progressively transformed into a collection of superficial celebrity figures heavily associated with commercial sponsorship deals and media appearances rather than the merits of their acts and/or artistry. In instances where Black music was once encoded with radical countercultural politics, the anti-capitalist messages are stripped away as performances become increasingly commodified through visual advertisements, music videos, films and other screen-based formats, transforming the performers into exciting and almost superhuman yet unreal, soulless 'icons'. This process of reducing real people to physical and sexual tropes generates familiar and recognizable yet fundamentally racist stereotypes of black people which underpin modernity's dominant narratives, promoting commodities in the most efficient manner yet underselling and distorting what it means to be a member of African diasporas. By replacing the vigorous yet necessary work of remembering the atrocities of slavery with 'the simplistic work of association', the growing visualization and consequent 'iconization' of black performers negate the potential of musical expression from the Black Atlantic to undercut and challenge prevailing forces of modernity (Gilroy 1999: 266–7). In 2004, Gilroy witheringly states that:

> … elements of globalisation and the centrality of black cultures to popular culture, youth cultures, advertising, cinema, and sports have never been greater. However, this enhanced visibility does not mean that the black body is imaged in postures or roles that would be chosen as a means to articulate or complement black political interests. It can be argued that novel communicative technologies and the faceless forms of appropriation they foster impact negatively upon solidarity-building tactics devised in earlier periods and refined where black subculture moved above ground during the 1960s and 1970s. Consciousness of kind and synchronized action previously mediated by print and sound have been changed and have begun to break down in the different atmosphere created by communicative and representational regimes dominated by images. The growing power of visuality tips the balance away from sound and even from print to create new forms of minstrelsy and new remote audiences hungry for the pleasures they display and orchestrate. Music and dance, so long the core of the alternative public world in which dissidence was worked into a counterculture, reluctantly yield their traditional places of authority to pseudo-performances and video-based simulations. Black is not just commodified but lends its special exotic allure

to the marketing of an extraordinary range of commodities and services that have no connection whatever to these cultural forms or to the people who have developed them.

(Gilroy [2000] 2004: 214)

I quote Gilroy at length here because his words about 'the growing power of visuality' are absolutely central to the concerns of Joseph's work and this book as a whole. While Gilroy tries to remain open to the notion that forms of visual communication may indeed possess some redeeming features with the capacity to offer countercultural forms of social organization, his perspective towards the growing prominence of screen cultures and their relationships with the Black Atlantic becomes pessimistic. By distinguishing the visual and audial properties of Afrodiasporic cultural expression in instances where the two expressive forms overlap, a controversial binary is therefore subtly insinuated by Gilroy's stance.

When discussing geographic territories in relation to audial and visual modes of expression, the framing of the South as equating to sound and the North as equating to vision forms contentious binaries that commonly emerge in Eurocentric discourses. While Rousseau's understanding of a contemporaneous Mediterranean South would greatly differ from definitions of the regions and spaces that (purportedly) constitute the global South in the twenty-first century, Gavin Steingo and Jim Sykes observe that in Western thought 'the South has been associated with sound, music, body, presence, nature, and warmth' whereas the North, in contrast, 'sees itself as dominated by writing and vision – by a cultural coldness born of the snow-capped peaks of the Alps' (Steingo and Sykes 2020: 1). These dichotomous relationships are grounded on the assumption that sound and vision are ideologically loaded – progressive or regressive, bad or good, even Northern or Southern – dependent on one's subjective interpretation.

By articulating the political potential of instances where 'poiesis and poetics begin to coexist' at the heart of certain modes of Black cultural expression, Gilroy focuses on the merits of 'autobiographical writing, special and uniquely creative ways of manipulating spoken language, and, *above all*, music', basing his selection and hierarchical framing of these forms on the fact that all three 'overflowed from the containers that the modern nation state provides for them' (my emphasis) (Gilroy 1993: 40). He borrows the term 'populist modernism' from Werner Sollors to articulate the ways in which the popularity of James Brown's funk music and the writings of W. E. B. Du Bois, Toni Morrison and Richard Wright draw from the combinations of philosophy, biography and vernacularism that originated in Fredrick Douglass's literary work, rewriting traditional narratives through formal experimentation and committed engagement with language's general failure, or the 'inability of mere words', to communicate the traumatizing experiences and overwhelming sensations endured by their enslaved ancestors (ibid. 124).

One of the fundamental points of criticism undermining Gilroy's work, then, stems from the observation that 'the redemptive hermeneutics informing the *Black Atlantic* was scripted at the expense of the negative dialectic of the Middle Passage' (Gikandi 2014: 241). Inspired by Saidiya Hartman's *Scenes of Subjection: Terror, Slavery, and Self-Making in Nineteenth-Century America* (1997), the notion of 'Afro-Pessimism' emerged as writers began to draw parallels between manifestations of anti-Blackness in contemporary American civil society and 'the fungibility of the commodity … the captive body' underpinning the dehumanizing logic of Transatlantic Slave Trading across the Middle Passage (Hartman 1997: 7 and 19).

Gilroy's theorization of the Black Atlantic attempts to move beyond the historical framing of the Atlantic Ocean as 'a narrative of loss, suffering, and social death', seeking ways in which the tragedies of the Slave Trade could in fact signify a subversive entry point into modernity for Afrodiasporic communities and, in turn, transform the Middle Passage's 'negative dialectic' into a process of redemption, offering sources for future empowerment in the struggle for worldwide social equity (Gikandi 2014: 241). For proponents of Afro-Pessimism, however, the term 'Black' in contemporary discourses – including and extending beyond Gilroy's theorizations of the Black Atlantic – '*still* equals "slave" in the United States as well as in the Western or "white" world in general' (my emphasis) (Weier 2014: 420). Frank B. Wilderson III goes as far as contending that 'Blacks do not function as political subjects' in our present moment with the same agency as non-black citizens, instead suffering a new type of 'social death' whereby the 'flesh and energies' of African-American citizens 'are instrumentalized for postcolonial, immigrant, feminist, LGBT, and workers' agendas' (Wilderson III 2016). As well as emphasizing how new forms of everyday discrimination and subjugation continue to echo processes of suffering and dehumanization endured across the Middle Passage, an Afro-Pessimistic perspective struggles to move beyond framing the Atlantic as a source of trauma, perpetuating the situation wherein 'the position of black people is analogized to that of being eternally a slave, being put outside a human framework, incomparable to another position of other disenfranchised people' (Wekker in conversation with Gilroy 2020).

In generating a set of cultural relationships across the Atlantic while, at the same time, seeking to frame these relations as a new phase of humanity that moves beyond the traumatizing experiences of the Middle Passage, Simon Gikandi suggests *The Black Atlantic*'s insistence that 'the black subject's entry into modernity was part of a redemptive hermeneutics … however violent it had been' stems from Gilroy's own biases towards North American contexts at the expense of black citizens in various parts of Europe and – perhaps most glaringly – large portions of Africa (Gikandi 2014: 241). While Gilroy attempts to bring African, American, Caribbean and European producers together in conversation through the metaphor of the ship, or 'a living, micro-cultural, micro-political system in motion', his efforts to think about cultural formations beyond the limits of the nation-state struggle to balance the continents with equal weight (Gilroy 1993: 4). Although Yogita Goyal acknowledges that *The Black Atlantic* was a 'path-breaking book' inspiring a range of writers and thinkers across the world, she argues that in many ways Gilroy's text also inadvertently 'replicated the problematic exclusion of Africa from discussions of modernity' through its primary focus on African-American cultural producers (Goyal 2014: v).

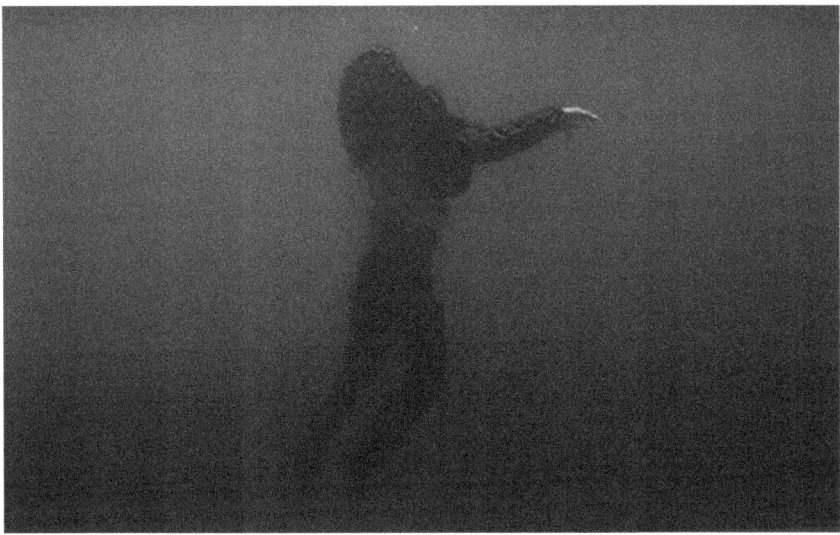

Figure 1.4 *Until the Quiet Comes* (2012), Kahlil Joseph and Flying Lotus © Warp Records.

Discussing *The Black Atlantic*'s emphasis on the countercultural capacities of African-American musicianship at the expense of black African and British musicians, Gikandi observes that Black-British intellectuals such as Gilroy who were writing in response to Thatcherism's crisis of national citizenship had started to turn 'to North America for lessons about how people defined as minorities could be acknowledged as citizens' (Gikandi 2014: 242). From the UK's perspective, Gikandi argues, 'the African American appeared to have successfully made the passage from the margins to the center' as a result of their cultural production, 'recognized as *citizens* rather than *subjects* … once they were considered to be major producers of American popular culture' (my emphasis) (ibid.). While an Afro-Pessimistic approach might deem the foundations of this shift (from subjecthood to citizenship by way of popular music production) particularly problematic as a result of the negation of the traumas experienced during the Middle Passage, Gilroy worries that contemporary theorists who wish to (re-)shape the future cannot 'afford the luxury of pessimism' despite any feelings of frustration and desperation towards the current state of the planet (Gilroy in conversation with O'Hagan 2020). Gloria Wekker echoes these sentiments in a separate conversation with Gilroy, suggesting that an Afro-Pessimistic position offers 'no answer' for those who seek change or wish to improve worldly relations for disenfranchised people both within *and* beyond its Afrodiasporic communities (Wekker in conversation with Gilroy 2020).

Gikandi suggests that Gilroy's omissions of various zones of Afrocentric culture (including Guyana, the birthplace of his mother Beryl Gilroy) do not exhibit 'a certain terror toward forms of blackness that are not blessed by the hand of modern Europe' but instead illustrate 'the kind of work he was asking the black [population] in North America to perform in order to provide a lesson to the black British' (Gikandi 2014: 242). In seeking lessons from the American communities through which Black-British subjects could learn how to negotiate their own minority statuses in the UK, the alternative sense of marginality that Africa and the Caribbean offered – 'not one of race or racialism, but of economic and political marginalization in a modernizing world' – was, according to Gikandi, not prioritized by Gilroy's investigations (ibid.).

While such observations ignore the issues of race and racialism that were occurring in areas like South Africa and Zimbabwe when Gilroy was writing, throughout my own examinations of Kahlil Joseph's collection of work I seek to address the imbalances in *The Black Atlantic*'s original arguments, focusing on processes of racialization as well as forms of economic and political marginalization which Joseph's non-US-based collaborators experience in a range of contexts and settings. For example, by examining the experiences of the local Sierra Leonean extras who contribute to the music-film *Process* (2017) as well as highlighting the actions of Afro-Brazilian songwriter-actor Seu Jorge as his character attempts to understand dreamlike appearances of the Yoruba spirit Oshun in music video-advertisement *The Model* (2010), I endeavour to draw attention to a range of Afrodiasporic voices and experiences across and beyond the scope of the Black Atlantic. While Gilroy's writings offer a valuable point of departure through their construction of the Black Atlantic as a 'rhizomatic, fractal structure of … transcultural, international formation', this project aims to highlight how Joseph tries – more so than many of his predecessors – to incorporate (if not centre) continental Africa and African voices (Gilroy 1993: 4).

In line with my efforts to address *The Black Atlantic*'s geographical imbalances (foregrounding African cultural producers in my discussions and, at some points, even broadening my research's scope beyond the Atlantic Ocean), this project will also endeavour to address the medium bias in Gilroy's writings which privileges audial forms of communication over the visual. Gilroy emphasizes the centrality of music throughout his argumentations for the Black Atlantic's challenge to modernity in the West, and yet the capacity for musically imbued Afrodiasporic *audiovisual* expression – such as films, music videos and installations – to 'overflow' across geographical boundaries and likewise contribute to the Black Atlantic's complex processes of countercultural subversion across a broad range of international locations remains largely underexplored by his work. In fact, Gilroy's core critique of 'visuality' and 'visualization' stems from the idea that such processes occupy prominent positions in Nazi Germany's 'constitution of the fascist polity and the fascist public sphere' (Gilroy 2004a: 150). Although contemporary advertisers and musicians do not consciously borrow from Nazism's controversial deployment of iconography to categorize the nation's political and ethnic groups, Gilroy argues that the legacy of the swastika's image in de-individualizing German citizens and reorganizing the nation in racialized solidarity (or estrangement) subtly shapes how modern marketing techniques quickly and effectively associate ideas and preconceptions with products and spokespeople through logos and branding.

The swastika, however, was originally supplanted from its Asian contexts by Adolf Hitler, its meaning changed from a symbol of peace and well-being in Sanskrit and Hinduism to a form of political iconography connected to a racialized manifestation of European nationalism. While imagery of the swastika played a pivotal role in imbedding an understanding of the Nazi party in the collective conscience of German citizens, oral forms of communication such as anti-Semitic radio propaganda and Hitler's grand public speeches likewise contributed to the rise of Nazism in interbellum Germany, indicating that both audial *and* visual modes of communication are loaded with the capacity to serve a variety of ends, rather than pre-programmed with any particular essence. In Rwanda, for example, radio played a pivotal role in stoking up the violence and hatred that culminated in the Genocide in 1994, emphasizing the importance of considering contexts of production, circulation and consumption in order to understand a media form's effects, rather than hierarchizing particular mediums through essentialist systemizations (McCoy 2009; Yanagizawa-Drott 2014).

Paradoxically, then, in suggesting that the Southern origins of certain sounds might be offered 'as radical *alternatives* to the dilemmas of modernity', Gilroy's positioning of sound above vision reaffirms disputable systems of hierarchies and binaries on which modernism is based, thereby indirectly reinforcing the framework of Western rationalization which he seeks to challenge and dismantle (Steingo and Sykes 2020: 2, their emphasis). Sound and vision must therefore be conceptualized as both *in* and *from* the North *and* South in order to activate their countercultural capacities, offering valuable ways to negotiate the possibilities and pitfalls associated with modernity through the fashion in which Eurocentric *and* non-Western codes of value and meaning are both imbedded *and* subverted through their communicative functions. Discursive analyses of Kahlil Joseph's audiovisual works, I argue, thus present rich opportunities for navigating the contradictions of our contemporary era of globalization precisely because these cultural products draw together an array of interwoven elements both audial *and* visual, optimistic *and* pessimistic, progressive *and* problematic.

Despite his own pessimistic framing of contemporary forms of visual communication, Gilroy's theorizations of African diasporas and Black music have continued to prove inspirational sources of understanding and debate for scholarship in the postmillennial era. Alexander Weheliye develops Gilroy's phonocentric countercultural arguments for Afrodiasporic expressive cultures in his book *Phonographies: Grooves in Sonic Afro-Modernity* (2005), expanding on the intersections of technology, sound and Blackness. Although Weheliye's discussions generally centre around audial forms of communication, he acknowledges 'sonic modernity and visual modernity do not stand as diametrical opposites' but, instead, 'articulate different modes of becoming-in-the-world for modern black subjects in the West, which, although not entirely the same, cannot quite be disentangled from one another' (Weheliye 2005: 50).

Weheliye's work recognizes the subversive potential of Black music's challenge to modernity through its ability to communicate beyond the limits imposed by language barriers, thus he argues for a theorization of 'sonic Afro-modernity' which stems from the 'glaring rupture' of sight and vision through the invention of the phonograph

(Weheliye 2003: 100). While on the one hand representing an attempt to separate sound from its original sources in a hitherto unprecedented manner, *Phonographies* suggests that this machinic development paradoxically 'occasions not so much a complete *disappearance* of the human as much as a *resounding* through new styles of technological folding' (my emphasis) (Weheliye 2005: 7).

For Weheliye, one of the ways in which these new sound technologies 'resound' or 'retune' human expression stems from their subversion of Eurocentric and predominantly White formations of modernity. For example, the Enlightenment's emphasis on logic and reason over dogma and superstition was built on various understandings of the 'Man of Reason' (Foucault 1961; Lloyd 2002). This abstract idealization of humanity's rationality neatly coincides with 'masculinity, transcendental reason, rational consciousness and European civilization' because it centres the perspectives of white European men, privileging socially constructed masculine traits over feminine characteristics, emphasizing the experiences of people who identified as white cis-gender over non-white LGBTQ+ voices (Braidotti in Braidotti and Gilroy 2016: 10).[8]

The non-verbal and oftentimes ineffable sounds captured by the phonograph therefore challenge Enlightenment scholars' 'self-perception as rationality and disembodiment incarnate' because these noises exist as inescapable parts of modernity through their attachment to new machinic advancements, merging the audial components of music and speech with the physical presence of sound-producing technologies, generating innovative ways to engage with and thereby centre contemporaneous Black experiences (Weheliye 2014: 183). Sonic and visual formations of Blackness, then, 'operate paradoxically as both central to and outside of Western modernity', capturing the contradictions that emerge when amplifying black peoples' experiences through (dis)embodied forms of sounded technologies (Weheliye 2005: 5). While Weheliye's discussions of Blackness's paradoxical 'inside-outside' status primarily focus on the development of sounded technologies, one may apply the same arguments to the film technologies adopted by Joseph, thereby illustrating how (audio)visual forms of communication capture both the centrality *and* marginality of Black cultural expressions in relation to Western formulations of Eurocentric modernity.

Weheliye's writing offers valuable contributions to the discourses surrounding Afrocentric music's countercultural capacities, highlighting technology's pivotal role in facilitating contradictory flows of cultural participation in *and* resistance to modernity when aligned with Black expressive forms. However, Daphne Brooks observes that *Phonographies* misses a chance to amplify non-white female voices whose lived experiences also constitute the realities of sonic Afro-modernity, pointing towards Zora Neale Hurston's 'angular voice' and the use of sound in her discursive ethnographies as a way of disrupting modernity while simultaneously and productively

---

[8] For further discussions on performativity and the social construction of gender, see also: Judith Butler's *Gender Trouble: Feminism and the Subversion of Identity* (1990) and *Bodies That Matter: On the Discursive Limits of Sex* (1993).

interrupting 'the phonographic projects of the literary "race men" …. who sit at the forefront of Weheliye's cogent study' (Brooks 2010: 623). In a similar fashion, Joseph's collaborations with women (Alice Smith, Beyoncé, Kelsey Lu and FKA Twigs) are dwarfed by his number of partnerships with men (Aloe Blacc, Arthur Jafa, Jesse Williams, Kendrick Lamar, Flying Lotus, Sampha, Seu Jorge, Shabazz Palaces and Storyboard P). On the broader level of 'unseen' personnel assisting the production of his projects, Joseph frequently collaborates with his wife Onye Anyanwu as producer, yet his other regular collaborators in terms of production and cinematography – Malik Sayeed, Matthew J. Lloyd and Omid Fatemi – are predominantly men.

Obioma Nnaemeka's concept of 'nego-feminism' is especially useful here for scrutinizing the forces of gender and sexuality affecting Joseph's work because she argues that feminism 'for African women … is an act that evokes the dynamism and shifts of a process as opposed to the stability and reification of a construct or framework' (Nnaemeka 2004: 378). By echoing the ways in which Gilroy frames the Black Atlantic as a 'rhizomatic, fractural structure' in a constant state of flux, 'nego-feminism' offers an understanding of feminism that likewise shifts and evolves, embracing change and fluctuation (Gilroy 1993: 4). Nnaemeka also observes that 'to meaningfully explain the phenomenon called African feminism, it is not to Western feminism but rather to the African environment that one must refer' (Nnaemeka 1998: 9). 'Nego-feminism' thus stands for: 'the feminism of negotiation' as well as 'no ego' because 'the foundation of shared values in many African cultures are the principles of negotiation, give and take, compromise, and balance' (Nnaemeka 2004: 377–8).

One can adopt Nnaemeka's concept as means of uniting the most insightful aspects of various other feminist voices and theoretical perspectives while, at the same time, retaining an awareness of the African contexts which shape ensuant debates and frame new concepts. In turn, a 'nego-feminist' reading of *Phonographies* highlights how the African continent is glaringly absent from Weheliye's discussions of the intersections between Black music and technology. While Weheliye examines in great detail the global reach of Black American music and its relationships to technology, Africa is 'consciously bracketed' by *Phonographies* in order to focus on the Black diasporic cultures that traverse the Americas and Europe, narrowing what the 'Afro-' prefix signifies in the term 'sonic Afro-modernity' (Weheliye 2014: 186). By framing a rift between African and African-American cultures in a manner reminiscent of Gilroy's original writings, Weheliye misses a significant opportunity for developing discussions on the complex cultural flows which take place between continents and countries, the restlessly omnidirectional and transnational movements which energize musical expression across and beyond the Black Atlantic. The noticeable exclusions from Weheliye's otherwise thought-provoking and illuminating text thus illustrate that deep and holistic analyses of Black cultural expression across the diasporas – and especially in the case of Kahlil Joseph – necessitate acknowledging the circulation of art, ideas and people to and from Africa *and* the rest of the world.

In her book *Africa in Stereo: Modernism, Music and Pan-African Solidarity* (2014), Tsitsi Ella Jaji develops Gilroy's original lines of thought while bridging some of the conceptual gaps in *Phonographies*'s arguments, developing a theoretical framework termed 'stereomodernism'. Jaji, originally from Zimbabwe, moved to America to study piano performance, and she draws from her positionality and personal experiences – moving across the Atlantic, adjusting to different environments – to emphasize that empowering forms of cultural exchange may shift back and forth Africa and America through musical performances and other related modes of expression. In doing so, she creates an understanding of the Black Atlantic that highlights how many women 'inhabit the contact zones enabling such travel', thereby bringing 'a gender analytic to bear on what has often been naturalized as a neutral field of action' and, in turn, echoing Nnaemeka's nego-feminist lens by challenging 'the masculinist tradition within diasporic internationalism' (Jaji 2014: 17).

As well as acknowledging that popular manifestations of pan-African solidarity adopt multidirectional, gendered routes between the pre-established spatial boundaries of particular nation states, Jaji's work is especially enlightening in relation to Kahill Joseph's oeuvre of contemporary audiovisual art because she locates the border-crossing work of filmmakers alongside that of musicians, distinguishing her position from the predominantly audiophilic groundwork of Gilroy's arguments and, in turn, channelling Weheliye's understanding of the connections between sonic and visual forms of Black cultural expression. She thus reasons that both African filmmakers and musicians 'recognised in African American forms not only artistic merit but also a compelling model for articulating resistance forged in the crucible of slavery and the long struggle for civil and human rights', echoing Gilroy's suggestion that it was precisely the performance and articulation of a 'counterculture to modernity' which made Black music from America 'so appealing' to consumers in Africa, and vice versa (Jaji 2014: 14–15).

Myriad theorists warily approach the capacity for popular cultural forms – especially cinema, it seems – to empower black people. Pearl Bowser and Louise Spence, for example, qualify their detailed analysis of early African-American filmmaker Oscar Micheaux and the radical possibilities of his pioneering film projects by positing: 'Can popular culture be political? Can it resist forces of oppression, racism, and the denial of African humanity and still remain popular?' (Bowser and Spence 2000: xii). Even Jaji recognizes the difficult obstacles complicating *Africa in Stereo*'s mission to establish Pan-African solidarity through cultural expression, raising a very important issue at the heart of Gilroy's project: 'How does one address the danger in calling the consumption and recycling of cultural exports from the world's (and history's) most dominant capitalist power, the U.S., a form of solidarity?' (Jaji 2014: 9). Jaji, however, understands that the radical countercultural powers of Black Atlantic cultural expression and 'stereomodernism' are not limited to a single form but instead require a variety of means of expressive communication to effectively overcome 'the challenges of new forms of exploitation … [which are] so acute and pervasive' (Jaji 2014: 8). In this sense, *Africa in Stereo*'s positioning of Black film alongside Black music in offering resistance to – and alternatives of – modernity through its laying bare 'the many complications of aspirational consumption' contrasts starkly with Gilroy's pessimistic position in relation to the visualization of Afrodiasporic cultures (Jaji 2014: 111).

Since the circulation of Gilroy's *The Black Atlantic*, and both before and after the publication of Jaji's *Africa in Stereo*, a range of scholarly voices have recognized the entangled relationships between sound and vision in filmic expression. Michel Chion's *Audio-Vision: Sound on Screen* (1994) is one of the first academic works to argue that 'sound film' is experienced as a trans-sensory whole, engaging the faculties of seeing and hearing concurrently rather than separately. Mathias Bonde Korsgaard builds on this idea in *Music Video After MTV: Audiovisual Studies, New Media, and Popular Music* (2017) by placing the music video form within the context of the fledgling sphere of 'Audiovisual Studies', focusing on the relationships between sound and image explicitly as opposed to 'the specifically visual or the specifically aural' (Korsgaard 2017: 7). However, as Chion acknowledges in 2013, the audiovisual approach may also be deemed 'audio-divisual' because, in each instance of sound and film combination, the effects are amalgamated 'in a way that is neither symmetrical nor complementary but conflictual' (Chion in Richardson, Gorbman and Vernallis 2013: 77). As illustrated by the overlaps *and* diversions which both connect *and* distinguish Gilroy's audial countercultures of modernity, Weheliye's sonic Afro-modernity and Jaji's stereomodernism, tensions between music, sound and moving images within the spectra of contemporary Black cultural expression are helpfully articulated by an approach that likewise shifts between audiovisual *and* audio-divisual frameworks.

In her discussions of the emerging Audiovisual Studies field, Carol Vernallis observes that digitalization blurs rigid compartmentalizations which distinguish sound and images because 'both now share an ontological ground of being code … an adjustment in one medium can spur a modification in the other, and then back and forth again, nearly effortlessly' (Vernallis in Vernallis, Rogers and Perrott 2020: 7). However, while there are instances when an 'audiovisual' cluster of theories suit Joseph's explorations of the relations between sight and sound, there are also moments where my research adopts the unevenness of Chion's 'audio-divisual' approach, privileging image-based theories over sound-based concepts, and vice versa, to encapsulate the multidimensional *and* polytonal diasporic flows of Joseph's work. Recent academic works such as *Music/Video: Histories, Aesthetics, Media* (Arnold et al. 2017), *Music Video After MTV: Audiovisual Studies, New Media and Popular Music* (Korsgaard 2017), *Transmedia Directors: Artistry, Industry and New Audiovisual Aesthetics* (Vernallis, Rogers and Perrott 2020), *The Rhythm Image: Music Videos and New Audiovisual Forms* (Shaviro 2023) and *The Media Swirl: Politics, Audiovisuality, and Aesthetics* (Vernallis 2023) contend that the music video is a chameleonic, hybridized form of artistic expression, positioned 'on a series of fault lines between music, sound and the visual, between high and popular culture, between dominant and alternative representations' (Arnold et al. 2017: 3).[9] Building on the research of a range of contemporary music video, film, new media and popular music scholars, I attempt to evaluate and access inconsistent 'fault lines' and 'crossroads' on which Joseph's works

---

[9] See also: *Unruly Media: Youtube, Music Video, and the New Digital Cinema* (Vernallis 2013), *Digital Music Videos* (Shaviro 2017), *Cybermedia: Explorations in Science, Sound, and Vision* (Vernallis et al 2021) and *Youtube and Music: Online Culture and Everyday Life* (Rogers, Freitas and Porfírio 2023).

rest, assessing the outcomes and effects as a variety of new media forms, music styles and academic frameworks compete, contest and overlap.

In true 'audio-divisual' fashion, literature centring around sound, music and moving image combinations in Afrodiasporic art does not necessarily offer clear, identifiable patterns but, instead, unfolds in an erratic manner, likewise balancing both modalities in a syncretic way before privileging image-based theories over sound-based theories, or vice versa. However, among these juxtapositions and disharmonies, there are moments when media scholarship recognizes 'audio-divisual' tensions latent in certain audiovisual expressions across the Black Atlantic, thereby offering fruitful avenues through which to articulate and assess the formal complexity and multifaceted forms of Afrocentricity and pan-African solidarity at the crux of Joseph's art. I therefore attempt to articulate these instances of tension throughout the book, reflecting the complex cross-cultural formations and affiliations underpinning Joseph's multidimensional media artworks as the filmmaker attempts to resist and subvert modernity's unilateral Eurocentricity and Whiteness by drawing from resources and concepts across Europe, North and South America and Africa. As well as merging traditions from across the Atlantic and indeed the rest of the world, I examine the inevitable tensions that arise as these diverse legacies compete and contest, colliding at various 'crossroads' in our contemporary neoliberal moment.

1.3.1 Crossroads of cultural traffic

In an attempt to understand these complex instances when cultural flows from Africa, America, Europe and the Caribbean intersect in various states of tension, the 'crossroads' metaphor from Elam Jr. and Jackson's *Black Cultural Traffic: Crossroads in Global Performance and Popular Culture* (2005) emphasizes the significance of movement when negotiating the complexity of contemporary forms of cultural communication. Jackson expresses an appreciation for Roger Chartier's modelling of printed text cultures in the French Renaissance (Chartier 1987), foregrounding the attention paid to 'the circulation of cultural artifacts *across* social boundaries … the fact that both elite *and* common people constantly imitate and borrowed each other's cultural forms' (my emphasis) (Jackson in Elam Jr. and Jackson 2005: 8), and Stephen Greenblatt's understanding of 'cultural mobility' as 'not the expression of random mobility but of exchange' is cited as shaping the theorization of Black cultural traffic as a series of omnidirectional negotiations between both producers and consumers (Greenblatt 1990: 229). However, despite considering Chartier's model and Greenblatt's definition 'helpful' for *Black Cultural Traffic*'s theorizations of motion in relation to cultural production and consumption, Jackson states that *The Black Atlantic* is 'the most seminal work promoting black cultural traffic', highlighting the circulatory model of movement for black cultural forms in Gilroy's chapter 'Jewels Brought from Bondage: Black Music and Politics of Authenticity' (Jackson, in Elam Jr. and Jackson 2005: 7).

In 'Jewels from Bondage', Gilroy explores the mobility of Black Atlantic cultural expression by focusing on the Fisk Jubilee Singers and their singing tour of Britain in 1870. This was the first time a choir group performed African-American folk forms of spiritual singing on public platforms in the UK. Understandably, the singers initially struggled to find a sustainable ecosystem for Black music produced by black performers because they were competing with the fifty years of 'blackface' minstrel entertainment to which Britain had become accustomed.

While white groups impeded the choir by refusing to hire the musicians or prohibiting their touring party from booking accommodation, many black music fans were protective of their musical heritage, worrying that their musical traditions would become disfigured by being made to compete against 'the absurd representations of popular culture offered by minstrelsy's pantomime dramatization of white supremacy' (Gilroy 1993: 89). Nonetheless, despite frequent encounters with race-based discrimination, the Fisk Jubilee Singers' gradual growth in popularity in Britain spawned a host of similar touring companies across Europe and South Africa, generating 'new constituencies among working people and elites' (Jackson in Elam Jr. and Jackson 2005: 8) through the construction of 'an aura of seriousness around their activities ... [projecting] the memory of slavery outwards as the means to make their musical performances intelligible and pleasurable' (Gilroy 1993: 89).

Jackson argues that the discussions of the Fisk Jubilee Singers's tour of England, Ireland, Wales and Scotland in 'Jewels from Bondage' shape his co-authored book's focus on mobility because Gilroy extrapolates the tensions that emerged as aspects of Europe, America and Africa's interrelated histories collided through the group's UK performances without becoming 'daunted by the complexity of black cultural traffic' (Jackson in Elam Jr. and Jackson 2005: 8). For example, the Fisk Jubilee Choir published and sold historical accounts of their group members' journeys, at once supplementing their income *and* contextualizing their struggles. While at first the publication of autobiographical histories to accompany the choir's music and lyric sheets might be disregarded as an 'unusual combination of communicative modes and genres', Gilroy explains that the group's merging of textual and literary material is a sophisticated blending of cultural markers, offering a helpful entrance point 'for anyone seeking to locate the origins of the polyphonic montage technique' that was developed in *The Souls of Black Folk: Essays and Sketches* (1903) and W. E. Du Bois's usage of the 'Sorrow Songs' (Gilroy 1993: 89).

Du Bois frames each chapter of his text with a fragmentary part of the 'Sorrow Songs' – a mixture of slave songs and poem-songs originally recited by plantation workers – in order to capture in textual form the 'echo[es] of haunting melody from the only American music which welled up from black souls in the dark past' (Du Bois 1903: 1). Gilroy suggests that these fragments 'both accompanied *and* signified on the Euro-American romantic poetry that comprised the other part of these double epigraphs', expressing the double consciousness of Black experiences in the West 'in the double values of these songs which are always both American *and* black' (my emphasis) (Gilroy 1993: 91). Gilroy here captures the 'complexity' of Black cultural traffic's movements between divergent cultural spheres, demonstrating how Du Bois's multimodal form of Afrodiasporic cultural expression draws from the fragmentation of plantation slave songs, transforming the pieces of these poem-songs through the Fisk Jubilee Choir's promotional activities as the group travelled to and across the UK.

Black cultural traffic's omnidirectional and intergenerational movements across the Black Atlantic are in turn mirrored by the flows of academic discourses between the aforementioned writers, the manner in which Du Bois's usage of fragmented slave songs shapes Elam Jr. and Jackson's 'crossroads' metaphor by way of Gilroy's analysis of the Fisk Jubilee Choir's activities in Britain. The analogy of constantly shifting sets of conceptual crossroads allows both *The Black Atlantic* and *Black Cultural Traffic* to trace 'black intellectuals' nationalist ideas as they travelled to and fro across the Atlantic' while, at the same time, tracking 'the travels of popular culture, specifically black music' (Jackson in Elam Jr and Jackson 2005: 7). However, by recognizing that exemplars of Black popular culture which include *and* extend beyond musical forms can be adopted as the theoretical mortar that binds these conceptual bricks, one may thus begin to build crossroads *between* other imagined crossroads, exploring the complexity of Joseph's contemporary screen texts as nodal points where disparate yet overlapping networks of ideas, contexts and cultural affiliations meet, compete and contest, struggling to reach a state of equilibrium, never grinding to a halt.

1.3.2 Crossroads of capital

As demonstrated by the discursive strands connecting Du Bois and Gilroy to Elam Jr and Jackson, crossroads between theories and cultural products become more complex and increasingly sophisticated as they stretch across both time and space, bridging the gaps between our networked empirical reality and the immateriality of our thoughts and ideas, thereby allowing theorists to build deep connections between a range of subjects. Akinwumi Adesokan, for example, is a Nigeria-born academic now living in America who uses the notion of the West African marketplace 'to flesh out' what he terms 'the crossroads of capital', drawing from his own experiences across the Atlantic to capture tensions between artistic practices and the neoliberal world system that are produced by 'the shuttling between the economic and the cultural spheres' (Adesokan 2011: 6).

In acknowledging that the imbalance between supply and demand throughout the world 'sustains the market and the fact that capitalism thrives on uneven geographical development', Adesokan recognizes that aspects of the market(place) are 'gendered, hierarchical, corrupt and socially oppressive … far from democratic, much less progressive' (ibid. 7). However, he also draws from Manthia Diawara's understanding of the marketplace as a space where 'the collective unconscious' of African citizens is moulded by certain manifestations of globalization that cannot be governed efficiently by state interference (Diawara 1998: 115). Past merchants managed to maintain traditional practices and long-standing commercial methods that were demonized by the colonial powers (Adesokan 2011: 7–8), and many continue to resist foreign modes of being that might otherwise transform contemporary marketplace workers into the sort of 'modern business bureaucrats and entrepreneurs' that today epitomize neoliberalism's core 'free market' values (Diawara 1998: 118).

The marketplace thus becomes 'a complex site of resistance' that operates inside the neoliberal framework yet, at the same time, offers its own ways for negotiating this particular world system (Adesokan 2011: 7). In a similar manner, Joseph's screen texts exist at the crossroads of capital, or the marketplace's 'complex site of resistance', inescapably wedded to neoliberal capitalism because they exist within our contemporary economic framework while, at certain points, channelling Black Atlantic music and film's resistance to Eurocentric versions of modernity through their implicit critique of capitalism's dehumanizing effects. Adesokan's crossroads of capital concept are therefore particularly helpful for emphasizing how 'capitalism's uneven geographical developments' affect Joseph's audiovisual works when he operates in diverse contexts and settings, thereby necessitating deep and thorough engagement with the various contextual factors that shape the filmmaker's work in a range of environments across America, Europe and Africa (ibid. 11).

Echoing the undercurrents of *The Black Atlantic* which energize Elam Jr and Jackson's ideas with their restless, omnidirectional motion, Gilroy's influence on the crossroads of capital concept is especially emphasized by Adesokan's discussions of the writer Caryl Phillips. When articulating the inherent tensions that appear 'in unexpected places and … unexpected forms' as uneven processes of globalization affect divergent contexts and settings across the world in different ways, Adesokan notes that although the renowned historian, journalist and Marxist writer C. L. R. James 'wrote and worked with the aim of undermining, even destroying, capitalism … who envisaged the maverick address proposed in the figure of Phillips?' (ibid.). Phillips was born in the Caribbean, raised in England and now predominantly resides in the United States, moving between the three core continents which constitute the Black Atlantic, capturing his experiences in writing. While Phillips's collection of essays *A New World Order* (2001) ruminates on one's dislocation from cultural spheres, pluralistic approaches to identity formations, and the erosion of concrete national boundaries, his travel book *The Atlantic Sound* (2000) traces the author's journeys to three major city ports of the Atlantic Slave Trade – England's Liverpool, Cape Coast in Ghana and Charleston in America's South Carolina.

The Atlantic Sound exemplifies the inherent instability of the Black Atlantic self by adopting a multi-generic style of writing, switching literary forms for each of its sections to capture the ceaseless shifting of the Atlantic Ocean. Adesokan, however, is particularly struck by Phillips's 'geographically informed conception of identity' (Adesokan 2011: 135). While living in the United States yet retaining a home in London as well as British passport, Phillips's essay 'The High Anxiety of Belonging' from *The New World Order* communicates his uneasiness maintaining concurrent affiliations to divergent cultural spheres. The writer struggles to tie any sense of belonging with concepts of 'race', and concludes by opting for a shifting, territory-based notion of the self wedded to the fluidity of the Atlantic Ocean, or, in Phillips's words, 'my increasingly precious, imaginary, Atlantic world' (Phillips 2001: 308). Although Phillips's sense of belonging is tied to the spatial arrangements of the Atlantic Ocean and therefore remains 'largely geographical', residues of racialization remain imbedded in his sense of self because the legacies of 'race' and racism are inextricably tied to the spaces that constitute the Black Atlantic, meaning these residues continue to influence Phillips's geographical affiliations *despite* his attempts to move beyond racial categorizations (Adesokan 2011: 135).

The problematic and fragmentary remnants of 'race' in Phillips's Atlantic-based understanding of the self, Adesokan observes, are articulated by Gilroy's framing of 'race' in quotation marks in *Between Camps: Nations, Cultures and the Allure of Race beyond the Colour Line* (2000/2004).[10] Gilroy's work highlights the antagonistic relationship between 'race-thinking' across the Black Atlantic (metaphysical notions and ideas which constitute 'race') and the real-life implications of institutional racialization within *and* beyond the American context which are, in turn, shaped by 'race-thinking'. Discourses of racialization here signify 'the lore that brings the virtual realities of "race" to dismal and destructive life', collapsing frail boundaries that artificially separate art and reality's entwined branches, thereby refusing to disentangle art's discourses from their real-world effects (Gilroy 2004a: 11).

At the 'crossroads of capital' – where myriad intellectual frameworks commingle as the cultural and economic spheres collide – the uneven developments of 'race-thinking' are exemplified by Phillips's realization that, in the same year as *The Atlantic Sound*'s publication, he moved to New York's Greenwich Village neighbourhood, a short distance from Charles Street where 'the great American writer Richard Wright endured much difficulty and unspeakable humiliation trying to live and write as a free man in the country of his birth' (Phillips 2001: 27). Wright achieved financial security after selling 250,000 hardcover copies of *Native Son* (1940), a fictional narrative exploring the institutionalized sense of racialized self-hatred endured by protagonist Bigger Thomas. Although Wright sought to escape the racial tensions surrounding his Brooklyn home by purchasing a property in Charles Street in the 1940s, he discovered that the area was marred by similar issues of underlying racial tension, eventually choosing to move to France permanently in 1947 after an epiphanic trip to Paris (Briones 2003; Moskowitz 2008).

Wright turned to Europe as a haven from forms of racism tied to the American context, whereas Phillips sought refuge in America as means of counteracting the fractious sense of belonging engendered by his European upbringing. Although the fragmentary yet tangible remains of 'race-thinking' in these separate geographical spaces have resulted in progressive outcomes such as 'the kind of institutional power that enabled Phillips to make a home in Greenwich Village', the freedom to emphasize one's geographic connections is never completely race-less, or void of the residues of racialization, as a result of the overlapping histories which bind the Black Atlantic's distinguishable yet interrelated territories (Adesokan 2011: 155). Stuart Hall, for example, uses the phrase 'Cross-Currents of Diaspora' to capture the implicit tensions at

---

[10] *Between Camps* was first published in Britain by Allen Lane The Penguin Press in 2000, and then republished by the Taylor & Francis Group's Routledge imprint in 2004. The book was published in America under the title *Against Race: Imagining Political Culture beyond the Colour Line* by Harvard University Press in 2000.

the heart of Caribbean identity formations, recalling the sensation of being 'absolutely staggered' when he first discovered the cultural *and* ethnic diversity of these islands (Hall 1995: 5). At the same time, he suggests that 'it is impossible to locate in the Caribbean an origin for its peoples', highlighting the extermination of the indigenous Arawak communities at the hands of European colonizers for profit, as well as pointing to the differences between the Cuban, Haitian and Dominican cultures which flow throughout and concurrently characterize the region (ibid.).

The crossroads, or underlying 'Cross-currents', of these diverse and simultaneously interconnected economic and cultural areas engender complex, problematic processes of 'race-thinking' and racialization across geographical spheres while, at the same time, also generating countercultural moments of resistance, disturbing the primarily Eurocentric foundations on which 'race-thinking' and our economic world system are grounded. Joseph's audiovisual works are therefore 'complex sites of resistance' where the crossroads and imbalanced relationships between 'race-thinking', commercial legacies and territory-based constructions of Black Atlantic identities may converge, competing as they draw from influences from a rich array of contexts and settings across Africa, America, Europe and the Caribbean while, at the same time, remaining subject to the 'uneven geographical developments' enacted by our contemporary economic framework (Adesokan 2011: 11).

1.3.3 Crossroads of aesthetics

In the digital age, Rosi Braidotti observes that 'global consumerism, while promoting an ideology of "no borders", implements a highly controlled system of hyper-mobility of consumer goods, information bytes, data and capital … [wherein] people do not circulate nearly as freely', thus digital products such as Joseph's audiovisual works may traverse the spatiotemporal limitations imposed on human movements and, in turn, share information and ideas across large geographical territories (Braidotti in Braidotti and Gilroy 2016: 11). Joseph's combinations of audial *and* visual expressive cultures are thus fruitful sites of enquiry when attempting to negotiate processes of neoliberal globalization in our contemporary moment. Audiovisual art can actively 'construct and perform social relations, forms and feelings' associated with our networked present (Shaviro 2010: 6) by performing and tracing certain traits of the globalized world-system, capturing elements of a zeitgeist that is 'unrepresentable' in its entirety yet, crucially, comprehendible in small, meaningful ways through the sensations and signs produced by artistic representation (Jameson 1991). As complex amalgamations of a variety of sound, music and image-based practices, the form(s) of Joseph's works harmonize with his content by mimicking the heterogenous elements of contemporaneity's global network systems, thereby allowing viewers 'to understand change in a world too enormous to see but vital to imagine' (Mirzoeff 2015: 12).

When striving to theorize and unpack aspects of a planet as vast and diverse as ours, the fast-paced emergence of new trends and issues in the creative and cultural industries makes the task of processing such phenomena increasingly messy. Clive Chijioke Nwonka thus adopts the term 'Black Neoliberal Aesthetic' to articulate the controversial presence of urbanized black male violence in forms of Black-British cultural representation that might otherwise consider themselves liberal or progressive, attempting to process the ways in which our global economic system affects the content and production of made-for-television films in the UK. The British film and television industries have attempted to expand the presence of black media workers both on and off the screen, basing their actions on the contested assumption that 'diversity' policies in the workplace (within and beyond the screen) would automatically negate institutionalized forms of racism (Malik, Chapain and Comunian 2017; Nwonka and Malik 2018). Nwonka, however, observes that new challenges arise when projects such as the BBC Two's made-for-television film adaptation of Zadie Smith's novel *NW* (2012) from 2016 purport 'to operate as a liberal disavowal of racism and racial exclusion' yet contradict themselves through overreliance on stereotypical representations of violent Black masculinities, which, in fact, 'constitute neoliberal racialisation' (Nwonka 2020: 844).

Nwonka's construction of the Black Neoliberal Aesthetic is rooted in the writings of Stuart Hall. Hall sought to emphasize that the increased presence of Blackness on screen does not adequately challenge processes of racism and racialization if such representations continue to circulate clichés and mischaracterizations; thus he asserted that viewers should not accept filmic texts uncritically 'by the virtue of the fact that they deal with the black experience' (Hall 1988: 28). Nwonka finds Hall's observation insightful, yet he recognizes that the decision to apply Hall's discourses to contemporary media representations of Black-Britons is undermined by the gulf that separates the theorists' respective contexts. Hall was responding to problematic depictions of black people which dominated British film and media cultures in the late eighties and early nineties, writing when a sense of weariness towards the hostile social conditions created by Thatcherism had emerged within the national psyche, the threat of further recessions and yet another spike in mass unemployment hinting that Margaret Thatcher's turbulent third term in office would be her last.

Nwonka, on the other hand, writes from the aftermath of Tony Blair's failed New Labour project as consecutive Conservative governments have continued to shift further and further into the realms of authoritarianism. In a period marked by stark nationwide rifts as a result of David Cameron's brutal austerity programme and the subsequent political fallout of the Brexit referendum, the scandalous treatment of the Windrush Generation and the victims of the Grenfell Tower disaster emphasize how biases relating to one's race and class continue to manifest, echoing in part – yet also drastically diverging from – the social and economic issues underpinning the Thatcher regime. Although Hall and his contemporaries were especially preoccupied with the moral panic which had started to surround increased reports of 'muggings' on Britain's streets, Nwonka justifies reappropriating Hall's arguments by focusing on the latest articulation of 'black convention' with regard to film and television dramas, which, in today's neoliberal environment, he worries 'often positions criminality and casualty as a central tenet' (Nwonka 2020: 844).

By creating an argument that echoes Nwonka's justifications for applying Hall's ideas to a contemporary context, one may theorize ways to ride these 'Cross-currents of diaspora' across the Black Atlantic, applying the Black Neoliberal Aesthetic concept to – and thereby enhancing – our understandings of Joseph's works. The award-winning film *Until the Quiet Comes* (2012), for example, incorporates elements of Bantu-Kongo Cosmology throughout its depictions of the Nickerson Gardens Housing Project as means of uniting African diasporas across national borders and the boundaries of race and class. However, *Until the Quiet Comes* also incorporates vivid representations of black male figures wounded and killed by gunfire, reinforcing stereotypes which harm the same black communities that are otherwise empowered by other aspects of the film. As Nwonka argues, his reading of neoliberal filmmaking practices resuscitates Hall's understanding of the '*seduction* of racial difference' in a capitalistic society, 'where the legitimacy of neoliberal reconstruction at the very fabric of cultural life merges at its most powerful and undetectable when aligned to blackness' (my emphasis) (Nwonka 2020: 849). Although Joseph's public persona as a filmmaker is grounded on the 'celebration of black life' that frequently characterizes his audiovisual works (Solway 2019), Nwonka's ideas help us process and disentangle the moments of contradiction which counteract the celebration of black peoples' lives and experiences, allowing theorists to recognize how the tensions in Joseph's art mimic the complexity and paradoxes of the neoliberal world system.

When examining how neoliberal conditions in the British context shape cultural production and reception, Nwonka asserts the Black Neoliberal Aesthetic phenomenon is 'both textual and structural', that *NW* was the result 'of a combination of manoeuvres of diversity politics *and* the narrativization of media discourses over black gun-crime in London' (my emphasis) (Nwonka 2020: 853). The legalization of gun ownership in America is but one of many factors which fundamentally distinguish manifestations of street-level violence in the United States from similar acts in Britain. Nonetheless, as illustrated by the transnational and intercultural crossroads generated by Gilroy's Black Atlantic construct *and* the multidirectional crosscurrents underpinning Hall's sense of Caribbean identity formations, the conditions of neoliberal existence for the diasporic communities in Europe, Africa and the Americas share many similarities which extend beyond both time *and* space.

Certain aspects of Joseph's works, then, reproduce elements of Nwonka's Black Neoliberal Aesthetic because, in the same vein as the filmic version of *NW*, they capture the reflexive relationships between the textual elements of a media form and the infrastructures beyond the screen through which that piece of media is produced, circulated and consumed. Rather than existing in a vacuum, the narrative themes of these works shape the empirical world by sharing 'the same neoliberal continuum' and blurring neat boundaries that separate art from its influences in real life, capturing the pressing need to unpack and process these contemporary media discourses if we are to understand how processes of neoliberal racialization continue to operate through – or are counteracted by – combinations of music, sound and moving images in the twenty-first century (Nwonka 2020: 854).

As demonstrated by Nwonka's recontextualization of Hall's writing in response to British television and, in turn, my own recontextualization of the Black Neoliberal Aesthetic in response to Joseph's filmic output, the flows of media arts and their discourses across the Black Atlantic are characterized by fluctuation and mobility, shifting and changing as they negotiate divergent cultural spheres across different configurations of time and space. The social value of Black music *and* moving images thus stems from these intercultural movements, the moments when an artwork's discursive meaning escapes its interiority and influences our lives in the real world 'by communicating information, organizing consciousness, and testing out or deploying the forms of objectivity which are required by political agency' (Gilroy 1993: 36).

Nwonka is by no means the first scholar to attempt to theorize Afrocentric audiovisual aesthetics. For example, Arthur Jafa – a close friend and collaborator of Kahlil Joseph[11] – poses in 1992 the ambition to create 'Black Visual Intonations', a filmmaking style that mimics 'the tendency in Black music to "worry the note" – to treat notes as indeterminate, inherently unstable sonic frequencies rather than the standard Western treatment of notes as fixed phenomena' (Jafa in Dent 1992: 254). Jafa argues that classical Western music traditions emphasize the precision and clarity of specific tonalities dictated by a single commanding rhythm, whereas traditional African music heritages include a broader range of tonal formations coordinated by 'polyrhythms' which sometimes possess as many as four rhythms at once. Based on the interpretation that the uneven 'call and response' bends and stretches of later Afrodiasporic musical forms – trembling blues bars, wobbling jazz notes – are indebted to the freeform, improvisational structures and energizing, communalizing functions central to continental African music and its associated rituals, Jafa theorizes that, if filmmakers find a way of capturing similar senses of music-imbued indeterminacy in their work: 'Black images [can] vibrate in accordance with certain frequential values that exist in Black music' (Jafa 1992: 254).

In many ways, Jafa's ideas about 'Black Visual Intonations' have the capacity to reinforce Gilroy's understanding of the Black Atlantic, offering an Afrocentric perspective of reality which challenges modernity's Eurocentricity. However, Jafa's manifesto is largely predicated on using the irregular speeds of a 'nonmetronomic camera rate' to replicate musical rhythms (Jafa 1992: 255) and he claims to have designed 372 'alignment patterns' or 'fixed frame replication patterns' which might be used to create the visual equivalences of 'samba beats, reggae beats, all kinds of things', relying heavily on visual aspects of sound-image amalgamations at the expense of the sonic (Jafa 1992: 254). By focusing on the possibilities of experimental editing structures, Jafa's early writings inadvertently neglect the curious hold of sonic reverberations over human emotions, the fundamental neurological and physiological effects at the heart of musical experiences which can affect our behaviours, and shape the ways people interact with the world. As a result, Jafa's theorization of 'Black Visual Intonations' indirectly separates music and moving images from some of the complex webs of experiences and lived realities in which Black Atlantic artworks are inevitably entangled. Tina Campt therefore attempts to

---

[11] Arthur Jafa's work *Love Is The Message, The Message Is Death* (2016) has been screened at Joseph's Underground Museum, and together the pair created the experimental 'docu-poem' *Dreams Are Colder Than Death* (2014).

bridge some of the conceptual gaps in Jafa's theories by drawing from her work with the Practicing Refusal Collective – an international black feminists' forum – and her own attempts to theorize 'the visual frequency of black life' or, in other words, the ways in which combinations of sound and moving image allow us 'to see the affects of sound' on Black Lives, and thereby 'visualise the impact of music' on everyday existence (Campt 2019: 30).

Campt states that Jafa's often quoted desire 'to make Black cinema with the power, beauty and alienation of black music' (Jafa in conversation with Sargent 2017) is an 'ambitious, aspirational' approach to filmmaking, or a 'deceptively simple ... [yet] intentionally moving target' with the potential to challenge and shift 'the definition of what constitutes (or what might constitute) "black film"' (Campt 2019: 30). However, while Jafa's early writings pose the question: 'How can we analyze the tone, not the sequence of notes that Coltrane hit, but the tone itself, and synchronize Black visual movement with that?' (Jafa 1992: 253–4), Campt similarly argues that Jafa's films 'require us to focus our attention not on the notes that comprise them but on the tonality of how they are rendered' in a manner akin to the compositions and performances of John Coltrane, suggesting that audiences 'must dwell in the tonality of the images and their capacity to depict black bodies in a state somewhere between stillness, movement, and motion' (Campt 2019: 30).

In order to articulate this complex state between static and stationary representations of black peoples' experiences in Jafa's work – the precarious and unpredictable state of Black existence in our contemporary moment platformed through combinations of the sonic and the visual – Campt turns to her experiences with the Practicing Refusal Collective. The feminist group originally convened in 2015 under the stewardship of Campt and her friend and collaborator Saidiya Hartman as means of exploring 'a rejection of the status quo as liveable ... a refusal to recognize a social order that renders you fundamentally illegible and unintelligible' (ibid. 25). Drawing from a rich range of feminist voices (from Angela Davis, Pat Parker and June Jordan to Audre Lorde, bell hooks and Ida B. Wells) the collective refuses 'to embrace the terms of diminished subjecthood with which one is presented' and, instead, searches for new ways 'to use negation as a generative and creative source of disorderly power ... striving to create possibility in the face of negation' (ibid.).

Inspired by her work with the Practicing Refusal Collective, Campt formulates an aesthetic category termed 'still-moving-images'. From an ocular perspective, she argues that still-moving-images in Jafa's collection of work 'hover between still and moving images; animated still images, slowed or stilled images in motion, or visual renderings that blur the distinctions between these multiple genres'. However, by complicating and challenging the boundaries between various generic forms as their content shifts between euphoric and agonizing depictions of Black experiences, Campt argues that these images 'require the labor of feeling with or through them' as one engages with both their content *and* form (ibid. 31). Still-moving-images thus offer diverse representations of contemporary black peoples' lives that hover between states of 'power, beauty and alienation', much like Coltrane's quivering notes as they hover between tonalities, communicating the complex and oftentimes paradoxical experiential dynamics of contemporary Black life in a manner that transcends the limitations of oral dialogue (Jafa in conversation with Sargent 2017).

Although audiences might struggle to engage with 'what, on first sight, appears to be a troubling and painful collection of images', Campt reasons that certain still-moving-images demand 'the effort required to position oneself in proximity to, or in a place of discomfort and, for some, potential complicity with, black precarity' (Campt 2019: 26). A prevailing sense of racialized insecurity in the quotidian experiences of black people justifies urgently circulating distressing imagery because, for Campt, the circulation of this discomforting content highlights the pressing need to address such racialized disequilibria in our contemporary epoch. Otherwise unseen instances of Black precarity are rendered visible through certain forms of audiovisual communication, thus still-moving-images encourage audiences to make an effort to feel the pain of Afrodiasporic experiences, communicating visceral sensations of discomfort as means of emphasizing the urgency with which a more just and fair society must be created.

While Campt argues that audiovisual representations of Black violence are necessary for enacting social change in the world beyond the screen, Nwonka's theorization of the Black Neoliberal Aesthetic challenges the assumption that the circulation of such images can effectively counteract stereotypical representations of Afrodiasporic communities. Campt turns to Jafa's 'power, beauty and alienation' mantra, arguing that contemporary black (audio)visual artists such as Kahlil Joseph are imagining 'the inseparability of black pleasure, beauty and suffering' in such a way that 'challenge[s] us to think differently about the labor required by forms of black visuality' (Campt 2019: 26). Nwonka, on the other hand, reasons 'the spectacle of black urban male death' on film and television purportedly disavows certain clichés surrounding Black masculinity and violence, while, at the same time, circulating and thereby inadvertently sustaining such stereotypes (Nwonka 2020: 846).

Although the works of Jafa and Joseph 'are engaging and recreating the visual archive of black precarity in new and transformative ways' (Campt 2019: 27), Nwonka's critique of the audiovisualization of Black violence highlights implicit tensions which complicate arguments for Campt's aesthetic category. Oscillating somewhere between Campt's still-moving-images and Nwonka's Black Neoliberal Aesthetic, Joseph's works thus operate at the crossroads and crosscurrents of aesthetic categories, capturing the relentless cross-cultural flows of Black music and moving images in our contemporary moment, while, at the same time, communicating the unstable, frequently precarious set of conditions under which Afrodiasporic identities exist across divergent spatiotemporal formations. Campt and Nwonka occupy different spaces across the Black Atlantic – the United States and Britain, respectively – which in turn illustrates how Joseph's audiovisual works are both meeting points *and* sites of contestation where different parts of the world interact, thereby continuing the intercultural conversations as articulated by Gilroy's earlier theorizations.

Campt's aesthetic category allows us to imagine 'the inseparability of black pleasure, beauty and suffering' (Campt 2019: 26), while Nwonka's ideas remind us that 'predominantly white dominated institutions derive cultural, social or economic values from non-whiteness' in such a manner than can rupture 'strategies for tangible social transformation' (Nwonka 2020: 849). Although the merging of black people's joys and pains through music and moving images in Joseph and Jafa's work has the possibility to challenge and disrupt hegemonic modes of being in our contemporary neoliberal moment, one must also remember that the commercial imperatives to which contemporary forms of audiovisual expression are inextricably wed complicate readings that would otherwise neatly categorize Joseph's aesthetics – and, in turn, the affective properties of his aesthetics – into rigid compartmentalizations, or singularizing narratives.

During a public discussion with Campt and Alexander Weheliye titled *Frequencies of Blackness: A Listening Session*, Zara Julius and Jenn Nkiru build on Campt's ideas about Black music and moving images, exploring how the aesthetics of Afrodiasporic cultural expression can communicate on a range of levels – or through a variety of countercultural frequencies – that challenge the West's prevalent discourses and, in turn, shape alternative ways of being across the globe (Campt, Julius, Nkiru and Weheliye 2020). Julius suggests that certain modes of performance have the capacity – if only for very short periods – to disrupt and challenge the foundations on which humans build their experiences of 'marketed time'. Marketed time, for Julius, is a sense of being tied to one's capacity to work: the condition of existing in a human form when the prevalent societal framework in which that person is situated is predominantly characterized by one's function as a labourer. Moments of rest, or periods that at least feel free from labour, are in fact inevitably framed by a person's relationship to the economic world system (Julius in conversation with Campt, Nkiru and Weheliye 2020). The need to continue generating commerce once a break period is over – and to repeat this process over and over, again and again, until financial security is achieved, or incapacitation intervenes through injury or death – involuntarily influences one's thoughts, actions and behaviours on an unending and unrelenting basis, manifesting in unhealthy, dehumanizing ways of being.

Responding to Julius's arguments for the disruption of marketed time through particular types of performance, Nkiru suggests that certain combinations of Black music and moving images can draw percipients into fictional worlds underpinned by intensified sensations of liberation, especially when an artwork blurs the boundaries between motion, time and space through audial and visual forms, merging the senses in such a way that almost feels as though one 'sees music' or 'hears film'. When the senses of seeing and hearing seemingly overlap and commingle, Nkiru emphasizes that these sensations of incongruity can disrupt marketed time and, instead, induce an alternative, freer sense of modernity deemed 'Black/boundless time'. During such instances, percipients momentarily escape the physical confinements imposed on their commodified body, deeply engaging with an audiovisual artwork or artistic performance on a sensate level and, in turn, tapping into an unverbalizable yet recognizable frequency of interhuman communication. Spoken communication serves to give other humans a sense of one's internal thoughts and feelings, whereas the sensations or frequential levels on which this particular form of expression operates effectively 'cut out that middle man', moving directly from one person's feelings to another to communicate sensory experiences, rather than relying on words to preserve, articulate and then express such feelings (Nkiru in conversation with Campt, Julius and Weheliye 2020).

While European theorizations of time emphasize linearity and fixity, Nkiru argues that sensations of Black time and boundlessness through audiovisual communication draw from African spirituality, building on the ways in which understandings of time and place from the continent explore 'poly-complexities … the collapsing of different times and different spaces in one moment'. Nkiru thus suggests that the feeling of unbounded time that emerges through certain forms of Afrodiasporic cultural expression is in fact 'a birth right and an ancestral right' for descendants of Africa (Nkiru in conversation with Campt, Julius and Weheliye 2020). When one momentarily escapes the ways in which their corporeal existence is imbedded in contemporaneity's prevalent sense of marketed time and in turn involuntarily tied to the ebbs and flows of capital, an Afrocentric sense of boundlessness offers an alternative understanding of time, thereby challenging, interrupting and decentring the Eurocentric foundations on which modernity *and* capitalism are based.

The idea that modernity is a period of American and European history that the rest of the world then followed is a highly problematic assumption, especially since large elements of what made the West modern had been imported or stolen from its colonies. Fredric Jameson, for example, goes as far as suggesting that the term 'modernity' should be replaced with 'capitalism' to refer to the viral expansion of the free market across the world which, in turn, was accelerated by the global spread of colonization, enslavement and slave-trading (Jameson 2002: 215). Joseph's combinations of music and moving images can be said to interrupt marketed time – the all-encompassing nature of capitalism, our personal relationships to Eurocentric modernity's prevalent economic framework – by generating these alternative senses of Black or boundless time. Nwonka's theorization of the Black Neoliberal Aesthetic in part challenges Campt's original arguments, especially her justifications for audiovisual representations of black male violence. However, Campt's attempts to theorize how audiovisual expression can allow audiences 'to see the affects of sound and visualize the impact of music' through the still-moving-images concept offer fruitful ways to understand the value of Black music and moving image combinations whose aesthetics challenge modernity's Eurocentric underpinnings and, instead, engender a sense of Black or boundless time (Campt 2019: 30).

Campt frames her discussions with Julius, Nkiru and Weheliye by questioning how certain sonic and visual frequencies – much like oscillatory waves of the Atlantic Ocean – might 'help us to see, hear *and* feel the power of black life's irrepressible desire and drive towards creating a different kind of futurity' (my emphasis) (Campt in conversation with Julius, Nkiru and Weheliye 2020). In order to think beyond the dehumanizing effects of Eurocentric modernity and neoliberal capitalism (to which the Black experiences depicted by Joseph's work are inescapably wed) and, in turn, create alternative futures characterized by liberation and freedom, one must thoroughly engage with the aesthetic crossroads at which Joseph's audiovisual projects reside, rather than reducing these visual forms to a singular or totalizing category.

By analysing the moments when Joseph's works hover between still-moving-images *and* the Black Neoliberal Aesthetic – or, in Campt's words, by scrutinizing 'a continuum of terror *and* joy' where certain audiovisual representations of black peoples' experiences fluctuate (my emphasis) (Campt 2019: 43) – I aim to assess how both marketed *and* unbounded senses of time compete and flow simultaneously alongside each other in various states of tension throughout the filmmaker's oeuvre. I hence attempt to disentangle Joseph's aesthetic crossroads from the crossroads of capital *and* cultural traffic at which his works' audial and visual components shift and transform across the Black Atlantic's diasporic crosscurrents, examining the points at which the filmmaker's combinations of music and moving images can disrupt the Eurocentric flows underpinning modernity, as well as exploring the moments when certain works in fact reinforce the contemporary societal forces which constitute neoliberal hegemony.

Gilroy reminds us that Black Atlantic music is able 'to demonstrate the reconciliation of art and life' if percipients liberate this form of cultural expression 'from its status as a mere commodity' (Gilroy 1993: 124). I thus contend that Joseph's new media works – the music *and* moving images of the Black Atlantic's crossroads, the ebbs *and* flows that dynamize the Audiovisual Atlantic's crosscurrents – likewise perforate barriers which forcibly and superficially separate contemporary forms of cultural communication from the external realities that they constantly and relentlessly shape. Joseph's films,

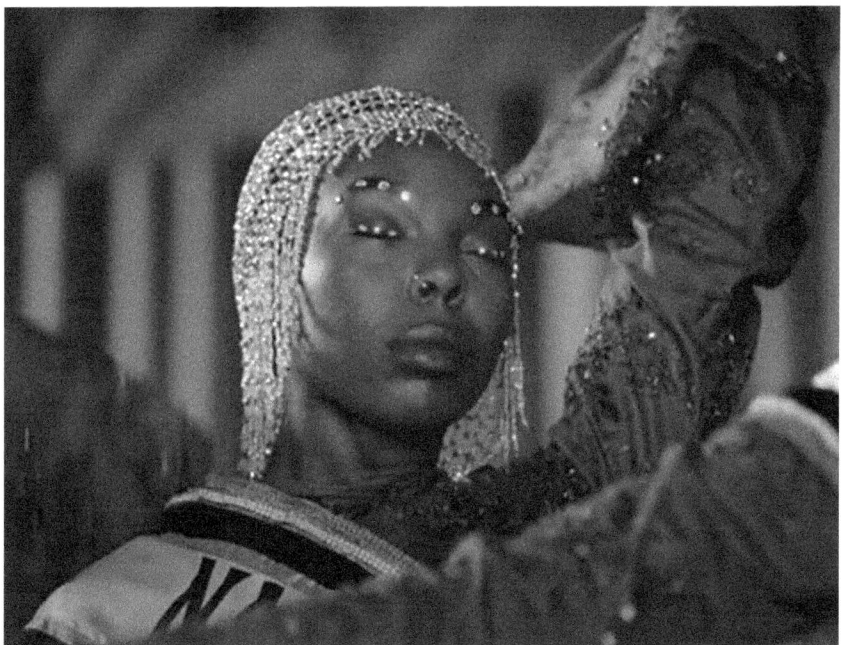

Figure 1.5 *Hub-Tones* (2018), Jenn Nkiru and Kamasi Washington © Young Turks.

music videos and advertisements challenge rigid, outdated notions of race, nationhood and identity, illustrating how the 'deeper impulses' at the heart of (post)national liberation movements and contemporary decolonization projects 'remain alive' at the crossroads of capital, alternative and established spaces, and new audiovisual aesthetics (Adesokan 2011: 11).

As the crosscurrents between these crossroads manifest in Joseph's media artworks, flowing across and between America, Europe and Africa, the impulse to challenge the Eurocentric perspectives that underpin modernity begins 'appearing in unexpected places and taking unexpected forms' as a *result* of – rather than *despite* – the uneven contextual developments enacted by our current economic framework's global reach (ibid).

1.4 Book structure and chapter overview

Having outlined this book's theoretical framework – the crossroads of cultural traffic, capital and aesthetics that manifest as music and moving images overlap across the Black Atlantic; or, in other words, the ebbs and flows of the Audiovisual Atlantic – I now turn to the main body of my research. A media form's genesis remains a contentious issue as a result of its innately collaborative processes, and tensions surrounding the 'co-authorship' of a film (Gaut 1997: 22) echo the ways that music video scholars might dispute positioning 'the figure of the performer as the artistic centre' over framing the director as the 'controlling creative hand' of a project (Railton and Watson 2011: 67). While a range of industry figures (from cinematographers, actors and sound designers to runners, location scouts and costume designers) contribute to the overall creation of a media form and its encoded signs and significations, for pedagogical reasons I mainly focus on the contributions of Kahlil Joseph and the primary musician(s) involved in each case study, occasionally touching on the input from other collaborators where relevant to my discussions about Joseph, his musical counterparts and the creation of their co-authored screen texts. In this way, I emphasize the collaborative nature of Black Atlantic music and moving image hybridizations while at the same time assessing the moments of tension that emerge as musical artists attempt to work on a project together with Joseph and indeed other contributors across a range of film and music professions. Collaborative, communitarian arts collectives remain as vital as ever – and the forms of compassionate, synergetic making and learning that true artistic friendships enable likewise deserve scholarly attention.

In what follows, I divide my work into five chapters. Starting with the beginnings of Joseph's solo career, I create a chronological map that follows the themes and transformations in his art since 2010. While I trace in part the moments in Joseph's career pathway – and development as an artist – that can be described as linear (such as his transition from a film and music video director to a site-specific installation artist, which I argue relates to his growing experiences as a contemporary media practitioner at a similar time as the establishment of the family's Underground Museum) I also document the anomalous instances which undermine any straightforward arguments for the linearity of his career trajectory and artistic development (namely, the complicated appearances of the Black Neoliberal Aesthetic in Joseph's work as he gradually starts to move away from digital distribution platforms towards exhibition spaces, when his creative practice otherwise ostensibly undergoes a period of 'maturity').

At the beginning of each chapter, I offer a contextual section that situates the ensuing content in relation to the key histories and academic discussions of relevant media forms and movements, examining the environments in which these media forms were first conceived, discussing the artistic and academic figures whose works are most relevant to my discussions of Joseph's works. After historicizing these media forms by examining the broader and more localized environments from which they evolved, each chapter focuses on two or three screen texts as case studies. I evaluate how Joseph's screen texts adhere to or challenge traditional parameters of certain media forms at Audiovisual Atlantic's crossroads of cultural traffic, capital and aesthetics, capturing his work's transcontinental and interdisciplinary movements as well as their paradoxes and tensions. *Kahlil Joseph and the Audiovisual Atlantic* thus aims to guide its readers through different frameworks for Black audiovisual culture via Kahlil Joseph's oeuvre. The book uses Joseph's filmic work as a pretext for addressing 'bigger' questions surrounding the Audiovisual Atlantic's enmeshed sonic *and* visual histories, flowing from tight, focused examinations of Joseph's collaborative screen texts towards broader, wide-ranging discussions of Afrodiasporic music *and* new media in different transatlantic contexts.

In Chapter 2, I frame Joseph's early works in relation to Los Angeles's key arts scenes, exploring how the director attempts to blend his emerging artistic persona with the existent cultural traditions that shape the city. Kahlil Joseph moved to Los Angeles for his undergraduate studies, leaving Loyola Marymount University before officially graduating in order to gain industry experience in the area. Drawing from the convincing case made by the *liquid blackness* research group's Alessandra Raengo and Lauren McLeod Cramer for situating Joseph's works in dialogue with the countercultural and intercontinental energies of the LA Rebellion filmmakers (Raengo and Cramer 2020), I also situate Joseph's merging of Black Atlantic music and moving images in relation to the new jazz-hip hop fusion scene, a contemporary phenomenon which has revived the legacies of the city's Central Avenue jazz club sector through the rebellious attitudes and D.I.Y approaches of the West Coast's gangsta rap movement (Solis 2019; Viator 2020).

I then focus on three screen texts – *Belhaven Meridian*, *Cheeba* and *The Model* – which demonstrate Joseph's mixing of jazz-hip hop's hybrid, multi-layered elements with the countercultural tradition of the LA Rebellion filmmakers, thereby illustrating how his audiovisual works operate as complex sites where the interdisciplinary flows of the city's film and music scenes compete and converge.

In Chapter 3, I move my focus away from Los Angeles and examine early Joseph works set in other parts of America. While the legacies of the LA Rebellion and new jazz-hip hop fusion scenes offer useful departure points that aptly encompass the manner in which Joseph's works engage the faculties of seeing and hearing concurrently, there are certain elements of his oeuvre which extend beyond these influences, especially the instances where his works promote external products using music and moving images, channelling certain formal characteristics akin to contemporary audiovisual advertisements.

Since Joseph's works operate on the boundaries of various structural parameters, I therefore frame my discussions in Chapter 3 around the influences of the 'music video' and 'advertainment' media forms (Korsgaard 2017; Armoo 2017), arguing that Joseph's screen texts blur film, music video *and* advertisement properties as means of creating formal parameters that mirror the complexity and sophistication of the experiential dynamics that span across the Black Atlantic.

I then compare two music videos commissioned to accompany Aloe Blacc's *I Need a Dollar* song: one directed by Derek Pike, set in Las Vegas, and created in a traditionally commercial environment; one directed by Joseph, set in Harlem, and produced within a more 'independent' setting. I explore how different institutional and industrial situations are shaped by uneven flows of capital and in turn nuance the intersections of cultural traffic and aesthetics, drawing from Emily J. Lordi's theorization of 'soul' performances to articulate Joseph's more 'soulful' approach to filmmaking (Lordi 2020). In the final part of Chapter 3, I focus on the short film promoting Shabazz Palaces's 2011 album *Black Up* (2011), examining how filmic and sonic lineages are recontextualized to market contemporary music products.

Chapter 4 contextualizes Joseph's turn towards installation art by examining the development of community arts groups and spaces dedicated to African-American artists since the Civil Rights Movement, drawing parallels between the Underground Museum's role in the local community with such pioneering examples as photographer Roy DeCarava's Kamoinge Workshop in Harlem. I then discuss three screen texts produced by Joseph between 2012 and 2014.

In 2012, Joseph's family established the Underground Museum using inheritance money gifted by his father Keven Joseph Davis. By 2014, the filmmaker would create his first piece for gallery exhibition. The project began as a series of stage visuals to accompany Kendrick Lamar on the 2013 Yeezus tour with Kanye West, until Joseph – following advice from his brother Noah Davis – transformed the work into a media installation showcased at the Joseph-Davis family's museum. While this collaboration with Kendrick Lamar represents the filmmaker's first foray into gallery spaces, the short films *Until the Quiet Comes* (2012) and *Wildcat* (2013) would later find themselves recontextualized by Joseph as exhibition pieces, thereby illustrating the malleability of his works' formal parameters as well as articulating the gradual shift in Joseph's artistic sensibilities in the direction of installation art.

By exploring the controversial presence of the Black Neoliberal Aesthetic in these works during a period when the formal complexity of Joseph's artwork hints towards a 'maturing' period of sorts – as well as recognizing how the director turned to installation art two years *after* the Underground Museum's establishment – I discuss how the crossroads of our contemporary world order generate inconsistencies and contradictions in a manner akin to the paradoxes and complications of Joseph's artworks, suggesting that one's development or 'progression' as a media practitioner or indeed a global citizen seldom follows an entirely linear trajectory.

I contextualize Joseph's works in relation to a range of key American filmmakers *and* British installation artists in Chapter 5. Following the release and widespread popularity of Spike Lee's *She's Gotta Have It* (1986), Manthia Diawara argues that there was a missing 'Black New Wave' in American independent cinema, regretting how the film's rampant commercial and critical success 'did not lead to a new language of Black cinema' (Diawara in conversation with McCluskey 2006: 10). During the same period, however, groups of Black-British media artists such as the Black Audio Film Collective and the Sankofa Film and Video Collective were offering countercultural ways of being through combinations of music, sound and moving images, gesturing towards the emergence of a new filmic vernacular predicated on the musical elements of Black Atlantic audiovisual communication as well as its Afrodiasporic roots. By adopting a transcontinental *and* interdisciplinary lens through which to locate the missing Black New Wave, I emphasize how one cannot understand Joseph's contemporary oeuvre and his movements towards the gallery without acknowledging these fundamental flows of cultural traffic across the Black Atlantic.

I then examine two screen texts directed by Joseph in collaboration with two British musicians. While *Video Girl* (2014) does not directly reference the African continent, the video uses the execution of an Aryan Brotherhood member through lethal injection as a metaphor for singer FKA twigs overcoming discrimination, connecting the Germanic roots of the racist American organization with the singer's status as a British citizen while articulating the residues of what Gilroy terms 'race-thinking' across the Black Atlantic (Gilroy 2004a).

Secondly, I focus on the music-film *Process* (2017), an experimental project that moves between city spaces in Sierra Leone and England to communicate the concurrent cultural affiliations of singer-songwriter Sampha. *Process*'s content eloquently articulates the complications engendered by the musical artist's concurrent cultural affiliations across the Black Atlantic, yet I also discuss how the project's initial release on Apple Music's exclusive platform – as well as its subsequent screenings across America and Europe – illustrates a failure to provide fair access to African citizens (including the dancers and actors who contributed to the final version of *Process*) which, in turn, captures the tensions that emerge when commodifying contemporary forms of audiovisual communication such as the 'music film' (Tobias 2020).

In Chapter 6, I discuss Joseph's most recent site-specific works and his adherence to what Jenny Gunn and the *liquid blackness* group term the 'music art video', an audiovisual work with flexible structural parameters that consciously attempts to drive its combinations of music and moving images towards 'more formally daring *and* theoretically informed ends' tailored to both online and offline spaces (my emphasis) (Gunn 2020: 163). After contextualizing Joseph's work in relation to key contemporary artists of the Audiovisual Atlantic, I discuss his media installations *Fly Paper* (2017) and *BLKNWS* (2018), exploring relationships between spatial factors and art's significations.

In the closing chapter of this book, I summarize Africa's role in what Joseph and Djibril Diop Mambéty term the 'reinvention' of cinema. As well as offering new foundations from which scholars *and* media practitioners alike may build deeper understandings of the director's oeuvre, I argue that *Kahlil Joseph and the Audiovisual Atlantic* develops new forms of knowledge about audiovisual expression's broader relationships to the world's prevalent economic system and the ways we negotiate modernity's underlying Eurocentricity. "We find ourselves," after all, in the words of Campt, "in the midst of a Black artistic renaissance" (2021: 5). She notes that exemplars of this special period of creativity "hail from the US, the UK, the Caribbean, and the African continent," adding "their impact is felt across multiple media, from music to dance, criticism, video, film, artwork, fashion and design" (ibid). Without further ado, then, let us dive headfirst into this complex and expansive Audiovisual Atlantic, navigating the transcontinental, interdisciplinary flows of Kahlil Joseph's first forays into the media production sphere.

2

The early works of Kahlil Joseph

2.1 Merging scenes: from Los Angeleno rebels to contemporary jazz hip-hop

As well as featuring the launch of his solo career as a filmmaker, 2010 became one of the most productive periods for Joseph in terms of output, marking the creation of six new media works – or seven, if one counts the experimental two-part advertisement *The Model* as two separate screen texts rather than two chapters that constitute a single piece of work. Although Joseph grew up in a seaport city, on the great isthmus of Seattle, he gravitated towards Los Angeles and the numerous opportunities that it presented – studying at the region's Loyola Marymount University, interning at the Directors Bureau (a thirty-minute drive away from his academic institution's campus) and working for a range of filmmakers and photographers who constituted the city's creative community. As a result of spending key formative years in the area, a large portion of Joseph's early works are set in Los Angeles, together generating a vivid portrait of the city's Afrodiasporic communities as well as capturing the interwoven relationships between the region's various art scenes.

Los Angeles is of course the home of Hollywood, the central region of the city which became shorthand for the American film industry due to its national and, eventually, worldwide recognizability. However, a group of African-American and African students who studied at UCLA's Film School Programme between the late 1960s and early 1990s felt troubled by the unrealistic and problematic representations of black peoples' lives which were circulated by Hollywood's prevalent filmmaking cultures. Inspired by the rebellious, countercultural spirit of Los Angeleno civil protesting (firstly, the Watts Riots in 1965; and secondly, the Rodney King Riots of 1992) that brought attention to the law enforcement's violent treatment of African-American citizens as well as the inhospitable living conditions that the city's black communities endured, these UCLA graduates started to produce and direct a series of works that retaliated 'against the form and content of the [Hollywood] tradition they were being taught' (Snead 1994: 117). Although these artists were independent in the sense that they made their films based on individualized perspectives and singular artistic visions, their contributions to 'emancipating the image' and decolonizing their filmic content demonstrate a shared preoccupation with representing and treating black people and their communities' lives and concerns with levels of dignity, respect and care which were otherwise absent in the works of their cinematic counterparts from Hollywood (Caldwell, cited by Field, Horak and Stewart 2010). As such, the group of LA-based filmmakers formed a type of pan-African solidarity that took inspiration from the anti-colonial Third Cinema movement, originating in Latin America before moving into Africa through filmmakers such as Sarah Maldoror and Joaquim Lopes Barbosa as Angola, Mozambique and many other nations struggled for liberation against imperial forces throughout the 1960s and 1970s, thereby capturing the transatlantic flows on which Black Atlantic (counter)cultural expression is grounded (Thomas 2013; Buchsbaum 2015).

This particular moment in Black independent filmmaking history has been retrospectively named the LA Rebellion Movement for the ways in which filmmakers rejected conventionalized Hollywood filming and editing techniques in favour of a style of cinema that 'set about *recoding* black skin on screen' (his emphasis) (Snead 1994: 115) through what was perceived as 'the revolutionary act of humanising Black people on screen' (Field, Horak and Stewart 2015: 1). Charles Burnett, for example, independently directed, edited and shot a feature-length drama called *Killer of Sheep* (1978). In drawing from the tradition of Senegalese cinema by reimaging the mask from Ousmane Sembène's *La Noire De …* (1966) and referencing the moments of animal slaughter from Djibril Diop Mambèty's *Touki Bouki* (1973), *Killer of Sheep* emphasized the transatlantic connections underpinning LA Rebellion filmmaking. Although Burnett submitted an earlier version of the film to UCLA as part of his Master of Fine Arts thesis project in 1977, Paul Dallas argues that the official release of *Killer of Sheep* to the public 'heralded the emergence of a new black independent cinema in America' through its merging of music and moving images to create a neo-realist portrayal of life for an African-American slaughterhouse worker's family (Dallas 2017: 139).

In 2010, Joseph re-enacted a scene from *Killer of Sheep* in his short film *Belhaven Meridian*. During the original scene, a determined, resilient wife confronts two gangsters who are attempting to recruit her husband for a violent task, before remonstrating with her partner on their porch for being tempted to use his 'fists' rather than his 'brains' to solve their financial issues. Alessandra Raengo and Lauren McLeod Cramer of Georgia State University's *liquid blackness* research group thus acknowledge that the spirits of experimentation *and* political awareness foregrounded by the filmmakers of the LA Rebellion shape and nuance Joseph's contemporary work, thereby bringing 'film studies and film education, artistic space and praxis, popular culture, and the experimental and avant-garde into a fluid exchange' (Raengo and Cramer 2020: 139).

While Joseph's direct reference to the doorstep scene from *Killer of Sheep* attempts to generate a filmic lineage between Burnett and his own work in 2010, a range of personal and professional relationships further emphasize the crossroads and crosscurrents across cultures and generations which link Joseph's contemporary projects to the Rebellion filmmaking movement. Haile Gerima, the Ethiopian filmmaker who earned a BA and an MFA from UCLA during the LA Rebellion period, trained Joseph's close friend and filmmaking collaborator Arthur Jafa (as well as their mutual friend, collaborator and cinematographer Malik Sayeed). By introducing the works of UCLA Rebellion filmmakers Burnett and Julie Dash to his then-student Jafa – who, in turn, proceeded to mentor and collaborate with Joseph and Ghanaian-British filmmaker Jenn Nkiru – Gerima's tutelage exemplifies the intergenerational relationships across the Audiovisual Atlantic which connect Joseph's new media works with several key figures associated with the LA Rebellion (ibid).

Manthia Diawara argues that the LA Rebellion filmmakers 'were using films in a very powerful manner … they had a Black aesthetics that one could compare to Black music – you know, the Blues, the vernacular', thereby illustrating how the works of Burnett, Dash and Gerima continue to shape Joseph's contemporary audiovisual artworks as he amalgamates Black Atlantic music and moving images for the purposes of radically redefining the communicative potential of Black filmmaking (Diawara in conversation with McCluskey 2006: 10). Music, of course, plays a pivotal role in Joseph's own work – especially the contemporary fusions of LA jazz-hip hop. Central Avenue, encompassing downtown Los Angeles's southern region and passing through Watts, was once 'the economic and social centre of the black population of a segregated Los Angeles' (Isoardi in Bryant et al. 1998: xv). The jazz club would showcase a range of famous jazz musicians from Art Tatum and Nat Cole to Charlie Parker and Charles Mingus through the 1920s and the early 1950s – before succumbing to a noxious concoction of lost leadership, police harassment and antagonism from white gangs (ibid).

The city's early hip-hop scenes, on the other hand, were originally disparaged as a 'diluted' manifestation of rap in comparison to the music emerging from New York's Queens neighbourhood in the 1970s, threatening to turn 'a street-based urban music style created by poor black and brown kids into something palatable for a white, more privileged, California crowd' (Viator 2020: 74). Inspired by the widespread popularity of Los Angeles's underground mobile DJ parties, the management team of Queens rappers Run-DMC eventually recognized the potential revenue streams that these party-goers offered for their burgeoning clientele, thus hip-hop started to migrate from the East to the West Coast through a flurry of tours headed by Run-DMC.[1]

When Run-DMC's Raising Hell tour came to the Los Angeles's Long Beach Arena in 1986, the promotion model worked as efficiently as predicted, grouping large portions of the city's youths together for the show. However, a spate of violent incidents between rival gangs had marred the tour's visits to other venues and cities over the summer, and the event on 17 August was forced to shut down as physical altercations between the crowd's factions of Bloods and Crips commenced in the venue and spilled into the parking lot (Kiersh 1986). The tour's scheduled show at the Hollywood Palladium on 18 August was also cancelled (despite Run-DMC twice performing at the event space before the 'rap riot' without any serious issues) yet the publicity and notoriety that the

---

[1] The mobile dance events took place in rented spaces such as hotel ballrooms and conference centres as well as cheaper solutions in garages and warehouses, coalescing around transportable sound systems and the prized vinyl music collections of local DJs and informal promoters (Jiménez 2011; Viator 2012). Los Angeles's vibrant DJ scene traversed gang rivalries and their territory lines, thus the mobile dance parties were embraced by the notorious Bloods faction as well as their counterparts from the Crips, indicating to Run-DMC's label that new modes of music entertainment would be readily consumed by a range of young black Americans (Viator 2020).

Long Beach Arena outburst generated for the rap group were sufficient to maintain their steady ascendency atop the music charts, cement their act in the public's psyche and establish Los Angeles's emerging rap scene as a more serious – even dangerous, and, therefore, more 'real' and respected – musical phenomenon than cultural commentators and the New York purists had given it credit for (Wahl 1999; Sullivan 2003).

Although a moral panic swept the nation as conservative voices interpreted the rap group's provocative, forthright brand of music as encouraging the latest wave of depraved actions committed by the youthful generations (Taylor 2020), Run-DMC's rapping style articulated aggrievance with and defiance towards America's racist systems of societal oppression, the violence at Long Beach Arena *revealing* the simmering discontent affecting black youths rather than *fashioning* these frustrations from thin air. On the back of Run-DMC's explosive yet nonetheless profitable relationship with the Los Angeles audience, rap music migrated away from the Bronx's dense urban environment and began to evolve in the presence of idyllic Californian beaches and towering palm trees. In turn, this migration generated a new type of gangsta rap predicated on street-level respect, commercial viability in the hands of black youths and frustration towards the city's racialized status quo (Garofalo 1997).

New York's early hip-hop culture was grounded on similar values, yet West Coast musicians Eazy-E, Ice Cube and Dr Dre emerged in the 1980s and 1990s as stalwarts of a kind of Los Angeleno rap music entrepreneurship 'rooted in the reality that those same toughs and gangsters were LA's most loyal rap fans … the counterintuitive belief that their stories were marketable' (Viator 2020: 123). By treating American society's forgotten youths in Los Angeles as the foundation for their new business model, gangsta rappers embraced the younger sections of society who were alienated and marginalized by the era's white hegemony, offering new forms of entertainment as well as presenting an alternative (albeit, in many cases, highly competitive) employment pathway through professional rapping by which to escape difficult living conditions that exacerbated poverty, encouraged criminal activities, and throughout the years provoked various forms of civil disobedience (Quinn 2004).

Today, Los Angeles is experiencing a revival period for its jazz heritage through a fashioning of new music that draws from the city's widespread popularity of gangsta rap. While the contemporary jazz scene's divergent roots extend back to the prime years of Central Avenue clubs when 'all races and classes gathered in the clubs' to listen to jazz and rhythm and blues (Isoardi in Bryant et al. 1998: xv), the new fusion of musical legacies merges the city's heritage of inclusive, desegregated jazz with the militant, anti-institutional energy of West Coast rap, cultivating the countercultural properties of Black Atlantic music's roots by exploring the overlapping lineages between old and new jazz musicians *as well as* old and new hip-hop pioneers. Saxophonist Kamasi Washington, a key figure at the heart of Los Angeles's new fusion movement, observes: 'We've now got a whole generation of jazz musicians who have been brought up with hip-hop. We've grown up alongside rappers and DJs, we've heard this music all our life. We are as fluent in J Dilla and Dr Dre as we are in Mingus and Coltrane' (Washington, cited by Lewis 2016). The countercultural elements of Los

Angeles's gangsta rap movement are thus channelled into the jazz-hip hop sounds of the new scene, forming a series of sonic markers whose liminal statuses and polygenericism echo the double-consciousness of African diasporas and, simultaneously, refute modernity's universalizing, all-encompassing grand narratives.

Jazz music evolved in New Orleans from a three-stroke pattern known in Afro-Caribbean and Latino cultures as a 'tresillo' (Sublette 2008; Peñalosa 2010), hip-hop emerged in New York through the popularity of Jamaican outdoor sound-system cultures (Forman 2000; Brunson III 2011) and both jazz *and* hip-hop were nuanced by the 'call-and-response' patterns of slave songs from the plantations (DeVeaux 1991; Hamlet 2011). Adopting polyrhythmic styles *and* collaborative approaches to music creation married to everyday aspects of life, the roots of these Afrodiasporic traditions challenge the tendency in traditional Eurocentric formulations of Western culture to assign musical authorship to a sole creator, instead emphasizing a communal approach to musicianship (Munyaradzi and Zimidzi 2012). Joseph – through collaborations with a range of contemporary Los Angeleno jazz-hip hop musicians, including Flying Lotus, Kendrick Lamar, Thundercat and Shafiq Husayn – has thus produced interdisciplinary audiovisual projects that mirror the intergenerational and transatlantic energies of Los Angeles's contemporary jazz-hip hop fusion scene as well as similar traditions from the LA Rebellion filmmaking movement.

In order to illustrate how the early new media works created by Joseph in collaboration with contemporary musicians in certain ways challenge Eurocentric formulations of modernity through instances of Black Atlantic audiovisual expression, I now discuss three screen texts filmed in 2010 and primarily set in various parts of Los Angeles, scrutinizing a range of African, American and European sources (including the UCLA Rebellion tradition as well as traces of the city's emergent jazz-hip hop fusion music) which dynamize Joseph's cultural traffic with their transnational flows across the Audiovisual Atlantic.

2.2 Where lamb killers tread: resisting the slaughter in *Belhaven Meridian* (2010)

Belhaven Meridian (2010) is Kahlil Joseph's first video project to promote musical material, created in partnership with the independent production company What Matters Most and published on their Vimeo and Youtube accounts for free access on 23rd and 27th March, respectively. The digital screen text amalgamates film, music video and advertisement properties in order to market three songs written and performed by Seattle-based musical artists Shabazz Palaces. However, the video's content shifts beyond Joseph and Shabazz Palaces's home city, instead exploring a local resident's negotiation of urban gang culture in Watts, Los Angeles. The young African-American man strolls through his neighbourhood before encountering a gang; rather than joining their ranks or instigating violence, the young man summons an African mask for assistance, evading the rabble by finding non-violent means to overcome the harsh environment that threatens to consume its inhabitants.

The strain of inner-city life in Watts largely stems from the Second Great Migration between 1940s and 1970s wherein large numbers of African-American citizens moved to burgeoning industrial cities in the North, Midwest and West seeking employment opportunities at newly formed companies (Boehm 2009; Brown, Vigil and Taylor 2012). Los Angeles's local government struggled to cope with the wave of mass movement to Watts, mishandling the situation by resisting the provision of economic support through federal antipoverty funds and ignoring the grievances of its citizens (Bauman 2008). The outbreak of civil disobedience during the 1965 riots quickly became narrativized by media outlets as representing the unwarranted complaints of a minute fraction in what was an otherwise a satisfied and untroubled community (Sears 1969), yet re-emergence of such large-scale rioting in 1992 emphasizes that on both occasions large numbers of Watts residents were openly and severely disturbed by the lack of governmental support and investment. In the twenty-first century living conditions in Watts have gradually improved, and three of Watts's toughest housing projects experienced a 50 per cent drop in violent crime rates in 2013 (Siegler 2013). However, a series of empty lots scattered across the area point to the chaotic periods of looting and arson which injured and killed civilians, destroyed local businesses and left many buildings beyond repair (Reyes and Jennings 2017).

Reflecting the complexity of the protagonist's double-consciousness (Du Bois 1903), *Belhaven Meridian*'s 'unruly' formal elements resist simplistic categorization (Vernallis 2013). Shot in one long take, *Belhaven Meridian*'s measured treatment of Watts's gang dynamics eschews the 'zaniness' (Ngai 2010: 949) and 'pulse and reiteration' (Vernallis 2013: 130) that characterize YouTube's intensified audiovisual aesthetics. Similarly, by indicating that the protagonist turns to his African heritage for spiritual guidance when resisting gang culture pressures, *Belhaven Meridian* rejects 'hypersexed, spoonfed, commercialised' clichés (Osumare in Elam and Jackson 2005: 267) which saturate certain examples of hip-hop music video culture (Connell and Messerschmidt 2005, Miller-Young 2008). The screen text, instead, remediates aspects of Charles Burnett's independent film *Killer of Sheep* (1978). David Bolter, Richard A. Grusin and Vernallis identify 'remediation' as an aesthetic quality of modern screen cultures writ large, encapsulating twenty-first-century music videos, post-classical cinema and clips on YouTube (Bolter and Grusin 2012; Vernallis, in Richardson et al. 2013). However, as Nicholas Cook and Philip Tagg elaborate, audiovisual interpretations of musical forms may develop 'sticky' properties by inviting multiple cultural associations both intentionally *and* inadvertently (Cook 2001; Tagg 2005). For example, while Joseph references a scene from *Killer of Sheep* in *Belhaven Meridian* – and goes as far as to signpost this influence in the music video through a non-diegetic textual superimposition of the film's title – the music video's representation of an African mask forgery echoes aspects of *Killer of Sheep*'s remediation of Ousmane Sembène's film *La Noire De* …. (1966) in an inviting yet subtly more indirect manner. Following the plight of Senegalese maid Diouana who finds herself trapped and mistreated in France, *La Noire De* … is the first feature-length film from sub-Saharan Africa as well as 'the first African film to gain critical recognition in the Western world' (Dima 2014: 56); thus allusions to Sembène's film in *Killer of Sheep* and *Belhaven Meridian* raise a series of poignant questions relating to the roots and influences that shape a media form's genesis across historical spheres and cultural crossroads.

At the conclusion of *La Noire De …*, a young boy wears the fake African mask and grips a fence's wire mesh, before removing the item to reveal his solemn face. In *Killer of Sheep*, Stan's daughter Angie wears a rubber dog mask and stands against the backyard's barbed wire fencing as a young boy stares into empty space, then turns to peer at the mask in a blank manner. Aboubakar S. Sanogo reasons that the film's 'quasi-restaging of the Sembènian shots … evokes the implacable entrapment Stan and his family find themselves in, not unlike Diouana in Antibes' (Sanogo 2014: 220). Alessandra Raengo develops Sanogo's thoughts further, arguing that Joseph's *Belhaven Meridian* depicts Diouna's mask in a manner that is 'reinterpreted but still connected' to Sembène's original source material, drawing from both an 'Afrocentric' *and* 'cinematic' past (Raengo 2016).

In an interview about *Killer of Sheep* with National Public Radio, Howie Movshotiz claims: 'Burnett says his eyes were really opened when he saw the work of the celebrated director from Senegal, Ousmane Sembène, which showed African people filmed from an African perspective. Burnett says he'd never seen black people on screen presented as human beings. The experience made him see the possibilities for his own movies' (Movshotiz in conversation with Siegel 2007). While Clyde Taylor suggests that: 'The basic palette of [Charles Burnett's] indigenous Afro-screen is closer to that of Italian Neo-realism and third world cinema than that to Southern California' (Taylor 1983: 47), James Naremore de-emphasizes the connections to Italy by arguing that Burnett's 'distinctive style of black neorealism … owes less to the Italians than to the Brazilian "cinema of poverty" and the films of Ousmane Sembène, which Burnett had seen as a student', thereby capturing how the uneven crossroads of capital, cultural traffic and aesthetics – in a manner akin to the migration of forged masks – manifest across continents in oftentimes messy and complicated patterns, engendering a range of reactions (Naremore 2017: 100).

Although the visual and thematic similarities of the shots in Sembène and Burnett's films imply that a conscious decision was made by the latter to channel the ideas and styles of a colleague whom he openly admired, the task of determining *La Noire De …*'s influence on *Belhaven Meridian* is complicated by Joseph's decision to visibly signpost *Killer of Sheep* as source material. While Joseph's signposting technique communicates very clearly that Burnett's film plays an important role in shaping and nuancing the music video's encoded meanings, the lack of clarification relating to the forged African mask's appearance in *Belhaven Meridian* might imply that no other direct links to filmic sources are intended. The chained fences that separate Watts's properties and backyards in *Killer of Sheep* act as a metaphor for the claustrophobic neighbourhood's simmering tensions, the lack of opportunities to overcome or 'escape' cycles of poverty and violence in the environment's cage-like, repressive atmosphere. In *La Noire De …*, however, the chained fence appears on a bridge at the film's conclusion when a masked boy stalks Monsieur, effectively chasing Diouana's former employer away from her family's neighbourhood in Dakar when the Frenchman visits Senegal in a lacklustre attempt to make peace. These underlying themes of attempting to access certain areas

– or cross difficult bridges – with varying degrees of success could simultaneously create a case for *and* against drawing connections between Sembène's film and Joseph's music video, using the transparent reference to *Killer of Sheep* as both a barrier and a stepping stone for the respective strands of interpretation.

Reading the music video through the lens of media semiotics, the presence of the 'uncited' forged mask still creates within *Belhaven Meridian* a complicated network or crossroads of overlapping signs and symbols, thereby allowing contradictory interpretations of the music video's past and present meanings to coexist in states of constant tension and fluctuation (de Saussure 1916; Barthes 1957; Hall 1973). Whether by design or chance, all emergent significations in *Belhaven Meridian* therefore qualify as valid interpretations, and one may develop grounds for following Raengo's line of argument by reasoning that the music video's direct reference to *Killer of Sheep* acts as an indirect bridge from Joseph's music video to Sembène's film. The various debates and 'associative chains' instigated by Joseph's 'remediation' of the fences and masks from *La Noire De ...* and *Killer of Sheep* here expose the structural complexity of *Belhaven Meridian*'s short film and music video hybridization, the formal and ideological sophistication of Joseph's Black Visual Intonations and still-moving-images that I endeavour to access and evaluate (Vernallis 2013: 460). While the precise meanings of any audiovisual artefact are never finished or absolute, messages encoded within a medium 'must be perceived as a meaningful discourse and meaningfully decoded' (Hall 1973: 18), thus *Belhaven Meridian*'s entangled crossroads remain a paradox for each percipient to unravel using their subjective experiences and positionalities. As long as each interpretation is heard, understood, scrutinized and – perhaps most importantly – respected, then *Belhaven Meridian*'s complex crossroads of signs and symbols are not forged in vain.

Belhaven Meridian was released across What Matters Most's Youtube and Vimeo accounts as, in their own terms, an 'allegorical short film/music video'. In turn, the fictional screen text combines media forms as means of advertising musical material written and performed by Shabazz Palaces. The group is comprised of two members: multi-instrumentalist Tendai 'Baba' Maraire is son of the mbira master Duminsani Maraire, recognized for 'introducing the music of his native Zimbabwe to the United States' (Kirby 2012), and rapper Ishmael Butler who previously worked with the band Digable Planets, specializing in infusing elements of jazz and rap. Inspired by 'a desire to protect and exalt our culture', Baba and Butler incorporate Africa's musical heritage into their collaborations (Butler in conversation with Snoad 2014); *Belhaven Meridian*, for example, culminates with gentle mbira sounds extracted from the song *Blastit* (2010). While Baba's father is an obvious source for the Afrocentric dimensions of Baba's work, Butler similarly claims that his family's musical preferences have nuanced the African drumbeats and jazz elements of his works (Cullen 2011; Moinzadeh 2016). By using electronically recorded samples that feel 'as much about beads and wicker ... [as] about plastic and circuitry' (Burke 2017), Shabazz Palaces align themselves with attempts to 'redefine culture and notions of blackness for today and the future' (Womack 2013: 9).

The blurring of fixed spatiotemporal boundaries in *Belhaven Meridian* draws from 'Afrofuturism', a concept originating in Mark Dery's *Black to the Future: Interviews with Samuel R. Delany, Greg Tate, and Tricia Rose*. In his 1994 essay, Dery challenges the 'sublegitimate status of science fiction as a pulp genre in Western literature' because the framing of the literary form in this particular way 'mirrors the subaltern position to which blacks have been relegated throughout American history' (Dery 1994: 180). Basic definitions of Science Fiction detail a narrative style that explains falsehoods and impossible events with scientific rationale, justifying the differences between empirical reality and a text's projected reality with technological developments or redefined laws of science (Abernethy 1960; Byrne 2004). Although one might critique the ways in which Science Fiction's framework uses fallible justifications to support outlandish concepts and ideas, Dery draws from the speculative, countercultural energy of this literary form and, in turn, positions it across a wide range of Afrodiasporic artforms. While acknowledging that Hollywood must 'reaffirm the status quo', Dery argues that the emergence and consumption of new forms of Afrofuturist expression will force American filmmaking to open itself to alternative narratives from a diverse range of perspectives, 'creating a rupture they may not be able to suture' (Dery 1994: 221).

While traversing the 'crossroads' of geographical settings and media structures, *Belhaven Meridian* movements across the Audiovisual Atlantic also oscillate on the boundaries between African and African-American cinemas' respective conceptual frameworks. The unnamed character approaches a menacing gang skulking the streets of Watts when, suddenly, the scene moves into supernatural territory as a digitally animated African mask – translucent and glowing – hovers over his head. The young man turns and snatches the object: the mask develops an opaque, material structure as he charges into the heart of the raging gang, fearlessly fending off physical blows while clutching the mask to his chest. In response to the threat of gang violence in a contemporary American area, the character channels the African spirit world for inspiration and strength, turning to African iconography for guidance and protection.

While certain aspects of the mask – the narrow eye-slits and high, bulging brow – depict the *deangle* spirit from the Dan cultures of Liberia and the Ivory Coast, the cross motif on the mask's forehead represents the *Mwana Po* figure from the Chokwe societies in Angola, Zambia and the Democratic Republic of Congo (Bleakley 1978; Fischer and Himmelheber 1984; Jordán 1998). It is highly likely that the mask is a forgery, a hybrid of distinctive cultural markers manufactured in West Africa and exported to the rest of the world for commercial gain (Shelton 1976; Steiner 1994). At once a composition of divergent African cultures and a rootless, itinerant forgery, the ruptured identity of the main character's African mask at the crossroads of capital and cultural traffic acts as a metaphor for the 'confusion and doubt' of the African diasporas' double-consciousness, the 'peculiar sensation' (Du Bois 1903: 3) produced by the symbiosis between contradictory ways of thinking, being and seeing as a member of the Black Atlantic (Gilroy 1993: 127). However, both the *deangle* and *Mwana Pwo* figures are also vital feminine forces within their respective societies (Johnson 1986; Cameron 1998; LaGamma 2004). The African mask's dislocation from the continent echoes the problematic repositioning of the forged mask in the film *La Noire De ...*, thereby channelling the artistic sensibilities and 'feminist strategies' of Senegalese director Ousmane Sembène whether inadvertently or by design (Kindem and Steele 1991: 56).

In French, the title of Sembène's film means both 'The Black Girl From ...' and 'The Black Girl Of ...', establishing the protagonist's ambiguous status as a native from Senegal and a transatlantic dweller in France, a nanny supporting her Senegalese family and a de facto slave in the French middle-class couple's possession.[2] The film's narrative articulates the danger of losing one's roots while seeking new life in a foreign land, and the mask is reimagined as a trophy of cultural conquest – hung in the couple's apartment, alone on an empty white wall – becoming a vivid visual representation of Diouana's social alienation.

The protagonist's suicide at the film's denouement is a challenging spectacle, complicating the film's focus on race-related gender issues. Jude Akudinobi describes the 'self-referential feminism' of Sembène's later works as 'a mode of agency and subjectivity deriving from culturally specific life experiences, social institutions, personal challenges and collective tribulations rather than reductive categories' (Akudinobi 2006: 181), thus Diouana's suicide may be interpreted as a drastic means of reclaiming autonomy over her trapped, disempowered body. However, by circumventing the 'aggressive masculinities' of American gang and mainstream hip-hop cultures (Aronson and Kimmel 2004; Hurt 2006), *Belhaven Meridian*'s African mask echoes elements of these feminist energies of *La Noire De ...* without, crucially, warranting bloodshed, allowing the protagonist to emerge from the altercation unscathed by summoning the wisdom and strength of an African cultural heritage which Diouana – tragically, fatally – ignores for too long.

Voiceovers communicate the sadness, frustration and fear that Diouana cannot verbalize aloud, thus a large part of *La Noire De ...* takes place in silence. Diouana becomes increasingly quiet the longer she spends in the apartment, gradually transforming into a silent object controlled by the whim of her French employers until suicide silences the young woman forever. By contrast, in *Belhaven Meridian*, Shabazz Palaces's meditative style of music evokes sensations of calm and equanimity without employing the stillness of silence. The song's tranquillity, however, is subtly subverted by the forthright, almost confrontational messages of frontman Ishmael Butler, who delivers passionate, uncompromising 'lesson[s] to the weak' for members of American society who 'use guns to write [their] poems' with such finesse that their antagonistic energy may pass undetected.

Silence reflects Diouana's loss of selfhood, whereas passionately delivered lyrics juxtaposed against cosmic sounds in *Belhaven Meridian* communicate the young man's determination to challenge the external forces shaping his environment. Sound thus articulates autonomy in *Belhaven Meridian*. The young man's freedom to resist

---

[2] The official English title for the film is *Black Girl* rather than 'The Black Girl From ...' or 'The Black Girl Of ...'.

The Early Works of Kahlil Joseph 59

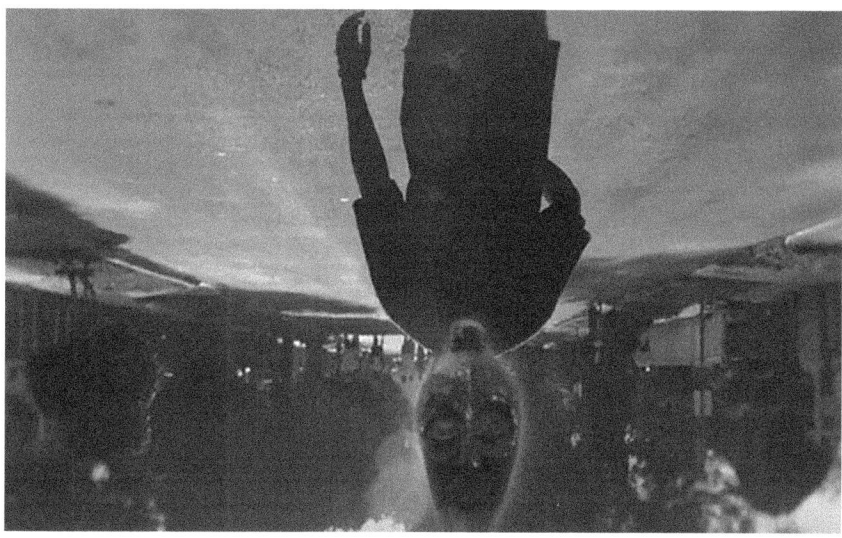

Figure 2.1 *Belhaven Meridian* (2010), Kahlil Joseph and Shabazz Palaces © What Matters Most.

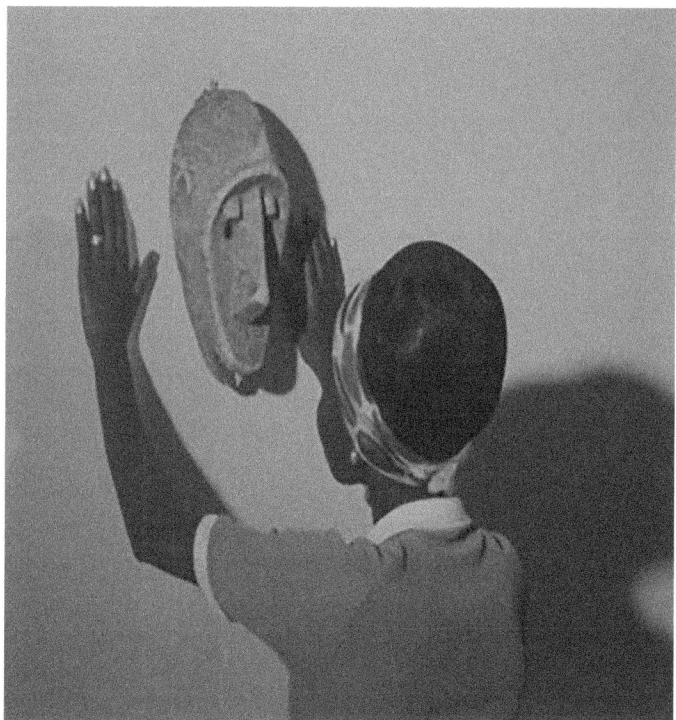

Figure 2.2 *La Noire De …* (1966), Ousmane Sembène © Filmi Domirev and Les Actualités Françaises.

and overpower America's imbalanced social infrastructures is represented by lyrical musings and combative proclamations set to the Shabazz Palaces's heterogeneous blend of introspective, calming and hazy experimental music. Sometimes known as 'avant rap' or 'Afro-celestial hip hop', Shabazz Palaces's music in *Belhaven Meridian* draws directly from African sources such as the stringed mbira instrument from the *Shona* music of Zimbabwe (Cullen 2011). The soft and playful mbira sounds emerge at the music video's denouement when a convoy of motorcyclists in possession of the forged African mask ride into the distance without a fixed destination. Text on the screen responds to a vague question posed during *Belhaven Meridian*'s opening 'Where are we going?' with the unspecific yet liberating answer 'Wherever we want'. Jafa is eager to explore the visual equivalences of 'samba beats, reggae beats, all kinds of things' in his original theorizations (Jafa 1992: 254), thus Joseph's visual articulations of the mbira's sweet tones in part capture the playfulness with which the motorcyclists and Shabazz Palaces reconfigure African sources (the mask and the instrument), controlling the future's destination through styles of their choosing.

While music correlates with empowerment in *Belhaven Meridian*, Diouana's imprisonment is represented by a silent void in *La Noire De* .... broken only by her internal thoughts and simmering fury. Although Dalia Rodriquez recognizes that silence may serve as form of empowerment by helping feminists of colour 'gain clarity as to making sense of racism' so that one may develop the self into 'a catalyst for social change', she also warns that silence in the face of such unjust social frameworks possesses certain dangers and risks (Rodriquez 2011: 589–90). Diouana constantly assesses her situation introspectively – roiling at the injustice of her predicament, resisting the colonization of her mind – yet the character only converts these thoughts and ideas into decisive action when she makes the irreversible choice to take her own life. Rodriguez declares that 'breaking our silence is critical as marginalized people, leading to changing our social conditions' but, at the same, cautions 'If we remain silent, accept our subordinate position and accept white supremacist notions of being less than, [we] will only contribute to our victimisation' (ibid. 590 and 596). Although one might reason that the protagonist in *La Noire De* ... liberates herself by deciding to become a martyr, another could counter-argue that Diouana's eternal silence in death is a tragic instance of self-erasure, her decision to end her own life failing to challenge the social systems that forced the victimized character to such drastic action in the first instance.

The music video's remediation of the forged African mask echoes aspects of *La Noire De* ...'s focus on gender and race, as well as the complicated, morally ambiguous manner in which Diouana chooses to liberate herself through suicide. Crucially, Black cultural traffic's 'capacity to move within black communities' (Elam Jr and Jackson 2005: 6) is exemplified by the manner in which *Belhaven Meridian* details a production crew re-enacting an impassioned scene from *Killer of Sheep*. Burnett's influence in the music video is articulated in univocal terms through inclusion of the film's name as a non-diegetic text-based title. As a result, the music video's scene channels the emotional energy and political significance of *Killer of Sheep*'s infamous doorstep scene, a heated altercation between Stan's wife and two criminals.

In *Killer of Sheep*, disillusioned slaughterhouse worker Stan must butcher animals for a living while struggling to support his family. During the doorstep scene at the start of *Chapter Four: Be A Man If You Can*, two local gang members knock on the door to Stan's house, seeking a weapon. Stan's wife overhears their doorstep conversation and confronts the gangsters. One gangster responds: 'That's the way nature is. An animal has its teeth, and a man has his fists … You be a man if you can, Stan.' Stan's wife, incensed, argues: 'There's more to it than just rich fists … You use your brain, that's what you use.' Her rejection of the neighbourhood's gang culture is mirrored by the main character's refusal to succumb to the institutional and localized social structures which, through the prospect of conflict, threaten to endanger his safety. Stan's wife recognizes the tempestuousness of life in Watts yet also emphasizes the sagacity of rejecting gang culture's idealized notions of hegemonic masculinity in the same vein as the protagonist (in)advertently channelling *La Noire De* … 's feminist strategies, resisting the cycles of violence that these notions perpetuate.

Freya Jarman-Ivens argues that the 'masculine-dominated nature of the music industry is notorious' because 'dominant ideologies of gender' have developed and sustained an imbalanced and sexist hegemony in broad societal terms (Jarman-Ivans 2007: 3). These gender-based imbalances likewise codify behaviours and actions within the film business, and Joan Mellen observes 'the fabrication in American films of a male superior to women, defiant, assertive and utterly fearless' (Mellen 1978: 3). Joseph's tendency to collaborate is similarly marked by an implicit bias towards the

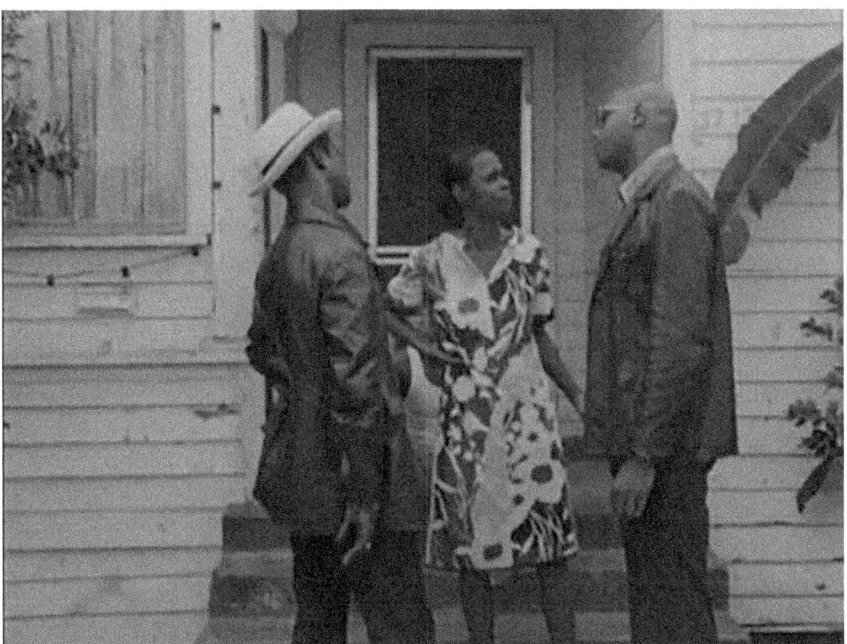

Figure 2.3 *Killer of Sheep* (1978), Charles Burnett © UCLA & Third World Newsreel.

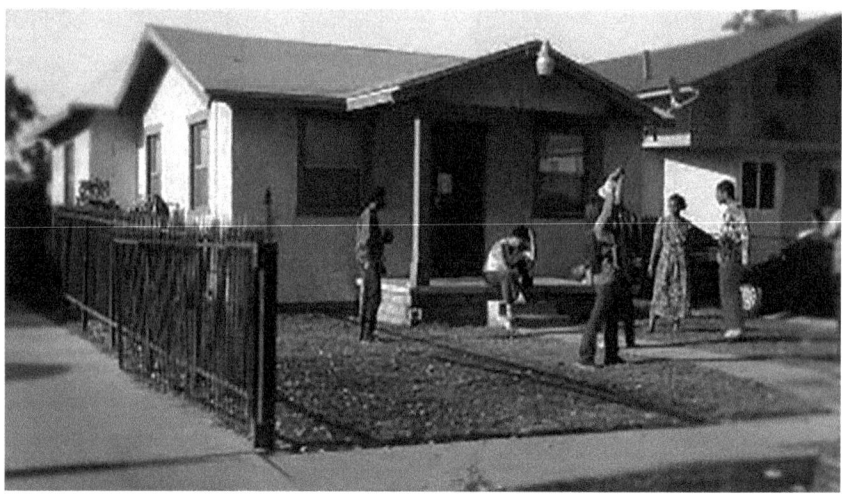

Figure 2.4 *Belhaven Meridian* (2010), Kahlil Joseph and Shabazz Palaces © What Matters Most.

patriarchy, whereby his collaborations with female musicians (Beyoncé, Kelsey Lu, FKA twigs, Alice Smith) are outnumbered by partnerships with men (Aloe Blacc, Kendrick Lamar, Flying Lotus, Sampha, Seu Jorge, Shabazz Palaces). While the content of such works as *Belhaven Meridian* mirrors the biases of Joseph's operational procedures and tend to privilege black men's experiences, Jared Sexton argues that certain examples of contemporary Black independent films offer 'a promising counter-cinema wherein a critical appraisal of Black masculinity [hitherto neglected and underrepresented] can be more fully developed' (Sexton 2017: xxvii). Sexton focuses on ground-breaking representations of masculinity in Barry Jenkins's *Moonlight* (2016) and Stephen Dest's *I Am Shakespeare: The Henry Green Story* (2017) which challenge the traditional hegemonies that compartmentalize and thereby deny the merging of masculine and feminine traits in black men's behavioural patterns. However, in light of Sexton's observations, one must acknowledge that Joseph's *Belhaven Meridian* similarly offers an important filmic representation of Black masculinity which, in the same vein as Jenkins and Dest's works, defies stereotypes and assumptions surrounding contemporary constructions of gender and race.

Rather than positioning *Belhaven Meridian* within a Western framework exclusively, it is vital to recognize the work's transmedia *and* intercultural properties through the Audiovisual Atlantic's crossroads of cultural traffic, capital and aesthetics. Indeed, by exemplifying 'the transnational and transcontinental cinema that African cinema has become today' (Orlando 2017: vii), the screen text oscillates on the boundaries of African-American *and* African filmmaking, echoing the ways *Killer of Sheep* and *La Noire De ...* overcome 'aggressive masculinities' while mimicking the complexity of the unnamed figure's double-consciousness. Although 'force ... violence and segregation' often generate or affect the flow of Black cultural traffic, Elam Jr and Jackson note that 'those vicious flows have rarely had the final say in the outcomes of traffic' (Elam Jr and Jackson 2005: 17). Lindiwe Dovey's assertion that African film directors promote 'the implicit message that making films about violence can help exorcise and explain violence in a way that either the taking up of arms or solely rational, disembodied discussion cannot' (Dovey 2009: 277) is thus supported by *Belhaven Meridian*'s use of African spiritual guidance and the wisdom of an African-American housewife to negotiate gang culture's masculinized mentalities. Using an artistic creation rather than 'solely rational, disembodied discussion' to consolidate African heritage with contemporary life in Watts, Joseph adopts Senegalese filmmaker Djibril Diop Mambéty's mantra of 'stylistic research [over] the mere recording of facts' (Mambéty, cited in Pfaff 1988: 218) as well as Sembène's theorization of film as 'a political instrument of action' (Busch and Annas 2008: 12). Thus, through art's profound ability to oscillate on the boundaries between didacticism and entertainment, one can create a lineage of African and Afro-American filmmakers – in the vein of Sembène, Mambéty, Burnett and now Joseph – who share 'as their cinematic project' the wish to 'increase the intensity of the presence' of Africans and African-Americans throughout the globe (Sanogo 2014: 220). Vitally, these artists use film to 'capture and extend one's imagination' (Bogle 2016: 477) in the hope of forming new realities in the empirical realm which – especially in the case of *Belhaven Meridian* – circumvent cycles of violence fuelled by American ghetto culture's toxic masculinity.

2.3 Activating A-Free-Ka: rolling through the smoke in *Cheeba* (2010)

Cheeba (2010), one of Joseph's earliest music videos, was described by a reviewer as feeling 'like a short film, or a montage in a movie' for its abstract, cinematic style (Tewksbury 2010), thereby exemplifying the manner in which Joseph's crossroads of aesthetics generate underexplored 'possibilities in Black cinema' through combinations of music and moving images (Jafa 1992: 254). The music video's song is the first single from multi-instrumental artist Shafiq Husayn's debut solo project *En' A-Free-Ka* (2009), featuring the soulful vocals of singer-songwriter and producer Bilal Oliver, and the musical craftsmanship of Stephen Lee Bruner.

Husayn – one-third of Sa-Ra Creative Partners, and collaborator with the likes of Egyptian Lover, Afrika Bambaata and Erykah Badu – claims that the *En' A-Free-Ka* album is an attempt to articulate 'freedom of the mind' in the form of a soundtrack, exploring the myriad ways in which 'freedom is reflected in the music' (Husayn 2009). In the same way that *Cheeba* glides across genre boundaries by combining in polymorphous fashion gentle funk sounds and soft echoes of bluesy horns with the neo-soul singing of Bilal (Bilal Oliver's stage name) and the legacy of cyclic Rastafarian Nyabinghi beats, Joseph's smooth camera movements and fluid transitions link visual representations of an underground recording studio, an unspecified space in France, and a rollerblading rink in Los Angeles. The director's vision of 'A-Free-Ka' is liberated from strict spatiotemporal boundaries and moves beyond the African continent, thus engendering gentle, contemplative sensations as means of conveying in audiovisual terms the fluidity and freeness (or 'A-Free-Ness') of the song's heterogeneity as well as the screen text's negotiation of various media formats. In turn, such sensations of boundless time disrupt the prevalent sense of marketed time characterizing Eurocentric modernity and, instead, present an alternative form of being that flows across different parts of the Audiovisual Atlantic unencumbered by the spatiotemporal limitations of one's physical form.

Bilal's captivating vocal delivery has resulted in certain commentators categorizing his style within the framework of 'neo-soul' which, broadly defined, marks the amalgamation of R&B and hip-hop with aesthetic attributes extracted from soul music of the seventies (Huff 2012; Okoth-Obbo 2017). However, the singer has repeatedly refuted rigid systemizations of his singing technique, arguing that his classically trained falsetto merges and blurs genre boundaries, thereby extending beyond any fixed definitions. In fact, many commentators suggest that William 'Kedar' Massenburg trademarked the term 'neo-soul' during the nineties, as the genre's scale of popularity increased, in order to accelerate its inevitable commodification, illustrating how the crossroads of capital and aesthetics reinforce or undermine certain musical – or vision-based – categories (Pais 2018; Nero 2019).

As well as drawing from Bilal's singing abilities, the hypnotic electric bass in *Cheeba* is provided by Stephen Lee 'Thundercat' Bruner. Thundercat grew up across South Central, Compton and Watts, starting his career as a bassist in the thrash crossover group Suicidal Tendencies before pursuing work as a sessions player and solo artist. His instrumentation offers integral frameworks for Flying Lotus's albums *Los Angeles* (2008), *Cosmogramma* (2010) and *Until the Quiet Comes* (2012) – for which Joseph provided a short promotional film – and the bassist also partnered with Kendrick Lamar when the rapper was starting to generate ideas for his third studio album. The pair's conversations about seminal jazz artists Miles Davis, Herbie Hancock, Ron Carter and Mary Lou Williams would form the West Coast rapper's core inspiration for the jazz-infused elements of his Grammy-nominated record *To Pimp a Butterfly* (2015).

Gabriel Solis locates Bruner's music – and Los Angeles's new jazz-hip hop fusion scene as a whole – in relation to the blurring of past, present and future in prevalent Afrofuturist discourses, the form's traversal of genre-boundaries through new audial technologies creating an 'in-between-ness' or 'both/and-ness' for understanding where intercultural crossroads sit 'at the intersection of the biological, the technological, and the cosmological' (Solis 2019: 25). *Cheeba* thus offers a rich site for critically examining the broader flows of cultural traffic moving through Los Angeles from Africa, Europe and other parts of America because the interlocking film *and* music industries were and continue to be arenas of paradox and conflict, shaping the nation's social realities through their production of myriad racialized discourses while, at the same time, remaining in turn constantly shaped and influenced by the very same societal structures that their narratives affect. The film *and* music scenes of Los Angeles past, present *and* future, then, exemplify a complicated and unending state of tension between the physical factors determining an artistic work's production and, on the other hand, their representational capacities on a discursive, metaphysical level.

To communicate the freedom with which cultural traffic flows through *Cheeba*, Joseph adopts subtle green filters and lighting during the screen text's roller-skating rink scenes, indirectly evoking hazy sensations connected to the psychoactive effects of *cheeba*: a transnational slang term for cannabis or marijuana, rooted in the Spanish word for 'young goat' or 'kid' (Merriam-Webster 2002). Sensations of strangeness and dreaminess established by the green lens filter are thus accentuated by innocuous posers sedated in the smoking area and the romantic affection of sensual dancers grinding together rink-side. By capturing such feelings through visual depictions of the dancing roller skaters partaking in dynamic recreational activities, *Cheeba* combines Husayn's mesmerizing singing with hallucinatory moving images to communicate feelings of lightness and detachment induced while under the influence of a cannabinoid 'high'. The complex feelings of surrealness and time-warping spirituality engendered by Joseph's visuals are rooted in the percolating sounds of Husayn's song, which, in turn, echo the tradition of enhanced spirituality communicated by Rastafarian Nyabinghi rhythms.

The term 'Nyabinghi' was originally adopted by a secretive anti-colonial society in East Africa, rumoured to have been led by Ethiopian monarch Haile Selassie I (Tafari 1980; Edmonds 2003). Although the time and location of the first Nyabinghi Assembly organized by Rastafarians remain a contested issue,[3] it is vital to note that these congregation sessions celebrate important dates in the Rastafari calendar explicitly tied to the religion's African origins, such as the birth of Haille Selassie I, or the anniversary of his first visit to Jamaica to commemorate African Liberation Day. A group of oftentimes unappointed or unelected organizers from the Rastafarian faith known as an Assembly of Elders dictate proceedings at Nyabinghi congregations, wherein cyclic, hypnotic drumbeat rhythms build walls of sound in tandem with traditional chants, heightening the spirituality of those in attendance (Barnett 2005; Kiyaga-Mulindwa 2005). Smoking *cheeba* may form a key aspect of the religious ceremonies as Elders encourage the discovery of one's 'inner consciousness' through an altered state of perception (Edmonds 2012: 49), thus the Rastafarian roots of *Cheeba*'s Nyabinghi Afro-rhythms are visually represented through the green lens's subtle allusions to the cannabinoid 'high' warping and affecting the experiences of the roller skaters in present day Los Angeles.

A nostalgic homage to the multitudinous local, regional and global factors that shape Husayn's creative output, Joseph imbues notions of globalization with solemn respect for past and future movements of black families in *Cheeba*'s establishing shots. Sampling *En' A-Free-Ka*'s multi-stylistic track *Le'Star* (2009) in the screen text's introductory moments, nostalgic accordion sounds and extracts of a French

---

[3] Despite the fact that famous public Rasta conventions summoned by Prince Emmanuel Edwards in 1958 and Claudius Henry in 1959 are often cited as the original Nyabinghi Assemblies (Dijk 1995; Barnett 2005), Verena Reckord argues that a 1949 gathering in the Wareika Hills on the outskirts of Kingston is most likely the first large-scale gathering of Rastafarians (Reckord 1998). Ennis Barrington Edwards echoes Reckord's stance, claiming that large gatherings took place in hill-based Rastafarian camps prior to 1958 yet the seclusion of the Warieka Hills has most likely obfuscated details of those events and consigned these meetings to the margins of history (Edmonds 2003).

lamentation are set to black and white footage of a woman with a packed suitcase conveying her struggles to a tiny child. The young boy – a physical manifestation of Husayn's spiritual lineage, representing members of the African diasporas from previous generations – stares innocently into his worried mother's eyes as she sighs: 'La famille ça va pas,/Je n'ai pas d'argent.' By infusing the language of colonizers into both *En' A-Free-Ka*'s title and the parent's complaint, the backdrop of the locked door which frames the mother and child as she sorrowfully acknowledges absent family members symbolizes the restrictions, or closed opportunities, endured by African diasporas during and after the height of imperialism, wherein family units are broken, loved ones separated from relatives, close groups forced by circumstance to disperse and relocate to new, oftentimes alien areas. However, after recognizing the severity of her plight, the mother continues to speak: 'Mon pseudo-copain n'est pas la,/Alors je t'attends,/Viens me chercher.' Embracing the possibility that a change in her fortunes is forthcoming as she softly utters this optimistic invitation, an aeroplane's underbelly soars overhead. Gently shifting *Cheeba*'s diegetic transmedia screen world across the Audiovisual Atlantic, the screen text moves away from the undisclosed Francophone and lands, instead, in contemporary Los Angeles.

Although the French word 'en' harks to the colonial language of past oppressors, the word 'ka' means in Ancient Egyptian 'the ethereal shape of the man [representing] the personality as a kind of astral body … the idealised self' (Carus 1905: 420), thereby imbuing linguistic construction of Husayn's album title *En' A-Free-Ka* with emphasis on the liberation of one's spirituality through discursive constructions of 'Africa' and 'A-Free-Ka' without denying the existence of imperialism's prevailing legacies. While the introductory scenes establish connections between A-Free-Ka, Europe and the United States in order to emphasize the forces of displacement which characterize

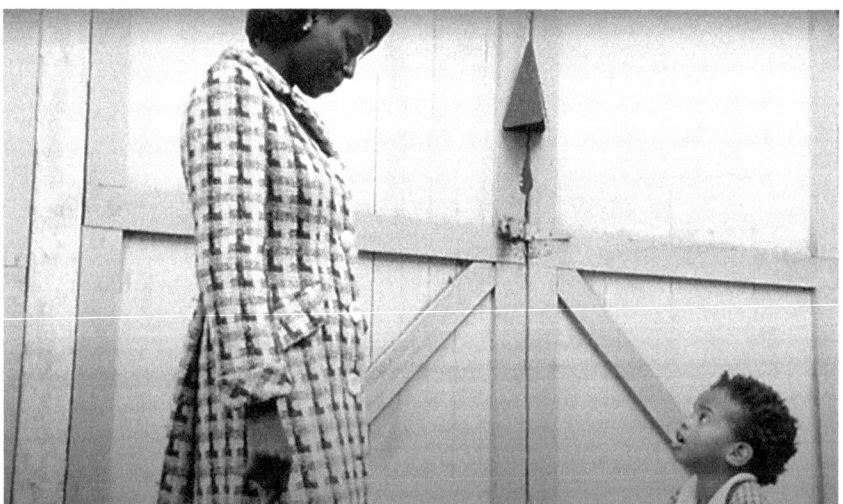

Figure 2.5 *Cheeba* (2010), Kahlil Joseph and Shafiq Husayn © Plug Research.

the grand trajectories of the African diasporas' historical movements, the final words of hope at the understated climax of the mother's lament communicate her dignity and composure in the face of enforced familial dissolution, an unswayable desire to control her destiny in spite of the nefarious colonial frameworks conspiring to displace and disempower by closing significant doors on her innocent son's future.

Echoing the fluidity with which Husyan's heterogeneous collage of sounds and musical styles fluctuate and flow, the depiction of Afrodiasporic characters moving effortlessly between continents and epochs throughout *Cheeba* emphasizes the mother's focus on the liberating aspects of her situation rather than the limitations imposed by the effects of colonialism's brutal structures. *Cheeba*'s components thus communicate the album's core concepts – the myriad formulations of freedom and liberation which may empower the geographical and indeed spiritual movements of the African diasporas – by articulating in audiovisual terms the smoothness with which Husayn's production skills effortlessly blend gentle, trembling brass instruments, serene keys and synthesizers, and hypnotic percussion sounds with Bilal's soulful vocals.

Although Bilal's 'neo-soul' comparisons place him in the company of esteemed artists Erykah Badu and D'Angelo, his impassioned croons also echo James Brown's gospel-inspired soul music and the pining blues sound of Louis Armstrong, thereby propelling Husayn's and Bilal's musical experimentations into exciting new territories through *Cheeba*'s sonic labyrinths of competing styles and sounds. Indeed, Bilal's tender, trembling voice harmonizes with the song's smooth, soulful combinations of horns, electronic keys and metronomic percussions in order to exemplify the unreservedly emotional and sentimental feelings that have come to constitute the very 'soul' of soul music (Landau 1976). The music video thus captures in visual terms the rupturing of one's sense of time and space while under soul music's mesmerizing spell, forming a montage of disparate locations and timeframes to create the impression of a soul singer lost in the heat of the moment, the passion of the performance.

The screen text also features black-and-white vignettes of joyous dance moves in a recording studio at an improvised jamming session. The dancers wear 'retro' suits and dresses reminiscent of socializers from a paradigmatic Central Avenue jazz club in downtown Los Angeles, intensifying the retrospective, soul-meets-blues qualities of *Cheeba*'s heterogeneous sound. In turn, this amalgamation of sonic and visual markers communicates the musical diversity associated with the region's jazz music peak, when the area was a hedonistic space flouting both physical and sonic forms of segregation and separation. Oftentimes coupled with a gritty lens effect to create the impression of low-quality filmstock's material decomposition, the worn, grainy texture of the recording studio's black and white footage compounds the retrospective, nostalgic styles of the enthralled participants' classic formal attire. *Cheeba* here offers a pastiche of glamorous lounges, fizzing cocktails and polished shoes plucked from the backdrop of a dizzying Langston Hughes or F. Scott Fitzgerald novel. The raucous energy of Central Avenue's community and its 'nonstop, vibrant club scene' are thus channelled into the video's underground studio as sweat drips from entranced band members' heads, wine and whiskey glasses clink, and dancers cool themselves with ornate fans (Bryant et al. 1998: xv).

At the same time, the area's decline and eventual destruction in the 1965 Watts riot fires are captured by the tone of reminiscence pervading the hazy, black-and-white footage, communicating the complex, overlapping sensations of happiness *and* regret engendered by recollection of Los Angeles's former vibrancy as a haven of Black jazz music. Joseph's music video here positions a series of America's most popular recreational activities in an unlikely dialogue, juxtaposing recording studio scenes against footage of the modern multi-purpose entertainment complex equipped with roller-skating rink and bowling alley, thereby channelling the liberty and swagger of the Roaring Twenties' social libertarianism and economic prosperity within a popular yet unglamorous venue from a section of present day Los Angeles struggling to resist waves of inflated building prices.

At their respective peaks in Los Angeles, the Bloods gang claimed Compton's *Skateland USA* while their counterparts the Crips were associated with *World on Wheels*, thus the setting of *Cheeba* possesses an undercurrent of territorial gang affiliations. Although *Cheeba* hints at the city's rap roots through the presence of a grainy low fidelity hip hop beat, Joseph's audiovisual depictions of suited, stylish dancers in an underground recording studio emphasize the history of Los Angeleno jazz music over the city's 'gangsta rap' heritage. However, in the aftermath of the 1965 riots, the jazz clubs were disfigured or destroyed, leaving 'decaying buildings and rubble-filled lots, some surrounded with chain-link fencing, [which] seemed to contain few secrets … a terribly aged outpost' (Isoardi in Bryant et al. 1998: xv).

The gradual downturn of *World on Wheels* in its latter years is implied by Joseph's framing of the recreational facility in relation to the ghostly memory of Central Avenue's once-thriving jazz scene, suggesting in a forlorn manner that a similarly problematic fate reminiscent of the jazz clubs' progressive transformation – and eventual decline – could likewise deprive the city of its iconic multipurpose rink. Indeed, *Cheeba*'s merging of the city's forgotten jazz club legacies with its declining entertainment facilities proved an astute observation. Despite offering fifty-two years of service to the local community and even surviving the civil unrest of 1992's Los Angeles riots 'that left its neighbours burned out hulks', *Cheeba*'s setting *World On Wheels* closed in 2013 after its owner AMF Bowling Worldwide filed for bankruptcy for the second time, citing 'a cash crunch' as well as '[failure] to find a buyer for the business' (Griffin 2013).

Margins of time and space, past and present, become interwoven and entangled through the music video's homage to the liberating qualities of the Nyabinghi Order's borderless, cheeba-saturated visualizations of A-Free-Ka, forming a polymorphic transmedia screen world that likewise fluctuates at genre boundaries and spatiotemporal borders. Since the marijuana plant spread from the vast fields of its native homes in Central Asia as a paste-like form in Ethiopian pottery and the travel-bags of wandering Sufis in Egypt, the hallucinogenic properties of tetrahydrocannabinol have been extracted through smoking pipes and edible forms for ritualistic, recreational and medicinal purposes in various parts of the world (Rubin 1976; Clarke and Merlin 2013). However, certain depictions of *cheeba* in American popular music cultures deviate from the spiritualistic and contemplative values of introspection associated with early usages of the plant, extracting child-like humour from the degradation of one's quality

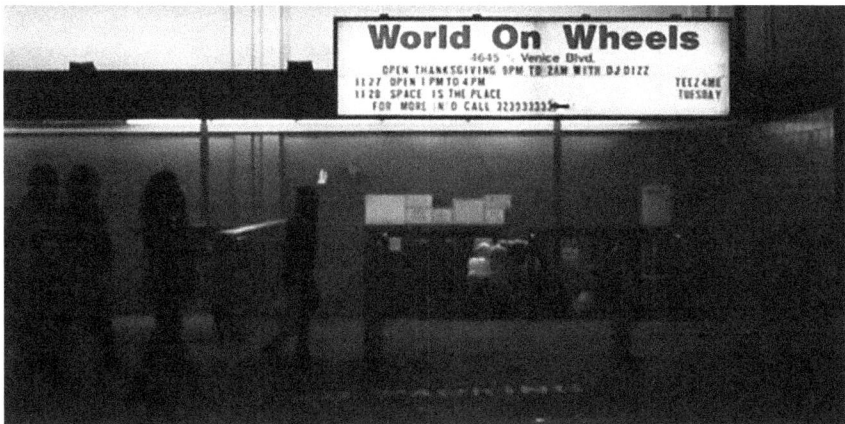

Figure 2.6 *Cheeba* (2010), Kahlil Joseph and Shafiq Husayn © Plug Research.

of life as result of cannabis overconsumption in a fashion similar to Cheech Marin and Tommy Chong's feature-length film *Up In Smoke* (1978) and Afroman's music video *Because I Got High* (2000).

Conversely, Husayn and Bilal's lyrics explore the ways in which a mysterious, nameless female figure permits 'ancient routes to glory' in the present moment, establishing flows between the mystical entity's origins and her present manifestations by emphasizing how 'she sets [him] free' through a state of profundity as natural and awe-inspiring as 'the sun and sea'. Husayn's abstract lyrics may therefore refer to a variety of things: possibly The Muse, who we see protecting her son in the music video's earlier scenes; perhaps *cheeba*, the plant with the power to grant the roller skaters new dimensions of introspection and understanding, moving across African, American and European territories in the same way that the Spanish term's original slang meaning for 'young goat' traversed national territories and transformed; or even music *writ large*, the sounds and styles from different generations and genres which uplift the jazz community and inspire Husayn's *En' A-Free-Ka* album. Representing in audiovisual terms the album's core concept, the music video constructs conceptualizations of the Muse, *cheeba*, and music's liberated spirit simultaneously. Husayn's audiovisual explorations of his African heritage's various branches and roots negate tropes of enslavement and restriction, exploring the contents of an abstract, spiritual A-Free-Ka that moves across geographical boundaries and temporal limitations. The screen overcomes physical barriers and obstacles in the same manner as the free-flowing drift of ghostly vapour, decolonizing the mind by placing impetus on both spiritual and bodily freedoms for the displaced African diasporas (Thiong'o 1986).

The crossroads theory from Harry J. Elam Jr and Kenneth Jackson's *Black Cultural Traffic* articulate the 'transformation, change and hybridity' of various Afrodiasporic cultural forces within the screen world of Joseph's *Cheeba* (Elam Jr and Jackson 2005: viii). The complexities of *Cheeba*'s overlapping sonic and visual jazz, soul and

Rastafarian influences echo how significations associated with notions of 'B/blackness', 'Africa' and 'African diasporas' may freely transform from subject to subject, person to person, generating intricate networks of meaning and (mis)understanding. The emphasis on plurality within the intersecting crossroads of *Cheeba*'s cultural markers challenges any interpretations which are totalizing or singular, counteracting the threat of racial essentialism's (pseudo)scientific grounds by emphasizing the semantic freedom of the terms 'African diasporas' and indeed 'A-Free-Kan diasporas' as their meanings continuously shift and constantly fluctuate in different settings and situations. Joseph's project therefore operates in tandem with Husayn's music writing abilities, Bilal's soothing vocal deliveries and Thundercat's emphatic bass guitar, generating polymorphous diegetic transmedia screen worlds wherein conventional boundaries of time and space are ruptured. A collaborative working environment or synergetic transmedia screen world likewise emerges in the non-diegetic or 'real' space beyond *Cheeba*'s fictional realms, exemplifying the practical benefits of Joseph, Husayn and Bilal's co-authored project together with the aesthetic merits of such work.

Since the original notions of Black Visual Intonations were theorized by his friend and collaborator Arthur Jafa, it seems fitting that Joseph's multifaceted diegetic and non-diegetic transmedia screen worlds are based on precepts of collaboration. Although Joseph is assigned as director for *Cheeba*, the project frequently channels and foregrounds the talents and artistic personae of colleagues Husayn, Bilal and Thundercat, capturing how future waves of artists may work together effectively when generating new artworks across visual and audial modes of communication. The collaborative construction of these aesthetics thus offers fruitful avenues for new generations of filmmakers, musicians and beyond. By challenging rigid compartmentalizations for media forms *as well as* reductive systemizations of humanity, we can develop our understandings of cultural pluralism, seeking underexplored opportunities to subvert Eurocentric ways of thinking about modernity.

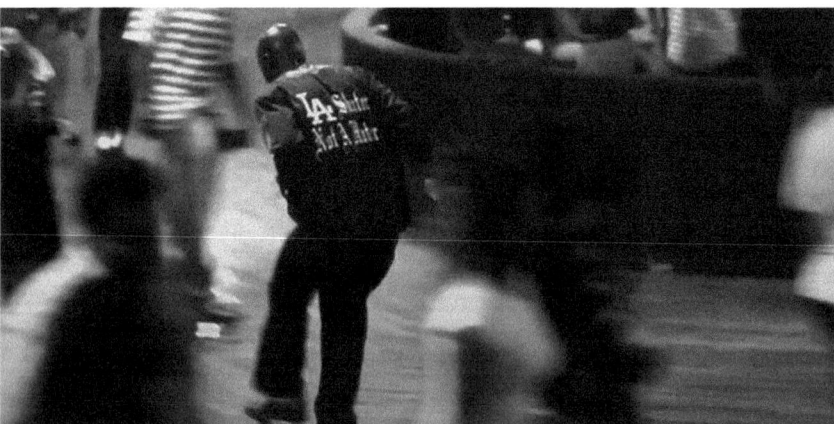

Figure 2.7 *Cheeba* (2010), Kahlil Joseph and Shafiq Husayn © Plug Research.

Jafa argues that Black Visual Intonations – the combined phonic and visual materialization of Afrodiasporic music, the audiovisual encapsulation of 'Black voices' in both musical *and* discursive senses – are exemplified by oscillating, oftentimes uneven combinations of sound, music and moving images (Jafa 1992). Mimicking paradoxical sensations of the simultaneous liminality and fixity of Afrodiasporic positionalities within our contemporary networked environment, Joseph's *Cheeba* epitomizes a pioneering new form of audiovisual artistry which draws from the polyrhythmic and multi-tonal roots of continental African music to 'audio-visualize' and thereby communicate complicated sensations associated with the African diaspora's negotiation of concurrent cross-cultural affiliations.

At the same time, however, at *Cheeba*'s crossroads of aesthetics a sense of boundless time emerges during its representations of A-Free-Ka, offering alternative ways of understanding the past, present and future that extend beyond the physical confinements of our commodified bodies. In part, these sensations are generated by still-moving-images throughout the screen text, echoing aspects of Black Visual Intonations' uneven and oscillating hybridizations of music and moving images. However, according to Tina Campt, still-moving-images 'hover somewhere between still and moving images' in a challenging manner that demands its percipients 'engage the overlapping sensory realms of the visual, and the sonic, the haptic', thereby encouraging us to experience 'the affective labor that constellates in, around, and in response to such images' (Campt 2019: 27).

As Joseph's camera glides between the underground studio and aging rollerblading rink, the speed of the dancers and rollerbladers slows and shifts in pace, until finally an unnamed lady is left alone – staring into nothingness, almost stationary but not quite perfectly still – before fading away into nothingness like a wisp of smoke. All at once she represents the Muse, cheeba and music's liberated spirit; yet at the same time she is none of these things, as much a person enjoying themselves in the rink's green light as the soul of Los Angeles's lost or degenerating spaces. By creating a still-moving-image that momentarily engenders these sophisticated sensations and incongruities before disappearing into the void, we are encouraged to feel vividly the paradoxical togetherness and temporariness of sensations as liberating as one's A-Free-Kan identity, a hallucinatory cheeba high or the disruption of marketed time. *Cheeba*'s prescient concluding sequence – a still-moving-image that disintegrates into dust much like the gradual decline of the final shot's 'real world' setting – captures the frailty of unbounded moments of time, highlighting how precious and precarious such sensations are for those who inhabit a world system otherwise defined by strict governance of what one can (and cannot) do with one's body at certain times, in certain spaces.

2.4 Sleepless in Hollywood: material richness and spiritual longing in Chapters One and Two of *The Model* (2010)

The Model (2010), directed by Joseph, is a two-part YouTube and Vimeo promotion campaign for the eponymous covers album by musician Seu Jorge and the band Almaz.

Both the content and formal structure of *The Model* exemplify 'radically new ways of manufacturing and articulating lived experience' yielded by the intersection of digital technologies and neoliberal social relations, combining a medley of contesting cultural markers in an audiovisual format and, in turn, examining the possibilities generated by convergent media forms (Shaviro 2010: 2). *The Model*'s 'unruly' chameleonic energy represents the 'instability and mutability of identities which are always unfinished, always being made' (Gilroy 1993: xi) for members of African diasporas while, simultaneously, challenging 'business conventions forged throughout modernity' as a postmodern marketing device (Andrews 2015: 14), thereby resisting simplistic categorization by forming a complex hybridization of disparate media forms.

In the first chapter *The Model: Marcello in Limbo*, Jorge plays singer-guitarist Marcello, a man of leisure restlessly meandering through his stunning Hollywood residence. Shot in one long take, Joseph's short film illustrates the character is driven to distraction by dream sequences controlled by Oshun, a Yoruba deity, incarnate as a model. In the second chapter, *The Model: Oshun and the Dream*, Marcello details his confusion, obsession and insomnia to a peculiar therapist figure as the deity continues to dominate his visions, drifting through a series of dream-like non-locations set in America, Asia and Africa. All the while, subtle gestures towards Seu Jorge and Almaz's covers album indirectly promote the Afro-Brazilian group's music: the album's songs *The Model, Everybody Loves the Sunshine, Cirandar* and *Cala Boca, Menino* constitute the screen text's soundtrack, and band-members feature as actors within *The Model*'s narrative.

Published across *Now Again Records*'s Youtube and Vimeo channels, *The Model* is fundamentally a marketing strategy for Seu Jorge and Almaz's self-titled music project, for Joseph cannot escape the need to promote the band's work. Bernice Kanner

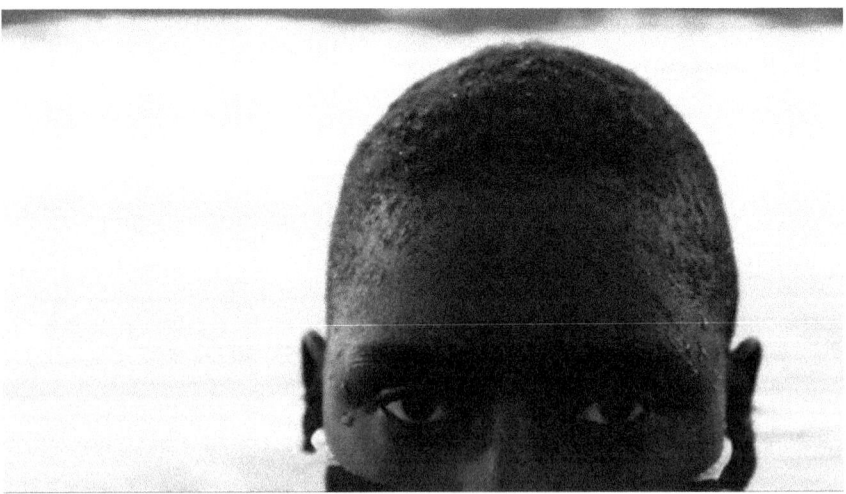

Figure 2.8 *The Model – Chapter One: Marcello in Limbo* (2010), Kahlil Joseph, Seu Jorge and Almaz © What Matters Most.

emphasizes: 'Life today is about selling: selling products, selling ideas, selling ourselves' (Kanner 1999: xviii), illustrating how commercialization becomes increasingly entwined with humanity's everyday activities in the neoliberal era. The pervasive nature of capitalism fosters transactional relationships, thus careful negotiation of these dynamics is required to ensure that Joseph's screen text creates meaningful contact with Jorge's audiences. While manipulative aspects of advertising 'have been spoofed in print, film and television' (Tungate 2007: 3), the artistic, unconventional aspects of *The Model* attempt to champion the covers album in such a way that foregrounds the merits of creatively engaging with consumers, rather than overemphasizing the 'dehumanizing logic' of capital and consequently devaluing the interactions between sellers and their viewership (Flakierski and Sekine 1990: 131).

The Model uses Hollywood's formulae for teasers and trailers, as well as advertising methods from the radio and music industries, to straddle various forms of audiovisual production, creating a multifaceted media piece with film, music video, television episode and radio advertisement properties. For example, *Marcello in Limbo*'s ending cuts dramatically after revealing that Oshun is the source of Marcello's restlessness, playing on the ways in which episodic television series situate themselves within 'cliffhanger tradition[s]' by ending with unresolved issues (Hilmes et al. 2014: 29) and, at the same time, echoing key elements of the 'cliffhanger continuity' which characterized comic strips across early print media (Lambert 2009: 8).

The ways in which *Marcello in Limbo* introduces *Oshun and the Dream* (and thus acts as an advertisement for an advertisement) complicate matters because the viewing order for the chapters is flexible and spans across YouTube and Vimeo's respective platforms. The screen text(s) may therefore stand alone or form a single piece of work, and finishing a chapter on one channel may lead to discovering the second on another, because the release of *The Model* across media channels expands the ways in which one consumes the screen text(s). These 'salient and experimental' aspects of postmodern marketing techniques represent an attempt to address the evolution of consumption practices in the wake of rapid technological developments (Andrews 2015: 3). *The Model*'s amalgamation of film, advertisement and music video properties at the crossroads of capital and aesthetics thus manipulates contemporary marketing paradigms while, simultaneously, mimicking the plurality of contesting cultural ties that nuance Marcello's diasporic experience as an affluent Afro-Brazilian musician residing in America. Adapting to the conditions of neoliberal capitalism to form a cultural artefact which is at once a marketing device and a piece of cinema, *The Model* paradoxically serves the derivative purpose of advertising for another cultural form while, concurrently, operating as an experimental exploration of Marcello's existential malaise.

Fred Moten develops the rich legacies of jazz music to articulate experimental uses of sounds and images across a broad range of artistic practices. He identifies 'improvisation' (as a method of producing art) and the 'ensemble' (as a way to structure groups of artistic producers) as strategies that are both frequently used as formulae among some of the most radical Afrodiasporic artists when creating art (Moten 2003). Indeed, Joseph's artistic approach when shooting *The Model* supports Moten's theories about artistic creation. The director elaborates: 'The biggest inspiration for this film was actually inspiration itself. I didn't know what I was going to do when Jorge and I met, so we just talked ourselves through the film until it was finished. The whole thing could almost be described as an exercise in improvisation on the part of the actor and the filmmaker' (ibid.). Joseph and Jorge's creative process when filming the project thus demonstrates similar traits to the musical extemporization of jazz ensembles, developing a 'call and response' approach that relies on participants to negotiate collaboration through a willingness to improve and adapt to unforeseen circumstances, traversing the fluctuating statuses of their own working relationships. In turn, this jazz-inspired approach is mirrored by the manner in which viewers 'improvise' when consuming *The Model*, moving across digital platforms and engaging with the chapters in unexpected and unanticipated ways.

Although it is possible to purchase physical copies of Seu Jorge and Almaz's album and stream the songs on Spotify and Apple Music's online platforms, the project is available for free on Seu Jorge's YouTube channel in the form of a series of uploaded videos. While each video possesses the audial properties of one of the album's songs, the visual material for each video is a static image of the album's front cover. The group's decision to advertise the album using *The Model*'s audiovisual materials thus encourages consumers to access the songs for free because Joseph's YouTube content shares the same digital platform as the freely available version of the album. When one engages with either *Chapter One: Marcello in Limbo*, *Chapter Two: Oshun and the Dream* or indeed both videos on YouTube, the platform's search bar and Recommended Viewing algorithm provide the cheapest and quickest routes to the music.

As well as releasing a range of solo musical material since the early 2000s, Jorge has formed a career as an actor, featuring in Fernando Meirelles and Kátia Lund's *City of God* (2002) and *House of Sand* (2005) directed by Andrucha Waddington. In Wes Anderson's film *The Life Aquatic with Steve Zissou* (2004), Jorge sings Portuguese covers of David Bowie songs, and the British singer stated: 'Had Seu Jorge not recorded my songs in Portuguese, I would never have heard this new level of beauty which he has imbued them with' (Bowie, cited by Maciel 2016: 252).

Although the commercial elements of producing, distributing and consuming a project are inescapable aspects of existing within an economic framework predicated on neoliberal capitalism, Jorge combines the sonic properties of his music with his visualizable presence as an actor in a manner that privileges creative merits of his craft over the financial rewards that such talents proffer. Joseph recalls their initial encounter during *The Model*'s shoot, stating: 'When I met Jorge, one of the first things he said was: "I don't make music videos … I make films." And that essentially became my maxim from that point forward … We really tried to take a new approach to the way music is incorporated into film' (Joseph and What Matters Most 2010). Joseph's statement articulates a shared vision between himself and Jorge in terms of challenging the traditional distinctions between media structures, and their approach privileges the artistic elements of the work rather than the need to generate (or even maximize) their profits. Joseph's *The Model* thus acts as advertisement for the music that is less concerned with the manner of the music's consumption *as long as* consumption takes place.

The Oshun figure in Marcello's dream represents a complicated combination of cultural sources between Africa, Europe and North and South America. Oshun has travelled from Iseja country in Nigeria to Brazil, Cuba, the United States and the UK as a religious icon and traditional myth, shifting form and meaning as she crosses rivers and oceans, journeys from region to region. Known in disparate cultural spheres as Oshun or Osun, Oxum or Mama Oxum, her name means 'the source' of rivers, people and children as well as 'that which runs, seeps, flows, moves as water does' (Murphy and Sanford 2001: 2), thus Oshun's most crucial characteristic is the fluidity of her identity as she traverses cultural boundaries, her ability 'to make herself anew whenever she comes to consciousness' (Murphy and Sanford 2001: 6).

By depicting the model as an entrancing, mysterious figure, the manner in which Marcello conceives the deity echoes Afro-Brazilian manifestations of Oshun, especially incarnations of the deity in Rio de Janeiro, Sao Paolo and other cultural centres shaped by the Umbanda religion. The word 'Umbanda' has contested meaning. Roger Bastide argues that it derives from the Bantu words 'Quimbanda' or 'ymbanda' which designate 'black magic', 'witchcraft' or 'Supreme Leaders' of religious groups in Angolan contexts, concluding that 'Umbanda' communicates a rudimentary form of 'white magic ... [a] jumble of objects and rite' with the aim 'of lifting spells ... driving out these [black magic] spirits prior to any ceremony in the tent' (Bastide 1960: 300, 329–30). On the other hand, Bastide's student Renato Ortiz and the scholar David J. Hess dispute the position that separates notions of 'Umbanda' and 'Quimbanda', suggesting that aspects of the two words overlap within the Umbanda religion in more profound terms, creating 'a unified system with a coherent grammar' which communicates 'an expression of national ideology rather than one restricted to a specific race and class' (Hess 1992: 138–9).

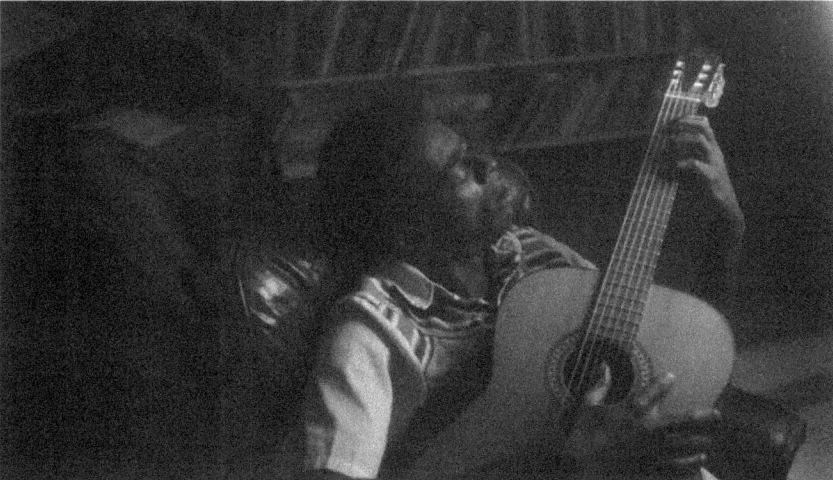

Figure 2.9 *The Model – Chapter Two: Oshun and the Dream* (2010), Kahlil Joseph, Seu Jorge and Almaz © What Matters Most.

Indeed, Umbanda is a syncretic Afro-Brazilian religion at crossroads of cultural traffic that merge Roman Catholicism with indigenous African and American beliefs, oscillating from organized forms of worship to more localized traditions and beliefs in a manner which echoes the fluidity of its etymological roots. For many Umbanda followers or Umbandistas, Oshun represents 'seductive beauty', and her 'exuberant sensuality' is celebrated through extravagant dance ceremonies which imbue the deity with erotic characteristics (Hale 2001: 214). Oshun's identity in *The Model*, however, is complicated by the presence of small children frolicking in Marcello's dreamscape. As two curly haired children – possibly his children, possibly his siblings – climb on Marcello's back, we see the musician smile for the first time across the two videos, finally expressing happiness during his state of limbo. Oshun adopts maternal qualities for certain sections of the Umbanda religion when she takes the form of Oxum or Mama Oxum, otherwise known as 'protector of birth, defender of mothers' (Silva, cited in dos Santos 2001: 69). Oshun thus epitomizes fearless eroticism *and* maternal tenderness concurrently, unabashed sexuality imbued with the tender instincts of a protective mother. In conceptualizing the significance of one's Oshun, whether through religious devotion or artistic creation, Lindsay Hale argues that Umbandistas are 'exploring their selves, carving out a place in the shifting fields of ethnic and gender ideology, expressing and working out aspects of their sexuality' (Hale 2001: 227). Hess echoes these sentiments, arguing that specific manifestations of Umbanda worship are nodes 'of a single system which has many interstitial points' (Hess 1992: 150). Oshun the model, therefore, represents a subconscious, heritage-based manifestation of Marcello's sexuality, exploration of his carnal desires tied to the roots of his cultural legacies.

In the dream, the unsettled musician, speaking Portuguese, and a therapist, speaking English, discuss how Marcello cannot accurately discern 'the exact forms … of the people, the figures, the environments' of his visions. The eeriness of this inconclusive verbal exchange is in turn exacerbated by the therapist's facelessness, her visage shrouded in shadow as though the ambivalence of Oshun's spirituality pervades the 'real' universe beyond the dream, rupturing both Marcello *and* the therapist's respective identities. Joseph acknowledges that 'the journey and the confusion, the symbols, the children, the therapy dynamic' in *The Model* are influenced by the 'Soul and God' verse in Carl Jung's *The Red Book* (Joseph and What Matters Most 2010). Addressing his soul during a conscious dream experiment, or, in his own terms, a state of 'mythopoetic imagination' (Jung and Jaffé 1961), Jung envisions a series of disjointed symbols and icons, concluding that the chaos of his dreams, 'the dregs of [his] thought', are in fact 'the speech of [his] soul' (Jung 2009: 233).

Oshun, in the form of a model, thus depicts an abstract articulation of Marcello's soul, subconscious communication from the immaterial, spiritual energy which distinguishes men from other animals, Marcello from other men. Joseph acknowledges that: 'Using Oshun as the character of *The Model* was important … because of her prominence in Brazilian culture and religion, and her attributes as the very embodiment of "beauty." But I also knew I wanted her character to operate on an archetypal level. Orishas very often mystically reveal themselves to people in their dreams, something

Carl Jung would consider incredibly important' (Joseph and What Matters Most 2010). Indeed, the fragmented and ambivalent manifestation of Oshun in Marcello's mind – part child-bearing seductress, part caring mother offering solace to her lost son – reveals a confused and agitated sexuality. Marcello's desires oscillate from carnal lust to familial companionship, which, in turn, communicates a fractured, wandering soul, a stray Afro-Brazilian spirit seeking comfort and consolation across cultural spheres and in unfamiliar spaces.

Marcello experiences an existential malaise, yet, specifically, his inner turmoil is connected to his status as an Afro-Brazilian musician residing in America. In turn, Marcello's attempts to decipher and process his dreams of Oshun drifting through the luxurious Hollywood Hills accommodation communicates broader existential anxieties connected to Afrodiasporic experiences across the planet. Gilles Deleuze accounts for such uneven processes of globalization through his explorations of 'de/reterritorialization'. In his co-authored text with Félix Guattari *Anti-Oedipus: Capitalism and Schizophrenia* [1972] (1983), the pair acknowledge that the flows of neoliberal capitalism's global world system subsume and reposition national subjects. In turn, these subjects subsume and reposition forms of popular culture in their new territories in relation to cultural configurations that characterized the geographical locations from where they were originally displaced (Deleuze and Guattari 1983: 34–5). The Oshun figure is hence de/reterritorialized by *The Model*, generating complex sensations of incongruity as Marcello strives to harmonize affiliations to divergent cultural settings.

Deleuze coins the phrase 'cinema of the seer' to articulate how style may express one's lack of agency in the face of 'situations we no longer know how to react to, in spaces we no longer know how to describe', characterizing emergent tensions between film characters and their harsh, external environments in the aftermath of the Second World War (Deleuze [1985] 1989: xi). Deleuze uses the Second World War as the key 'break' distinguishing his aforementioned 'cinema of the seer' theory from previous manifestations of filmmaking (ibid.). Despite having the potential to overcome the Eurocentricity at the heart of the 'seer' concept, Deleuze does not apply de/reterritorialization to this film theory in a particularly deep manner. However, the 'seer' is deterritorialized from postwar European contexts and thus deterritorialized in new spacio-temporal contexts, an updated version of Deleuze's theory may assist the negotiation and analysis of screen cultures which extend beyond Europe, as well as developing explorations of screen texts whose structural forms extend beyond rigid notions of what constitutes 'cinema'. For example, a deterritorialized model of the 'cinema of the seer' facilitates scrutiny of a variety of media forms across geographical contexts. One can thus position Jorge's portrayal of Marcello throughout *The Model*'s hybridization of film, music video *and* advertisement forms in relation to portrayals of 'seers' from a key feature-length film set in Ghana: Haile Gerima's *Sankofa* (1993).

Gerima was a member of the LA Rebellion Movement. Born on 4 March 1946 and raised in the Ethiopian city of Gondar, he emigrated to the United States in 1968 to study theatre, initially enrolling in acting classes at Chicago's Goodman School of Drama. He then moved to attend UCLA, studying in the film department that produced prominent black filmmakers Charles Burnett and Julie Dash. A militant social activist as well as a dedicated cinema theorist, Gerima has generated a reputation among filmmaking communities 'for his dedication and perseverance in preserving and creating independent Africana films that raise audience consciousness' (Turner and Kamdibe 2008: 969).

In *Sankofa*, an African-American model named Mona is transported by the magic of a Divine Drummer from a photo-shoot in contemporary Ghana's Cape Coast Castle to a plantation at the peak of the Southern United States' slave trade era. Silently roiling, the oppressed Africans from the past are described by Kara Keeling as Deleuzean 'seer-slaves … mutely witnessing an intolerable present' as means of surviving the slave-owners' brutality (Keeling 2007: 62). However, the ferocity of their stares mirrors the Divine Drummer's intensity as he witnesses the disrespectful transformation of Cape Coast Castle from its origins within Atlantic Slave Trade to tourist attraction. Eventually, the model's bewildered stares transition from incapacitated shock to steely fury, imitating the Divine Drummer and her enslaved ancestors by nearing a state of captivated meditation. At the film's conclusion, Mona shuns the photographer when she returns to the present and, instead, joins Divine Drummer's intense ritual, developing profound respect for her ancestral roots that were previously ignored.

'Sankofa' is a word from the Twi language of Ghana, meaning: "To go back and get it." The phrase is usually associated with the proverb "Se wo were fi na wosankofa a yenkyi," which roughly translates as: "It is not a taboo to return and fetch it when you forget" (The Adinkra Dictionary [Willis] 1998).[4] Mona, initially, shares with Marcello an inability to recognize the profundity of embracing ancestral roots as a distinct demarcation of identity. However, while Marcello never manages to reach an epiphanic moment of reconciliation with his past, Mona's inactive stare switches from overwhelmed hysteria to calculated passion, rejecting her modelling career when she embraces her ancestry and instead locates solace in the comforts of Ghanaian spirituality. Gerima has spent most of his adult life producing films in the United States, teaching at the historically Black institution Howard University for approximately forty years.

During this time, the artist has remained dedicated to using cinema 'as a mechanism for offering up politicized counternarratives' which situate African preoccupations at the heart of their discussions, echoing the Twi 'Sankofa' mantra that necessitates an understanding of the past and a willingness to engage with one's cultural heritage (Elam Jr and Jackson 2010: 27). *The Model*, meanwhile, subverts *Sankofa*'s depiction of modelling as the epitome of Western evils, with actress and model Jodie Turner-Smith creating a multifaceted, transcontinental representation of Oshun as Marcello's dream interpretation deterritorializes the Yoruba myth.

Although *The Model*'s raison d'être is to promote the band's covers album, Joseph's artwork implores viewers to acknowledge the deeper, more profound values of Seu

---

[4] In Britain, the Sankofa Film and Video Collective similarly drew from this African saying for inspiration when they formed in 1983.

Jorge and Almaz's work which extend beyond maximizing profits or reducing their music to a purely commercial endeavour. At the same time, simplistic readings are destabilized by the work's concurrent affiliations to different cultural contexts across the Audiovisual Atlantic. Structural tensions tied to *The Model*'s combination of media forms thus communicate the complexity of the screen text's content, the presence of the sacred Yoruba figure warped by Marcello's dreams and reimagined in an expensive yet soulless Western environment. As Marcello drifts aimlessly within his luxurious dream-world, these concurrent affiliations – as well as his present sensations of rootlessness – become manifested in the model's discomforting and indefinable presence. By calling 'sankofa' in her own way, she thus encourages the musician 'to go back' and discover the roots of his ancestral heritage in order to make sense of where he now finds himself. Knowledge is power; se wo were fi na wosankofa a yenkyi.

3

Webs of expression

3.1 Internet music videos and new forms of representation

While elements of Joseph's transatlantic, interdisciplinary body of work are shaped by the innovations of pioneers such as Charles Burnett, Halie Gerima and Julie Dash, his combinations of music and moving images oscillate between filmic *and* music video forms, thereby necessitating an understanding of some of the film *and* music video contexts that his works simultaneously channel and challenge, support or subvert. However, the precise moment of the music video form's arrival, whether linguistically, conceptually or materially, is contested and today remains unclear. Some commentators attribute the first adoption of the term 'music video' to American disc jockey J. P. 'The Big Bopper' Richardson in 1958 (Palmer in conversation with Cornish 2011); others argue it emerged in Czechoslovakia when Ladislav Rychman created promotional material for the song *Dáme Si Do Bytu [Let's Get to the Apartment]* in the same year (Hrabalik 2014); Tony Bennett also makes a claim for creating the first music video in 1956, combining his version of song *Stranger in Paradise* (1953) with footage of a short walk through London's Hyde Park (Keppler 2016).

As network executives across the globe began to develop their understanding of increasingly expanding audiences and, in turn, diversified the content of their channels and programmes, cinema establishments were forced to compete with new televised formats of audiovisual entertainment. In response, musicians and directors began to develop artistic and promotional materials with analogue sound-on-film technologies, experimenting with new combinations of music, sound and moving images. During the mid-1960s, a rich variety of music-imbued media started to appear. The Beatles starred in their first feature film, the 'rockumentary' *A Hard Day's Night* (1964), separating musical sequences with comedic sketches and, in turn, blurring the boundaries between reality and fiction; director Kenneth Anger's short experimental film *Scorpio Rising* (1964) rejected dialogue, blending religious iconography and abstract visuals of queer and biker subcultures with popular songs from the sixties; Alex Murray, producer and co-manager of The Moody Blues, promoted his version of *Go Now* (1965) with footage filmed on 35mm at London's Marquee Club, securing a Number 1 in the UK Pop Music Charts and Number 10 in America.

Although the release of music video material remained far from ubiquitous, isolated examples of experimentation among artists indicated a growing curiosity for innovation through new audiovisual formats, amalgamating moving images, sound and music in stimulating and previously underexplored ways. In the mid-to-late seventies, several new television programmes became dedicated to playing promotional film clips from both emerging *and* established acts. For example, Australian TV shows *Countdown* and *Sounds* both premiered in 1974, offering national television platforms for publicizing the release of new music (Wilmoth 1993; Kruger 2011).

In 1975, Queen employed television director Bruce Gowers to create a promotional video for new single *Bohemian Rhapsody (*1975), which was shown on British programme *Top of the Pops* in lieu of the show's regular broadcasting format involving 'live' performances from featured singers and bands (Giles 2015). The *Bohemian Rhapsody* video was particularly significant because it illustrated a 'desire … to invest in new communicative forms, beginning with the video clip, until then unexplored in combination with music' (Bizzo 2007: 205). As previously discussed, many prototypical combinations of music and moving images preceded the televised format of music videos, yet Queen's release of official audiovisual accompaniments for their *Bohemian Rhapsody* single '*despite* television's initial reluctance to use the clips' consequently formed 'a relationship between music video, television and record sales that has proved commercially irreversible, of mutual benefit to both the music *and* television industries' (my emphasis) (Mundy 1994: 263). By combining media forms as means of sharing their audiences and, in turn, opening new markets for their products, the marriage between music and television started to evolve and accelerate.

In 1979, *Video Concert Hall* was launched in America to perform a similar function to *Countdown*, *Sounds* and *Top of the Pops*. However, the significance of *Video Concert Hall* in terms of cementing the music video as a key cultural form was overshadowed by the United States' introduction and runaway successes of the first 24-hour-per-day music channel: *Music Television*, otherwise known as MTV. The channel was launched in 1981 and at the time owned by Warner Communications and American Express, epitomizing 'the commercial logistics' of our global economic framework shaping the 'increasingly connected' music and television industries (ibid.).

Airing the music video for The Buggles' song *Video Killed the Radio Star*, the song's lyrical content presciently characterized the channel's ensuing success over the next fourteen years (Warner 2003; Tannenbaum and Marks 2012). During this period, cheap video recording and editing equipment became manufactured on large scales as rudimentary digital technologies made visual effects and image compositing simple to generate, in part removing financial boundaries that previously obstructed participation and, instead, encouraging DIY-approaches to video-making from burgeoning artists with limited resources as well as influential acts with financial backing. Reebee Garofalo argues that 'With the coming of MTV, the videos (or promotional clips, as they were called) offered a way of gaining entrance to the U.S. market that was more cost effective than mounting cumbersome and chancy transatlantic national tours', thereby illustrating how global financial flows shaped and moulded early manifestations of the music video form (Garofalo 1997: 326).[1] Indeed, as music videos became a normal part of a musician's promotional cycle, major acts such as Madonna and Duran Duran chose to invest time and money into the music video form, shooting on quality 35mm film stock rather than cheaper video options, adopting controversial themes and striking imagery that were more engaging than simplistic, low-budget 'band-on-stage' videos (Metz and Benson 2000).

Despite certain participatory boundaries being removed by the advancement of cheap video-making technologies, African-American artists were seldom shown on MTV until Michael Jackson's landmark music video – the high production-budget, 14-minute *Thriller* (1983) – sold over a million copies on VHS, pushing the form to new artistic heights by combining elements of horror films, B-movies and musical dance routines into a single audiovisual artefact (Griffin 2010). The music video won Grammy Awards in the *Best Video Album* and *Best Video, Long Form* sections, secured four MTV Awards, and was inducted into the American National Film Registry in 2009.

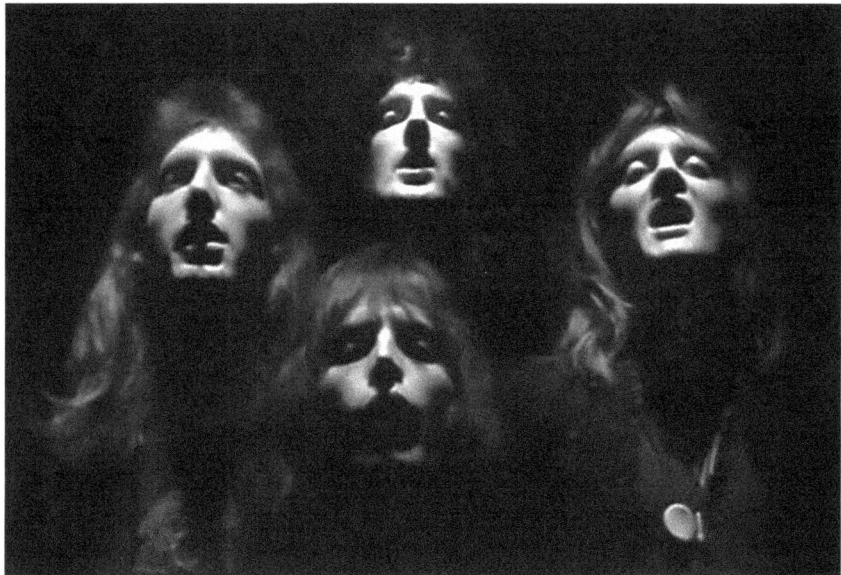

Figure 3.1 *Bohemian Rhapsody* (1975), Bruce Gowers and Queen © Hollywood Records and Virgin EMI Records.

---

[1] Reebee Garofalo argues that 'music videos had developed earlier in Britain [than other countries] because the paucity of radio stations in Britain and throughout Europe had caused British record companies to seek exposure for their artists on televisions such Britain's *Top of the Pops*', which, again, highlights the ways in which international forces of neoliberal capitalism nuance early histories of this particular audiovisual form (Garofalo 1997: 326).

However, before the release of *Thriller* and the resultant surge of black peoples' visibility on MTV, David Bowie famously criticized the ways in which videos created by 'the few black artists that one does see' were given the 'graveyard' broadcasting slots between 2:00 am and 6:00 am, when viewing figures were normally at their lowest (Bowie in conversation with Goodman 1983). Although the success of *Thriller* eventually encouraged TV executives to invest in new black artists, the organization's initial resistance to showcasing African-American talent on screen is an example of the racial biases which have historically plagued the overlapping music and moving image industries (Mahon 2004; Niddle 2020).[2]

MTV started commissioning non-music programmes such as stunt show *Jackass* (2000–02) and reality TV series *The Osbornes* (2002–05), and executive Van Toeffler declared: 'Clearly, the novelty of just showing music videos has worn off. It's required us to reinvent ourselves to a contemporary audience' (Toeffler cited by Hay 2001: 68). While music videos still featured sporadically on MTV, the form migrated away from television sets and started to materialize across the internet, welcoming the digital phase of postmillennial music video history. Although the MTV franchise commanded over 100 worldwide channels at its peak in 2004, the subdivisions of the station similarly experienced decline as the internet's popularity soared, eventually leading to the cancellation of its week-long music specials and annual summer events, gradually focusing on 'ordinary celebrities' or more 'relatable' reality television subjects rather than emphasizing the lavish lifestyles of musicians, athletes and actors (Grindstaff 2012).

Eventually, key technological shifts curtailed MTV's dominance over music's visualization. The channel's audience numbers were starting to decline in the mid-to-late nineties as appetite for the internet overtook television; while television had previously overthrown cinema as the era's 'dominant' audiovisual media outlet (Jameson 1991), the rising popularity of the internet was challenging – and would eventually surpass – television's position.

The introduction of user-generated content and improved interoperability of web designs throughout the 2000s shifted the balance of power within the media-sphere. The development of person-to-person music sharing was facilitated by the invention of the MP3, a coding format for digital audio which went public in 1998. In response to the public release of this pioneering technology, Napster (1999 to Present) was formed as a peer-to-peer file-sharing site which, unlike other file-distribution sites such as Hotline (1996–2006) and Usenet (1980–Present), specialized in sharing music files through its user-friendly front-end interface. At the time, no legislation existed to negotiate the overwhelming influx of readily-available online music, thus the service was accused of 'depriving copyright holders of revenue that they might otherwise have received if individuals purchased those works in tangible form' (Ku 2002: 264). Legal action

---

[2] Despite the singer playing a pivotal role in improving the possibilities for African-American representation within the music industry, the accusations against Jackson made writing this section very difficult. However, it is necessary to acknowledge *Thriller*'s influence on the history of music videos, regardless of the crimes and controversies attributed to the performer.

against Napster's 'piracy' was coordinated by a range of musicians and their labels, and prominent lawsuits from major artists such as Metallica, Dr Dre and Madonna and the 'Big Four' recording companies Universal Music Group, Sony Music Entertainment, EMI and Warner Music Group (and their subsidiaries) culminated in Napster shutting down its entire network in order to comply with injunction orders. Napster liquidated its assets and became acquired by software developers Roxio through a bankruptcy auction, undergoing a rebrand campaign as a legitimate business under the name Napster 2.0 (Burkart and McCourt 2004).

The legal saga between Napster, its artists and the record labels demonstrates the slowness with which the music industries responded to the challenge of online media dissemination, highlighting the recurring issue of distribution within the new digital economy. From tablet devices, smart phones and laptop computers to interactive installations and virtual and augmented worlds, the omnipresence of the internet facilitates access to new media content such as contemporary digital music videos through various platforms and technologies. The phrase 'Web 2.0' was invented by Darcy DiNucci in 1999 to characterize the gradual shift of internet content from static, isolated sites to user-generated content and increased interoperability between systems and products, thereby facilitating the rise in 'smart' devices across mobile phones and television sets. In turn, Steven Shaviro characterizes the digital present as a 'post-cinematic' moment wherein smaller screens such as phone devices and television supersede and consequently replace 'the big screen' (Shaviro 2010).

While websites such as Napster and iFilm (1997–2008) offered the first instances of file hosting and peer-to-peer sharing opportunities for music videos, the launch of website YouTube in 2005 has had an extraordinary impact on the music video's contemporary condition. The site allows users to upload their own audiovisual content online for public consumption, thereby reducing the barriers to music video production in a powerful new way. The band OK Go demonstrated how YouTube facilitates exciting new possibilities for up-and-coming musicians when their treadmill-based dance routine for song *Here It Goes Again* (2006) achieved viral status and accumulated millions of views, catapulting the band into stardom. Social media platforms allow video links to sites such as YouTube, Vimeo and Dailymotion to be shared or embedded within their sites, and handheld mobile technologies permit downloading, streaming and sharing video content in essentially any geographical location on earth (James 2020). Although platforms such as Bebo, MySpace and Vine have lost relevance over time, Facebook, Twitter, Instagram and TikTok remain major outlets for the digital distribution and consumption of new music video content.

As the music video form continues to evolve and develop across new online spaces, Mathias Bonde Korsgaard argues that: 'There was a time when music videos were highly standardized – partly due to constraints imposed by television. While the days of the traditional three-minute clip are not entirely over, music video today has transformed into unimaginable shapes and entered into new relations with other media' (Korsgaard 2017: 200). Death Grips created an interactive online installation for their song *Retrograde* (2012) called the 'Death Grid', wherein tiny looped sequences or sounded GIFs of the band performing can be played in a variety of patterns. Halsey adopted an

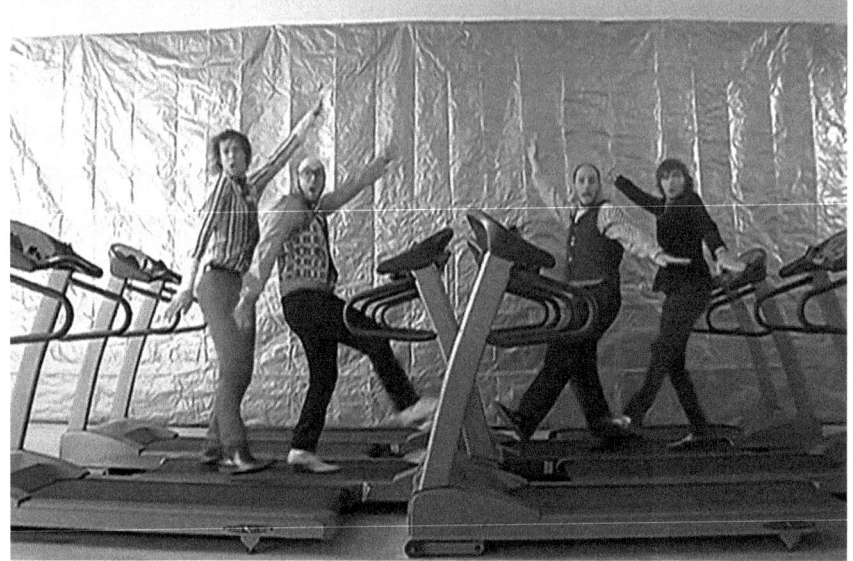

Figure 3.2 *Here It Goes Again* (2006), Trish Sie and OK Go © Capitol & EMI.

alternative 'vertical music video' format to accompany the song *Without Me* (2019), meaning that the new audiovisual material was designed especially for mobile devices. Music videos to accompany Björk's eighth studio album *Vulnicura* (2015) were created using virtual reality and made available to download through the project *Vulnicura VR* (2019). Subscription services such as TIDAL and Apple Music now turn music video releases – such as Joseph and Sampha Sisay's collaborative project *Process* (2017) – into exclusive events, thus, as Korsgaard notes, new forms of music video are developing and dispersing at rapid rates across myriad digital locations.

Joseph's audiovisual works are being constructed during this intensely digitized era, and the development of the internet operates in tandem with humanity's growing dependence on new technologies. From handheld communication devices to new digital platforms, these machinic advancements constantly shift the ways that commercial campaigns may connect and interact with consumers through combinations of music and moving images (which, in turn, constantly transforms how consumers may likewise negotiate and engage with contemporary forms of audiovisual advertising).

Early music videos created during MTV's embryonic stages were in fact 'conceived as a form of promotion' and 'their producers and directors were drawn from the ranks of advertising', meaning that the form's early manifestations became 'dominated by the aesthetics of advertising – fast cuts, ever-changing camera angles, eye-catching visuals, and a panoply of special effects' (Garofalo 1997: 326). In contrast, Joseph's blurring of the boundaries between film, music video and advertisement does not punctuate advertising aesthetics in the same manner. *Belhaven Meridian* (2010), *The Model* (2010) and *Black Up* (2011) are at once promotional materials for separate musical projects *and* audiovisual forms of art in their own right. For example, *The Model* (2010) creates a narrative about a somnambulist figure named Marcello across two short videos, marketing the latest covers album produced by singer-songwriter Seu Jorge and the band Almaz while, at the same time, functioning as an experimental media artwork in its own right. Similarly, Joseph's *Dawn in Luxor* (2014) and *Music Is My Mistress* (2017) ostensibly function as advertisements for various clothing ranges created by fashion label KENZO, yet the works also operate as experimental films connecting musical pieces to unusual visual materials (and Joseph has even presented *Dawn in Luxor* at the Los Angeles's Underground Museum and the Frye Art Museum in Seattle as part of gallery installations).

Joseph's work exemplifies the contemporary phenomenon of 'advertainment', whereby advertisements converge with entertaining content produced by celebrities and influencers to create new and increasingly covert commercials. 'Advertainment' manifestations fit seamlessly with other digital media posts and do not stand out or 'feel' like traditional audiovisual advertisements because they avoid unnecessary interruptions, attempting to enhance the consumer's experiences with marketed materials without resorting to intrusion (Armoo 2017). The self-regulatory Dutch Advertising Code, however, reasons that 'advertisements should be recognisable as such', attempting to police the complicated online landscape of social media platforms wherein advertisements and regular posts frequently overlap and commingle (Arayess and Geer 2017: 529). In this sense, the blurring of media boundaries throughout Joseph's artwork raises ethical questions surrounding the commercialization of contemporary African-American experiences through music and moving images. Paul Gilroy might criticize the 'deskilling, dehumanizing' processes of visualization that subvert countercultural forms of Audiovisual Atlantic expression and perpetuate Eurocentric hegemony (Gilroy 1999: 267). After all, as Akinwumi Adesokan's crossroads of capital metaphor remind us, Joseph's works present 'conflicting impulses within a particular system' where contradictions of the neoliberal world order manifest (Adesokan 2011: 11).

3.2 Of soul and capital: comparing Derek Pike and Kahlil Joseph's *I Need a Dollar* projects (2010)

Two music videos were released to accompany Aloe Blacc's song *I Need a Dollar* (2010), the theme song of HBO series *How to Make It in America* (2010–11). The secondary Nevada, Las Vegas version was published via the YouTube account of skateboard apparel vendor LRG Clothing on 17 March 2011, and prolific music video specialist Derek Pike is credited as the project's director. The original Harlem, New York version of the music video was directed by Kahlil Joseph, released on 4 April 2010, and publicized on both YouTube and Vimeo by the What Matters Most media production collective.

In a fashion similar to the ways certain directors of feature-length films adopt recognizable styles and traits to carve out their own artistic identity, one can distinguish Joseph and Pike's respective approaches to making music videos through their projects' amalgamations of sound, music and moving images. While studying at New York's Tisch School of Arts, Pike became one of the youngest directors to have a music video featured on MTV. Now an experienced director of over 100 music video projects across various genres, Pike has collaborated with a vast array of high profile musicians, including: RedOne, Waka Flocka Flame, XXXTentaction, Wiz Khalifa and Enrique Iglesias. Pike's version of the *I Need a Dollar* video portrays Blacc hitchhiking across the Nevada desert until the singer stumbles across a casino in Las Vegas, landing a jackpot on the slot machines using a coin rescued from the floor. Joseph's music video, on the other hand, uses a split-screen effect to follow a young man's fruitless attempts to find employment on a harsh wintery day in Harlem in the wake of the financial crisis while, simultaneously, juxtaposing black-and-white footage of Blacc crooning melancholically from the comfort and shelter of an apartment's room.

While both music video adaptations for *I Need a Dollar* have garnered widespread popularity, the reflective mood of Joseph's version communicates the vulnerability of Blacc's lyrics and his soulful sound more delicately than Pike's screen text which,

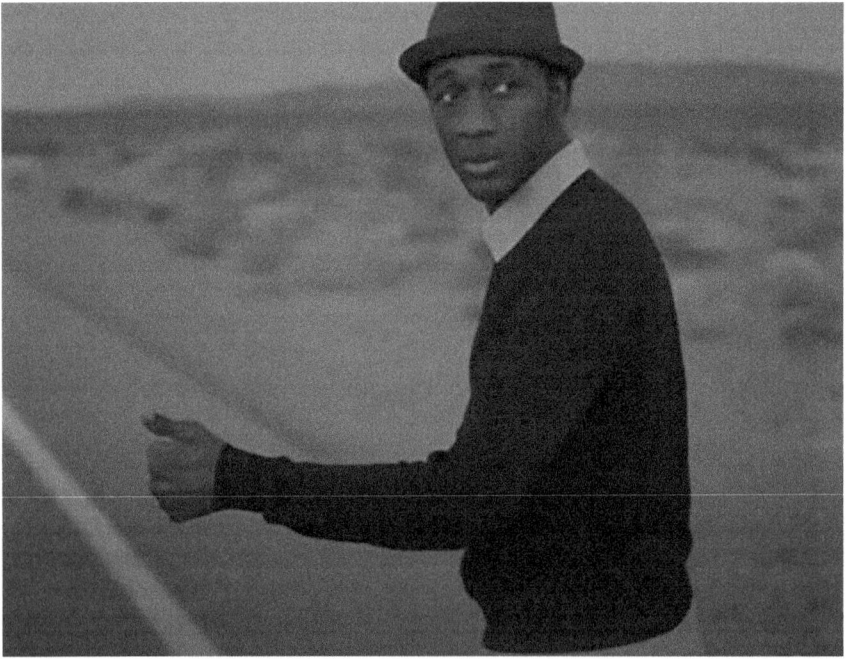

Figures 3.3 *I Need a Dollar [Nevada version]* (2010), © Derek Pike and Aloe Blacc © LRG/Lifted Research Group.

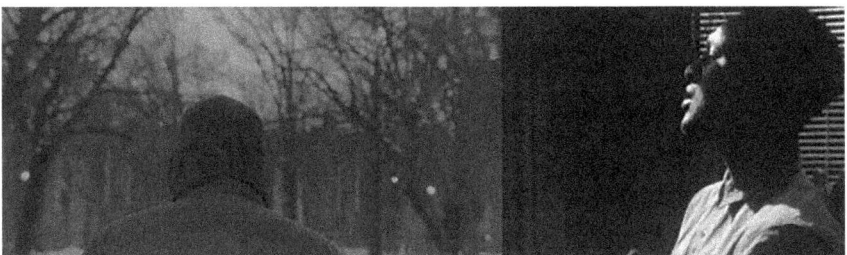

Figures 3.4 *I Need a Dollar [Harlem version]* (2010), Kahlil Joseph and Aloe Blacc © What Matters Most.

instead, aims to appeal to a broader audience, drawing from music video genre tropes yet in certain ways omitting or de-emphasizing some of the politicized undercurrents of Joseph's Harlem version. Pike suggests that aspiring music video directors should 'just keep on shooting … as much as you can' in an unselective fashion because this was how he gained 'exposure', working with a range of famous names that eventually 'legitimized' his status as a video director (Pike interviewed by Yeoh 2010). He thus endorses developing one's reputation through an efficient turnover of projects and clients in lieu of choosing creative partners systematically or predominantly on the terms of their art. Indeed, Pike's professional approach to video-making is conventionally commercial in the sense that he openly admits that the direction of his videos is ultimately dictated by his clients. Tellingly, his use of the word 'client' when articulating his creative process illustrates a transactional approach to music video production dependent on establishing the providing and receiving ends of service, a thorough and effective professional approach to building one's status as a reliable music video director within the highly competitive and predominantly unstable industry (Stubbs 2019). When asked about his creative process directly, Pike responds: 'This usually depends on the client. Sometimes a label will get in touch and say we need an idea for a video by tonight … And I sometimes I have a week to turn in the treatment, a couple days to shoot, and a month on the edit.' When pressed about his favourite music video, Pike illustrates entrepreneurial nous by adopting a coy, neutral stance: 'I usually don't like this question because I don't want any of my clients to feel left out, so I generally just say this … my favourite is always my next video' (Pike interviewed by Yeoh 2010).

Operating within the global economic framework of neoliberal capitalism, Joseph must similarly establish effective working relationships with clients and in turn produce income through his art to sustain a livelihood. While most art forms are woven into the uneven oscillations and unpredictability of volatile market environments, independent filmmaking is especially tied to its ability to remunerate the work of various different parties and departments, from actors and cinematographers to distributors and salespeople. When positioned alongside the complicated situations and circumstances that contemporary artists must continuously negotiate, music videos such as *I Need a Dollar* are thus connected to the complex and paradoxical relationships and contributions of both film *and* music practitioners – as well as the complexities and paradoxes of their visual *and* sonic content – at the Audiovisual Atlantic's crossroads of capital, cultural traffic *and* aesthetics.

Joseph outwardly claims that his processes for determining future collaborators are particularly selective, declaring that his preference for partnerships with mainly black clientele such as Blacc is driven by a thirst for artistic development and success based on the merits of the collaborators' work, a competitive yet passionate meeting of minds whereby: 'Black talent is exponentially propelled by other black talent … Steel sharpens steel' (Joseph in conversation with Abraham 2017). Although the vast majority of Joseph's collaborators are black, the filmmaker has worked with the predominantly white band Arcade Fire and one of his most regular cinematographers, Matthew J. Lloyd, is white. While his artworks often 'display a set of experiences that are intimately tied to blackness' (Sarantis 2018), Joseph thus shares with Pike the propensity to work with collaborators beyond any rigid notion of colour lines *despite* the predominantly Afrocentric focus of his work.

Joseph states publicly that his motives are not entirely dictated by securing profits. When multimillionaire Beyoncé contacted Joseph for assistance with her project *Lemonade* (2016), the artist is adamant that: 'It wasn't until she really came at me and said: "I wanna collaborate with you, versus you work for me," then I was, like, let's talk' (Joseph in conversation with Abraham 2017). Although Joseph's approach is underscored by a willingness to collaborate on mutually respectful terms (creating working relationships that at least *feel* more profound than a hierarchical, transactional partnership between two business parties devoid of connection), one should process Joseph's claim with an element of scepticism because the need to generate money is an inescapable aspect of existing within our economic framework, and all artists – including Beyoncé, Joseph and Pike – must engage with the market system out of necessity *despite* their ideological positions, *regardless* of their resistance to or compliance with our dominant economic framework.

While Joseph initially struggles to find terms to articulate his mindset, he ultimately suggests that his approach is grounded on 'integrity' rather than 'radicality', reasoning that one of the main reasons he would never include the final outcome of the *Lemonade* visual project in one of his own exhibitions is because: 'For me, there's a clear distinction between my own work, and work for hire' (Joseph in conversation with Lissoni 2017). Problematically, however, the creation of working relationships based solely on this loose definition of 'integrity' seems naïve or unrealistic given the dominance of ruthless competitiveness within our contemporary epoch, and staunch anti-capitalist commentators may criticize Joseph for 'selling out' to and thereby perpetuating the demands and prevailing infra/supastructures of neoliberal capitalism's world-encompassing economic frameworks (Gastil 1971; Harvey 2007; Woodhouse 2009). As Paul Gilroy argues, influential figures and organizations within the cultural industries are willing 'to make substantial investments in blackness provided it yields a user-friendly, house-trained, and marketable "reading" of the stubborn [black] vernacular that can no longer be a called a counterculture' (Gilroy

2004a: 242), thus Joseph's approach to filmmaking in *I Need a Dollar* – while in some ways more sensitive to the complicated dynamics of cultural pluralism *and* more critical of whiteness's hegemonic status than Pike's video (and other similar approaches conducted by directors black, white and beyond) – does not challenge the status quo in particularly radical terms and therefore remains a commodified and consumable packaging of black peoples' experiences, adhering to and thereby perpetuating the free market's prevalent dehumanizing and racially biased logic (Sidanius and Pratto 1993; Mason 1996; Bhattacharyya 2017).

In terms of understanding how Joseph negotiates the flows of our global financial framework as an artist bound to such an economic system by necessity rather than choice, elements of the director's 'integrity' conceptualization may generate fragile yet valuable avenues for characterizing the artist's creative processes, offering a compassionate humanist's lens through which to process and understand our oftentimes harsh, frustrating and divisive world order. Gayle Wald observes that: 'one can *have* soul, *be* soulful, and play *soul music*' (her emphasis) (Wald 1997: 147), thus it is possible to develop overlaps between Joseph's idealistic form of 'integrity' and more frequently constructed notions of 'soul' and 'soulfulness', encompassing elements of Blacc's music *as well as* the artistic 'integrity' which Joseph claims is a fundamental component driving his creative processes.

Drawing from Wald's arguments, Emily J. Lordi theorizes 'soul' as 'a logic constituted through a network of strategic performances … meant to promote black thriving, if not liberation', illustrating how similar understandings of 'black thriving' may account for and even commend the high number of digital views which Joseph's projects of self-defined 'integrity' have accumulated (Lordi 2020: 5). Joseph's delicate yet potentially useful notion of 'integrity' is thus strengthened when informed by Lordi's more robust conceptualization of 'soul'. Understanding 'soul' as a mindset or logic of resilience and resistance rather than an essence or quality innately imbedded in the artistry of certain black performers allows us to negotiate clichéd situations (such as Joseph's) wherein the artist's resistance to commercialization and the influences of external industrial contexts is based on anecdotal self-praise. Instead, this conceptualization of 'soul' grounds such passionate and heartfelt (yet nonetheless precarious and unstable) ruminations on artistic intent within a long-standing tradition of countercultural performance, striving to articulate and preserve the racial-spiritual 'self-consciousness, self-realization, [and] self-respect' at the heart of black music, black art, black souls (Du Bois 1903: 5).

Joseph's filmmaking activities, then, take place within 'an era of targeted precision marketing' and the size and scope of his audiences affirm that 'the appeal of black faces and styles need no longer be restricted to black consumers' (Gilroy 2004a: 242). However, while one must critically and diligently digest and process the conveniently self-constructed 'integrity' concept shaping Joseph's creative processes, one should not completely dismiss the tone characterizing Joseph's approach when collaborating with like-minded artists, especially if, crucially, this interpretation of 'integrity' is regarded as a rhizomatic offshoot stemming from 'soul' and its popular discourses. When exploring his inspirations for partnering with and dedicating a piece of work to the singer Alice Smith, palpable enthusiasm is evident when Joseph declares that Smith shares with jazz musician Alice Coltrane 'this really deep soul thing ... [which] isn't really interested in the marketplace' (Joseph in conversation with Dallas 2017: 143). By facilitating alternative pathways for existence within our present economic framework which 'preserve principles of social collaboration and interdependence' (Harvie 2013: 193), Joseph seeks from his co-authors those elusive and somewhat fanciful elements which are grounded in emotions and sensations, yearning for something closely resembling 'soul'.

Although such characteristics communicate Joseph's clichéd wishes to imbue his artistic process with a self-defined and therefore problematic understanding of righteousness, at the same time his preoccupations with 'integrity' illustrate a sensitive, humane approach to creativity rooted in the countercultural tradition of certain Afrocentric art performances. The mechanics of what Joseph determines as Smith and Coltrane's 'deep soul thing' thus signify a subtle shift from a Du Boisian conceptualization of 'soul' as 'a deep spiritual-racial consciousness' to something which might be better understood as 'the special resilience of black people ... surviving the historical and daily trials of white supremacy' which, in turn, breaks down barriers between art and reality, bestowing through artistic expressions and collaborative projects '*worldly gifts* such as emotional depth and communal belonging' (my emphasis) (Lordi 2020: 5).

There is a long history in American popular culture of ascribing politics to forms of African-American cultural production, thus the manner in which Pike's video offers entertainment should be recognized on its own terms. At the same time, however, one must not dismiss the ways in which Joseph's video attempts to amplify the soulful qualities of Blacc's song, attempting to communicate in visual terms certain signs and significations embedded in the original record. Without creating a simplistic dichotomy that frames Pike and Joseph's videos on opposing ends of the same spectrum, I now consider the content of the two *I Need a Dollar* music videos, exploring the ways in which the music video directors balance commitments to their clientele on the one hand with audiovisual articulations of Blacc's interpretation of a soul music song on the other.

Blacc's song is a complex hybrid of various musical styles and forms: driven by choral rhythms and soulful keys, the 'call-and-response' structure of his plaintive vocals in *I Need a Dollar* echoes John Lomax's field recordings of chain gang members and farm workers 'down on their luck ... making a plea for help' (Blacc interviewed by Green 2011). Both the Nevada and Harlem music videos channel these sonic themes by exploring the fortunes of two young black figures searching for ways to generate money in contemporary America. Pike presents a suited singer traversing the desert without any immediate signs of danger or hardship and thus augments the playful dimensions of Blacc's soul music interpretation, whereas Joseph depicts his protagonist's journey as a hurried, intensified attempt to secure financial stability, which, when the outcome goes awry, has problematic, dangerous repercussions that emphasize the resilient and resistant elements of the soul music tradition.

Many of the great paradoxes at the heart of both Blacc's music and Joseph and Pike's music videos stem from the notion that Afrodiasporic experiences are rendered more complex by states of limbo. Relentless oscillations between cultural states and affiliations thus engender a precarious and challenging existence for certain sections of the African-American population who lack sustainable income for food and shelter, commanded to adhere to societal expectations without certain opportunities and advantages that innately form within America's societal framework(s). The settings of the music videos are thus similarly loaded with both contradictory *and* common signs and significations. Famed for its vibrant nightlife and lax betting laws, Las Vegas is a historical site of friction between the dominant Nevada State Government and the ancestors of indigenous Native Americans as the two factions compete for control of natural resources, land ownership and gambling rights (Hanes 1982; Pasquaretta 1994; Thornton 2005). The self-defined 'Gambling Capital' or 'Entertainment Capital of the World' perpetuates the glamorous aspects of casino lifestyles and pleasure-seeking in clubs without addressing the social frictions that simmer beneath the city's surface, tensions between government and indigenous people on which Las Vegas's modern environment of indulgence is founded (Macarthur 2016; Liu 2019).

Las Vegas's governing bodies have also clashed with black citizens throughout the years. Racism's prevalence in the area fluctuated in tandem with 'economic recessions and times of prosperity', meaning that Las Vegas experienced a shift from 'cordial relations' between blacks and whites at around 1905 to 'an acrimonious state of affairs' in the early thirties (White 2004: 71). Gambling in Las Vegas casinos became legalized in 1931 yet white tourists and workers did not want to engage with local black citizens who had recently migrated the area in search of new employment opportunities (Eadington 1999; Gray and DeFilippis 2015). Racist city officials would only issue licenses to black-owned businesses if they moved themselves away from the most popular parts of Las Vegas to the Westside of the newly built railroad tracks; thus the local black community sought new opportunities from the enforced dispersal (such as replicating businesses and services already provided in the downtown area) as they prepared 'to live a different social, cultural, and economic lifestyle' (White 2004: 76).

Over the years, racism and inequality continued to mar the city's self-idealization as an American utopia. Although top artists earned large sums of money as white consumers began to enthusiastically purchase the influx of Black records from the 1950s, Las Vegas developed a reputation as 'the Mississippi of the West' as a result of its strict and unjust segregation policies – for example, black entertainers were oftentimes prohibited from staying overnight at the hotels where they performed (Cook 2013; Pearce 2014). Pike's Nevada music video depicts an improbable get-rich-quick scheme which plays on and exploits interpretations of Las Vegas as a hedonist's playground, a space where the rich congregate to escape (further) their social responsibilities, rather than a site of tumultuous and complex race relations. Although Blacc is captured hitchhiking through the Nevada desert and across the historic railway lines in his search for financial security, the neatness of his ironed shirt, chino trousers and trilby hat undermines the plausibility of his march through the desert's inhospitable conditions while attempting to hitchhike, missing opportunities to draw connections between the precariousness for black workers in the city at present and the Jim Crow period of Las Vegas's rich and complex history. While visual representations of

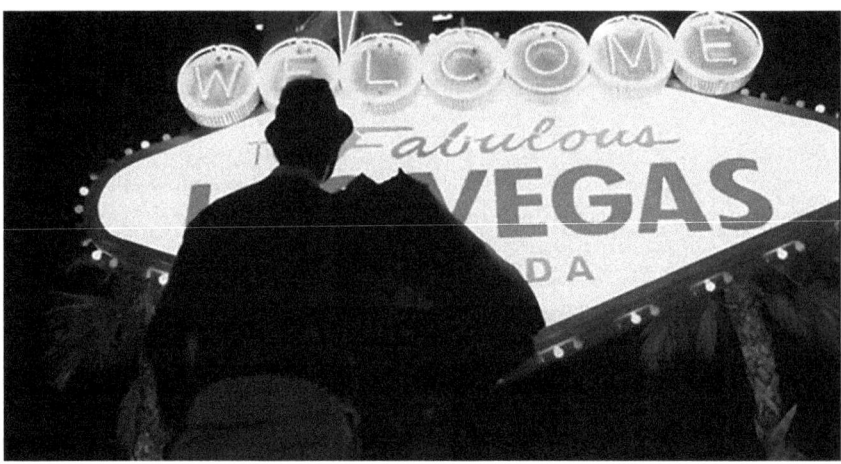

Figure 3.5 *I Need a Dollar [Nevada version]* (2010), © Derek Pike and Aloe Blacc © LRG/Lifted Research Group.

Blacc in Pike's music video depict a struggling African-American man attempting to procure financial stability in the same manner as the Harlem video, Pike frames the protagonist's quest for money in an improbable fashion, stripping the *I Need a Dollar* song of the potentially sincere and emotional energies with which it was originally charged, and, in turn, characterizing Blacc as a contemporary performer unable or unwilling to reconcile the historical past of his ancestors with the status of the black community in the present. The protagonist's transformation from unlucky troubadour stranded in the Nevada desert to suave gambler parading in the heart of Vegas's casino district metaphorized the safety of Blacc's wager beyond the screen. On the surface, Blacc appears to take a gamble by entering the precarious and intensely competitive music industry as an artist. However, the manner in which his song draws from the countercultural legacies of soul music yet, paradoxically, packages these qualities into a consumable popular form becomes a savvy business strategy rather than a speculative risk or genuine attempt to process and understand hardship for African-American workers.

Harlem is as complicated and paradoxical a site as Las Vegas, loaded with overlapping histories and contradictory legacies of race relations. On the one hand, Harlem has long been characterized as the 'Cultural Capital of Black America' by historians and commentators since the advent of the Harlem Renaissance (Schoener 2007; Gill 2012; Taborn 2018). From writers Langston Hughes, Richard Wright and Countee Cullen to musicians Duke Ellington, Ethel Waters and Billie Holiday, photographers Gordon Parks and James Van Der Zee to politicians Marcus Garvey, Malcolm X and Adam Clayton Powell Jr, numerous powerful and inspiring black figures demonstrate and articulate aspects of the 'spirit of play and optimism' (Huggins 1995: 10) which defined Harlem's exceptional period of intellectual, social and artistic output. Problematically, however, certain Harlem Renaissance figures became reliant on white systems of patronage, meaning that Black voices were forced to 'perform' in a manner that adhered to white values and tastes in order to receive money (Story 1989; Parascandola, Bone and Wade 2010).

In Pike's music video, the director adheres closely to a straightforward definition of the music video form by using audiovisual material to promote a single song which, in turn, contributes to the transformation of Blacc's song into a more conventional music video. By diluting the screen text's subversive 'soul' features, a greater sense of marketed time permeates the video, its neat yet implausible ending with the slot machine victory reminding us of the 'constructedness' of the screen text as a commodity tied to external commercial imperatives. Joseph, on the other hand, frames a teaser trailer for *I Need a Dollar* with an audio recording of black activist James Baldwin discussing his childhood experiences of inhospitable sections of Harlem. Baldwin details: 'I was born in Harlem, Harlem Hospital … we used to play on the roof and – I can't call it an alley but near the river – it was a dump: a garbage dump …' as the trailer's unnamed protagonist walks across icy terrain. The camera is flipped upside down to mirror the precariousness of the ice underfoot, communicating the fragility of Baldwin's upbringing in Harlem's twenties and thirties as well as hazards and insecurity of the nameless protagonist's social situation in the present day as he navigates the contemporary Harlem cityscape across the ice and into the streets.

In refusing to develop promotional material that reduces Blacc's music to an apolitical form of audiovisual entertainment, Joseph's music video and its trailer attempt to capture the frustrations of Afrodiasporic existence within predominantly white societies through complex combinations of music and moving images, channelling elements of Lordi's 'soul' paradigm while, simultaneously, drawing from the explorative spirit of Black independent cinema by attempting 'to discern or depict the full spectrum of black American life and culture' through experimentation with audiovisual forms (Snead 1994: 115). As well as drawing from Black musical resources and cultural traffic whose lyrical content foregrounds the relationships between poverty and urban racism – such as Marlena Shaw's *Woman of the Ghetto* (1969), Oscar Brown Jr's *Dime Away From A Hotdog* (1972), Donny Hathaway's *Little Ghetto Boy* (1972) and Grandmaster Flash and the Furious Five's *The Message* (1982) – the 'retro' sound of Blacc's music explicitly echoes the 'soul realism' that characterizes Curtis Mayfield and Marvin Gaye's respective oeuvres. The sombre, gritty content of Joseph's visual content thus connects ideas about 'soul' and contemporary Harlem through its sonic *and* visual features, generating a shape-shifting filmmaking style.

At the crossroads of cultural traffic Blacc's *I Need a Dollar* is an amalgamation of numerous sonic influences, many of which are shaped by Bill Withers's song *Ain't No Sunshine* (1971). Both musicians adopt a baritone style of singing and feature the A minor scale to reflect their lyrics' respective explorations of the pain and desperation surrounding pursuits of money and love. Although the melodies of both *I Need a Dollar* and *Ain't No Sunshine* have similar shapes, Withers's song tends to hold the note as though letting his articulation of personal anguish linger a little longer for cathartic purposes, whereas Blacc's phrasing is more purposeful and upbeat, reflecting his determination to secure economic stability by diagnosing the main issues of his misfortune, directly reaching out for assistance.

During the middle eight section of Blacc's song, the music's pitch shifts upwards as though the musician begins to reach heavenwards for help, forming a desperate prayer in the face of worldly tribulations and relentless uncertainty. At this point in Pike's video, Blacc's neatly dressed hitchhiker sings atop a desert rock formation and reaches into the air, before catching a ride into the heart of the city's brightly lit gambling district. In Joseph's version, the protagonist takes a break from negotiating his urban environment, meeting an acquaintance to smoke something while sitting on a snow-covered bench in the middle of an icy park, quickly fist-bumping in such a way that could be interpreted as both innocuous greeting and illegal exchange.

Although the prayers of Pike's protagonist are answered by the anonymous car driver, his pristine style of clothing throughout the ordeal undermines the severity of this situation, suggesting that the character is grossly inconvenienced rather than forced to face the sort of extreme social or financial hardship which underpins Lordi's 'soul' logic of resistance and resilience. Contrastingly, in Joseph's video the higher octave of Blacc's voice reflects the temporary 'high' achieved by pausing to inhale the undefined substance. Whether drawing from a joint or cigarette, or sitting with a friend or business contact, the character's relief in momentarily halting the day's activities communicates the underlying stress of his daily routine, implying that near-constant states of tension in Harlem's wintery citified landscape are temporarily alleviated by the comfort of such brief yet thoroughly welcomed moments of reflection and reconciliation. Through subtle depictions of both smoking and selling an unknown substance, the 'soul' logic of resilience embedded in Blacc's song is emphasized by Joseph's visual allusions to the underlying presence of illegal activities. Although both videos explore the pressures that their protagonists' respective lines of work entail, the moment of respite in the middle eight section of Pike's version results in a drastic reversal of fortune, whereas the undercurrents of tension examined in the same section of Joseph's video continue to broil and are never satisfactorily resolved.

Sam Cooke's *Chain Gang* (1960) and Lee Dorsey's *Working in the Coal Mine* (1966) exemplify the tradition of the 'work song' in Black music wherein lyrics detailing the hardships of toil are accompanied by harmonious and upbeat music to form a bittersweet reflection on black society's relationships to the hegemony of whiteness or, in the words of Lordi, 'a kind of virtuosic survivorship specific to black people as a group' (Lordi 2020: 5). Although Blacc attempts to construct his '*own* chain gang song' (my emphasis) (Blacc interviewed by Green 2011) through a lyrical representation of hardship whose musical features are rooted in the early 'call-and-response' field songs of America's African slave population, Pike's video incongruously concludes with the unlikely event of Blacc's character winning a large jackpot after finding a single dollar on the Las Vegas streets. Rather than emphasizing the grittiness of the opening lyrics' plea for money and the soulful qualities of the song which explore a character's resilience in response to socio-economic hardship, Blacc's performances in Pike's video in both the bar and the desert entertain the music video's viewership through the contagious enthusiasm of his professional vocal delivery, his emphasis on the song's playful musical elements undermining the fundamental countercultural qualities of 'soul' which otherwise charge the song with its emotional weight. While both music videos capture the 'soul' roots of Blacc's bluesy musical and lyrical styles through frank accounts of their protagonist's struggles to negotiate modern societies, the tongue-in-cheek moments of Pike's video thus flirt with but never reach convincingly such levels of sincerity, only communicating in part the 'unabashedly sentimental' feelings and heartful emotion at the core of soul music (Landau 1976: 210).

As the directors navigate the unevenness of the crossroads of capital in different ways, Lordi's 'soul' definition and Joseph's 'integrity' mindset offer helpful avenues for articulating feelings and sensations which transcend the impersonal logic and mechanics of the marketplace as different institutional and industrial situations generate two distinguishable music videos. In turn, these volatile – and nonetheless valuable – ways of articulating approaches to production capture how screen texts created within particular contexts can foreground or understate a piece of music's countercultural content.

While Pike's music video is a professional interpretation of the song's musical content largely emptied of controversial subject matter, Joseph's gritty and darker portrayal of an unemployed wanderer searching through wintery Harlem in the music video and its trailer draw attention to America's dire social schisms. In doing so, Joseph's work focuses on the countercultural qualities latent in Blacc's music, augmenting certain features within the song which are momentarily explored – or altogether ignored – by Pike's video. *I Need a Dollar*'s lyrics emphasize that 'all that glitters ain't gold' for those attempting to negotiate the myriad obstacles and opportunities underpinning the creative and cultural industries across different parts of the Audiovisual Atlantic, which makes recognizing, scrutinizing and understanding the unlikely moments that do shine all the more valuable – for practitioners and scholars, across film and music, alike.

3.3 Fragments of a fever dream: piecing together Shabazz palaces in *Black Up* (2011)

On 15 November 2011, a short film to advertise Shabazz Palaces's feature-length album *Black Up* was released on YouTube by Sub Pop Records and through What Matters Most's Vimeo account. While Joseph's footage captures civilians and animals negotiating busy New York locations and Puerto Rico's spacious green wilderness, a medley of songs from the album, audio samples from across the web and a selection of Shabazz Palaces's previously unreleased material provide the screen text's soundtrack. Puerto Rico is a Caribbean Island that is considered part of North America, thus the video's intense visual collage of urban and rural environments marks the first-ever hip-hop release from grunge, punk and rock label Sub Pop while, at the same time, exploring the cross-cultural connections which shape Joseph's collaborations with Shabazz Palaces.

The project was ultimately deemed 'Video of the Year 2011' by *The Seattle Times* and featured in Kara Walker's *Ruffneck Constructivists* exhibition at the ICA Philadelphia in 2014 alongside Joseph's *Until the Quiet Comes* (2012).[3] While *Belhaven Meridian* in part promotes Shabazz Palaces's album *Of Light* (2009) in an indirect manner, *Black Up* operates in the same vein as *The Model* because the videos specifically share titles with particular musical albums, advertising these musical projects across digital platforms while, at the same time, attempting to convey in audiovisual terms similar themes and styles which shape the sonic materials of Shabazz Palaces and Seu Jorge's respective musical releases.

In terms of producing a work of 'advertainment', *Black Up* is one of Joseph's most difficult works to process for casual digital audiences and non-specialist media consumers, since the screen text's formal complexity is influenced by the sophistication of the video's musical sources. Although Eric Grandy states that Shabazz Palaces's frontman Ishmael Butler 'lets some sunlight in, breathes fresh air' with his contemplative lyrical content and calming vocal delivery throughout the musical album, he qualifies this statement by adding that *Black Up* is not entirely comprised of 'easy, uncomplicated songs' (Grandy 2011). Shabazz Palaces's Zimbabwean mbira rhythms and philosophical rap meditations are set to wobbling bassline drops and evocative synthesizer samples in a manner reminiscent of *Belhaven Meridian*'s soundtrack, creating a compelling range of soundscapes that oscillate from the euphoric and uplifting aspects of soul music to a 'cerebral and at times utterly baffling' concoction of genres (Bakare 2017).

The idea that 'no real taxonomical equation' can compartmentalize all of the songs featured in the *Black Up* album is thus developed by the screen text's combination of film, music video and advertisement properties (Young 2011). Paul Dallas argues that the *Black Up* video explores the 'fragmentation' of audiovisual forms and ideas of identity, whereas *Belhaven Meridian* examines the 'fluidity' of such notions (Dallas 2017: 144). In this sense, Joseph's 'integrity' approach manifests through *Black Up*'s emphasis on the complexities of cultural traffic and its dedication to artistic practice for its own sake, on its own – even if difficult or obtuse – terms, rather than emphasizing the project's status as a cultural commodity (which, in turn, may have resulted in somewhat less sophisticated audiovisual project in order to market Shabazz Palaces's work to as broad an audience as possible).

Verdant space plays a prominent role through *Black Up*'s combinations of film, music video and advertisement properties, communicating the allegorical depth of 'Blackness' through 'green' manifestations of the concept. The video's motionless opening shots capture the lush Puerto Rican jungle emptied of human activity. As birdsong and insect trills emit from somewhere deep within the thick vegetation, abstract text appears on screen and Butler's voice interrupts the wilderness's comforting array of natural sounds, verbalizing an extract from Shabazz Palaces's song *Bronny on a Breakaway (Bop Hard)*. 'Pilgrim Marketing Plan Rebuttal', he declares, dramatically enunciating the track's opening line before adding in a tongue-in-cheek manner: '…

---

[3] Founded in 1986, Sub Pop gained notoriety after signing contracts with the celebrated Seattle bands Soundgarden, Mudhoney and Nirvana.

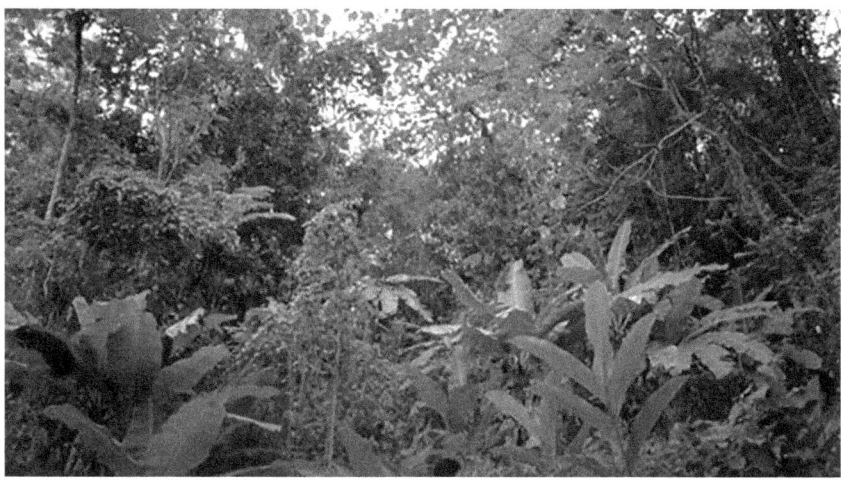

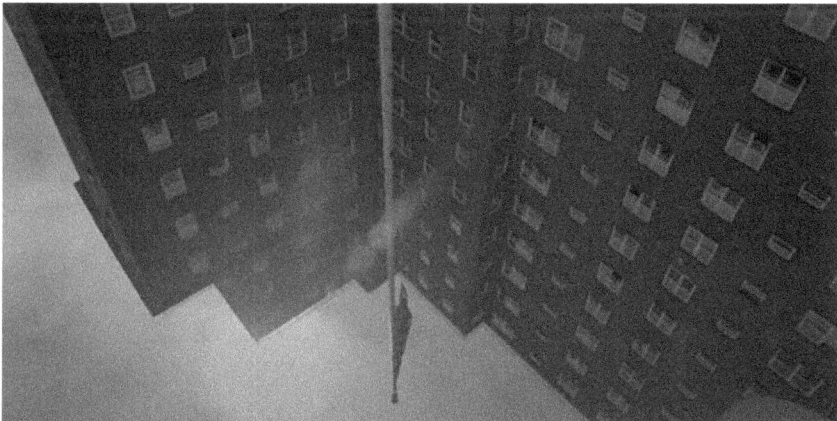

Figures 3.6 and 3.7 *Black Up* (2011), Kahlil Joseph and Shabazz Palaces © What Matters Most.

Take Seven'. While the word 'pilgrim' likens the experience of seeing and hearing *Black Up*'s messages to religious devotees travelling to sacred spaces in pursuit of profound spiritual enrichment, the phrase 'marketing plan' refers to the modern phenomenon of businesses coordinating and executing advertising strategies for a specific demographic. Joseph creates a paradoxical, controversial new term wherein 'Pilgrim Marketing Plan' denotes a cynical commercial strategy targeting unsuspecting spiritual wayfarers as they participate in revered journeys of worship and self-discovery. A noise-editing effect adds a robotic sound to Butler's voice, thereby articulating tensions between tradition and modernity as well as the sacred and profane.

Vitally, the refutation or 'rebuttal' of this business tactic by Butler's lyrics implies that Shabazz Palaces privilege spiritual awakening and new forms of devotional expedition over the contemporary era's commercially driven priorities. However, the comical acknowledgement that the song is the seventh attempt at successfully metamorphosing the misanthropic 'Pilgrim Marketing Plan' is thus reimagined by the *Black Up* film in cinematographer's terms, implying that this opening section of *Black Up* is in fact the project's seventh version or 'take' at transforming the questionable ethics of the business plan into something earnest and heartfelt.

The inclusion of the words 'Take Seven' foregrounds the rehearsed or artificial nature of producing art, positioning amateurish film-making techniques alongside Shabazz Palaces's bold and grandiose attempts at producing heartfelt, sincere art while operating within the constraints of a capitalistic economic framework. Paradoxically, however, the 'Take Seven' disclosure acknowledges that the artists strive to preserve the solemnity and sanctity of traditional examples of pilgrimage by embracing the subversive and droll. Joseph and Shabazz Palaces recognize that they must produce art within the confinements of neoliberal capitalism's free market. At the same time, the artists attempt to create something thought-provoking and sincere that is not primarily driven by augmenting profit margins, protecting and serving the pilgrims of today with a 'Marketing Plan Rebuttal' that lauds and explores a broad range of human characteristics and emotions – from humour and joviality to remembrance and solemnity.

By transforming the screen text's 'Pilgrim Marketing Plan' from calculated advertising strategy to a philosophical film art, the complexity of *Black Up*'s formal structures echoes the Shabazz Palace album's heterogeneous constructions of stereomodernism. As percipients engage with the screen text's movements between film, music video and advertisement forms, the act of processing *Black Up* mimics aspects of an uneven spiritualized journey. The opening fifteen seconds populate *Black Up* with meaning in a manner reminiscent of Joseph's representation of the dense jungle thicket, at once stripped of superfluous detail yet, at the same time, subtly emphasizing how broader complexities and contradictions remain hidden from plain sight, skulking within the deep.

After the opening shot of the empty rainforest merges with the appearance of *Bronny on a Breakaway (Bop Hard)*'s introductory lines, the film's audiovisual material intensifies as rapid editing speeds create a disorientating montage of both urban and rural spaces. Dancers cackling in Puerto Rican bars and worn-out tyres being replaced commingle with empty passageways and side-alleys, broken streetlights flickering overhead, and cars in convoy navigating busy streets. The silhouette of a Zebu ox's skull momentarily appears in front of the green forest's lush and healthy backdrop, before dead pigs are filmed hanging from the ceiling in a slaughterhouse, their necks slashed and faces set alight by flamethrowers in preparation for consumption.

Joseph's inclusion of the hanging pigs forges a connection between the *Black Up* screen text and Charles Burnett's film *Killer of Sheep*, wherein slaughterhouse worker Stan must support his family through the arduous daily task of killing animals, regularly returning home exhausted to fix his broken house, drifting apart from his stoic yet tired partner. The hanging sheep carcasses thus create a visual metaphor for the brutal conveyor belt on which Stan and his family struggle on a routine basis, unable to escape cycles of poverty dictating the lives of so many Watts citizens. Their daily struggles are thus echoed by the grotesquery of *Black Up*'s hanging pigs. The silhouetted image of a Zebu ox's skull which briefly appears in *Black Up*'s dizzying opening montage further develops the cinematic lineage of Joseph's screen text, opening up a poignant relationship between Shabazz Palaces's promotional video and Djibril Diop Mambéty's seminal experimental feature-length film *Touki Bouki* (1973).

In *Touki Bouki*, cowherder Mory and student Anta dream of fleeing Dakar in favour of Paris. Mory straps a Zebu ox's skull onto the handlebars of his treasured motorcycle and together the pair navigate Senegal's opportunities and pitfalls, performing different money-making schemes across the country as means of producing sufficient capital for their journey. However, when the pair finally have enough money to leave their country, Mory is tormented by scenes of butchery and barbarity from an abattoir as he approaches the ship to Europe, haunted by resurgent memories – that were initially presented in the opening sequence of *Touki Bouki* – of a terrified ox drawn away by the horns for inevitable slaughter. Mory halts abruptly on the gangplank and then abandons Anta, fearing a fate similar to the bewildered animal as the ship sails into unexplored territory. Although *Touki Bouki* and Burnett's *Killer of Sheep* have little in common thematically, Sarah O'Brien draws parallels between the two films because both portray 'the metaphoric weight of slaughtered animals … compelling them to stand in for analogous images of death' (O'Brien 2016: 33).

In this sense, Joseph's *Black Up* channels the ways that *Touki Bouki* warns against abandoning one's roots, implying that to forget the legacies of one's African ancestors may result in physical and spiritual capitulation. However, Mambéty complicates any simplistic or totalizing readings of the film's ending. When Mory flees from the ship in pursuit of his modified bike, he remains tormented by traumatic images of the beast struggling against the rope, panicking as it senses impending doom at the hands of the slaughterhouse workers. As Mory darts through the city with increasing panic, he finally locates his vehicle smashed to pieces in a traffic accident. This incident snaps the Zebu ox's horns from the motorcycle's skull ornament and, as Mory attempts to process the situation, memories of a gruesome cascade of blood pouring from the ox's lacerated neck agonize him. Mambéty creates a paradoxical denouement in *Touki Bouki* wherein Mory remains in Senegal without integral components of his life and identity, in part preserving his African roots yet losing Anta and suffering the destruction of his motorcycle. The complexity of Mambéty's film is thus channelled in *Black Up*'s abattoir scenes, generating similarly problematic situations for members of African diasporas wherein escape from societal determinism seems impossible no matter one's mindset and action.

Black Up's footage of the slaughtered pigs and silhouette of the Zebu ox's horns thus creates a cinematic lineage connecting both *Touki Bouki* and *Killer of Sheep* across the Audiovisual Atlantic. Sergei Eisenstein's *Stachka [Strike]* (1925) is one of the first cinematic works to convey complex allegorical meaning through images of slaughtered animals, representing the violent suppression of a workers' strike in pre-revolutionary Russia through cross-cuts between battlefield scenes and startled cattle brutally killed. However, Eisenstein's work lacks the racial dimensions of *Touki Bouki*, *Killer of Sheep* and *Black Up*'s filmic heritage, wherein bestial murder communicates the internalized dilemmas born from negotiating African ancestry rather than the literal massacre of an uprising political class. All three audiovisual artworks adopt striking and disturbing sequences of dying animals trapped in slaughterhouses, illustrating that the paradoxes and complications of developing selfhood in relation to Africa and its diasporas may involve navigating frustrating, cage-like borders. In turn, such processes of navigation extend beyond simple, neatly defined parameters and – ultimately – rarely possess clear, straightforward answers.

A key factor that distinguishes *Black Up*'s animal slaughter metaphors from *Touki Bouki* and *Killer of Sheep* is the manner in which sounds and music play pivotal yet differing roles. Vlad Dima argues that Mambéty's alternations between synchronous and asynchronous sounds in the *Touki Bouki* '[separate] his work from sound's more conventional use as soundtrack in the context of West African cinema' (Dima 2012: 38). The jarring sonic attributes of *Touki Bouki* especially augment and shape the significance of the film's slaughter scenes because, as Charles Mudede suggests, parts of *Touki Bouki* reach 'the condition of a music video' through the film's combination of sonic and visual materials in nonchronological fashion (Mudede 2016). For example, a peuhl flute's soft, hypnotizing melody links the film's opening shots of herders performing their duties in vast open spaces before abruptly cutting to oxen drawn into the abattoir against their will, the beasts' rattling chains and the slaughterhouse workers' animated cries. An intense sonic concoction of wild seagulls squawking and Anta's aunt laughing dementedly at the thought of Mory jumping from a cliff is positioned alongside graphic footage of the goat's lacerated neck. Soon, Anta rests her head against the rock face's crags in dismay as the gulls fly and glide serenely above the open sea, far from the violent ritual taking place on land.

Music plays a much more conventional role in developing the meaning of the slaughter scenes in *Killer of Sheep*. Ashley Naftule argues that *Killer of Sheep* was a lost classic for decades because the director used music from highly esteemed African-American performers such as Dinah Washington, Louis Armstrong, Scott Joplin and Earth, Wind and Fire. Since the film's overall budget was $10,000 and the licensing fees for the selected songs greatly exceeded this figure, *Killer of Sheep* was unable to secure distribution rights until UCLA preservationist Ross Lipman restored the film, establishing a DVD sales contract through the assistance of production house Milestone Films and filmmaker Steven Soderbergh (Naftule 2017).

In the original, uncirculated edition of *Killer of Sheep*, Washington's version of the romantic ballad *Unforgettable* (1961) plays in the film's closing moments as sheep are herded for slaughter, forming a bittersweet farewell to Stan and his family's 'unforgettable' situation trapped amid Watts's cycles of poverty and hardship. However, rights for *Unforgettable* were too expensive for the preservation project's budget, thus Washington's melancholic track *This Bitter Earth* (1961) is adopted in the alternative soundtrack for the film's updated version. The majority of *This Bitter Earth*'s lyrics lament the inevitable passing of time that grinds love and life's strongest forces into eternal oblivion, the solemn realization continuously whispering from the back of one's mind that all the wonderful aspects of existence will one day disintegrate and drift away 'like the dust/that hides the glow of a rose'. However, the final verse of *This Bitter Earth* finds solace in the fact that someone might 'answer' one's calls of desperation in spite of life's inevitable and impeding void of nothingness, thus Washington ends the song with epiphanic optimism, concluding 'this bitter earth/may not be so bitter after all'. In the final shots of *Killer of Sheep*, Stan and his wife – having endured so much and seemingly confined in Watts to endure so much more – slowly dance together in their dilapidated house, two lost lambs desperately clinging to the transient respite of the other's companionship.

In *Black Up,* Joseph combines *Killer of Sheep*'s conventionalized use of music as an accompanying soundtrack with elements of asynchronous, jarring sounds that distinguish the various aural realms of *Touki Bouki*. For example, Joseph connects shots of slaughtered pigs with the reverberating drums of an ominous digital soundscape created by Shabazz Palaces. A mixture of distorted cries echo and repeat as the pulsating drumbeat quickens, intensifying the slaughterhouse's noxious atmosphere as carcasses hang from the ceiling, blood drips from severed throats and flames smother lifeless, charred faces. However, the warm, invigorating keys and steady, repetitive claps of Shabazz Palaces's song *Are you ... Can you ... Were you? (Felt)* suddenly feature at this juncture, offering a recognizable and comforting musical structure within Shabazz Palaces's sonic minefield of disorientating noises.

In visual terms the rack-focus effect denotes the camera moving a shot in and out of focus, and Dima extrapolates this idea by exploring usages of the 'sonic rack-focus effect' in Mambéty's work, whereby 'sounds and noises are mixed, are played at varying volume levels, and take turns as the primary (loudest) source of sound' (Dima 2012: 41). In *Touki Bouki*, the 'sonic rack-focus effect' is used when the cattle are slaughtered, and most of the sequence's sounds work in tandem with images. However, Mambéty gradually muffles the sounds of the animals dying to the point that listeners 'cannot make out the details ... our senses are so overwhelmed that they are no longer trusted' (ibid. 45). In similar fashion, Joseph adopts the 'sonic rack-focus effect' during the slaughtered pigs sequence as sound levels of acoustic instruments, electronic noises and Butler's voice fluctuate and shift.

Dima and Michel Chion argue that the meanings of a film's sounds must not be reduced to vague abstractions through generic contrasts with images, thus it is imperative to locate the specific meaning of these sounds in relation to an audiovisual piece's visual dimensions (Chion 1994; Dima 2012). While the hanging pigs of *Black Up*'s introductory scenes mirror the intensity of *Killer of Sheep*'s symbolic, music-infused representations of murdered animals, *Black Up*'s rhythms change pace as new songs *and* soundscapes are introduced, thereby exploring a range of moods associated with Afrocentric identities in a manner akin to *Touki Bouki*. One may argue that the moments of 'fragmentation' between Joseph's sound, music and moving images in *Black Up*'s collaboration with *Shabazz Palaces* thus communicate an African style of filmmaking rooted in the audiovisual experimentations of Mambéty's debut feature-length film (Dallas 2017: 144). By collaborating with a band who explore both American *and* Zimbabwean cultural roots through the audial components of their songs, the 'audio-divisual' moments in *Black Up* sonically and visually echo Mambéty's combinations of sound and moving images 'in a way that is neither symmetrical nor complementary but conflictual', thereby challenging traditional filmmaking frameworks and thus situating the project in pan-African, globalized contexts (Chion 2013: 77).

As the song *Are you ... Can you ... Were you? (Felt)* starts to play, an intimate close-up of a man and woman embracing under glorious sunlight evokes sensations of sentimentality and optimism. By combining an instance of profound beauty amid New York's bustling streets with a simplistic yet uplifting beat, the scene's visual and sonic aspects communicate the uncomplicated bliss of proximity shared with a loved one, the closeness and warmth of humans experiencing life's precious moments together. During a similarly intimate and soothing moment in *Black Up*, a hooded lady rests her head on Butler's shoulder while queuing for an ATM machine. The pair wait patiently with their backs to the camera, tender body language cementing the pair's close relationship in spite of the fact their facial expressions remain hidden. The film then transports itself to a mysterious beach far away from the urban cityscapes and – shooting directly into the sky – captures a tiny glimpse of a 'micromoon' floating in the evening's jet black sky, sea breeze softly blowing the highest leaves of a palm tree.[4] The moon is positioned at the centre of the frame, creating the illusion of a pinpricked hole in the sky's canvas, a tiny gap emitting light akin to projecting film through a great blank sheet.

Although the couple's tenderness in the busy city space feels spontaneous, *Black Up*'s visual allegory for film projection draws attention to the mechanics of calculated filmmaking processes which nuance the film's diegetic universe. By creating an intellectual montage that thematically links the distinguishable city and beach scenes, the short film thus reminds percipients that the footage of the pair queuing together in the busy city space is as painstakingly crafted as the mesmerizing images of the tiny full moon amid the great dark sky, emphasizing that every frame in *Black Up* is delicately loaded with meaning *despite* the filmic illusions of randomness and chaos which are augmented by the Mambétian disparities between audial and visual planes (Dima 2012).

As demonstrated by the myriad sources and influences within Joseph's screen text, the musical heterogeneity of Shabazz Palaces's album is communicated by the bricolage nature of the advertisement's shots and sequences which, in turn, channel the diverse artistry of a range of black filmmakers, poets and musicians. At times, *Black Up*'s aesthetics may feel smothering and intense, an anarchic amalgamation of ideas and theories chaotically stitched together in some sort of wild cinematic frenzy, or, as What Matters Most's Vimeo account defines: 'a fever dream induced by the music of Shabazz Palaces'. In this sense, the project fails to offer an alternative to the Eurocentric frameworks of marketed time which pervade contemporaneity because it feels cluttered and confused.

---

[4] While the term 'micromoon' is not accepted by all astronomists, it colloquially refers to the smallest form of a full moon, or the opposite of a supermoon (Amatulli 2019; Torregrossa 2020).

And then – out of the bedlam, swiftly – *Black Up* provides the chance for one to reach epiphanic instances of clarity. At one of the film's most striking moments, Joseph offers a glimpse of a small boy staring into the sky, spying sunlight through the windows of an abandoned building covered with emerging plants and saplings. Green shoots from an intrusive branch cover part of the frame as columns of darkness either side of the tiny boy merge with the windows' shadows, threatening to engulf and stifle his fragile curiosity. At this point in the short film, Butler's words from *Are you … Can you … Were you? (Felt)* declare: 'I woke up to it: heavy, alight with trueness' while the song's warm, comforting melodies wobble and reverberate. Once again, we experience the 'sonic rack-focus effect' that features similarly in *Touki Bouki*. From the visual and audial chaos, clarity emerges within *Black Up*'s complex audiovisual whole. In the same vein as the young boy staring in silent wonderment beyond the tiny saps of a branch, Joseph's combination of film, music video and advertisement properties illustrates how Butler 'woke up' to something large and bright – high above the lush forests of foliage, far removed from the cities' dense concrete buildings – connecting all of the universe's multitudinous manifestations through an unbounded or Black sense of time, the pervasive sense of liberation reminding him of the universe's sheer size and our minute, insignificant roles within it.

While promoting Shabazz Palaces's new release, the *Black Up* video seeks to communicate moments of connection and harmony that ripple and flow throughout the band's musical projects, drawing from and sustaining the heritage of African and Afrodiasporic artists such as Djibril Diop Mambéty and Charles Burnett through crossroads of cultural traffic. Indeed, Paul Dallas argues that Joseph's collaborations with Shabazz Palaces echo his work with Flying Lotus and Sampha because the screen texts develop 'these moments of transcendence, for a lack of a better word, where the combination of music and imagery seem to take flight' (Dallas 2017: 148). Dallas struggles to articulate in appropriate terms instances of harmonization and asynchronization between the sonic and image-based dimensions of Joseph's work, thus communicating the filmmaker's Mambétian ability to shift 'from a visual plane onto an aural narrative one' (Dima 2012: 38) as well as instances where boundless sensations of time are evoked by Afrodiasporic art forms.

Exemplars of African cinema such as *Touki Bouki* are complicated by the manner in which their storylines 'circle as they circulate, so that their fabric contains many interlocking stories and permutations of stories' (Teshome 1989: 60). The overlapping and oscillating nature of *Black Up*'s dense combinations of Black music and moving images creates a complex audiovisual artwork that shifts between film, music video and advertisement forms as well as Western and African cultural influences. In promoting Shabazz Palaces's new album, one may locate *Black Up*'s transmedia qualities alongside *Belhaven Meridian*, *I Need a Dollar*, *The Model* and *Cheeba*'s merging of film, music video and advertisement forms, as well as their multilayered crosscurrents that connect various African, American and European media sources across the Audiovisual Atlantic.

4

Exhibiting resilience

4.1 To popularize the underground: movements towards the community arts space

In the years following Kahlil Joseph's prolific output in 2010, two major tragedies befell his family. When his father Keven Joseph Davis contracted brain cancer and passed away in 2011, the Joseph-Davis family were left an inheritance with which to create the Underground Museum, a community space dedicated to Afrodiasporic arts. Following the establishment of the Underground Museum as 'not only one of the most important destinations for black art in the country' but at the same time 'a crucial gathering place for its working class Arlington Heights neighbourhood', Noah Davis contracted a rare type of soft tissue cancer, passing away in 2015 (Pogrebin 2020). While their father's parting gift provided monetary means to establish a community centre focused on African-American arts and cultures, Noah's advice to his brother detailed situating the *m.A.A.d.* project in this radical gallery setting.

The Underground Museum represented a departure from conventionalized curatorial practices because, from the classical era to the present day, museum and gallery spaces in the West have been predominantly 'built as temples of culture and art, reflecting images of Europe as the ideal' (Catlin-Legutko 2019: 42). Some of the major problems associated with the formal display of art in designated exhibition spaces are the oftentimes uneven and exploitative relationships between the original creators or owners of materials on display on the one hand and the host institutions that commission, purchase or originally 'stole' such works on the other (La Follette 2017). While Cinnamon Catlin-Legutko believes that exhibition spaces possess 'power to change lives, inspire movements, and challenge authority', she also notes that historically 'we find non-Indigenous people acquiring the belongings and remains of people from other cultures' which, in turn, means that art galleries and museums are 'colonizing spaces' as well as sites capable of disseminating new forms of knowledge and disrupting hegemonized historical narratives (ibid. 41). Using the Museum of Contemporary Art – where in fact Joseph's *Double Conscience* (2015) and *One Day at a Time: Kahlil Joseph's Fly Paper* (2018) exhibitions have been hosted, featuring his audiovisual works *m.A.A.d.* (2014) and *Fly Paper* (2017) respectively – as an exemplar of these issues, his sister-in-law Karon Davis observes that: 'Conventional cultural institutions, whether it's fashion or movies or museums, they're born of 300 years of whiteness' (Davis, cited by Solway 2017).

As well as forming 'temples' dedicated to Western ideologies, museums and galleries have also been misused as centres for disseminating misleading information. Depictions of Africa both in the West *and* on the African continent were often 'reconstructed as the product of a monolithic imperial propaganda', justifying the colonial project's barbarity under the guise of a civilizing mission 'with savages of an inherently inferior order, both intellectually and morally, to the white coloniser' (Coombes 1997: 2). Munyaradzi Mawere elaborates by suggesting: 'There is no doubt that the colonial regimes in Africa played a fundamental role in the establishment of museums at least as they are known today, particularly the construction of buildings designated to the storage and exhibition of cultural, historical and artistic objects' (Mawere in Mawere et al. 2015: 1). Various artefacts and other miscellaneous manifestations of material cultures were stolen from African people and displayed in African and Western museums and galleries as both trophies of conquest *and* proof of pseudo-scientific race-based social orders, at once teaching people about the values and features of African societies and, simultaneously, framing these portrayals of Africa within misleading narratives that legitimized the harmful actions of the colonizing parties. Catlin-Legutko articulates the complicated sensations of dehumanization that emerge when groups recontextualize such materials from their original locations, stating: 'For many Euro-Americans, inclusion in a museum exhibition may instil pride and signify achievement. For colonized populations, it feels like being captured and isolated in a glass case or like being collected for display on a velvet-covered card' (Catlin-Legutko 2019: 41–2).

The Underground Museum's organizers needed to negotiate similar tensions when seeking to transform the museum from a 'colonizing space' to one instead characterized by decolonial curation (ibid). By emphasizing community values and cooperation between large- and small-scale museums as means of counteracting the problematic infrastructures and gatekeeping processes that tend to privilege and reinforce modernity's Eurocentric 'whiteness' at the expense of other voices, the Underground Museum evoked the spirit of resistance and solidarity of the Underground Railroad, a network of secret routes and safehouses that enslaved African-Americans and abolitionists created to help escapees reach free states and neighbouring Canadian territories. In turn, the Underground Museum followed in the radical tradition of various artists, curators and activists who have similarly attempted to forge their own spaces centred on Afrodiasporic arts. The Civil Rights Era, for example, saw some of the most progress made in terms of platforming Afrodiasporic voices in specialist art spaces. Following the assassinations of Malcolm X in 1965 and Dr Martin Luther King Jr in 1968, new spaces dedicated to Black artistry started to emerge with more frequency. The Brockman Gallery was established by brothers Dale and Alonzo Davis at Los Angeles's Lemeirt Park area in 1967. The annual Brockman Gallery Film festival that was arranged throughout the 1970s showcased experimental films from Afrodiasporic directors, and many of these artists 'drew from West Coast assemblage practices … the predicament and aspirations of Black Americans' in such a way that would result in the Brockman becoming 'the hub for a community of black artists' over the years, attracting creative figures from a range of backgrounds and across a variety of expressive forms (Godfrey and Whitley 2017: 28). In similar fashion, Suzanne Jackson's Gallery 32 and Samella Lewis's Contemporary Crafts Gallery were key venues for the display of African-American art in Los Angeles during this period: while Gallery 32 hosted a Black Panther fundraising event centred around the poster works of Emory Douglas (Peter and Willick 2012), Lewis became known for her *Black Artists on Art* publication, a series co-edited with Ruth G. Waddy that platformed key figures in the Black arts sphere (Lewis and Waddy 1969).

Although the era's Black Arts Movement was predominantly involved in the literary and theatrical arts by uniting a range of 'Afro-American dramatists, poets, choreographers, musicians, and novelists', the poet Larry Neal envisioned 'an art that speaks directly to the needs and aspiration of Black America', elaborating that: 'The Black artist takes this to mean that his primary duty is to speak to the spiritual and cultural needs of Black people' (Neal 1968: 28). Indeed, the Chicago-based artists collective AfriCOBRA – the African Commune of Bad Relevant Artists – applied similar ideas to their paintings and poster art, leading visual artist Jeff R. Donaldson to emphasize that the group's work throughout the 1960s and 1970s drew from 'the whole family of African people, the African tree' (Donaldson 2012: 80).

Likewise drawing inspiration from continental Africa, the prize-winning photographer Roy DeCarava became the first director of the Kamoinge Workshop and its gallery in 1963. DeCarava was a Guggenheim Fellowship Awardee who specialized in capturing the richness and intimacies of African-American life in Harlem, and his sensitive portrayals of everyday experiences – especially his 1969 survey exhibition at the Studio Museum, which was originally formatted as a novella under the title *The Sweet Flypaper of Life* (1955) with text provided by the poet Langston Hughes – would later inspire Kahlil Joseph's video installations *Black Mary* (2017) and *Fly Paper* (2017).

The East African Kikuyu word 'kamoinge' signifies 'a group of people acting together', thus DeCarava's Kamoinge workshop sought to provide safe meeting spaces for the city's African-American photographers, which is in turn echoed by the Underground Museum's function for visual artists in the present. Although the group tended to 'meet *socially*, usually on Sundays, to listen to music, eat together and present their work to each other', the Kamoinge Workshop's attempts to create informal support networks and innovative spaces dedicated to the discussion and dissemination of their work illustrate the lengths that African-American artists were willing to go in order to forge and protect their own pathways in spite of the institutional Eurocentricity which underpinned the contemporary arts world (my emphasis) (Godfrey and Whitley 2017: 40).

Although the Kamoinge Workshop's brownstone gallery is no longer controlled by the group, the collective continues to participate in both individual and group exhibitions throughout America and across the world, offering a valuable support network of black photographers and artists. In this sense, the foundation of the Underground Museum mimicked elements of the Kamoinge Gallery's historical trajectory as well as the contemporary actions of the Kamoinge Collective, providing a space where support networks are built for the latest generation of Afrodiasporic visual artists and their communities.

In the following sections of Chapter 4, I turn my focus to three screen texts that capture Joseph's movement from combinations of film, music video and advertisement circulated online to new (trans)media works capable of being exhibited in gallery spaces, using the Underground Museum's establishment and development as the historical backdrop which frames my discussions. Before Joseph was inspired by his brother's suggestion to present *m.A.A.d.* at the Underground Museum in 2014, he released audiovisual works *Until the Quiet Comes* (2012) and *Wildcat* (2013) as short films, entering the former into the Sundance Film Festival (where it won the Special Jury Prize) and disseminating the latter on the Vimeo channel of What Matters Most and across NOWNESS's Vimeo, YouTube and Dailymotion platforms. However, the formal sophistication of *Until the Quiet Comes* and *Wildcat* made it possible for these screen texts to be retrospectively re-positioned in gallery contexts as installation pieces *after* Joseph had decided to frame *m.A.A.d.* in such a manner.

Jenny Gunn notes that the *liquid blackness* research group uses the term 'music art video' to describe the music videos of Arthur Jafa, Jenn Nkiru and Bradford Young that 'intentionally push the format to more formally daring and theoretically informed ends, creating work that lives as comfortably in the formal gallery space as it does online' (Gunn 2020: 163). Jeffrey Heinzl similarly amalgamates the terms 'art cinema' and 'music video', and he might classify Joseph's screen texts as 'art music videos' because the screen texts' fractured storylines and tenuously related streams of moving images form 'an ambiguous narrative ruptured by striking images that force a reconsideration of the previously provided narrative information' (Heinzl 2018: 3). However, the synthesis of 'art cinema' and 'music video' for Heinzl communicates the disintegration of distinctive formal and cultural boundaries which has come to characterize elements of today's digital file sharing, streaming services and online media dissemination, ushering in new types of distribution, circulation and reception (Shaviro 2017; Waldfogel 2017; Fehrle J. and W. Schäfke-Zell 2019). In this sense, Gunn's music art video category differs from Heinzl's theorization of the art music video because the former acknowledges a screen text's suitability for both online platforms and offline art exhibition spaces, whereas the latter refers to the collapse of linear narratives or 'audio-divisual' properties of a media form.

As a hybridization of home video footage and digital film, the materiality of *m.A.A.d.* works in tandem with the content of its diegetic screen world to form a malleable transmedia installation piece, drawing from a range of overlapping yet distinguishable formats from different parts of the Audiovisual Atlantic. While *Until the Quiet Comes* and *Wildcat* were originally circulated as films, their merging of film, music video and advertisement forms means that they also adhere to Gunn's 'music art video' definition, shifting formal parameters depending on the contexts in which they are situated. I thus aim to map the transatlantic *and* interdisciplinary crossroads of these three screen texts by emphasizing how their meanings and significations shift across physical and non-physical environments (namely digital platforms and exhibition spaces) in a manner akin to the transformations of musical expression across the Black Atlantic.

4.2 Dancing through death realms and dreamscapes: sculpting in time, activating African cosmology in *Until the Quiet Comes* (2012)

Flying Lotus is the artistic persona of musician Steven Ellison, a Los Angeleno jazz-hip hop musician – and co-creator of *Until the Quiet Comes* (2012) and *Wildcat* (2013) with Joseph – who fuses the repetitive tempos of rap music with warbling notes and electronically modified jazz samples. Flying Lotus is the grandson of singer-songwriter Marilyn McLeod and the great-nephew of jazz pianist Turiya Alice Coltrane and saxophonist John Coltrane, his energetic and diverse musical range drawing from all manner of influences, including and extending beyond the pioneering musical exploits of his family – who, in turn, incorporate myriad, frequently non-Western influences into their own music productions.

The artist is signed to Warp Records, an independent British record label founded in 1989 whose musicians and music video directors experiment with digital technologies across audial and visual practices (Wilson 2010), striving to be 'a synonym for adventures in sound and vision' while boasting a roster of artists who 'create groundbreaking music, videos and cinema … traverse mediums to explore new spaces' (Warp Records 2020). The organization is associated with 'intelligent dance/techno' – a controversial colloquial descriptor which first appeared on online forums to refer to music featured on Warp's 1992 compilation album *Artificial Intelligence*, articulating an emerging form of experimental electronic music designed for listening at home rather than dancing in the club (Reynolds 1998; Cardew 2017).[1] Flying Lotus's own independent record label, Brainfeeder, is based in Los Angeles and aims to support experimental electronic music in a similar fashion to Warp while, simultaneously, striving to counteract the connotations of elitism embedded in the original 'intelligent dance music' phrase.[2] Although the musician physically releases his personal material

---

[1] A Usenet message entitled 'Can Dumb People Enjoy IDM, Too?' was posted on 1 August 1993 criticizing the elitist and offensive connotations of the term, and two days later the list server's system administrator responded by emphasizing that 'intelligent' was encouraged by some Warp staff because the word already featured on the *Artificial Intelligence* compilation and its style was intended for consumption beyond the dance floor while, at the same time, 'leaving plenty of room open for interpretation and invention' (Behlendorf 1993).

[2] The 'hyper-abstract work' of Warp Records's most influential signing Richard David James – who performs under the stage name Aphex Twin – operates on the borders between electronic dance music and avant-garde art, creating unusual sounds and polyrhythms in a manner that is often very difficult to dance to (Bohn 2002: 100). His music video collaborations with director Chris Cunningham are characterized by disjointed imagery and jarring actions that subvert stereotypical patterns of behaviour associated with the music industry, parodying corporate excess and chauvinistic video performances in such a way that, according to Scott Wilson, marks 'a movement of withdrawal from Ibiza-style dance music to more cerebral forms of electronica' (Wilson 2010: 404). While the artist's experimental oeuvre across myriad genre forms rejects the formulaic 'build-and-drop' style designed for rave spaces in Ibizan super clubs, the word 'cerebral' here possesses similarly problematic connotations as the word 'intelligent'. Aphex Twin has criticized the 'intelligent dance music' category, stating 'I just think it's really funny to have term like that. It's basically saying "this is intelligent and everything else is stupid." It's really nasty to everyone else's music' (Aphex Twin, interviewed by Gross 1997). The artist's record label Rephlex releases a strain of music similarly designed for listening rather than solely dancing yet associates itself with a genre self-defined as Braindance, which Dave Segal has suggested is a 'snide dig' at the 'IDM' descriptor (Segal 2003).

through Warp Records, Brainfeeder has fostered 'a reputation as a home for the beat scene's more leftfield output', releasing the futuristic, pioneering sounds of British electronic music artists Aphex Twin, Iglooghost and Ross from Friends as well as offering an important platform for the city's new music scenes, circulating the work of Los Angeleno jazz-hip hop fusion musicians Thundercat and Kamasi Washington (Fintoni 2015).

Joseph's 2012 collaboration with Flying Lotus combines haunting imagery of African-American citizens from Los Angeles with sections of tracks *See Thru U*, *Hunger* and *Getting There* from Flying Lotus's fourth studio album *Until the Quiet Comes*. An ethereal portrayal of youthful characters negotiating the area surrounding the Nickerson Gardens public housing apartment complex in Watts, Joseph and Flying Lotus's audiovisual interpretation of *Until the Quiet Comes* plays with notions of time and space in a similar manner to the *Belhaven Meridian* video, weaving together sonic and visual components in a style that hovers somewhere between profound dream and realistic nightmare.

Although *Until the Quiet Comes* won the Special Jury Award at the 2012 Sundance Film Festival as a film submission – and is presented on both What Matters Most TV's Vimeo account and Warp Records' Youtube channel as a short film – the screen text's brevity, non-linearity and emphasis on its musical elements complicate straightforward or singularizing readings which reduce *Until the Quiet Comes* to exclusively a short film or solely a music video. In turn, the structural malleability of the project allows *Until the Quiet Comes* to shift and transform when it is located in different contexts and settings. For example, several years after the project's release, the cut-paper silhouette artist Kara Walker featured *Until the Quiet Comes* and the director's *Black Up* project in her 2014 exhibition *Ruffneck Constructivists* at the Institute of Contemporary Arts, University of Pennsylvania. At once shaped by Russian Constructivism's engagement

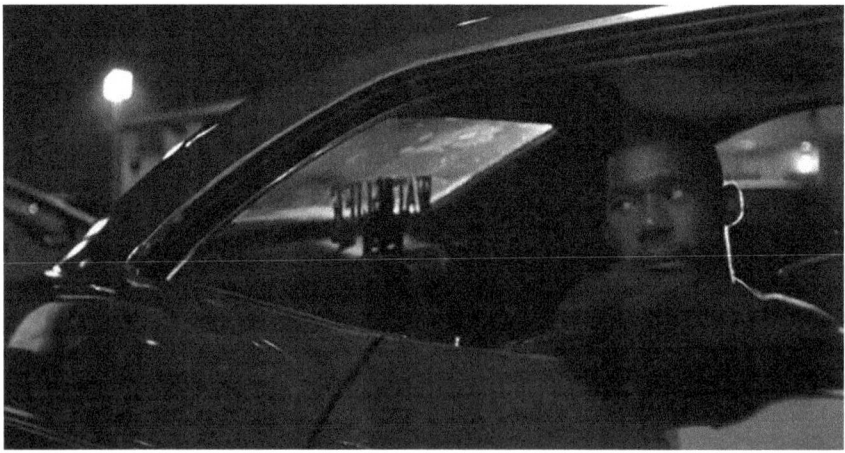

Figure 4.1 *Until the Quiet Comes* (2012), Kahlil Joseph and Flying Lotus © Warp Records.

with art and architecture as well as channelling the unapologetic bravado and idolization of street cultures in MC Lyte's hip-hop song 'Ruffneck' (1993), Walker positions Joseph's work alongside ten other contemporary artworks that similarly capture the crossovers and interactions between urbanization and new artistic practices across disciplines, vocalizing her hopes that 'the interaction between these very divergent works and methods could return a viewer to the questions of modernism, architecture, urbanism and the resistant bodies who reshape it' (Walker 2014).

Malik Sayeed and Arthur Jafa's artwork *Deshotten1.0* (2009) was included in *Ruffneck Constructivists*, featuring a shocking depiction of a shooting victim lying vulnerable and unguarded in a hospital bed as various visitors enter and leave his ward. While the intensity of *Deshotten1.0*'s soundscape captures subtle aesthetic similarities with Joseph's *Until the Quiet Comes* in sonic terms, visually the two projects are connected by their respective explorations of human vulnerability and the threat of gun violence. The opening scene of *Until the Quiet Comes* captures an unmoving young black man suspended underwater in an upright position, his red jacket contrasting sharply against an unending aquatic void's vivid colour scheme of ghostly shades of blue. Joseph's screen text then develops this subcurrent of violence by depicting a young boy mimicking gunshots in an empty swimming pool before, abruptly, falling to the ground wounded, a large puddle of blood streaming from his injured body.

For all the formal innovation and structural sophistication of the artwork, *Until the Quiet Comes* remains paradoxically reliant on its circulation of stereotypical images of young Los Angeleno African-Americans shot down in the streets, thereby reinforcing Nickerson Gardens' notoriety as the Watts housing project 'known for its wall of names that honoured the building's dead residents' (Moore 2020: 47) and, in part, circulating the misleading discourses that it seeks to dismantle through what Clive Chijioke Nwonka terms 'the Black Neoliberal Aesthetic'.

While Nwonka writes predominantly about the problematic 'diversity' agenda that has increasingly influenced the UK screen industry, one may apply his ideas to American contexts and thereby illustrate (by way of Stuart Hall) how media texts 'are not necessarily *good* because black people make them' (my emphasis) (Hall 1988: 28). In Hall's analysis, 'good' refers to whether a screen text is 'ideologically progressive through first conceptualizing what [comprises] the black experience and [then] how this singular identity conferred onto the black populace could be exploded, made heterogeneous and refer to a lived experience of difference and modernity' (Nwonka 2020: 848).

For Nwonka, the 'ideological progressiveness' of a screen text is complicated at its structural and textual levels by the neoliberal framework, thus black peoples' experiences become 'directly indexed to the cultural, material and epistemic praxis of mainstream black cultural value' (ibid. 17). Despite the fact that *more* Black experiences are being circulated through the mainstream via media forms such as films and music videos, these representations will reinforce rather than challenge stereotypes associated with African diasporas in the world beyond the screen if they only ever refer to 'male urban violence and death' (ibid. 13). Joseph's representations of the young boy lying shot in the empty pool – and the wounded man floating in an aquatic void – therefore threaten to perpetuate clichéd associations that circulate around the Nickerson Gardens's region, critiquing the violence that has occurred in the area while, at the same time, inadvertently perpetuating the sort of mischaracterization that results in forms of violence against the area's black communities, the racialized misrepresentations that are themselves acts of violence (Rock, in conversation with Slovick 2011).

While the presence of the Black Neoliberal Aesthetic in *Until the Quiet Comes* undermines its attempts to process and negotiate inter-gang violence in Nickerson Gardens, Joseph complicates the discursive significations of the unnamed man's physical suspension by using an unending aquatic void to communicate the sudden disintegration of support and familiarity that the man endures when he is shot in the chest. His slow, sinking movements beneath the water thus echo Tina Campt's aesthetic categorization for still-moving-images, challenging the binaries between 'motion and movement' as means of generating affective responses (Campt 2019: 27). Although *Until the Quiet Comes* does not elaborate the cause behind the man's abrupt suspension, the moving images of a young boy from Nickerson Gardens brutally shot in an empty swimming pool imply that the movements to and from the aquatic void and the Nickerson Garden neighbourhood in part reflect the complexities of shifting from non-existence to consciousness – and then life to death – in a cyclic fashion beyond human comprehension, oscillating between perpetual movement and eternal stillness. While the soul manifests in the boy's youthful form, his hostile physical surroundings are emptied of profound meaning during the act of slaughter. However, when the soul passes into the mysterious aquatic void beyond any fixed spatiotemporal geographical boundaries, the character's transcendence of physical limitations implies that newfound profundity shapes his condition, gradually drifting from hostility to calmness, from rapid movement to near-stillness and semi-fluctuation (Campt 2021: 54–65).

The spiritual water realm filling the empty swimming pool in part creates a visual metaphor for Gilroy's Black Atlantic conceptualization, the (meta)physical

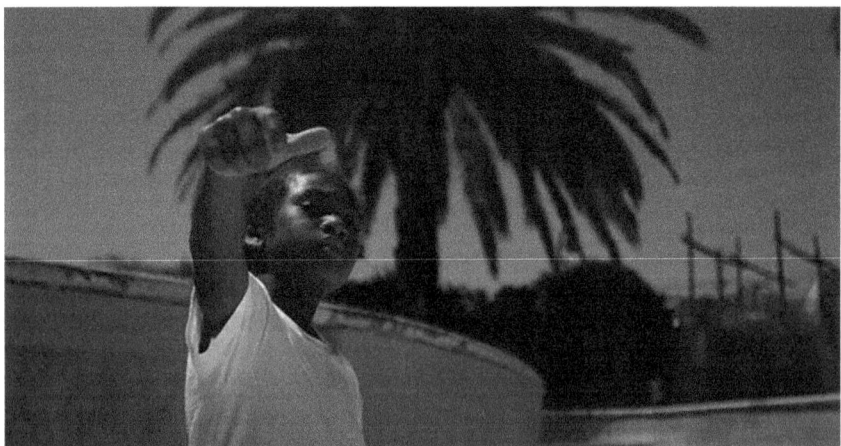

Figure 4.2 *Until the Quiet Comes* (2012), Kahlil Joseph and Flying Lotus © Warp Records.

roots and routes of historical and contemporary movements generating new forms of understanding as members of African diasporas attempt to overcome the physical limitations of their immediate surroundings. In fact, according to Campt, a still-moving-image requires the labour 'of sustaining affective kinship with black bodies suspended in the simultaneity of black joy and trauma', thus the aesthetics of *Until the Quiet Comes* actively perform the 'work' of this balancing act, attempting to steady the oftentimes contradictory flows of cultural traffic, capital and aesthetics across the Black Atlantic which facilitate both joyful *and* traumatic experiences (Campt 2019: 43).

Lauren M. Cramer suggests that these aesthetic explorations of suspension in *Until the Quiet Comes* form powerful artistic and discursive possibilities by 'unmooring [blackness] from the histories, policies and technologies that cohere the notion of blackness, *most notably in the realm of representation*' (my emphasis) (Cramer 2017: 142).[3] In this sense, Nickerson Gardens' narratives are unmoored from strictly African, American or European contexts, exemplifying the discursive possibilities – as well as the innate contradictions – of Black Atlantic audiovisual expression. At the same time, the Black Neoliberal Aesthetic illustrates how the 'aestheticization of black death' in *Until the Quiet Comes* 'sits within the general continuum of the cultural and generic hegemony of visualized urban male death' and must therefore retain a certain level of social responsibility as media depictions of Black violence shift from an artwork's diegetic world into the reality beyond the screen (Nwonka 2020: 855). Campt echoes Nwonka's continuum framework, characterizing 'the affective and visual frequencies' of still-moving-images within and beyond a media text's screen world as 'a continuum of terror and joy in blackness' with the power to generate strong emotional responses and forge new forms of kinship (Campt 2019: 43). It is therefore between a variety of positions – back-and-forth emotional states, geographical ties and formal media boundaries – that the Black Neoliberal Aesthetic *and* still-moving images converge in *Until the Quiet Comes*, capturing the possibilities and paradoxes of Black Atlantic audiovisual expression as Africa, America and Europe interact in a variety of states and conditions.

Although Joseph does not explicitly cite his sources in *Until the Quiet Comes*, Duane Deterville gleans depictions of Central Africa's circular Bantu-Kongo Cosmogram and the mythical Kalunga barrier from the short film's underwater suspension scenes as well as shots of the wounded child. In the Cosmogram, four key stages of human existence (birth, life, death and disembodied spirit form) are depicted as four quadrants of a circle (Gundaker 2011). According to spiritual figures of the Bantu-Kongo, the Kalunga is a powerful barrier, often characterized as a body of water, that separates the living world from the realm of our ancestors by dividing the Cosmogram into two halves (MacGaffey 1974; Fu-Kiau 2001).

In his two-part online essay, Deterville thus recognizes subtle allusions to birth and death constantly moving in a cyclical fashion as depicted by the Cosmogram through

---

[3] For further information see: 'Holding Blackness in Suspension: The Films of Kahlil Joseph' (2016b), a recording of the *liquid blackness* event which features a conversation with the filmmaker; and *Holding Blackness: Aesthetics of Suspension*, the October 2017 issue of the *liquid blackness* journal.

the hand positions of the child's motionless body within the circular swimming pool, arguing that the underwater suspension scenes represent the soul transitioning towards its disembodied form. By interpreting allusions to the Bantu-Kongo myth in these scenes as well the wounded boy's fixed hand positions within the emptied swimming pool, Deterville adopts what he defines as an 'Afriscape' critical lens when examining *Until the Quiet Comes* in order to process 'the deterritorialised cultural presence of Black/African people anywhere in the world' (Deterville 2013).

Naima Sutton suggests that the short film possesses 'an underlying understanding of traditional African cosmology' through references to Bantu-Kongo philosophy and the Cosmogram, yet Joseph at best references these facets of African cosmology obliquely, alluding to the four parts of the Cosmogram's soul-cycle yet never signposting such gestures in a direct manner (Sutton 2020). Similarly, while the specific manifestations of Central African culture that Deterville cites are not directly addressed by Joseph in interviews or press releases surrounding *Until the Quiet Comes*, Deterville's decision to deploy an 'Africscape' framework echoes Harry J. Elam Jr and Kennell Jackson's *Black Cultural Traffic*, understanding the complex global movements of today's Afrodiasporic cultural forms through the crossroads metaphor. While the relentless flows of these cultural forms may appear overwhelming and indecipherable at times, the crossroads concept takes into account complicated processes of transformation as artworks and artefacts negotiate both physical and abstract borders, becoming recontextualized in diverse new settings. Deterville's argument that the Afriscape lens 'tacitly connects the metaphysical spaces of Kalunga to the everyday spaces of urban Black communities' (Deterville 2013) thus mirrors Elam Jr and Jackson's motivation to decipher various complicated moments as the crossroads of Afrocentric cultural traffic 'end up in unlikely places, in contradictory alliances ... [taking] on new and unintended forms' (Jackson in Elam Jr and Jackson 2005: 5).

Deterville's 'Afriscape' theorization accounts for sections of *Until the Quiet Comes* which may (in)advertently channel aspects of the Bantu-Kongo Cosmogram and the Kalunga barrier. However, Joseph complicates a straightforward understanding of Deterville's interpretation by adopting aesthetics of suspension which, at the same time as echoing this particular branch of Central African cosmology, also echo recurrent images in Andrei Tarkovsky's feature-length film *Mirror* (1975). Caught between 'quasi-dreaming and pseudo-remembering' as memories and fantasy overlap and merge (Menard 2003), objects and people in *Mirror* float between states and forms as narrator Alexei attempts to piece together his personal history through the haziness and fluctuating reliability of his consciousness. During the film's non-linear explorations of thoughts, memories and emotions, a supine female figure simultaneously representing mother, wife and sister inexplicably materializes, suspended mid-air above her bed, and then hastily disappears from Alexei's visions, thereby capturing in Tarkovsky's words: 'Neither nightmare nor symbol; a sense of floating is what we all feel when all our support is gone' (Tarkvosky in conversation with Strick 1981: 72).

Elam Jr and Jackson's crossroads notion reminds us that Afrodiasporic cultural artefacts 'can synthesise radically disparate materials' (Elam Jr and Jackson 2005: 5), thus *Until the Quiet Comes*'s fluctuations at the borders of both Bantu-Kongo cosmology *and* Russian arthouse cinema negotiate underexplored psycho-geographic territories. In turn, such movements open up new possibilities for representations of 'African diaspora' and 'Blackness' over numerous boundaries both within and beyond the diegetic universe(s) presented on screen, traversing various points across the vast Black Atlantic. One may therefore argue that the screen text echoes Tarkovskian suspension of spatiotemporal laws through the suspended man's floating body in *Until the Quiet Comes*, since the abstract style of Joseph's collaboration with Flying Lotus does not offer clear or concise explanations within the filmic universe's setting(s).

As boundaries and borders between diegetic screen-based spaces are ruptured with increased frequency throughout the short film, various contradictions and complexities emerge with growing intensity. Although the music video depicts children running blissfully free with their friends across Nickerson Gardens' playing fields, the sky is digitally transformed to hellish crimson, echoing the red tones of the suspended man's jacket and wounded boy's blood in a dark, unsettling manner. Storyboard P, the dancer who portrays the wounded victim's older form inexplicably reanimated under the blood red sky, shifts the short film's setting between life and death through an euphoric reinterpretation of 'flex dancing' and thus creates a sequence of sublime resurrection, forming moments of hope and beauty in an otherwise dark and disturbing depiction of Afrodiasporic experiences in contemporary Los Angeles. Joseph's filmic direction and FlyLo's musicianship here combine with the exquisite, almost inhuman movements of flex dancer Storyboard P. In turn, the dancer's movement plays a vital role in communicating the screen text's fluidity in terms of both content and structure, mimicking the contesting flows of Afrodiasporic experiences and their representations across diverse cultural spheres by correspondingly fluctuating at the borders of distinguishable media forms.

'Flex dancing' originated in nineties Jamaica when young dancer Bruck Up – which, in Patois, roughly translates as: 'broken' – gained notoriety for his rubbery body movements and implausible contortions, eventually finding fame in Brooklyn's reggae clubs. Storyboard P develops Bruck Up's style by incorporating the delicate precision of Harlem voguers, the swagger of Memphis jookers and the aggressive gesticulations of Los Angeles krumpers, drawing from his experiences as a ballet dancer in his youth while also incorporating different types of 'street' performance (Weiner 2013; Raengo et al. 2018). Portrayals of aggressive masculinities captured by the fallout of violent shooting are unexpectedly imbued with feminized tenderness as a result of Storyboard P's 'vogue' influences and the subsequent 'queering' of the masculinized 'flex' dancing. His combinations of various dancing styles and techniques within his performances thus synthesize the agonies of violence and ecstasies of spiritual release into a mesmerizing visual showcase, connecting the streets of contemporary Los Angeles with a variety of distinguishable performance cultures across the Black Atlantic.

While Joseph and Storyboard P have partnered together for depictions of memory and misremembering Harlem life in digital installation *Fly Paper* (2017), their debut partnership in *Until the Quiet Comes* frames the abnormal twists and convulsions of Storyboard P's powerful style of flex dancing in such a manner that, according to

Deterville, 'presents us with an image of his body/soul in an effortlessly masterful and fluid drift towards its destiny' (Deterville 2013). The ambiguity of Deterville's 'body/soul' phrasing thus illustrates the ways in which Storyboard P's dancing abilities and Joseph's representations of those movements within the context of his short film together harmonize a variety of different cultural sources, thereby complicating simplistic interpretations of the 'African diaspora' notion.

Berys Gaut's theory of filmic 'co-authorship' (1997) – or what Gilroy deems a 'co-creator' of Black Atlantic expression (Gilroy in conversation with Henry 2020) – both emphasize the valuable roles played by Joseph's collaborators. Storyboard P's dancing, Flying Lotus's music and Joseph's direction weave together a 'co-authored' or 'co-created' compilation of *Until the Quiet Comes*'s interdimensional representations of Afrodiasporic life, death and rebirth across the boundaries of cultures and media forms. In turn, the fragile boundaries distinguishing art and life are ruptured by such a process. As Joseph acknowledges: 'Even with Storyboard P, *Until the Quiet Comes*, that, to me, was a watershed moment. My father had just passed away and, when I made that, I didn't know what to do with all that emotionality but I remember how I wanted the thing to feel. I feel like that was my therapy' (Joseph in conversation with Kane 2017). The project was deeply personal for Joseph as a result of its timing. Through a productive, collaborative relationship with Storyboard P, the filmmaker was able to undergo individualized catharsis, creating a form of audiovisual expression rich with a huge amount of idiosyncratic sentimentality for the director as well as retaining the countercultural spirit of Black Atlantic artistic expression, remaining sufficiently 'open' for interpretation from other perspectives as a result of its formal sophistication.

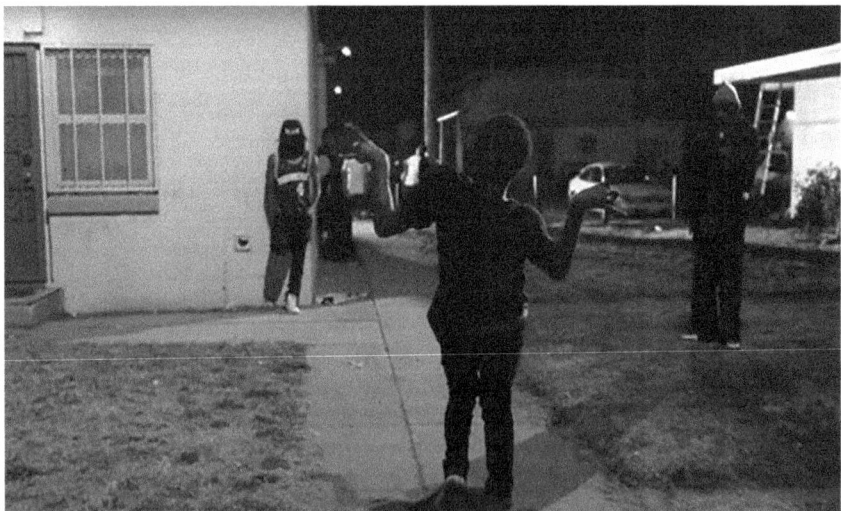

Figure 4.3 *Until the Quiet Comes* (2012), Kahlil Joseph and Flying Lotus © Warp Records.

Until the Quiet Comes's overlapping compositions of dance routines, musical scores and moving images at the crossroads of cultural traffic, capital and aesthetics thus illustrate the complex frequencies at which the still-moving-image, Black Neoliberal Aesthetic and Black Visual Intonations of Storyboard P, Flying Lotus and Kahlil Joseph's co-created work both harmonize *and* contradict. In turn, the dynamics of the triumvirate's working relationship in the 'real' space beyond the short film's artificial universe challenges the singularizing narratives of 'auteur' theory which credit the director as the sole artistic voice at work within a filmic piece's composite whole (Astruc 1968) and, in turn, risk narrativizing Afrodiasporic experiences as a single story (Adichie 2009). However, as Nwonka reminds us, the relationships between collaborators are redundant (even if groups adopt an 'integrity'-based method akin to Joseph's filmmaking approach) if the images themselves regurgitate controversial, even damaging representations of ostracized communities.

The *Until the Quiet Comes* project won its award at the Sundance Film Festival during a problematic two-year period for American cinema wherein a disproportionate amount of 'slave-master' narratives – from Oscar-winner Steve McQueen's *12 Years a Slave* (2013) to Peter Cousens's *Freedom* (2014) – were produced and widely consumed. In later years, Ryan Poll commends the handling of slave narratives in Jordon Peele's Academy award-winning debut feature film *Get Out* (2017) for the ways it recognizes 'how American slavery is not an institution confined to the past, not one locatable in a particular region (such as the South), but a national institution, practice, and affect that continues to shape and structure the present', refusing to locate Blackness's issues with racism solely in a bygone era but, instead, framing the interlocking forces in both the past and present as a way of negotiating and recognizing their problematic future trajectories for current and new generations (Poll 2018: 72). Although *Until the Quiet Comes* is not a direct exploration of the nation's historical representations of slavery, the film's melding of past and present through its framing of the Kalunga barrier and the Bantu-Kongo Cosmogram in Nickerson Gardens similarly illustrates how racist infrastructures will continue to adversely affect the experiences of black people in Los Angeles unless such forces of systemic racism are addressed. While *Until the Quiet Comes* thus deviates from the controversial strand of 'slave-master' filmmaking between 2013 and 2014 through its re-contextualization of Bantu-Kongo cosmology to process two disparate yet metaphysically connected gun attacks in Watts, the bloody images of the wounded man and boy complicate Joseph's marriage of gang culture's destructive masculinities with African spiritualization. By wedding the lives and deaths of two black Los Angelenos with stereotypical representations of gun violence, Joseph's film recirculates disingenuous narratives of African-American citizens, reinforcing the noxious, colonial discourses which, paradoxically, the countercultural energies of *Until the Quiet Comes* seek to challenge.

Such a complex representation of violence is echoed by Ngozi Onwurah's *Welcome II the Terrordome* (1995), 'the first independent feature' directed by a Black British woman (Ciecko 1999: 67). Named after the song *Welcome to the Terrordome* from American hip-hop group Public Enemy's third studio album *Fear of a Black Planet*

(1990), Onwurah's film riffs on depictions of a 'blackened planet … scorched by World War Three' from *Fear of a Black Planet*'s album cover and its songs' lyrical content, challenging 'associations of purity with goodness and virtue … the monopoly on purity historically attributed to "European" whiteness' while reminding audiences 'every human being can trace their ancestors back to Africa' (William 2011: 105–6). *Welcome II the Terrordome* shares with *Until the Quiet Comes* unsettling audiovisual representations of racialized violence towards young men, leading some critics to suggest that 'we've needed more than a quarter-century for its spiky refusal to be understood' because the film 'speaks more to 2021 than 1995' (Bradshaw 2021). Writing in the nineties, Anne Ciecko acknowledges that *Welcome II the Terrordome* and its 'somewhat ambiguous' political stance (Ciecko 1999: 69) may seem to replicate in part 'stereotypical representations, preconceptions, and common-sense assumptions … perpetuated by the media' which have in turn 'contributed to divisiveness within the black British community' (ibid. 70). However, she argues that the film offers 'a critical challenge to such images' (ibid. 69) and was in fact poorly received by mainstream film critics at the time of its release precisely because Onwurah 'touched sensitive nerves in [her] representation of race relations in a dystopic Britain' (ibid. 71).

There remains much gun violence in Nickerson Gardens – so perhaps leaving this complex constellation of overlapping issues unaddressed in *Until the Quiet Comes* would be disingenuous, or a distortion of what it means to live in this particular geographical space at a specific moment in time. Although the image of a gunned-down and bloodied African-American Los Angeleno is a reprehensible cliché born from and in many ways reproducing the controversial discourses on which whiteness's hegemony is built, Joseph's artwork communicates in a manner akin to *Welcome II the Terrordome* how the Black Atlantic's routes and roots are not neatly defined narratives with straightforward trajectories and solutions but are instead shaped by layers and layers of overlapping and complicated transnational flows. These oscillatory flows – even in their most grotesque and violent forms – must be acknowledged and addressed if indeed such problematic legacies are to be disentangled and counteracted.

The award-winning *Until the Quiet Comes*, then, through its transnational unification of the Kalunga barrier, Bruck Up dancing, Tarkovskian tropes and sonic-visual *Terrordome* synergies, attempts to process Los Angeles gang violence through non-violent means, capturing some of the underlying tensions of Audiovisual Atlantic expression. However, while Joseph aims to critique the unjust social realities on which such violent images are based, his project's circulation of these stereotypes also illustrates that even the most compassionate attempts to subvert violent clichés are not always sufficient on their own. Contemporary artworks that constitute the sights and sounds of the Black Atlantic must be interpreted and consumed in relation to other artists, or as part of a broader collection of artworks, if we are to form effective strategies and ways of being through which to offer alternative frameworks that subvert neoliberal hegemony and, in turn, challenge modernity's Eurocentricity.

4.3 FlyLo at the All-Black rodeo: cowboys and angels in *Wildcat* (2013)

Wildcat (2013) was originally promoted as both a celebration of the annual All-Black August rodeo in the Southern town Grayson and a filmic tribute to Janet Celestine, one of the event's original founders. The tribute features an original soundtrack composed by Flying Lotus, remixing and editing unreleased harp-based material created by the musician's great-aunt, the jazz legend and spiritual-devotee Alice Coltrane. Joseph's project is currently available to access freely online on NOWNESS's main website, Vimeo channel and Dailymotion account, as well as What Matters Most's Vimeo channel. However, the manner in which the film combines music video and art properties and, simultaneously, subtly advertises Grayson's annual rodeo event illustrates the collapse of traditional formal parameters within our contemporary mediascape's disruptive 'convergence environment' (Fehrle 2019: 8), pointing towards 'the degree to which film culture is being redefined by digital media' as forms of cultural traffic converge through crossroads of aesthetics (Tyron 2009: 2).

The sophistication of *Wildcat*'s aesthetic crossroads means that one may locate the screen text within the structural parameters of a variety of media forms. While the screen text's audial and visual components mirror 'structural relationships of music and images' which often define conventional music video forms (Björnberg 1994: 51), *Wildcat* was later featured as part of Joseph's gallery exhibitions at the McNay Art Museum in San Antonio and the Bonnefantenmuseum in Maastricht as well as the *Black Cowboy* show curated by Amanda Jackson at The Studio Museum in Harlem. Jenny Gunn and the *liquid blackness* research group's music art video categorization captures the ways in which *Wildcat* sits 'at the fluid intersection of art installation and experimental film' (Gunn 2020: 163), thus this section of Chapter 4 endeavours to analyse the screen text with a variety of media parameters in mind, evaluating the tensions that occur as the screen text's formal parameters shift and transform in relation to different contexts and settings.

In her later years, after the passing of her husband and iconic jazz musician John, Alice Coltrane became a *swamini* – a term meaning '[she who is] one with her self' that categorizes figures who have been initiated into the Hindi monastic order – and performed religious ceremonies while developing original melodies from a variety of traditional chants. As a result of this period, Coltrane is also known by her adopted Sanskrit name Turiyasangitananda, or Turiya Alice Coltrane. In the same vein as Turiya Coltrane, belief in the existence of one's spirit is a key aspect of Joseph's understanding of the universe. He states:

> Spirituality is everything. It's ultimately more important than anything else. We're clearly spiritual beings because we can't locate where life exists in someone's body. Science hasn't caught up to the moment yet but the evidence is overwhelming. For each person, it's a different thing. It's mixed with this idea of consciousness, which is related but also different altogether. Everything has consciousness – trees, land,

water, cities, individuals – and they all have different agendas. It's like all these different conversations are happening.

(Joseph, in conversation with Dallas 2017: 149)

Although one must analyse Joseph's decision to locate himself within such a broad and vague definition of 'spirituality' with a degree of scepticism, it is difficult to reject that sonic and visual representations of abstract and otherwise indiscernible spirit figures are integral parts of the *Wildcat* film. Turiya Coltrane was Flying Lotus's great-aunt and Janet Celestine was affectionately known as 'Aunt Janet' or 'Nana' among the Grayson community, and in *Wildcat* a local girl plays an angelic figure – in crude 'dress up' wings and a tiara – that represents the prevailing legacies of both deceased figures. *Wildcat*'s crossroads of aesthetics and Black cultural traffic articulate tributes to the intergenerational relationships between families, friends and communities. *Wildcat* thus channels the area's traditions by engendering a sense of boundless time, remembering deceased loved ones and the persistence of their spiritual legacies across spatiotemporal borders (Nkiru 2020).

Charles P. Linscott argues that *Wildcat* 'builds on the musical deconstruction and audiovisual mapping' found across Spike Lee's music video *Tutu Medley* (1986) for four tracks from Miles Davis's album *Tutu* (1986) as well as William Greaves's experimental film *Symbiopsychotaxiplasm*: *Take One* (1968) and songs from the Davis album *In a Silent Way* (1969) (Linscott 2020: 150). Lee's music video incorporates four different songs – *Splatch*, *Tutu*, *Tomaas* and *Portia* – and each visual section communicates the tone and feel of the respective musical pieces. While Jafa identifies *Tutu Medley* as the first instance of his experiencing the mapping of visual material in accordance with musical structures (Jafa in conversation with Joseph 2017), Linscott contends that this style of filmic construction originates in *Symbiopsychotaxiplasm: Take One,* another audiovisual work indebted to Davis's music.

At the end of the mastering process for the Davis album *In a Silent Way*, sound engineer and producer Teo Macero remixed and edited song structures formulated during a three-hour recording session. An array of talented jazz artists – from Wayne Shorter on tenor saxophone and Dave Holland on electric bass to drummer Tony Williams and keyboardist Josef Zawinul – contributed to the project, adapting original compositions and reworking particular sections. Greaves's *Symbiopsychotaxiplasm: Take One* echoes *In a Silent Way*'s experimental style of composition through the way that three separate film crews were hired to capture the production of a fictional documentary titled *Over the Cliff* in frequently conflicting ways, thereby 'riffing (like a jazz musician) on the concept of racial authenticity' by disrupting 'stable hierarchies and social categories' as different parties fight for control of the 'trainwreck' that the auteur Greaves mischievously orchestrates (Gottlieb 2013: 165). The filmmaker generates a multi-layered piece of meta-art by playing the role of an unprofessional and careless director during filming while, secretly, experimenting with the documentary film form, concepts of artistic authorship and the industry's expectations of Black independent filmmakers (MacDonald and Stewart in Greaves, MacDonald and Stewart 2021). Songs that would later form a part of *In a Silent Way* were used as

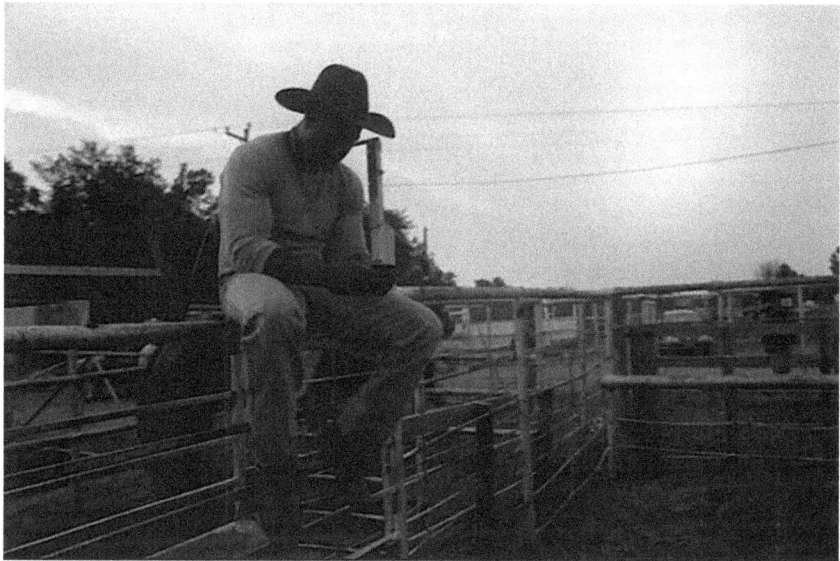

Figure 4.4 *Wildcat* (2013), Kahlil Joseph and Flying Lotus © What Matters Most and Brainfeeder.

Symbiopsychotaxiplasm: Take One's soundtrack, thus Davis's whimsical ululations warble and float in the background, uniting chaotic episodes of miscommunication and various arguments among actors, producers and camera crew in a manner that adopts 'music as a structure for a visual pattern' reminiscent of Jafa's categories for Black Visual Intonations (Jafa in conversation with Joseph 2017).

Linscott draws vital connections between the styles of framing moving images and music in Joseph's *Wildcat* and Greaves's *Symbiopsychotaxiplasm: Take One*, yet one must also emphasize the importance of the latter's film *The First World Festival of Negro Arts* (1966) in relation to the musical structures of Joseph's visual components. Greaves often plied his trade filming for large corporations and institutions, and the United States Information Agency commissioned the director to create a 5-minute news piece at the first-ever *World Festival of Black Arts* in Dakar, Senegal (1–24 April 1966). Greaves decided to turn his footage into a feature-length documentary film, adopting a jazz-infused soundtrack especially composed by James Hubert 'Eubie' Blake because the original filmic material was captured 'largely without synchronous sound' (Knee and Musser 1992: 16). In unifying the comprehensive yet loosely organized visual material through a structure explicitly connected to the rhythms and movements of Blake's music, *The First World Festival of Negro Arts* offered a framework for his combinations of music and moving images in *Symbiopsychotaxiplasm: Take One* and, in turn, nuanced the oscillations between Black Visual Intonations and still-moving-images in *Wildcat* – and indeed throughout Joseph's extended oeuvre – in more recent years.

Flying Lotus's sampling and reworking of Turiya Coltrane's compositions form the musical foundations on which *Wildcat*'s Black Visual Intonations are grounded, connecting Joseph's film to the music-based visual structures of Greaves's *The First World Festival of Negro Arts* and *Symbiopsychotaxiplasm: Take One* as well as Lee's *Tutu Medley*. Flying Lotus's score does not use formulaic beats associated with Western strong structures but, instead, adopts a more atmospheric framework, emphasizing tone and ambience in a manner that echoes the spiritual cassette album recordings of Turiya Coltrane's *swamini* years – *Turiya Sings* (1982), *Divine Songs* (1987), *Infinite Chants* (1990) and *Glorious Chants* (1995) – as well as her estate's posthumous collection *World Spirituality Classics 1: The Ecstatic Music of Alice Coltrane Turiyasangitanada* (2017) which draws from the four cassette tapes. While one must develop 'a sensitivity to musical and imagistic connections ... across historical lineages of Black filmmaking' in order to reveal the intricate layering of Black cultural forms and influences that constitute *Wildcat* (Linscott 2020: 150), it is also imperative to recognize the Eastern influences which shape the musical works of Turiya Coltrane, Flying Lotus and consequently, the audiovisual work of Kahlil Joseph. Through hybridizations of international cultural forms, Joseph creates transnational *and* intergenerational aesthetics that rely on movements across time and space in the same way that the traditions of the Grayson community unite generations and families in the present, relying on the newest wave of townsfolk to support and maintain the rodeo tradition.

While Flying Lotus's broad range of music styles resist rigid categorizations, Afrofuturism's attempts to 'Preprogram the Future' by collapsing strict temporal boundaries (Eshun [1998] (1999): 07[105]) are detectable in the ways that *Wildcat*'s soundtrack and filmic content both form an 'interpenetration of the past and the present' (Linscott 2020: 150). Samples of Turiya Coltrane's work and the angelic visual tribute to Aunt Janet represent the unforgotten spirit of loved ones influencing and shaping present forms of artistic creation. Joseph notes that 'from the perspective of quantum physics the past, present and future are all happening simultaneously', and *Wildcat*'s reworking of the past for sources of inspiration demonstrates that his contemporary audiovisual artworks envisage a future for music and moving images charged with new possibilities and permutations, teeming with as much vibrancy and as many opportunities for experimentation as Turiya Coltrane's *swamini* music compositions (Joseph in conversation with Jansen 2018). Stylistically, modern technologies permit hybridizations of new synthesized sounds with remastered Turiya Coltrane samples, thus Flying Lotus's fuzzy ambient score illustrates the audial amalgamation of past and present musical sources, paving the way for futuristic creations and genre-bending explorations of sound. Simultaneously, the merging of past and present in visual terms is likewise a key element of boundless notions of time, capturing how *Wildcat* negates sensations of marketed time by 'collapsing ... different times and different spaces in one moment' (Nkiru 2020).

There are thirteen historic All-Black towns that remain in Oklahoma, a reminder of the 1889 Land Rush wherein the state's territories were forcibly taken from local Seminole and Muscogee Creek Indians in the aftermath of the Civil War, and then offered by the government to non-Native Americans based in other parts of the nation.

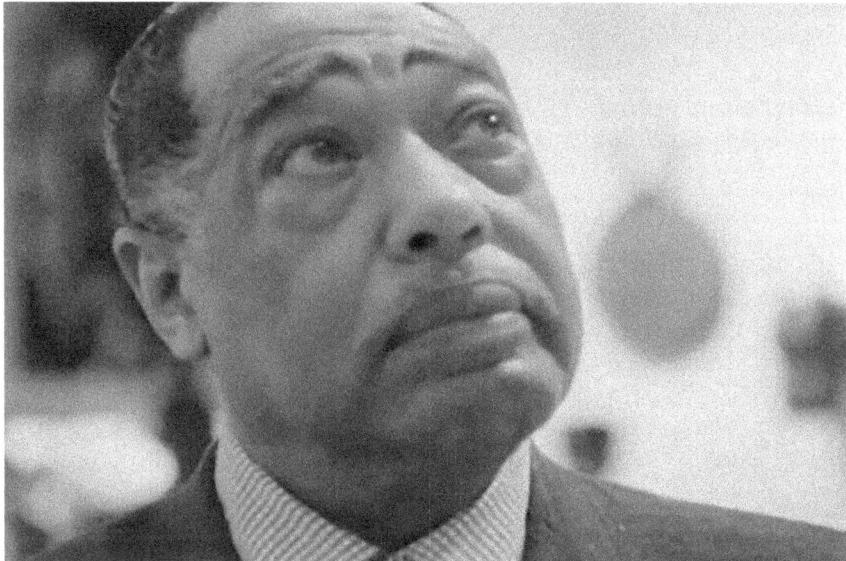

Figure 4.5 *The First World Festival of Negro Arts* (1968), William Greaves © Motion Picture and Television Service of the United States Information Agency.

A state auditor from Kansas named E. P. McCabe assisted the foundation of Langston during this period, encouraging other African-Americans to settle nearby as means of generating an African-American block of political power. Former slaves had started to group, travel and settle together after the War for 'mutual protection and economic security', and the encouragement of litigators, estate agents and public figures such as McCabe drew black groups to Okmulgee County and the South Central region of the United States, compelling family units to start afresh in the newly available spaces (O'Dell 2009). Even though grand visions of an All-Black state never fully came to fruition, from 1865 to 1920 African-Americans established more than fifty identifiable settlements in Oklahoma, thus a rich legacy of black communities started to bloom in the area and, in the case of Grayson, remain today (Tolson 1970; Drass 1986).

Grayson – in Okmulgee County, Oklahoma – is a small, tightly knit community which, according to the 2010 population census, features around 159 registered citizens (CensusViewer 2010). While Grayson is currently named after a businessman, merchant and writer named George W. Grayson,[4] the town was originally called Wildcat, a title which stood as the area's legal name until the 1960s despite the official establishment of Grayson Post Office in 1902. Rumours circulate that many people

---

[4] Grayson (1843–1920) had Muscogee Creek ancestry, and his indigenous name was Tulwa Tustunugge, which translates as: 'Wolf Warrior'. While he supported the proposal for the State of Sequoyah's recognition as a Native American state, his father owned a plantation and around seventy African-American slaves (Grayson 1988).

living in the area once secretly sold a type of homemade alcoholic drink named 'wildcat whiskey'. However, Maude Tucker, an 83-year-old who previously sold 'wildcat whiskey' when she moved to Wildcat from Louisiana with her family, disputes that the town's name originates in its legacy of homemade brewing. Six miles away in a rival town named Henryetta, she insists that the area's entrance was once marked by a makeshift sign, the words 'N – –, don't let the sun set on you' threatening visitors with the chilling message that their ground was particularly unsafe for black people during the darkness of night. In response to Henryetta's racist message, Tucker's town slaughtered a wildcat and attached the carcass to a pole, erecting the following counterstatement underneath: 'White Man, don't let the sun set on you here' (Tucker in conversation with Etter 1983).[5]

W. E. B. Du Bois first coined the term 'colour line' to articulate the internalized anxieties faced by black people when navigating certain white-dominated spaces, capturing a conundrum wherein rejection of the space might amount to the black person being 'blamed for indifference' while, at the same time, entering the domain risks having one's 'feelings hurt' as a result of 'unpleasant altercation' (Du Bois 1899: 325). The story of underlying tensions existing between Wildcat and Henryetta corroborates the idea that, in certain forms of popular culture and in various real-life settings, parts of the American South are comprised of citizens preoccupied with preserving racial dynamics and accompanying tensions related to the 'colour line' (Millner 1985).

Wildcat, however, challenges misassumptions associated with America's bull-riding cultures because, as Joseph observes: 'Black people are light years more advanced than the ideas and images that circulate would have you believe' (Joseph in conversation with NOWNESS 2013). Past hostilities between blacks and whites that mar the South's broad history – as well as the tensions between the citizens of the Wildcat and Henryetta towns which operate on a localized level – are ignored by Joseph's short film. Rather, local cowboys organizing the rodeo while Aunt Janet's spirit traverses the neighbourhood as ethereal protector communicate how townsfolk care about creating and sustaining interpersonal bonds, honouring familial connections rather than rupturing humanity's relationships and revitalizing bygone prejudices.

During the film's opening sequences, an extreme close-up shot of dainty angel ornaments made of glass establishes undertones of delicateness which similarly characterize *Wildcat*'s ensuing explorations of celestial beings and the filmic representations of abstract spirituality. Flying Lotus's adaptation of Turiya Coltrane's musical material reworks fluttering harp sounds of her jazz song *Galaxy in Turiya* (1972) as Joseph's camera hovers over the exquisite trinkets. According to Jayna Brown, music was, for Turiya Coltrane, 'an essential part of collective ecstatic worship as she and her bands and congregations created sound environments inseparable from spiritual expression' (Brown 2021: 59). Despite the fact that she was raised in

---

[5] The Sky TV series *Watchmen* (2019–Present) has brought the Tulsa massacre back to popular memory, and *Lovecraft Country* (2020–Present) from the same broadcaster has similarly started to reinsert the racially aggravated hostility of 'sundowner towns' such as the Henryetta into popular culture.

the Christian faith, played in Detroit's Baptist churches and received formal training on the piano and organ, 'her belief system was capacious and universalist, with her musical practices and forms of worship framed by Hindu philosophy' (ibid.). The harp is adopted by Saint Cecilia – the patroness of music celebrated by a range of Anglican, Catholic and Orthodox churches – as one of her defining musical possessions; thus the predominantly Christian values of Oklahoma and the American Southern region may in part magnify the certain connections between *Wildcat*'s angel icons, Flying Lotus's harp samples and cherubic music emanating from heaven's entrance gates, the Christian interpretation of an afterlife manifest in sonic form (Thorsen 2020). At the same time, however, the Hindi signification of the harp communicates the ritualistic aspects of a *swamimi*'s dedication to self-discovery and spirituality, articulating how the performer was 'more than Christian', marrying an array of influences across 'the black Christian church, jazz, and Hindu worship songs' (Brown 2021: 60).

Turiya Coltrane's song *Om Rama* (2017) was released as part of the posthumous collection *World Spirituality Classics 1: The Ecstatic Music of Alice Coltrane Turiyasangitanada*, drawing from aspects of her four cassette albums released between 1982 and 1995. *Om Rama* combines Western and Eastern influences in a similar way to the *Wildcat* soundtrack, amalgamating rippling harp sounds, handclaps and chants with a gospel church organ to develop the song's rich sonic texture in a manner that mirrors the all-consuming focus of Hindi prayer rituals and meditation (Knight 1985; Wade 1996; Lewis 2017). For Turiya Coltrane, the harp possessed powerful personal meanings because her late husband John bought the instrument towards the end of his life. It was not delivered until after his death, took approximately six months to build and remained predominantly unused in the family house, yet one day a strong breeze caused the strings to hum as though a spirit was attempting to communicate to Turiya Coltrane and her relatives directly (Hsu 2017; Smith 2017). The sonic and visual elements of the screen text thus operate in tandem to form Black Visual Intonations amplifying the holiness and spirituality of Joseph's Grayson interpretation, transforming a typical small town in America's heartland into a heavenly plain laden with sanctified meaning at once within *and* beyond Oklahoma's physical geographic boundaries. Turiya Coltrane was one of the few harpists throughout the history of professional jazz music, and one can detect in the work sampled by her nephew a fusion of cascading, rippling string arrangements, conveying a range of personal significations and broader intercultural meanings latent within the film's sonic components which thus complement the formal sophistication of *Wildcat* as an audiovisual whole.

Although What Matters Most's Vimeo account openly declares that the characters who populate *Wildcat*'s audiovisual world are both 'actual – cowboys; and envisioned – angels', the filmmaker blurs distinguishable boundaries between reality and imagination throughout his short film's depictions of Grayson. For example, the angelic figure representing the spirits of both Aunt Janet and Turiya Coltrane is played by a young girl in a white dress. At one moment, she hops onto the back of a lawnmower as a young boy steers the vehicle around the neighbourhood, effortlessly harmonizing with the dynamics of the rural universe in her immediate surroundings. Joseph's merging of fact and fiction in *Wildcat* thus mimics the manner in which the roots of the town's original name are inconclusive, riddled with mystery and hearsay. Although the word 'Wildcat' may originate from the area's home-brewing activities or indeed a militant response to Henryetta's blatant racism and hostility towards black people, a definitive understanding of Grayson's roots remains lost in the labyrinths of Southern America's complex yet largely undocumented history. The short film balances realistic, phenomenon-based portrayals of the All-Black rodeo with dreamy representations of a metaphysical noumenal plain inhabited by angels (Campt 2021: 48–54).

As well as mirroring the sonic richness of Turiya Coltrane's Eastern and Western musical sources, the amalgamation of physical and non-physical worlds shrouds Joseph's visual depictions of the small, rural town in limbo between cultural sources and conditions, oscillating between abstract states and concrete, empirical forms. Indeed, the ethereal, moody sounds of Flying Lotus's sample-laden soundtrack thus charge Joseph's mesmerizing images of the cherubic girl with intensified sensations of surrealness and awe. As the ghostly angel joins the town's children and negotiates the environment on her companion's pointedly unglamorous and unmythical lawnmowing machine, the soothing harp noises remind percipients that the short film positions the humble Grayson town in a celestial realm where definitive answers in the face of uncertainty become obsolete, liberated by the *swamimi* belief in the unknowable complexity of the universe beneath the superficial veneer of 'normality' and everyday occurrences (Vahed 1997; Kumar 2012).

While Joseph's *Black Up* (2011) channels *Touki Bouki* and *Killer of Sheep*'s heritage of Afrodiasporic cinema by combining the slaughter of animals with a powerful section of music, *Wildcat* captures muscular bulls charging around the dusty ring and energetic calves released for the rodeo's chasing games, stamina tasks and 'free-hand' riding challenges as the ambient hum of Flying Lotus's soundtrack reverberates in the background. Joseph's audiovisual content in *Wildcat* attempts to portray the ecstatic liberation of Afrodiasporic spirits as a result of the All-Black rodeo gathering, whereas the killing of animals in *Black Up*, *Touki Bouki* and *Killer of Sheep* represents the claustrophobic dread and perverse sensation of inescapable turmoil that are associated with certain experiential dynamics of Blackness in Africa and beyond the continent.

Although Joseph's framing of the animals performing their allocated roles delineates the activities and events which may define a typical rodeo gathering, his footage also subtly inverts the legacy of animal slaughter symbols which are traceable across the aforementioned Senegalese and African-American films. In *Wildcat*, the intense sensations of pain associated with slaughter scenes are irrelevant in relation to the wholesome pleasure of the All-Black rodeo amid Grayson's picturesque countryside world. Vibrant, healthy livestock reconfigure the existing animal motif, generating filmic portrayals of Afrodiasporic life in the American South that radiate the harmony and, in turn, capture the contentedness of the unforgotten angels, the memory of Aunt Janet and Turiya Coltrane and their consequent spiritual peace. Joseph's transformation of the slaughtered animal symbolism thus echoes the manner in which *Wildcat* draws from recognizable film traditions but, at the same time, combines music video, film and advertisement forms, thereby generating new, complex structural parameters merging past, present and future spirits of Afrodiasporic cinema and Black Atlantic audiovisual expression.

While the presence of the Black Neoliberal Aesthetic in *Until the Quiet Comes* undermines its potential to subvert the Eurocentric infrastructures that constitute modernity, the oscillations between Black Visual Intonations and still-moving-images in both *Until the Quiet Comes* and *Wildcat* capture the subversive elements of Black Atlantic music *and* moving images, the disruptive, unruly sights *and* sounds of the Audiovisual Atlantic. In turn, the formal sophistication of these works articulates how Joseph's works are complex sites where the crossroads of capital, cultural traffic and aesthetics interact, perpetuating aspects of Eurocentric hegemony and at the same time offering alternative modes of expression – and, in turn, new ways of being – that might help us negotiate the possibilities and pitfalls of modernity.

4.4 Mad city's children: remembering kid Kendrick's Compton in *m.A.A.d.* (2014)

Kahlil Joseph's first installation work – a short film of approximately fifteen minutes, made in collaboration with Kendrick Lamar – was titled *m.A.A.d.* (2014) after the musician's award-winning second studio album *good kid, m.A.A.d city* (2012). In *m.A.A.d.* Joseph weaves Lamar's family videos together with other sources of found footage as well as newly shot clips, deploying special effects to distort the speed of people's actions and layering the collection of moving images in a hallucinogenic, otherworldly style. Although the footage used in *m.A.A.d.* was originally intended to be framed as backing visuals for Lamar's live-show when he was supporting Kanye West's *Yeezus* tour (2013), their focus on and commitments to other projects meant that the artists were unable to coordinate and complete their collaboration within the allotted timeframe, leaving Joseph with some promising audiovisual material yet no outlet through which to showcase the work.

On the front cover of the *good kid, m.A.A.d city* album, an old photograph of the rapper as a baby sitting with two uncles and his grandfather is accompanied by the text: 'A SHORT FILM BY KENDRICK LAMAR'. Lamar here foregrounds his understanding of the musical project as a concept album with cinematic traits, a site where audial and visual components collide. Of course, Lamar's collaboration with Joseph transformed and changed over time: the 'SHORT FILM' that was initially destined to become a background piece for the rapper's contribution to the *Yeezus* tour evolved into a fine art installation incorporating footage from 1992 provided by Lamar's family members. At the suggestion of his brother Noah Davis, Joseph finished editing the material and installed the work as a double screen projection on a continuous loop at the family's Underground Museum, and *m.A.A.d.*'s favourable reception within this context resulted in the work being featured at the Museum of Contemporary Art in Los Angeles.

The Museum presented *m.A.A.d.* under the title *Kahlil Joseph: Double Conscience*, emphasizing the implicit duality of W.E.B. Dubois's famous 'double consciousness' theory, the warring sets of expectations associated with being an American citizen and, at the same time, one's status as a black person (1903), as well as, at the same time, drawing from the favourable reputation generated by Joseph's public persona and his emerging body of work to market the event. *Double Conscience* was consequently featured in a range of additional gallery spaces, including Art Basel in Switzerland and the Southbank Centre in England.

Reviewers of *m.A.A.d.* and its presentation as *Double Conscience* acknowledge that the Joseph's body of work 'falls somewhere between music videos and shorts films … usually watched on a laptop on Vimeo, not on museum walls' (Ducker 2015). However, the two-screen installation is 'lauded for saving the art of the music video' through its subversion of preconceived notions of structural parameters, exploring how meanings imbedded within a media form may fluctuate and alter depending on the manner in which one frames and presents the work, and, in turn, communicating Joseph's attempts to undermine predetermined or essentialist understandings of modernity (Jansen 2017).

While acknowledging that art is 'never produced in a vacuum' because an artist's personal aims both purposefully and unintentionally affect and nuance the various meanings of their work, Susie Hodge emphasizes the influence of 'situations, backgrounds, locations, materials and religions, and frequently the artist's own irreverence' as well as highlighting the significance of 'rules, tradition, convention, patronage or financial constraints' during these meaning-making processes (Hodge

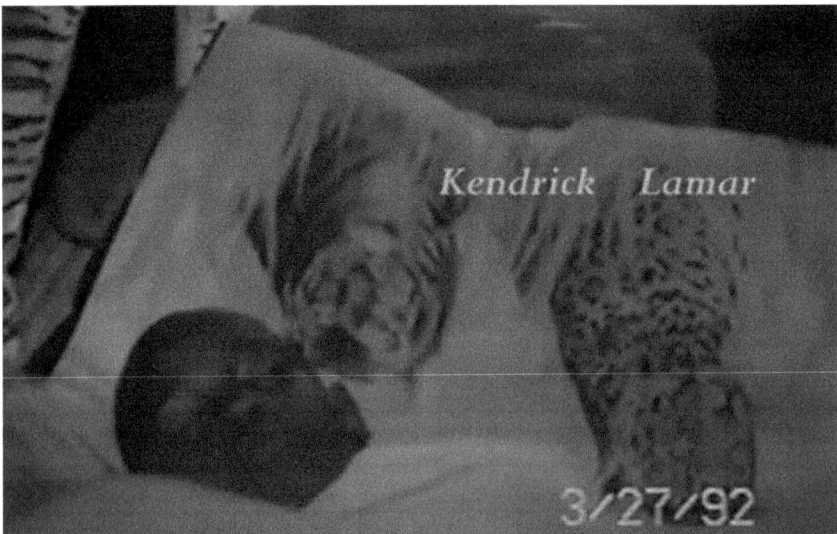

Figure 4.6 *m.A.A.d* (2014), Kahlil Joseph and Kendrick Lamar © Top Dawg Entertainment, Interscope Records and Aftermath Entertainment.

2016: 6). Indeed, although myriad overlapping and contesting forces influence the various overlapping signs and significations of Joseph's works during their encoding and decoding stages, the LA Rebellion filmmaker and media artist O. Funmilayo Makarah observes: 'The central elements of Video Installations are environment and experience. For instance, just as artists such as painters begin with a blank canvas, media artists creating Video Installations begin with an empty space that they transform' (Makarah in Bobo 1998: 130).

Although many factors cited by Hodge and Makarah (such as materiality and time) are indeed vital constituent parts which affect the interwoven meanings and significations of any artwork's cohesive whole, installations possess a special relationship with space, thus the form's situatedness oftentimes produces 'in spectators an expanded spatial awareness, a phenomenological sensitivity to all that is actual and present within a bounded space' (Elwes 2015: 1) since, as Holly Rogers reminds us, audiovisual installations specifically address 'the way objects interact in space' (Rogers 2010: 145). In order to situate Joseph's *m.A.A.d.* and its manifestation as *Double Conscience* within the broader contexts of contemporary Afrodiasporic filmmaking across a range of creative practices, then, one must process the relationships of his artwork with the spaces within which they are positioned, activating the similarities and differences between the Underground Museum, the public museum co-founded by Joseph's late brother, run by his extended family, set in a predominantly African-American and Latinx part of the city, and Los Angeles's Museum of Contemporary Art, a national institution founded in 1967 and spread across two large sites. With an awareness of the particularities of space here in mind, one may therefore assess both the seismic and more subtle shifts in meaning that occur when *m.A.A.d.* is framed in new gallery locations across art museum contexts.

The Museum of Contemporary Art has showcased *m.A.A.d.*'s incarnation as *Double Conscience* and the *One Day at a Time: Kahlil Joseph's Fly Paper* (2018) exhibition exemplifies the key issues which artists and curators continue to face in our contemporary moment because, as previously discussed, such spaces are 'born of 300 years of whiteness' (Davis, cited by Solway 2017) and oftentimes frame 'images of Europe as the ideal' (Catlin-Legutko 2019: 42). The characterizations of the Museum of Contemporary Art as a predominantly white institution and the Underground Museum as a black-led community space shift the meanings of their housed artworks because many controversial aspects of art curation in specialized spaces are rooted in the prevalence of cultural gatekeeping. 'Gatekeepers' are often defined as 'a person or organisation which exerts control over whether works are heard by a wider public audience or not, and mediates between those artworks and their potential audience, guiding their audience toward or away from that work' (Mills 2012: vii), thus those who hold positions of power within the organization of sites dedicated to cultural exhibition may govern *what* is exhibited as well as *how* artworks are displayed.

Similarly, as a result of the racialized cultural imbalances which, in broad societal terms, are perpetuated and augmented by the historical and ongoing schisms between colonizing forces and colonized communities, art curators in the West who determine whether Afrodiasporic cultural artefacts are displayed or rejected are frequently white, middle-class and male, thus the stakeholders who are imbedded within the heart of the local communities and cultures shaping the artworks in question are frequently marginalized or ignored by organizers (Hall 1993b; Golding 2013). Lonnie G. Bunch III, the Fourteenth Secretary of the Smithsonian Institution, recalls personal experiences of the racial imbalances in the arts curatorial profession that he faced during the early years of his career:

> When I first attended national meetings of museum professionals in the late 1970s, I was struck by how few people of colour were present. I remember searching the crowd for the nod of recognition or the acknowledgment and acceptance that comes from a common cultural connection. I knew we would find each other eventually, share effusive greetings, and joke once again about the "joys" of integrating the profession. In a corner of the convention centre, or in the rear of the vendors' marketplace, we would prepare ourselves for the sessions by singing the words of Al Green's 1971 hit, "I'm so tired of being alone, I'm so tired of being on my own." Invariably after attending a session, we would reconvene and someone, drawing on his knowledge of southern folklore, would say "There were just a few of us flies in the buttermilk." Reminding us, though we needed no reminder, that the museum field was awash in whiteness.
>
> (Lonnie G. Bunch III 2019: 3)

From Sethembile Msezane's embodiment of the chapungu bird at the University of Cape Town in 2015 to the performance art of Bree Newsome pulling down the confederate flag in South Carolina, vital Pan-African movements of public activism in the vein of Rhodes Must Fall and #BlackLivesMatter have in recent times spread awareness about the ingrained race-based inequalities within and beyond the arts world through savvy engagements with screen-based technologies. However, in spite of such anti-institutional moments of convergence between art and the camera, large imbalances between the number of black and white arts curators as communicated by Bunch III's experiences in the 1970s continue to exist throughout the globe at this present moment in time (Cooks 2011; Cahan 2016). The lack of diverse voices within the managerial branches of art institutions supports and thereby sustains systemic hierarchies of power which are, in turn, shaped by aspects of one's positionality. Factors such as race, class and gender affect a person's location within these hierarchies, and, when dominant points of view within the arts management systems centre and consequently privilege the experiences and perspectives of white people over non-white sections of society, works of art from global and diasporic communities oftentimes become marginalized or neglected, 'ticking boxes' mandated for diversity and inclusion programmes rather than forming the invaluable core or *raison d'être* of an exhibition.

The inclusion of works such as *m.A.A.d.* in the Museum of Contemporary Art locates and thereby contributes to the cementation of African-American voices in traditionally white spaces, spreading Joseph's Black Atlantic audiovisual expression to a broad audience. The Underground Museum, meanwhile, functioned as a grassroots, family-run gallery offering a space where Afrodiasporic experiences are centred, where

Black arts and its communities can exist and flourish at the heart of such cultural discussions rather than their periphery, thus *m.A.A.d.*'s inclusion within this space serves to augment the museum's reputation as a fundamental focus point or nexus of contemporary Black creativity.

Joseph and Lamar's collaboration calls for harmony between the various sections of Los Angeles's black communities, yet in order to activate this solidarity the audiovisual artwork transfers Lamar's discussions of Compton street life and the city's racial tensions into a visual format for gallery consumption. While *m.A.A.d* and its *Double Conscience* guise play on a constant loop, the section which might be described as the starting point of the work's unending feedback adopts the introductory bars from the album's eighth song *m.A.A.d. City* (featuring MC Eiht) (2012): 'If Pirus and Crips all got along,/They'd probably gun me down by the end of this song,' intones Lamar wistfully as contorted, wobbling footage captures an unidentified car slowly cruising along the street opposite separate pairs of bystanders one dreamy, ethereal night somewhere in Compton. While the dark humour of Lamar's lines might chime with patrons in a predominantly white space, this nihilistic depiction of the Pirus-Crips tension could resonate in a starkly different manner for citizens who have experienced the groups' disputes or live in proximity to areas of conflict.

Compton, one of the county's oldest cities, is situated in downtown Los Angeles yet remains known as the 'Hub City' as a result of its centralized location within the broader context of Los Angeles County. After the Supreme Court set the precedent in the Shelley versus Kraemer case (1948) that racially exclusive housing practices were fundamentally unconstitutional, large groups of middle-class black Americans migrated to the area in the 1950s, seeking new employment prospects and fair housing opportunities (Sides 2004). Despite this legislative breakthrough, however, de facto forms of racism beyond the courts still left the city's growing African-American population largely unsupported by its officials. After the initial surge in popularity, black and white citizens from the middle and upper-middle classes started to defect from the area towards nearby locations such as Artesia, Bellflower, Carson and Inglewood, where cities that were newly formed – or recently incorporated into the broader Los Angeles County municipality – offered lower crime rates and new sources of investment. Over the years, the imbalanced living conditions have proved fertile grounds for the development and evolution of street gangs, especially the factions named in Lamar's song: the Pirus and Crips.

The Pirus – otherwise known as the Piru Street Family, or the Piru Gangsters – are a criminal gang from Los Angeles founded on the streets in 1969, their name referring to the residential Piru Street area in Compton as well as forming the backronyms 'Political Inner-city Revolutionary Union' and 'Powerful Indestructible Revengeful United'. The Pirus established the notorious Bloods, or Blood Alliance, from LA County prison, creating a larger organization with another street group known as the Brims in 1974. Both groups had been victimized by (and were similarly antagonistic towards) the rival Crips gang, their territorial disputes ineffectively cloaking desperate attempts to control a portion of what little resources were available at street-level for their contesting factions of drug dealers, firearms traders, prostitutes and pimps. The

Blood Alliance was therefore formed as means of protecting the mutual interests of the Pirus and Brims as the Crips and other gangs began to coordinate both secretive ambushes and public attacks on their cliques of street hustlers, and indeed vice versa (Martinez 2008).

Although Lamar is no longer a member of a particular gang, he grew up surrounded by the influences and temptations of gangster culture: his father Kenny Duckworth was a member of the Gangster Disciples division from Chicago, and Lamar's wider circles of friends and family are reported to have connections with the Bloods. Lamar's mother Paula Oliver was the driving force behind the family's move from Chicago, where Kenny was a gang member, to Compton, where Lamar was born; and although Kenny was a caring father he remained 'a flawed man like the rest of us', his history of gang affiliations communicating the complicated and conflicting forces affecting his son's upbringing in proximity to the streets (Moore 2020: 42). Indeed, on the aforementioned album cover of his second album, a very young Lamar is pictured sitting on the lap of one of his uncles at a family gathering as the adult in question throws a Crips gang sign with his hand.

The eyes of his grandfather and two uncles in the photograph are censored while the eyes of young Lamar remain untouched, at once emphasizing how the coming-of-age narratives of the album are told 'through the eyes' or from the perspective of the rapper while, at the same time, offering tokenistic gestures of privacy for the family members featured in this particular scene. Lamar's phrase 'm.A.A.d.' stands for 'my Angry Adolescence divided', mirroring the tendency in gangster rap and its attendant cultures to creatively acronymize and thereby impose a certain element of order and control on aspects of the chaos and turbulence in their immediate surroundings. The inclusion of the photograph thus signifies Lamar's 'escape' from this particular environment rather than glorifying the gangster lifestyle while, simultaneously, illustrating how such a close, deep-rooted relationship with the gang cultures of his city has forged an inextricable connection to his own sense of identity.

'Seem like the whole city go against me ...' continues Lamar in *m.A.A.d.*, 'Every time I'm in the street I hear: YAWK YAWK YAWK YAWK'. The rhythms of various songs selected from *good kid, m.A.A.d city* dictate the speed of Joseph's editing, and, here, the sonic effects engendered by the rapper's onomatopoeic method for describing the resonations of gunshot fire are emphasized by the sudden disappearance of voice-like sounds which were otherwise echoing in the song's background, subtly growing with intensity. In turn, the rapid editing of *m.A.A.d.*'s footage contrasts sharply with the slow disfigurement of the car's previously languid movements, and short shots of a man staggering in the Los Angeles street merge with clips of another person dancing in his darkened kitchen under the illumination of frenetic strobe lights. Lamar's aggressive beats explode from the momentary lull in dramatic, ferocious fashion and the film's shots shift in time with the pulsating crash of each emphatic beat, amalgamating night and day as images of black men dancing and relaxing around various parts of Compton are interspliced with clips and still images of jarring violence from undisclosed areas: someone is pinned to the floor by armed officers; a group of policeman in riot gear jog in unison as the city burns; two lynched people hang from a tree as members of an all-white crowd pose for the camera smiling or point at the atrocity admiringly, threateningly.

One might argue that traces of the Black Neoliberal aesthetic form as Lamar's lyrics about life surrounded by gang culture operate in tandem with Joseph's visuals, circulating 'the spectacle of black death' even if only for a fleeting moment (Nwonka 2020: 856). The hanging bodies have their eyes hidden by black rectangles in the same manner as Lamar's family members on the album cover and indeed several other young men featured moving around the city in the opening visual sequence, thereby blurring the spatiotemporal boundaries between past and present, the living and the dead, as a reminder of the underlying racial tensions on which contemporary gun criminality and police violence in Los Angeles are grounded, the historical roots of black peoples' murder under the influence of Jim Crow laws in the South which manifest in contemporary Compton in new, insidious ways.

A particularly striking moment of the installation's introductory sequence captures turquoise light shining behind a baby's head, and, later in the piece, similar shots resurface: a baby plays with its feet on a learning mat depicting the sign-language alphabet: home footage from 27 March 1992 captures a four-year-old Lamar napping surrounded by blankets. The juxtaposition of these idyllic moments against antagonistic forces threatening the peacefulness of black peoples' lives reinforces the fact that Lamar's childhood was surrounded by institutional racism, his upbringing underpinned by the threat of violence from law enforcement officers as well as the Bloods and Crips.

Joseph describes the piece as 'a kaleidoscope of storylines and ideas that defy typical categorisation to explore new languages and new forms … probably more about Compton that anything else' (Joseph in conversation with Raiss 2014). Lamar, however, is an embodiment of young black masculinity defined by Compton's streets, thus the overlapping narratives weaving Lamar and Compton together possess inextricable bonds that cannot be wholly disentangled. Lamar, for example, gave Joseph the phone number of his childhood friend Tremell, whose mother performs skits for the official *good kid, m.A.A.d city,* for further assistance when gathering footage for the collaboration. The filmmaker says that Tremell applied his 'deep relationships with the community' to assist with the gathering of cast members, emphasizing the closely knit bonds between the rapper and friends from his upbringing which remain intact despite Lamar's newfound status as a famous artist (ibid.).

Echoing Lamar's relationship with Tremell, a close group of childhood friends (who met through the non-profit Compton Jr Posse organization) established the Compton Cowboys, an inner-city equestrian group aiming to negate disingenuous stereotypes about African-American citizens from the area while offering alternative pathways to Compton youths who might otherwise become tempted by the gangster lifestyle (Thompson-Hernandez 2018).[6] In many ways Joseph's portrayal of black equestrian communities is foreshadowed by his earlier work *Wildcat* (2013), wherein the

---

[6] The motto of the organization is: 'Streets raised us. Horses saved us' (Compton Cowboys Official 2020).

community of Grayson, Oklahoma, connect over the town's long-standing Black rodeo event. In his collaboration with Lamar, the calmness of the Compton Cowboys as they tend to their animals enacts a moment of serenity amid *m.A.A.d.*'s chaotic visualizations of police violence and gun crime. Joseph's shots of this subculture therefore operate in tandem with a period of brevity within the installation's soundscape, emphasizing the opportunities for self-reflection and reconciliation provided by looking after the cowboys' horses and, in turn, momentarily escaping the complications of Compton street life.

Gradually, cowbell noises from Lamar's anthemic song *Backseat Freestyle* (2012) build in the background: however, rather than going deeper, or more rural, with further representations of the Compton Cowboys and their agricultural practices, images of the city's complex network of crossroads merge with a gathering of revellers dancing and drinking in the streets, and Lamar's cries of 'Goddamn I feel amazing, damn I'm in the matrix' capture the hedonism, the sheer pleasure of existing, as a young black person born and raised in Compton. In this sense, Campt's theorization of the visual frequencies of Black experiences 'embracing the joy, beauty, horror and pain that is the afterlife of slavery' here captures the paradoxes of Lamar and Joseph's collaboration, at once circulating the tired images of Black violence yet simultaneously trying to break away from ways of being that perpetuate these repeating narratives (Campt 2019: 43).

Drawing from her personal experiences of the imbalances of representation within the curatorial professions, Cinnamon Catlin-Legutko identifies in the West 'a troubling practice of "othering" by those who work in museums, people who are predominantly white', as a result of the institutionalization of white perspectives and the privileging of white people's values within the Western arts curation sphere (Catlin-Legutko 2019: 42). This 'othering' phenomenon dehumanizes people's experiences and perspectives, illustrating the importance of accessing, processing and negotiating the cultural politics defining the spaces within which particular artworks are exhibited. While points of view from groups such as Native Americans and African diasporas tend to be marginalized and silenced by such unequal societal infrastructures, the hegemonic values of the white people at the heart of these systems oftentimes remain unchallenged, controlling the (in)visibility of particular forms of art and culture within their spaces and, in turn, affecting and nuancing the values and meanings of artworks as well as the day-to-day functioning of the spaces in which they are housed.

The significance of *m.A.A.d.*, then, through its centring of Lamar's discourses about growing up amid contemporary Compton's contradictory forces of violence and love – the pleasures and pains of city-life – becomes emphasized by the ways in which the work challenges the dangerous 'othering' at play in today's gallery spaces. While the installation subverts the hegemonic whiteness at the heart of Museum of the Contemporary Art through its focus on certain Afrocentric narratives which are otherwise marginalized, exploited or exoticized by predominantly 'white' exhibition spaces, in the Underground Museum the installation operates as a physical manifestation of the establishment's core values because it centres Black Lives and narratives in a pioneering 'Black' museum space. In this sense, *m.A.A.d.* offers a framework by which future audiovisual installations might reinforce and empower other spaces of alternative Afrocentric sociality through Black Visual Intonations. While its merging of music and moving images in certain ways challenge the Eurocentricity underpinning modernity by embodying in material form the countercultural values at the heart of the Black Atlantic's emancipatory projects, at the same time the subtle undercurrents of the Black Neoliberal Aesthetic problematize the efficacy of the alternative modernity communicated by *m.A.A.d.*, circulating stereotypical representations of certain Afrodiasporic experiences and thereby partially producing 'an endorsement of the very ideologies that it claims to counter' (Nwonka 2020: 859). While Joseph's movement into the gallery space highlights new opportunities for Black Atlantic audiovisual artists to work across media boundaries and challenge the underlying forms of whiteness which shape exhibition spaces and constitute modernity, the underlying elements of contradiction within the context of his work complicate such countercultural endeavours.

In numerous interviews, Arthur Jafa cites the influence of John Akomfrah's 'affective proximity' notion. Echoing Sergei Eisenstein's montage theory, Jafa details 'affective proximity' as the process 'when two things come together … [an image] demanding to be emancipated from the context in which it found itself and placed next to where it was supposed to go' in order to generate a new effect (Jafa in conversation with Obrist 2016). Akomfrah in turn states that: 'To begin to force many ways of being and living, I must work with the premises of the cinematic … Organising new spectacularity, new configurations, or what constitutes moving images – multiplicity, overlap, affective proximity, and subjectivity are very important' (Akomfrah in conversation with Canela 2018). *m.A.A.d* shares with Akomfrah's projects *Mnemosyne* (2010) and *Nine Muses* (2010) a similar strain of 'affective proximity' because all three works – which are concerned with memory past and present; the formation of new memories as well as the recalibration of old – have moved between cinematic and film-installation forms through processes of recontextualization, bringing divergent yet overlapping modes of audiovisual communication into conversation.

'Migrants were often filmed in relation to debates about crime or social problems, so that's how they get fixed in official memory', explains Akomfrah in a discussion about *Nine Muses*. 'But that Caribbean woman standing in a 60s factory isn't thinking about how she's a migrant or a burden on the British state; she's as likely to be thinking about what she's going to eat that evening or about her lover' (Akomfrah in conversation with Sandhu 2012). In similar fashion, *m.A.A.d*'s home footage captures a boy enjoying his youth, not knowing what the future might hold, unaware his third studio album *To Pimp a Butterfly* (2015) would receive seven nominations at the 2016 Grammy Awards. And now – as his story is told and retold again and again through the gallery, across multiple albums, via the Audiovisual Atlantic's music and moving images – we continue to see that child from different perspectives, under new lights, as the butterfly continues to transform and evolve.

5

Sights and sounds across the sea

5.1 Looking for Langstons: Black waves and British connections within a transatlantic paradigm

As I have discussed throughout this book, Joseph's audiovisual artwork is at once shaped by the transcontinental perspectives of Los Angeles's Rebellion filmmakers and installation artists as well as the new jazz-hip hop scene, fused to the influences of diasporic creators across Africa, Europe and different parts of America.

In the post-Civil Rights Movement climate, the evocative works of the LA Rebellion directors set the tone for new forms of Black independent film in America, within and beyond the Los Angeleno bubble, that would move away from blaxploitation's clichéridden formulae for commercial success. This period of filmmaking was short-lived. The works of Shelton Jackson 'Spike' Lee – whose influences on Joseph and Jafa by way of Greaves are captured by Linscott's 'audiovisual mapping' approach (Linscott 2020: 150) – epitomize the brief flow of Black New Wave films between the early 1980s and the mid-1990s which attempted to appeal to mainstream audiences while, at the same time, allowing directors to retain some authorial control of the overall filmic project.

During his first year studying at New York University Film School, Lee channelled the rebellious spirit of his predecessor Oscar Micheaux through his short twenty-minute film *The Answer* (1980). Lee's film is a satirical portrayal of a black screenwriter hired to rewrite D. W. Griffith's *The Birth of a Nation* (1915) for $50 million, echoing Micheaux's *Within Our Gates* (1920) by responding to Griffith's film and criticizing the director's support for white supremacism. Once finished, *The Answer* was poorly received by the film department whose members considered Griffith a founder of American cinema, culminating in a disciplinary hearing and nearly resulting in Lee's expulsion from the university for his work's rebellious and provocative tone (Loughrey 2016; Tillet 2018). However, the incident captures a defiant longing to promote Afrodiasporic perspectives through audiovisual experimentation which is likewise located in the efforts of such filmmakers as Arthur Jafa to communicate 'the enunciative desires of people of African descent' (Jafa 1992: 253).

The releases of Lee's *Do the Right Thing* (1989), Burnett's *To Sleep with Anger* (1990), Dash's *Daughters of the Dust* (1991) and Gerima's *Sankofa* (1993) were often interpreted as responses to 'the climate of long-muted black frustration and anger over the worsening political and economic conditions that African-Americans ... [continued] to endure in the nation's decaying urban centres' (Guerrero 1993: 24). However, powerful forms of 'frustration and anger' were not limited to the urban poor. Lee's *She's Gotta Have It* (1986) captures the restless cosmopolitanism of Brooklyn's Fort Greene, featuring a black woman named Nola Darling who challenges societal expectations of black women by maintaining three sexual partners at once.

Although the isolated, friendless nature of Nola's character combines with the absence of her mother (and indeed the omission of any significant female role model figures) to create a film that leaves 'black women silent in a discussion about sexuality' (Simmonds 1988: 19), Lee's problematic attempts to expand filmic representations of African-Americans beyond 'seeing blacks purely in terms of white norms and practices' illustrate a key independent Black New Wave film that mirrors elements of Joseph's Black Visual Intonation characterized by 'ignoring or at best belittling the toys and games of the dominant white culture' (Snead 1994: 118–19). Mary Neema Barnette's *Sky Captain* (1984), Wendell B. Harris Jr.'s *Chameleon Street* (1989), and Cheryl Dunye's *The Watermelon Woman* (1996) – as well as Lee's early films *Sarah* (1981) and *Joe's Bedstuy Barbershop: We Cut Heads* (1983) – similarly generated substantial mass appeal among black *and* white audiences *despite* their oppositional and rebellious qualities, demonstrating the commercial viability of Black independent films that could be quirky and, at the same time, confrontational.

Manthia Diawara, however, captures the crux of a major underlying issue when balancing the artistic and challenging imperatives of filmmaking with commercialization and the need to generate profit. When articulating the sentiments of attendees at a conference on Black independent filmmaking, Diawara – who was speaking of a cinematic world that pre-dated certain forms of Nollywood cinema as

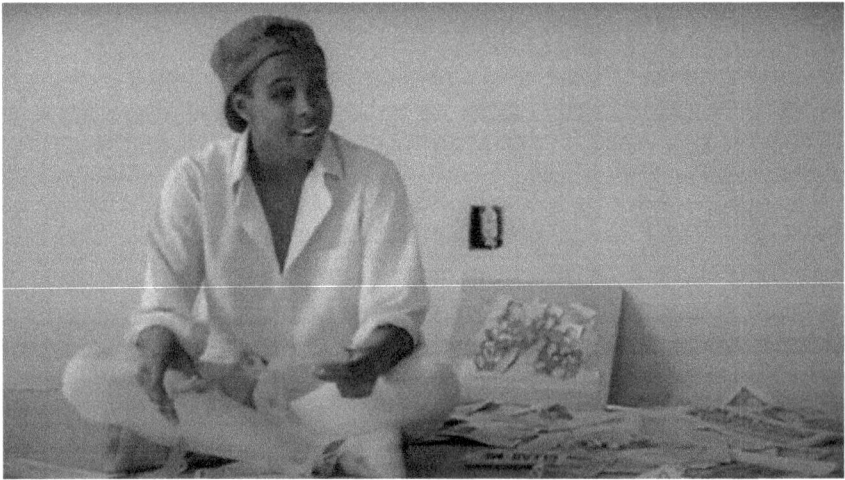

Figure 5.1 *She's Gotta Have It* (1986), Spike Lee © 40 Acres and a Mule Filmworks.

well as the contemporary 'golden era' of web-based Afrocentric media forms[1] – notes that filmmakers operating in the shadow of Lee's work could not replicate the levels of sophistication for Black artistry which were previously established by Burnett, Dash et al. associated with the LA Rebellion Movement:

> Then came Spike Lee's *She's Gotta Have It* (1986). Very edgy. Very interesting. Also, independent and its a movie that could be shown in movie theatres ... [Audiences] began to watch Spike Lee and he becomes the Black filmmaker. It was positive ... but it was unfortunate because it did not lead to a new language of Black cinema. It killed independent cinema ... Our whole conference was based on the question of where we are going after *She's Gotta Have It*.
> (Diawara in conversation with McCluskey 2006: 10)

While Lee's film offered a vital new strain of Black independent cinema by capturing Afrodiasporic experiences in a way that was both digestible and accessible for broad audiences, *She's Gotta Have It* also sparked a wave of Black filmmaking that emphasized the commercial viability of its projects over the radical and confrontational styles of earlier independent black directors who, in the vein of the Greaves, LA Rebellion and even Micheaux, rejected dominant Hollywood filmmaking vernaculars and were in many ways in closer proximity to art house cinema with their abstract, indirect and unconventional techniques. Important crime drama films of the decade such as John Singleton's *Boyz N the Hood* (1991), Ernest R. Dickerson's *Juice* (1992) and *Menace II Society* (1993) by Albert and Allen Hughes reflected on dangers of the hood-life and hustling the streets for young African-Americans, whereas light-hearted films such as Reginald Hudlin's *House Party!* (1990) and F. Gary Gray's comedy drama *Friday* (1995) with Ice Cube and Chris Tucker offered comic relief for audiences of young black adults.

However, what might have been a vibrant period of creativity for Black independent filmmaking following Lee's artistic and commercial successes in fact petered out (and, if anything, produced a lull in quality). In a manner that echoes Joseph's gradual movements towards exhibitions spaces from 2011 to 2014, one can adopt a transnational framework for diasporic filmmaking when searching for an alternative Black New Wave period that was otherwise deemed 'missing' from American cinema in the aftermath of Spike Lee. By following the crosscurrents of the Black Atlantic and turning to the era's wave of British installation artists, one starts to piece together a post-national, intercontinental collection of audiovisual art that draws from the countercultural energies of Black Atlantic music in order to challenge the inherent Eurocentricity underpinning Western formulations of modernity.

As activism started to counteract the institutional racism of established gallery spaces, Black-British artists would slowly embrace opportunities for the representation

---

[1] Joseph's collaborative works do not at present include Nollywood films or Afrobeat music videos, emphasizing how the rich convergence points of sound and image across the Audiovisual Atlantic may both encompass and extend beyond some of the most popular forms of Black cultural expression.

of Afrodiasporic cultures facilitated by the emergence of new media technologies. One of the most important groups to undertake the construction of a pan-African, anti-colonial filmmaking style and thereby pave the way for the future artists were Britain's Black Audio Film Collective. In a style that Kahlil Joseph's artworks would later echo, the Black Audio Film Collective's oeuvre between 1982 and 1998 blurred the boundaries between media forms by presenting their combinations of documentary films, animations and found footage in a menagerie of cinema, gallery and workshop spaces, drawing attention to fragile discursivity of concepts such as 'Blackness' and indeed 'film' which were commonly misperceived as possessing concrete and unfluctuating meanings.

In a mission statement penned by one of the collective's key founding figures, John Akomfrah declares: 'What, after all does "black independent filmmaking" mean when present film culture is a largely white affair?' (Akomfrah 2015: 58). While the Black Audio Film Collective sought to maintain the independence of their filmmaking exploits by resisting mainstream cinema's institutionalized Eurocentric hegemony, their decision to operate as a group was implicitly 'directed towards the deconstruction of the fetishistic attachment to the cult of the auteur which earlier independent avant-garde film-makers such as those of the French New Wave had embraced' (Enwesor in Eshun and Sagar 2007: 114). In a similar fashion to Joseph's collaborative approach to work, the co-authored nature of their productions challenges outdated notions of the 'genius' auteurs in the vein of François Truffaut, Alain Resnais and Jean-Luc Godard single-handedly controlling all the encoded meanings of a filmic product, relying on the contributions from a range of personnel rather than a single voice drowning out the other contributors (Gaut 1997; Dovey 2009).

While Godard's work similarly moved between traditional film spaces and unconventional gallery locations, the increasingly experimental nature of his works during the latter stages of his career illustrates a self-conscious effort 'to erase his image as a celebrated "director" and remove evidence of his hand as the "author" of his work' (Rush 2007: 43). The Black Audio Film Collective, on the other hand, had always openly grounded their work in collective action and thus incorporated the deconstruction of hierarchical power structures into the very fabric of their art's being. One of their major films, *Handsworth Songs* (1986), uses low-fidelity Jamaican dub music to mirror in audial terms the graininess of found footage and newspaper clippings surrounding the racially charged Handsworth and Brixton riots of 1985, pre-empting Arthur Jafa's formula for Black Visual Intonations by offering an audiovisual blueprint for future media artists who seek to harmonize depictions of blackness with the 'frequential values' of certain music and moving image combinations (Jafa 1992: 254).

Importantly, the Black Audio Film Collective echoes the Afrocentric art activism of AfriCOBRA, the Black Arts Movement and the Black Emergency Cultural Coalition from the late sixties and early seventies, leading Okwui Enwezor to argue that: 'the rise of these collectives was precipitated by the crisis that was then growing within the global social imaginary dominated by instruments of neo-liberal capitalism' (Enwezor in Eshun and Sagar 2007: 122). Indeed, another British group of filmmakers, named the Sankofa Film and Video Collective, were likewise motivated by needing to address societal balances between black and white people augmented by the globe's imbalanced economic framework, becoming 'committed to providing support for aspiring writers and directors, often trying to secure funds on their behalf' (Dixon 1995–6: 132).

Isaac Julien, for example, produced *Looking for Langston* (1989) with the help of the Sankofa Film and Video Collective, using the work of poet Langston Hughes (in a manner akin to Greaves) and the Harlem Renaissance of the 1920s to frame his exploration of black homosexuality. Although the Hughes Estate was provoked by the film's associations with the poet's work with black gay cultures and consequently sought an injunction to prevent screenings of the short film across America, Julien later hinted that he was 'more interested in complementing Hughes's works rather than dealing with his sexual lifestyle', hence why *Looking for Langston* forms 'a poetic, experimental [screen] text' through a montage of 'various archival materials, dramatized segments, poetry readings and music from the past and present' (Shin 2003: 201).

The nineties saw important black artists' media installations explore moments of tension associated with racialization and racism as well as many commonly addressed questions and concerns that had influenced media art since its inception. Steve McQueen won the 1999 Turner Prize and became the first black filmmaker to win an Academy Award for Best Picture in 2014 for his feature-length film *12 Years a Slave* (2013).

However, his early media works have been showcased in exhibition spaces throughout the globe, including the Johannesburg Biennale, Amsterdam's Stedelijk Museum and Documenta X in Germany, as well as New York's Marian Goodman

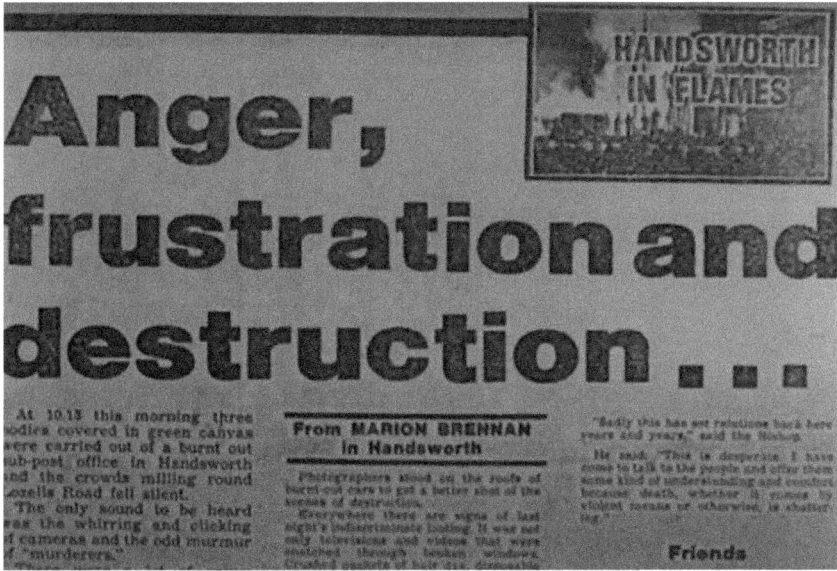

Figure 5.2 *Handsworth Songs* (1986), Black Audio Film Collective © Black Audio Film Collective (Lina Paul).

Gallery and Museum of Modern Art. The artist oftentimes features himself as an actor in his films, playing in his debut artwork *Bear* (1993) an ambivalent nude boxer who both fights and flirts with another naked man. The video is often installed from the floor to the ceiling across a single wall, yet the floors of the enclosed space must be highly polished in order to produce a reflection of the black-and-white projection which 'makes the experience far more intimate than normal monitor viewing ... The viewer really does feel inside the ring with these two boxers' (Rush 1997: 61).[2]

After Joseph's shift towards installation media from 2011 to 2014, he collaborated with two key Black-British artists between 2014 and 2017. In Chapter 5, I now discuss Kahlil Joseph's intercontinental collaborations with these two UK-based artists. Firstly, I explore the transmedia qualities *of Video Girl* (2014) with FKA twigs, a music video with filmic qualities that transforms racist abuse endured by the musician into an emphatic rebuttal of the Neo-Nazi Aryan Brotherhood *without* conspicuously alluding to elements of continental Africa. Secondly, I focus on Joseph's collaboration with the singer-song writer Sampha Sisay entitled *Process* (2017), a music-film exploring the London-born musician's relationships with his Sierra Leonean family, highlighting how rights-holder Apple Music's exclusion of Sierra Leone from its business model meant that many of the Sierra Leonean nationals who assisted the project could not initially access *Process*.

5.2 Performance in the face of bigotry: processing prejudice, negotiating the *Video Girl* (2014)'s demons

Kahlil Joseph released a screen text with FKA twigs through the musician-dancer's YouTube account, entitled *Video Girl* (2014). FKA twigs – whose real name is Tahliah Debrett Barnett – grew up in England's Cheltenham area. She came from a low-income family yet experienced a private education at a Catholic institution named St Edward's School, receiving an academic scholarship to pay for her tuition fees. Despite early explorations in creating music at nearby youth clubs, FKA twigs moved to South London aged seventeen to pursue employment as a professional dancer, working in the music industry as a backup dancer and assisting video projects for musicians Jessie J, Taio Cruz, Wretch 32, Ed Sheeran and Kylie Minogue. FKA twigs then delved into music-writing by mixing a range of styles and sounds with her soprano's voice, developing into a performer who, in her own right, is capable of both singing *and*

---

[2] In conversation with Paul Gilroy, McQueen suggests 'the only way' he can explain how his recent made-for-television film *Lovers Rock* (2020) merges the senses to communicate the importance of black music in peoples' lives is simply 'through music' (McQueen in conversation with Gilroy 2020), thereby echoing Jenn Nkiru's understanding of black/boundless time's ability to cut out the 'middle man' when communicating complex sensations through frequencies and emotions rather than language (Nkiru in conversation with Campt, Julius and Weheliye 2020).

dancing at the centre of an artistic project. One critic notes that Joseph and FKA twig's audiovisual project for *Video Girl* 'is *nothing like* any of the videos she ever danced in' (his emphasis) (Breihan 2014), thereby representing a major shift from her more 'conventional' projects with renowned pop stars to an experimental combination of music and moving images while, at the same time, echoing the complications of the music art video category at the crossroads of capital, cultural traffic and aesthetics.

As her career path's trajectories have shifted and changed over the years, FKA twigs claims that she was frequently perceived among industry figures as a specialist in supporting other artists rather than an autonomous artist possessing her own creative talents and self-determined artistic visions. She thus wrote the lyrics for *Video Girl* (2014) as means of processing 'what it was like, being a young girl who wanted to make a name for myself and not knowing how', channelling the frustrations of her career's embryonic stages into both the audial *and* visual dimensions of her art (FKA twigs in conversation with Lamont 2014).

The *Video Girl* video reimagines the resilience of the performer's primary years as an uncertain yet talented young performer negotiating the complex and ruthless entertainment business, focusing on racist abuse that FKA twigs has experienced rather than solely exploring her career path's trajectory during its formative years. David Olusoga notes that one of the issues that caused the 'deepest ruptures in Britain in the postwar era, as it had done during the war years' related to interracial relationships (Olusoga 2016: 504) yet on 28 September 2014 – on the day of the *Video Girl* shoot, in our contemporary postmillennial climate with the war years far behind us – FKA twigs endured racist online comments from sections of her (then-)boyfriend's fan base because she was black and he was white.

The group of followers who abused FKA twigs are named 'the Robsessed' after the subject of their fixation, the white English actor Robert Pattinson. Pattinson's fame from roles in *Harry Potter and the Goblet of Fire* (2005) and the *Twilight* saga (2008–13) inadvertently developed a section of 'Robsessed' young followers whose devotion to the actor manifested as jealous insults and racist remarks online. The fans were upset that Pattinson had chosen a black woman as his partner, rather than someone white and 'more famous' in the mould of his former acting colleague and ex-girlfriend Kristen Stewart. FKA twigs defended herself publicly by making a statement about the abuse, highlighting how she was 'shocked and disgusted' by the treatment and emphasizing that racist behaviour 'is unacceptable in the real world and it's unacceptable online' (FKA twigs via her Twitter account @FKAtwigs 2014). Joseph's direction for the *Video Girl* project articulates FKA twig's emotions in response to abusive behaviour of 'the Robsessed' by capturing the singer's complex sensations of anger and disappointment when she faces an Aryan Brotherhood member at an undisclosed prison complex. Joseph's music art video thus forms an audiovisual tribute to the performer's time spent as a frustrated, directionless youth in search of artistic recognition *as well as* her frustration in the aftermath of the abuse, synthesizing this tumultuous period in FKA twigs's career in order to thwart the racial prejudices of the online abusers and the industry figures who did not believe that FKA twigs could sustain a career as a solo singer.³ The soundtrack of Joseph's audiovisual interpretation of the *Video Girl* song combines the titular song with the *Preface* track of FKA twigs's collection *LP1* (2014). The music art video has two sections: the first, set to *Preface*, details the artist playing a forlorn character who watches from behind one-way glass as the member of the Aryan Brotherhood is strapped to a medical table by doctors and law officers and eventually given a lethal injection; the second section adopts the original *Video Girl* song as toxins seep through the arrested man's veins. FKA twigs moves beyond the glass barrier to sing into a microphone that hangs from the ceiling, dancing and jerking around the room and over the man's body while provocatively caressing the symbolic 'AB' tattoo on his motionless neck.

'Integrity' forms a vital part of Joseph's mindset when selecting a co-author for his work once it is fused with theorizations of 'soul' in order to form 'a narrative of belonging to and with other black people' (Lordi 2020: 9). FKA twigs partially echoes this line of thought by stating that it is important for an artist to have 'your friends, your family and your creative collaborators who make you feel amazing', placing her artistic partners on the same levels of importance as those with whom she shares close familial bonds (FKA twigs cited by Hunt 2020). However, although FKA twigs argues 'being able to collaborate is one of the great joys of being a human' (FKA twigs in conversation with Harris 2020), she does not explicitly emphasize the specific importance of a collaborator's relationship to the African diaspora in the same way that Joseph claims to be 'exclusively interested in the lives of black people' (Joseph in conversation with Nance and Jafa, cited by Orr 2017) and 'exponentially propelled' when collaborating with black artists (Joseph in conversation with Abraham 2017).

Discourses surrounding the complex musical styles of FKA twig's oeuvre *and* her motivations as a creator are problematic insofar as the artist believes mischaracterization continues to affect her work. Although FKA twigs has been described as 'one of the most compelling and complex acts in R&B' (Josephs 2014) and 'the UK's best example … of ethereal, twisted R&B' (Lester 2013), the musician attempts to reject such strict compartmentalizations. One must process the artist's claims carefully because she refuses narrow categorizations, while at the same time benefiting from the ways that genre is used to organize the contemporary music economy, her songs both applauded *and* critiqued for their parallel statuses both inside *and* outside the definitions of various formal parameters and genre configurations (Gorton 2014; Sampson 2014).

However, when activating similarities between FKA twigs's music and certain stylistic traits from which she attempts to distance herself, controversial undertones

---

³ The roots of the Aryan Brotherhood and other neo-Nazi white power skinhead groups in America can be traced back to the British skinhead culture of the late 1960s. During this period, British skinheads were influenced by British mod rockers and Jamaican rude boys, harbouring an open appreciation for black musical forms such as ska and soul music. However, Shadow Defence Secretary Enoch Powell's controversial 'Rivers of Blood' speech stirred Britain's underlying racial and societal tensions in 1968, and a phenomenon termed 'skinhead terror' by The Observer in April 1970 resulted in pockets of Britain's skinhead groups attacking the influx of Pakistani immigrants and other Asian minorities that were joining their estates, as well as targeting members of the gay community and proponents of the hippie movement (Marshall 1991; Tarasov 2001; Ashe, Virdee and Brown 2016).

arise if one does not examine and scrutinize her claims thoroughly. R&B, or Rhythm and Blues, evolved from inner-city African-American churches as a secularized version of gospel music between the late 1930s and early 1940s, gaining momentum when 'urbane, rocking, jazz based music with a heavy, insistent beat' became popularized and circulated by communities weary of war's bleak realities, searching for something soulful and profound in their everyday routines (Palmer 1982: 146). While thematic aspects of pain, anguish and heightened emotional sensitivity are prevalent in certain formations of the genre (Redd 1985; Gilroy 1993), FKA twigs contests that confining her music within neat R&B parameters is imbued with racial bias. In an interview with *The Guardian*, she argues:

> It's just because I'm mixed race. When I first released music and no one knew what I looked like, I would read comments like: 'I've never heard anything like this before, it's not in a genre.' And then my picture came out six months later, now she's an R&B singer. I share certain sonic threads with classical music; my song *Preface* is like a hymn. So let's talk about that. If I was white and blonde and said I went to church all the time, you'd be talking about the 'choral aspect'. But you're not talking about that because I'm a mixed-race girl from south London.
> (FKA twigs in conversation with Lamont 2014)

One might argue that FKA twigs's presentation of herself as a South-Londoner attempts to feed from the 'strong and well-deployed stock of social capital' which characterizes the merging of working- and middle-class values in large parts of this particular area (Butler and Robson 2001: 18), replacing her early life's connections to rural Cheltenham with the capital city's reputation as 'an extraordinary colocation and concentration of people' as well as a centre for 'ideas and creativity' (Bell et al. 2013: 1). However, the musician's blatant attempt to control and mould her own identity as an artist does not undermine the claim that processes of racialization may distort and mischaracterize the significations of her musical output, echoing the ways in which 'race-thinking' may mischaracterize or misrepresent one's understanding of the self (Gilroy [2000] 2004).

In the second section, Joseph maintains medium close-up shots to preserve the pre-established intimacy between FKA twigs and the camera, yet a shift takes places in the tone of the performer's body language and the video's music. FKA twigs's dancing becomes increasingly provocative as the music's intensity increases: she straddles the dying white supremacist's pelvis and feigns stabbing him in the chest, twisting in a jarring manner that echoes the unsettling convulsions of the man's poisoned body parts. While *Preface*'s ambient structure lacks drumming noises, metallic percussion sounds slowly clatter to give the *Video Girl* song a steady, hypnotizing beat. The intimate bond between FKA twigs's character and Joseph's camera thus becomes suffused with heightened senses of liberation and bravado through the section's new musical material and the dancer's writhing gestures, transforming the opening section's series of introspective shots into a provocative statement of defiant sensuality.

Neil Dougan argues that FKA twigs 'grapples with Catholicism's virgin/whore complex' in *Video Girl* through the manner in which the singer-dancer is 'both the girl staring helplessly into the cold sterile world of the execution chamber and the witchy dominatrix disrupting the ritual to straddle and claim the dying prisoner' (Dougan 2015). Sigmund Freud's original definition of the Madonna/Whore complex, however, is an outdated and misogynistic attempt to compartmentalize womanhood. Freud attempts to organize women into the binary positions of either chaste and maternal Madonna figures or, at the other end of the spectrum, as promiscuous as prostitutes, judging that such promiscuity is immoral by arguing that: 'where such men love they have no desire and where they desire they cannot love' (Freud [1912] 1959: 204). By projecting male impotency onto the behaviours and actions of women, the Madonna/Whore theory essentially forms an excuse to ignore a woman's autonomy, superficially positioning humanity's actions into two artificial camps rather than allowing our behaviours to manifest beyond these points.

FKA twigs produced an album in 2019 titled *Mary Magdalene* that actively attempted to challenge the ways the figure had developed into a symbol of the 'Virgin Whore' archetype, thus the artist did not see Magdalene 'as a person in the Bible … It was more looking at her as a woman and what she represented … what was her true story, how was it manipulated, how does that relate to the matriarchy in general' (FKA twigs in conversation with Shaffer 2019). Although FKA twigs did attend a Catholic school during her youth and learned about Mary Magdalene through the 'the virgin-whore' framework, the performer states: 'The virgin-whore is incredibly healing and empowering and important for women to embrace … She was this incredible herbalist, healer and doctor … So why did we learn about her in Sunday school as "the prostitute?"' (FKA twigs in conversation with Spanos 2019). The music art video thus portrays the performer vulnerably tearing in the witness area *as well as* straddling the dying racist provocatively, gloating at his execution. Joseph and FKA twigs therefore incorporate elements of this Freudian theory into the project as means of challenging

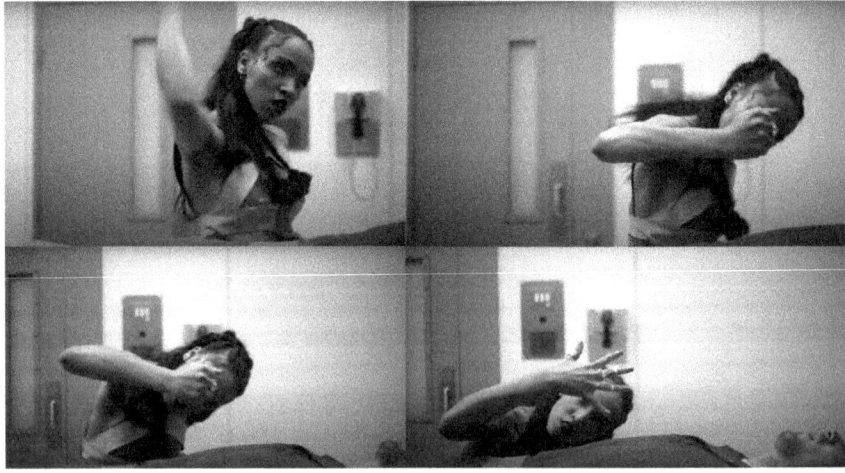

Figures 5.3, 5.4, 5.5 and 5.6 *Video Girl* (2014), Kahlil Joseph and FKA twigs © Pulse Films.

the misogynistic grounds on which it is based. *Video Girl* represents FKA twigs simultaneously within *and* beyond the Madonna/Whore binary's narrow confinements, disrupting Freud's formulaic constructions of womanhood by illustrating how women are allowed to be fully human rather than reduced to narrow compartmentalizations. Audre Lorde echoes the performer's attempt to challenge patriarchal constructions of womanhood, calling for a more complex understanding of black woman's sexuality:

> The erotic is a measure between the beginnings of our sense of self and the chaos our strongest feelings. It is an internal sense of satisfaction to which, one we have experienced it, we know we can aspire. For having experienced the fullness of this depth of feeling and recognising its power, in honour and self-respect we can require no less of our selves.
>
> (Lorde [1978] 1984: 54)

Building on Lorde's explorations of black women's power, one must also take into account the fact that FKA twigs's dancing atop the white supremacist may symbolize a reversal in power dynamics void of sexuality, a visual representation of the shift in their relationship that sees the victim of racial hatred dominant and in control of the perpetrator's fate. However, even the singer's more 'demure' character wears a revealing top in the video which, in turn, is framed in a provocative manner by Joseph's camera, thereby emphasizing that the power and complexity of FKA twigs's humanity extends beyond Freud's reductive framework, positioning the performer's strengths partially within and, at the same time, far beyond the realms of gendered, heteronormative sexuality, especially the narrow confinements of the 'Virgin-Whore' framework.

Elements of *Video Girl* imply that self-restraint is not necessarily a key aspect for her personal interpretation of modern Catholicism because, in the context of her own identity, expressions of sensuality are not necessarily sexual. Rather, the singer-dancer freely negotiates human impulses unperturbed by such narrow definitions of her womanhood. For example, when challenged about her tendency to cry in interviews and throughout her artwork, FKA twigs retorts: 'I'm proud of being sensitive. It's not a bad thing. The opposite of sensitive is insensitive' (FKA twigs in conversation with Edwardes 2016). While the performer's actions in the music art video at certain moments reject 'traditional prescriptions for female prudence' and, instead, 'carve new spaces for eroticism and sexual freedom' – especially in the second section, when the character pursues cathartic release and purges the racist demons through the sensualized dancing ritual atop the white supremacist – one must acknowledge the manner in which the co-authored screen text celebrates the variety of women's behavioural choices through the spectrum of actions that FKA twigs's character exhibits, shifting between phases, stages and desires of her humanity in a manner which oftentimes evades neat and systemic categorizations (Lee 2010: 128).

The traditional undertones of *Preface*'s choral music and the restrained, 'respectable' behaviour of FKA twigs's character are juxtaposed against her dramatic, modernized electro-soul music and the singer-dancer's powerful performance around the immobile prisoner's execution chamber. Both sections of the video are connected through the manner in which emphatic release of the dancing ritual depends on the solemnity and slower pacing of the opening section to augment the tension of the prisoner and mourner's respective situations. Arguably, the music art video's theatrical shift depends on both the mourning figure's composure and restraint during the initial mourning stages *as well as* her decision to defiantly release her unexpressed emotions through dancing, exemplifying a sophisticated exploration of sexuality that celebrates difference 'without classifying elements of difference as deviance … [enabling] Black women to continuously strive for radical Black female sexual subjectivities that are just right for them' (Stallings 2007: 10–11).

While certain types of mainstream music video demand 'triviality', echoing their 'pop song' source material by leaning towards 'the ephemeral and disposable rather than the lasting or durable' (Austerlitz 2008: 2), Joseph's music art video captures FKA twigs both loathing and relishing the racist's suffering in *Video Girl,* blurring the Madonna/Whore complex's neat moral categorizations and, in turn, creating a complex audiovisual exploration of ethical values in relation to the overlaps between race and gender. Karen Vintges observes that FKA Twigs 'speaks in a voice that is outspokenly anti-racist and implicitly feminist' (Vintges 2017: 161), thus the lyrical content of *Video Girl* attempts to convey how the performer is a far more complicated figure than simply 'that girl from the video' in the eyes of ill-informed industry commentators or racist 'Robsessed' fans. Miles White argues that the body gestures in hip-hop culture subvert '[traditional] Victorian models of proper decorum' on which idealized Western codes of social behaviours and gestures are based, thus the act of crotch-grabbing 'emphasises the lower bodily stratum that Victorianism denies … telegraphs defiance to a race-based order in which black masculinity has historically been contained and emasculated' (White 2011: 41), thereby affirming Vintges's argument that FKA Twigs refuses 'to conform to standard norms of heterosexual beauty' by the manner in which she merges masculine and feminine attributes into her artworks and performances (ibid.).

While FKA twigs rejects compartmentalization of her work within the parameters of R&B music on the grounds that her song possesses underexplored hymnal qualities, the fleeting instance of this particular dance move in *Video Girl* celebrates the prisoner's death with overt machismo and, at the same time, challenges strict parameters of Victorian propriety by which one might be tempted to frame the work and indeed her sexuality in light of her publicized rejection of R&B's performative codes and acceptance of traditional choral influences. Although one cannot entirely misposition Joseph's *Video Girl* video within the context of hip-hop music videos as a result of the momentary crotch-grabbing gesture, the inclusion of this specific movement illustrates that Joseph and FKA twigs openly draw from a range of cultural sources in their art, unrestrained by external expectations and, in turn, echoing critical debates which concern Afrodiasporic arts in the West.

At the dawn of the Harlem Renaissance, W. E. B Du Bois delivered a paper at the 1926 Conference of the National Association for the Advancement of Coloured People, arguing for the need to incorporate political elements into art that supported Black cultures on the basis that 'all art is propaganda and ever must be, despite the wailing of the purists' (Du Bois 1926: 296). In turn, Alain Locke responded in 1928 with an essay entitled *Art or Propaganda?*, rejecting overdetermined theorizations of art so that black artists could retain the choice between 'group expression' and 'free individualistic expression' and, in turn, freely pursue 'spiritual growth' or 'regeneration of spirit' based on one's own desires and instincts, unshackled by pre-established criteria shaped by other artists and voices (Locke 1928: 1). Similar debates concerning the necessity for propagandistic elements in Black artistry were replayed in America during the 1960s. As the Black Arts Movement emerged alongside the Civil Rights Movement, groups of writers and intellectuals whose understanding that their art 'must reflect and support the Black Revolution' were predicated on the Duboisian position that 'any art that does not discuss and contribute to the revolution is invalid' (Karenga [1968] (1972): 31). In the late 1980s, African-American arts started to openly enter and transform the American cultural mainstream as a new generation of artists grew up during and were encouraged by the societal developments and increased personal freedoms of the post-Civil Rights Movement climate. In response to these systemic shifts, Trey Ellis's article *The New Black Aesthetic* calls for a Lockean understanding of Afrocentric art that 'shamelessly borrows and reassembles across both race and class lines', thereby encapsulating 'much more than just Africa and jazz' for contemporary black artists (Ellis 1989: 234).

While Ellis's arguments capture a welcome sense of liberation in inviting African-Americans to freely construct identity from all available resources black, white and beyond, his articulation of the privileges that certain African-Americans are afforded in terms of interacting with and accessing particular cultural forms inadvertently neglects the various class divisions that exist within African-American communities. Ellis's 'New Black Aesthetic' notion thus ignores how artists positioned closer to the wealthy echelons of American society (or, in FKA twigs's case, the British elite at her private school in Britain's Gloucestershire region) benefit from neoliberalism's uneven economic framework in a manner that those with less capital – or fewer opportunities – simply cannot. Many specifications unique to different class sections of African-American society are essentially conjured out of sight by Ellis's theory, and Mark Anthony Neal bemoans Ellis's failure 'to mention the ways that hip-hop artists, for instance, also borrow across race and class, despite some of them not being second-generation new black middle class' (Neal 2001: 112). However, in marking out the manner in which the black middle classes may openly embrace all manner of cultural sources through the complex operation of forming and shaping one's own identity, Joseph and FKA twigs's exploration of the singer's Black-British self in *Video Girl* echoes certain aspects of Ellis's thought processes – *despite* the Americentric and class-based position of his 'New Black Aesthetic' theory.

As a privately educated individual born in an economically stable Western nation, FKA twigs is privileged in having access to certain influences, the choice to openly accept or reject African and Western sources within her artwork. Similarly, Joseph is the son of prominent arts educator Dr. Faith Childs-Davis and sports and entertainment lawyer Keven Joseph Davis, thereby locating the filmmaker's family within the upper echelons of American society in a manner echoing the position of Miles Davis, whose father Miles Dewey Davis Jr was an affluent dentist and landowner before his son became a prominent musician (Monson 1995; Tomlinson 2002).

While the privileges of their societal positions play a large role in shaping their respective outputs, one may therefore argue that Joseph and FKA twigs fall into a specific category of contemporary artists:

> … for whom black consciousness and artistic freedom are not mutually exclusive but complementary, for whom 'black culture' signifies a multicultural tradition of expressive practices; … [who] feel secure enough about black culture to claim art produced by nonblack as part of their inheritance.
>
> (Tate 1992: 207)

Although Kadiatu Kanneh reminds us that the absence of Africa may 'represent a homelessness and restlessness out of which new identifications are formed' (Kanneh 1998: 123), FKA twigs's blending of traditional choral sounds and modern dance moves in a sensualized, provocative manner throughout the video's critique of racist behaviour captures the work of an interdisciplinary artist who adopts cultural forms as she sees fit, unrestricted by the need to express herself in any particular predetermined manner. After all, as Alessandra Raengo from the *liquid blackness* research group reminds us: 'liquidity is almost *de rigueur* among multi-media and post-disciplinary artists from the post-black generation' (Raengo 2023).

In turn, Joseph's collaborations with artists such as Ishmael Butler and Tendai Maraire from Shabazz Palaces (for whom African influences form vital sources of inspiration) *as well as* a performer in the vein of FKA twigs (who explores complex issues surrounding race and feminism without necessitating specific references to Africa) likewise illustrate an approach to filmmaking unencumbered by the weight of expectation and responsibility tied to preconceived and rigid notions of B/blackness. While arguing that his artistic work is 'exclusively interested' in examining the experiences of black people, Joseph's audiovisual explorations of Blackness and African diasporas throughout his oeuvre capture these lives oscillating and changing *without* shying away from instances where Africa does not feature prominently (Joseph 2017). *Video Girl* thus exemplifies the ways in which two creators 'no longer need to deny or suppress any part of [their] complicated and sometimes contradictory cultural baggage to please either white people or black' (Ellis 1989: 235). Harnessing her impressive falsetto range while staring directly into the camera, FKA twigs emphatically reminds legions of Robsessed fans alongside the trapped Aryan Brotherhood member beneath her: 'Got something to say? I don't want to hear about it.'

5.3 Digital spirits and platform limits: between Sampha's Morden and Freetown in *Process* (2017)

In 2017 Joseph directed *Process*, a short film about first-generation British-Sierra Leonean musical artist Sampha Sisay. The musician, who performs under the mononym Sampha, grew up in South London's Morden area after his parents relocated from Freetown. A 'love-letter' to his formative years when his mother was still alive (Bryant 2017), *Process* captures captivating footage of Freetown and Morden's diverse residents and features, juxtaposing the primary cultural spheres which shaped Sampha's upbringing in order to articulate the musician's Afrodiasporic experiences, embracing the pain of his mother's passing while offering a speculative, solemnly hopeful vision of a future that channels the guidance of her spiritual presence. The 37-minute project features songs from Sampha's debut album in the same way that *The Model* utilizes music from collaborators Seu Jorge and Almaz, or *Until the Quiet Comes* adopts a range of songs written by Flying Lotus. James Tobias asserts the project is at once a music film *and* an essay film 'in conversation with the music-video form', thereby indicating the multi-layered nature of the project's formal boundaries (Tobias 2020: 157). Although the project was screened 'as an installation at interior and exterior locations in Brooklyn and London' (Cook-Wilson 2017),[4] *Process* was otherwise exclusively available to internet users with a paid digital subscription to Apple Music when it was first released.

While the rapid expansion of technologies permits innumerable possibilities for global communication in our contemporary digital epoch, Gilroy laments the 'deskilling, dehumanising' machinic developments by which black artists capture sound and images in digital formats (Gilroy 1999: 267). In the same way that André Bazin identifies painting as 'an *ersatz* to the processes of reproduction' (his emphasis) (Bazin 1960: 8), phenomenological quandaries arise during processes of digitally capturing moving images and sounds. Since file sizes, pixel numbers, editing software and image-capturing equipment may inscribe a particular meaning in the same way that types of materials or styles of brushwork imbue paintings with a certain code or expression, William J. Mitchell suggests that digital image files 'are ephemeral, can be copied and transmitted virtually instantly and cannot be examined (as photographic negatives can) for physical evidence of tampering' (Mitchell 1992: 51), thereby alluding to the dilemma of postmodern meaninglessness wherein sounds and images captured through digital technologies become unanchored from reality, losing their abilities to generate signs and significations (Metz and Benson 2000).

Although anxieties of authenticity may stem from questions surrounding artistic (re)production and the ontological tensions that emerge with sound and image digitization, Umberto Eco reminds us that 'absolute originality' is in fact a fairly unusual construct because, after all, 'much art has been and is repetitive' (Eco 2005: 203). While it is important to respect the ethical values of artists who carefully negotiate 'models of a real without origin or reality' in an effort to combat an ontological void of meaninglessness and endless fictionalization (Baudrillard 1988: 166), cultural commentators must not completely reject the ways in which contemporary artists such as Joseph do in fact choose to embrace the effects of digitalization within their art, openly adopting modern technologies as means of charging their works with a range of

---

[4] *Process* was showcased as a wallscape projection at Shoreditch High Street Station and Brick Lane in London and North 7th and Bedford in Brooklyn. It was also located in storefronts at London's 58 Great Eastern Street and 10 Dray Walk, and Brooklyn's 55 Wythe Avenue, 101 Bedford Avenue and 106 North 6th Street. There are no official records of the project being installed or screened in Sierra Leone or another African country.

significations. Carol Vernallis reminds us that sounds and images 'both now share an ontological ground of being code' through digitalization (Vernallis in Vernallis, Rogers and Perrott 2020: 7). Where Baudrillard fears the endless expansion of an ontological vacuum, then, one may counter-argue that the continuous (re)generation of new forms of value permitted by the digital turn thus allows artists to adapt to social and technological changes as they happen, capturing and communicating multitudinous hypothetical permutations of sociality which, in turn, may subvert pre-established frameworks for modernity.

As a project exclusively available for digital streaming, *Process* captures both the ontological (and more practical) tensions that emerge when an artwork becomes digitized, complicating ways in which one processes and consumes a media form. Apple Music boasts software fully integrated into Apple's IOS operating system, and the streaming service is currently the globe's second most popular – behind Spotify – as a result of the iPhone's ubiquity. 'Apple Exclusives' therefore represent the streaming service's most brazen attempt to challenge Spotify's dominance since restricted accesses to high-end releases rely on the Exclusive Value Principle to generate 'psychic needs rather than pure utility fulfilment', attracting a market of music fans that Spotify does not prioritize (Groth 1994: 8). As well as promoting the content of a music album, Tobias suggests that the launch of *Process* with Sampha and Joseph was 'part of a strategy by Apple on its entry into the streaming platform market to compete with more established platforms like Spotify' (Tobias 2020: 161).

Joseph has constructed a range of audiovisual advertisements in an era where it is very popular among large businesses to employ Black-British artists as means of popularizing their brand. In 2018, Nike announced a five-year commitment to supporting young Londoners, entitling their venture *The London Takeover*. The sportswear conglomerate launched their campaign with the *Nothing Beats a Londoner* commercial, a collaboration with the Wieden+Kennedy advertising group that unites

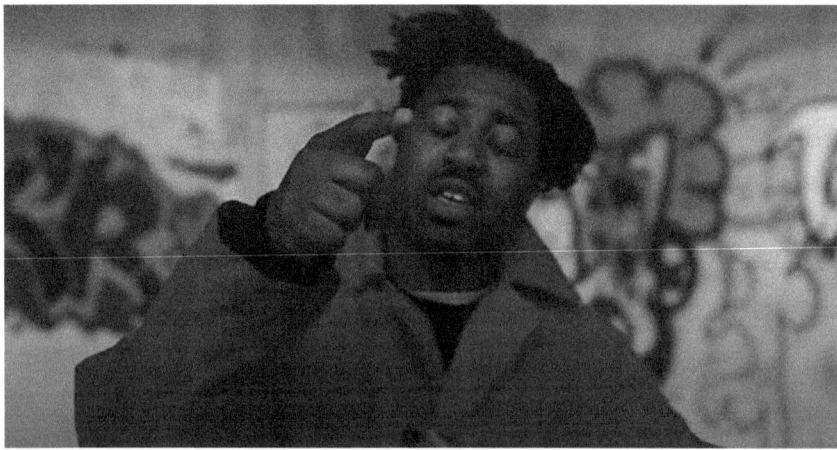

Figure 5.7 *Process* (2017), Kahlil Joseph and Sampha © Pulse Films.

cameo appearances from black musical artists such as Giggs, Jorja Smith and Big Shaq with the instrumental version of Skepta's song *Shutdown* (2015). Similarly, in the *Silence the Critics* campaign in 2019, advertising agency Mother coordinated a partnership between Swedish furniture company IKEA and an artist named Darren Dixon, the British grime musician who performs under the title MC D Double E as part of the Newham Generals group.

In some ways, the 'advertisement' marketing strategies of *Process, Nothing Beats a Londoner* and *Silence the Critics* might indicate a triumph of sorts for the artists themselves. The *Nothing Beats a Londoner* commercial raised Skepta's widely respected track to even higher levels of notoriety, and D Double E released an original music video entitled *Fresh N Clean* (2015) based on the musical material from his *Silence the Critics* project. Controversially, however, the *Nothing Beats a Londoner* advertisement excludes the rich and diverse groups of Asian citizens who form a large part of London city's communities, and *Silence the Critics* tailors and re-packages a fundamentally countercultural genre for the inoffensive tastes of white middle-class audiences, dislocating D Double E's music from its anti-institutional origins. Similarly, in 2020, Apple Music announced that part of its 'biggest geographical expansion' in a decade would involve the inclusion of fifty-two new territories, encompassing Sierra Leone (Dams 2020). However, at the time of *Process*'s original release, the project was unavailable to Sierra Leonean citizens as a result of Apple Music's business model. A range of local actors and dancers contributed to *Process* (including the Sierra Leonean National Dance Troupe), so for several years immediately preceding the conglomerate's territorial expansion these co-authors were unable to access their own work.

The crossroad of capital metaphor illustrates how Joseph's works are 'conflicting impulses within a particular system' (Adesokan 2011: 11) and – to some extent – Joseph embraces his works' position within the framework of neoliberal economics (as well as challenging systematic categorizations of film, music video and advertisement forms) in order to subvert systemic social configurations. In committing the cardinal sin of 'high art' theory by embracing the commodification of cultural forms and blurring the boundaries between commercial and 'serious' art (Shaviro 2017), one might therefore argue that Joseph offers a form of resistance to the contemporary world order, exploiting an economic framework rooted in colonial capitalism for financial and cultural (re)gain. While *Process* increases Apple Music's profit margins as well as earning Joseph and Sampha more money, it offers a countercultural representation of convergence between Freetown and Morden, between a British-Sierra Leonean musician and an American director, exemplifying the ways in which Black Atlantic audiovisual expression can generate flows and connections across fixed spatiotemporal borders.

While the crossroad of aesthetics generated by *Process*'s merging of Freetown and Morden captures the dynamism of the Black Atlantic, the issues surrounding the project's accessibility for African nationals and its relationships to the crossroads of capital and cultural traffic highlight how an audiovisual art form's complex webs of aesthetics, cultural traffic *and* capital must operate in a synchronous fashion in order to offer alternative ways of being that undermine modernity's Eurocentricity.

Otherwise, a screen text may balance the Black Atlantic's music and moving images in a transcultural, intercontinental fashion while, at the same time, sustaining the uneven flows of knowledge by harnessing an imbalanced framework for distribution, thereby perpetuating uneven states of development across the world *despite* purporting to challenge these worldwide discrepancies through its encoded messages and countercultural discourses. In lacking free accessibility and operating through geo-blocking strategies, the screen text undermines the countercultural messages that it articulates so eloquently.

As flows of *Process*'s cultural traffic compete and overlap, the screen text incorporates a variety of contesting media qualities, forming a dynamic artefact oscillating between the formal boundaries of music video, film and advertisements. *Process* acts as an additional component of the artists' respective franchises, a production for commercial consumption promoting Sampha's music to Joseph's fan base, Joseph's filmmaking to Sampha's audience. In *The Model*, for example, Marcello experiences an existential crisis because he neglects the spiritual aspects of his ancestral lineage and never reaches an epiphanic moment of conciliation between his African heritage and contemporary existence in the West, thus *The Model*'s unruly formal media boundaries reflect a fragmented soul who experiences – yet never effectively comprehends – the complexities of Afrodiasporic existence. Sampha, on the other hand, embraces both his British *and* Sierra Leonean roots, openly acknowledging and consolidating complicated connections between past and present in order to come to terms with his mother's passing, nurturing and encouraging his personal development as an artist as he processes her absence.

Although *Process* oscillates somewhere between an advertisement, a music video and a film in the same way that Sampha's complex diasporic experience fluctuates somewhere between Sierra Leone and Britain's disparate cultural spheres, the balance between *Process*'s film, music video and advertising properties thus echoes Sampha's acceptance of his double-consciousness's paradoxical affiliations, counteracting his existential anxiety by turning the solemnity of his mother's passing into a quietly powerful statement of hope and resilience. Moreover, the screen text draws from the 'creative energy' of Afrofuturism and time-distorting elements (Anderson 2016: 229) as means of processing the musician's past influences, thereby shaping Joseph's exploration of Sampha's diasporic experiences in a manner that is at once profoundly sombre yet tentatively hopeful, subtly marked by sadness yet determined to create a bright future by channelling Bintay's motherly spirit.

Process exemplifies the music video form's propensity to experiment with 'new modes of visualisation' through the latest forms of digital technology (Shaviro 2017: 8). One of *Process*'s key Morden sequences involves Sampha playing a small Rhodes piano on a cold dreary day, performing *Plastic 100°C* to no one in particular at a dilapidated, graffitied bandstand where 'a young teenage Sampha would sit years earlier and future dream the very moment that was being filmed' (Young Turks and Apple Music, published on Press Party website 2017). Sampha's hands and face subtly blur as he sings and plays, the 'realness' of Process's portrayal of Morden undermined by ghostly image distortion. Named the 'timewarp' effect on editing software *Adobe After*

Effects, the 'timewarp' displaces digital pixels on selected areas of the singer's body, creating the illusion of disfigurement and interdimensional travel. As Sampha dances in his seat, lyrics from 'So hot I've been melting out here' from *Plastic 100°C* mirror his physical mutations. Interdimensional travel is a key aspect of *Process* because Sampha and Joseph aim to create 'an omniverse where time and space lap over each other ... for it not to feel like it was set in one particular period' (Sampha 2017), thus *Process* uses the 'timewarp' effect to form an aesthetic which mirrors Sampha's fluid movement between social spheres as a member of Sierra Leone's diasporic community, channelling the spirit of his ancestors while empowered by familial love.

Bintay Sampha – Sampha's deceased mother, to whom *Process* is dedicated – is characterized as an interdimensional spirit emerging from a chrysalis, displaying time-travelling abilities in the same vein as her son. Joseph's representation of Sampha's mother as a time-travelling entity thus echoes British-Somali writer Warsan Shire's multidimensional portrayal of motherhood in the poem *I Have Three Hearts*.[5] 'Mother is a cocoon', writes Shire, metaphorizing her life's most powerful figure, a woman who has 'one foot in this world/one foot in the next'. While Joseph captures the dualistic essence of Sampha's double-consciousness by representing his ancestor as a dimension-traveller bestriding Freetown and Morden's metaphysical boundaries, the filmmaker's depiction of the musician's deceased mother emerging from a cocoon-like state also inverts the life cycle process, emphasizing that Bintay achieves an immortal existence beyond the grave as a source of love and inspiration in her son's heart and mind. A mother's body acts as a cocoon, housing and nurturing her offspring until he is ready to be born. However, by channelling Bintay's memory through his work, Sampha protects or 'cocoons' his mother's spirit, ensuring that her existence as a force of emotion driving his creative output overcomes her physical passing, transcends her material decomposition.

As still-moving-images mimic the liminal state of Bintay's spirit caught between noumenal and phenomenal realms during the song *Under*, Sampha croons: 'You're the ghost in my machine ...' above a complicated medley of synths and vocals, underscoring the unity between spirituality and machinery with a tenderness that is both vulnerable and powerful, pained by his mother's absence yet strong enough to unveil his suffering for all to see. Although Bintay's soul cannot realistically traverse space-time dimensions in an electronic machine, Joseph's metaphor counteracts the notion that postmodernity's technoculture is 'cold and soulless' (Lysloff and Gay 2003: 185) by ensuring that the legacy of Bintay's spirit continues to foster prosperity during Sampha's life, marrying the magic of Bintay's immortal, time-travelling soul with the fantastical possibilities of futuristic technologies.

Recalling Kodwo Eshun's 'alien discontinuum' as a framework through which to emphasise the transnational and intercontinental flows of *Process*'s cultural traffic across time and space and between machinic and organic forms, one may activate formal similarities between Joseph's project and various other forms of communication

---

[5] Shire's poetry is used throughout Joseph's 2016 *Lemonade* project with Beyoncé.

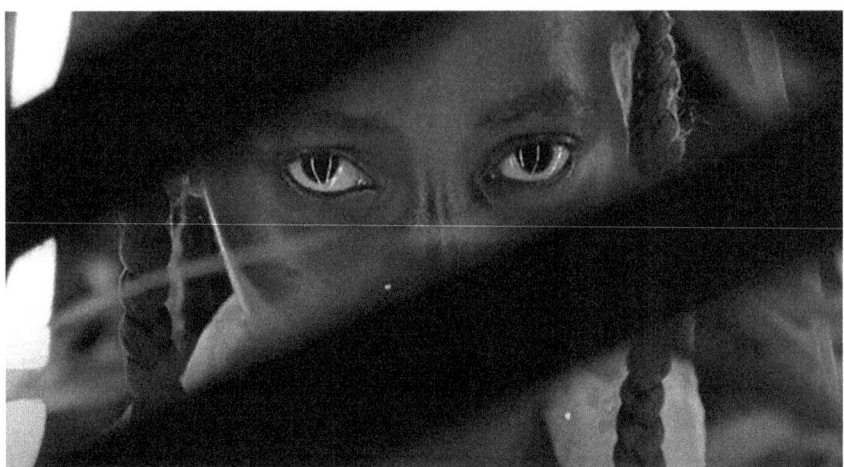

Figure 5.8 *Process* (2017), Kahlil Joseph and Sampha © Pulse Films.

that explore alternative ways of being human in our neoliberal framework and, in turn, distort more conventionalised or marketed senses of time (Eshun [1998] 1999; Nkiru and Julius 2020). Bintay's unusual mechanised cocoon also resists distinctive comparisons to any earthly cultural sphere or geographical setting, thereby forming a complex representation of Sampha's deceased mother that merges technological advancement with magical wonder, Afrofuturism's speculative musings with traditional African mysticism. Bintay – embodiment of Sampha's ancestral heritage – manifests between and beyond past, present and future representations of Sierra Leone and Morden, retaining her 'purity' in spite of these concurrent affiliations to disparate temporal realms and divergent social spheres, thereby emphasizing Sampha's conciliatory integration of British and Sierra Leonean cultures, his sagacious, wholesome understanding of double-consciousness and the tensions of its opposing passions.

Bintay's dimension-travelling capabilities are never questioned, yet the chrysalis which permits such movement between spacio-temporal spheres is partly mechanized, thus *Process*'s complicated amalgamation of formal categorizations reflects the complexity of Sampha's diasporic experience, straddling genre boundaries in the same way that Sampha's formative years are shaped by cultural influences from Sierra Leone and the UK simultaneously, neither sphere taking particular precedence. Using the lens of Afrofuturism to theorize how the metaphysical boundaries between Freetown and Morden, and life and death, are explored throughout *Process*, one can begin piecing together theories about how Sampha's mother disappears into a kaleidoscopic ether as she teleports through time in her mechanized chrysalis. After all, the logic-suspending technology of the time-travelling mechanized chrysalis, imbued with Bintay's freed and immortalized Sierra Leonean spirit, reflects 'the emergence of a black identity framework within emerging global technocultural assemblages' and the manner in which formations of Afrofuturism may grant awareness 'of the multitude and varied possibilities and probabilities within the universe' (Anderson and Jones 2016: vii).

Indeed, speculative representations of future societal formations and events play a pivotal role in nuancing Joseph's exploration of Sampha's diasporic experiences. Joseph's crossroads of cultural traffic refuse to be restricted by inflexible genre categorizations, rigid film theory frameworks and strict formal media configurations in the same way that Sampha refuses to be impeded by the tensions of his double-consciousness or even the limitations imposed by laws of spatiotemporal reality. The screen text solemnly celebrates Bintay's life as well as Sampha's British and Sierra Leonean roots, respectfully honouring the complicated, interconnected processes which shape past, present and future, the contesting flows of cultural traffic which continue to mould Sampha into a devoted, caring son shaped by Africa, Britain and indeed the world.

Akinwumi Adesokan argues that genre formations are 'predicated on the complex, intangible shuttling between the cultural and economic spheres' at the crossroads of capital (Adesokan 2011: 3). Despite the geographical unevenness of Apple Music's business model that for a short while prohibited Sierra Leonean citizens from viewing the projects that they helped to create, *Process*'s crossroads of capital, aesthetics and cultural traffic have in certain ways combined to generate a screen text that communicates the complexity of concurrent affiliations to divergent cultural spheres and, at the same time, allows such an encoded message to traverse physical borders in a manner akin to Afrodiasporic identity formations. Offering new ways of seeing and thinking as a source of inspiration within the neoliberal order, one might argue that *Process*'s content attempts to convert weakness into strength in response to 'an increasingly precarious and demanding world' characterized by globalization, commercial competition and interconnected networks (Srnicek and Williams 2016: 2). Indeed, Nick Srnicek and Alex Williams seek radical methods of overthrowing capitalism and lambast 'building bunkers to resist the encroachments of global neoliberalism' (ibid. 3) and Jen Harvie promulgates artistic practices that model 'alternative ways of being' grounded in the preservation of 'social collaboration and interdependence' (Harvie 2013: 193). Such principles are exemplified by the collaborative and interconnected aspects of *Process*, the ways in which its crossroads affect a range of stakeholders, and the manner in which its content merges depictions of Morden and Freetown to emphasize Sampha's experiences.

However, as Adesokan reminds us, tensions wrought by globalized neoliberalism are 'both contradictory and complementary' (Adesokan 2011: 178). Although *Process* offers alternative means of existence within the neoliberal order through its references to the countercultural possibilities of Black Atlantic music and moving images, accessibility is a major hurdle that precludes the screen text's ability to undermine Eurocentric modernity in *all* territories across the Atlantic, *despite* the conglomerate's recent expansion into new African territories.[6] Apple Music's paywall and its uneven expansion across Africa and indeed the globe undermine *Process*'s ability to present an

---

[6] In 2020, Apple Music expanded into: Algeria, Angola, Benin, Chad, Liberia, Madagascar, Malawi, Mali, Mauritania, Mozambique, Namibia, Republic of the Congo, Senegal, Seychelles, Sierra Leone, Tanzania, and Tunisia. The App Store, Apple Acade, Apple Podcasts and iCloud (as well as Apple Music) are now available in: Cameroon, Côte d'Ivoire, Democratic Republic of the Congo, Gabon, Libya, Morocco, Rwanda, and Zambia (Dams 2020).

alternative modernity in the most effective manner, emphasizing that inequalities will continue to manifest until all countries and continents are permitted free access to the same media networks.

The complex, contradictory qualities of Joseph's new media works are thus exacerbated by their statuses as cultural artefacts operating within the world-system's contemporaneous manifestation of neoliberal capitalism (Harvey 2007; Davies 2017). Philip E. Mirowski's blogpost *This Is Water (Or Is It Neoliberalism?)* (2016) draws from David Foster Wallace's essay *This Is Water: Some thoughts, delivered on a significant occasion, about living a compassionate life* (2009). Mirowski reworks Wallace's treatise for living a compassionate life in order to explain how the 'translucent outlines of a semi-coherent political movement all around [us].. nearly as invisible as water', go unnoticed in our daily lives, suggesting that members of Western society passively accept both the comforts and ramifications of free market liberalism by floating along wherever the current dictates, failing to engage with life under the conditions of our prevalent economic framework in sincere, meaningful ways (Mirowski 2016). While Mirowski contends that resistance to neoliberalism 'will not arise from within modern economics' (ibid.), other commentators champion forms of artistic practice which 'critically respond to the pressures of neoliberal capitalism' (Harvie 2013: 192) and thereby form conceptual spaces and conditions 'in which to assemble resistance against the neoliberal capitalist order' (Charnley in Sholette and Charnley 2017: 2).

Process offers in a part a critical alternative to the controversial world system by framing one's sense of identity beyond rigid national frameworks, thus Tobias goes as far as arguing that the project 'constitutes a contrapuntal island in the streams of national and transnational empire, downstream from global capital's technological rendering of the virtual as technical possibility' (Tobias 2020: 162). However, the earlier issues of accessibility surrounding *Process*'s release platform demonstrate that a thorough understanding of Joseph's oeuvre necessitates scrutiny of the European, American *and* African contexts in which his works are produced, circulated and consumed. In turn, such processes of examination emphasize how Black Atlantic music *and* moving images are unable to challenge the Western perspectives underpinning modernity if members of Europe, America *and* continental Africa are not included – and respected – as part of the same transcontinental conversations. For all the technical possibilities enacted and countercultural messages promulgated by the screen text, their potential to resist the dehumanizing effects of our global order will echo and reverberate into nothingness if they are only ever experienced – over and over again – in the same parts of the world.

6

The contemporary Audiovisual Atlantic

6.1 Intercontinental journeys and transmedia screen arts of the digital diasporas

Two of Joseph's most recent audiovisual works – *Fly Paper* (2017) and *BLKNWS* (2018 to Present) – have been promoted as media installations, with *BLKNWS* set to be transformed into a feature-length film (Greenberger 2022). However, at the time of writing this book, both projects are not legally available to view online on any platform. Joseph's shift towards situated exhibition art in recent years may in part relate to what he senses are the dwindling opportunities associated with traditional understandings of independent filmmaking. In an interview promoting the exhibition of *m.A.A.d.* in New York and Maastricht, he states:

> I don't know what's going on now in independent film. I think it's exciting because it seems like it has lost its path. It'll find its way, I know. If you look at the history of cinema, what we're experiencing happens every fifteen or thirty years. Attendance is at an all-time low; exhibitors and studios freak out; the movies look like cardboard cut-outs. I'm excited about the next wave, whatever it's going to be. The only thing that's ever moved art forward is a technological advance, like the shift from cutting film to nonlinear digital editing.
> (Joseph in conversation with Dallas 2017: 148)

Joseph here articulates how the ebbs and flows of independent cinema are cyclical aspects of an industry predicated on technological advancement, thereby demonstrating how the crossroads of capital, cultural traffic and aesthetics are linked by a screen text's dependence on machinic innovations (Vernallis 2023). At the same time, however, such periods of unproductivity and stagnation are connected to an absence of technological advancements as much as an absence of 'breakthrough' moments for practitioners using existent sound-image technologies. Independent filmmakers are thus inextricably tied to the emergence of new digital technologies *as well as* the manner in which they adopt and adapt existent technologies that are already accessible.

Although the independent filmmaking scene has for Joseph partially 'lost its path', in many ways certain forms of Afrodiasporic audiovisual culture across a range of mediums – including yet also extending beyond the film scene – have thrived in recent years. Texan filmmaker Terence Nance's debut project is a semi-animated film titled *An Oversimplification of Her Beauty* (2012) that blurs boundaries between fiction and reality. The film is partially based on Nance's own experiences, following an extravagantly idealistic artist who unsuccessfully pines for the affections of the film's muse, his friend Namik Minter, with whom Nance shares a complicated yet close relationship. The self-referential meta-romance premiered at the Sundance Film Festival in 2012 and adopts a complex range of futuristic soundscapes created by Flying Lotus – as well as an articulate and acerbic directorial voiceover reminiscent of the droll observations in Greave's meta-documentary *Symbiopsychotaxiplasm: Take One* – thereby sonically marrying past and present forms of Black Atlantic cultural expression.

Situated somewhere between the independent film and music video economies, Janelle Monáe published a feature-length visual album, or 'Emotion Picture', on YouTube in April 2018. Each track from Monáe's music album *Dirty Computer* is partnered with a music video, and each music video is connected by the narrative of Monáe's android alter ego, Jane 57821, attempting to escape the imprisonment of a homophobic future society. Heralded as a 'milestone ... [celebrating] queerness, female power, and self-worth' (O'Connor 2018) and an emphatic statement of support for 'those who don't fit in the Trump-era matrix' (Empire 2018), the album moved 51,000 album-equivalent units in its first week (Caulfield 2018).

At the heart of the mainstream music video landscape, in May 2018 actor-comedian Donald Glover – who produces music under stage-name Childish Gambino – published a music video on YouTube accompanying his single *This Is America*. Morbid sensations of discomfort, engendered by the song's sinister marriage of pulsating trap music and soulful choral singing, are accentuated by the video's unsettlingly brazen depictions of a daylight shooting alongside school children energetically recreating the South African Gwara Gwara dance. Accumulating 12.9 million views in 24 hours, the online response

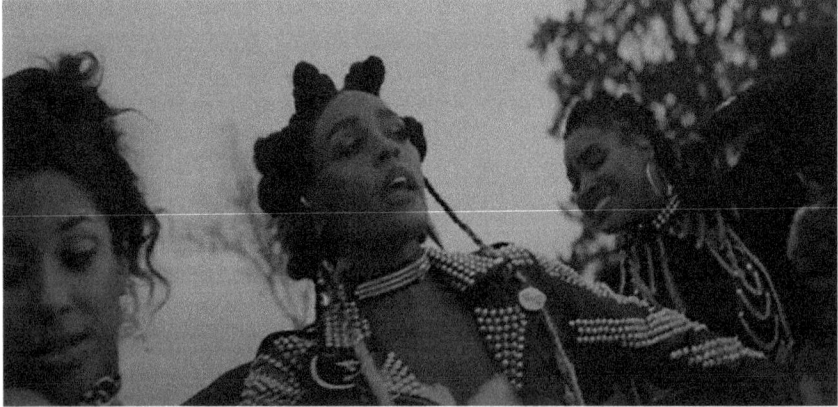

Figure 6.1 *Crazy Classic Life* (2018), Alan Ferguson and Janelle Monae © Wondaland.

to Glover's video – ranging from longform think-pieces and reaction clips to short, sharp 'tweets' and parody videos – reflects 'a gushing river of well-deserved praise' (Kornhaber 2018) and was described by American media conglomerate National Public Radio as bringing a 'Black Renaissance' to popular variety show *Saturday Night Live* (Carmichael 2018).

Beyond Nance's critically acclaimed debut, Monáe's 'milestone' visual album and Glover's wildly popular music video exemplify the commercial and critical success with which Afrodiasopric artists are embracing new media (Hassler-Forest 2022). Despite what Joseph perceives as a lull in creativity for Black independent film, a smorgasbord of commentators echo the NPR's praise by recognizing the flowering of a 'Black Renaissance' in terms of new media production across various forms of screen-based communication (Peas 2017; Silva 2017; Eferighe 2018; Wicker 2018). Indeed, Kenya Barris's television series *Black-ish* (2014 to Present), Barry Jenkins's *Moonlight* (2016), Donald Glover's series *Atlanta* (2016–Present), Justin Simien's Netflix series *Dear White People* (2017 to Present) and Jordan Peele's *Get Out* (2017) have received a variety of national accolades, and Ryan Coogler's *Black Panther* (2018), as well as winning a BET award, was the second highest grossing film of 2018.

Recent exponents of independent Afrodiasporic audiovisual art such as Baloji and Jenn Nkiru together represent with Joseph members of the Black Atlantic's contemporary digital diaspora, combining music and moving images in a subversive and experimental manner (Vernallis, Rogers and Perrott 2020; Vernallis, Rogers, Leal and Kara 2021) while, at the same time, engaging with 'inter-generational conversations among contemporary black filmmakers, visual and sound artists who carry out what Toni Morrison described as the "liquidity" of the black arts, i.e., practicing one artform *in terms of* another' (Raengo 2023).[1] The rapper – whose full name is Baloji Tshiani – was born in Lubumbashi, Congo-Léopoldville (now Democratic Republic of the Congo) to a Congolese mother and Belgian father. Gravitating towards projects that oscillate at the boundaries between media forms, he reasons he was forced to make his own music videos: 'Nobody really wanted to shoot my films' (Baloji cited by Reeves 2020). *Peau de Chagrin/Bleu de Nuit* (2018) explores Congolese Batwa wedding traditions and is characterized as 'a musical trip' as a result of its merging of music and moving images (Reeves 2020). His short fiction film *Kaniama Show* (2019) is a satirical portrayal of African propaganda television and 'the collusion of State and media powers', echoing the American music-dance show *Soul Train* (1971–2006) through 'a set stuck in the 70s that underscores an unwillingness to change' (Baloji in conversation with Tambini 2019). *Never Look at the Sun* (2019) – made in partnership with Joseph's frequent collaborators NOWNESS – examines the phenomenon of 'skin bleaching' as people with dark skin attempt to emulate Eurocentric beauty standards, adopting a poem written by architectural designer Thandi Loewenson (that is narrated by the decolonial

---

[1] Nance has also directed the avant-garde television show *Random Acts of Flyness* (2018–Present) which airs on HBO and is currently developing an installation under the working title *Day*, mimicking the manner in which Joseph between media forms.

thinker and race relations speaker Dorrie Wilson) as sounds and music designed by Baloji play in the background.

Baloji's most famous project, *Zombies* (2019), features songs *Spotlight, Glossine (Zombie)* and *Ciel d'encre* from *137 Avenue Kaniama* and offers a critique of the digital cultures that permeate throughout Africa and the rest of the world, exploring 'our fears of missing out on news, our visceral need to share events, our inability to choose where we want to be because we're in several places at once – but ultimately nowhere' (Baloji in conversation with Pellerin 2019). *Zombies* was selected as Short of the Year by MUBI and won Best Styling at the UK Movie Video Awards. After the project 'created a furore' at various short film festivals and received a range of awards (including the Prinzipal Prize at the Oberhausen International and selection for the London Film Festival), the artist was signed by the British production company Academy Films, further cementing his esteemed statuses as both a musician *and* filmmaker. Commentators noted that 'Baloji doesn't have the kind of perspective on the world that UK-based production companies like Academy Films are used to' (Von Trapp cited by Reeves 2020) yet the company's Head of Music Maurizio Von Trapp emphasizes the company's excitement 'to add Baloji's voice to our roster' because the filmmaker 'makes films for the future, he asks questions that aren't being posed, and he does it with dexterity and poetry' (Von Trapp 2020). The popularity of his interdisciplinary art has also resulted

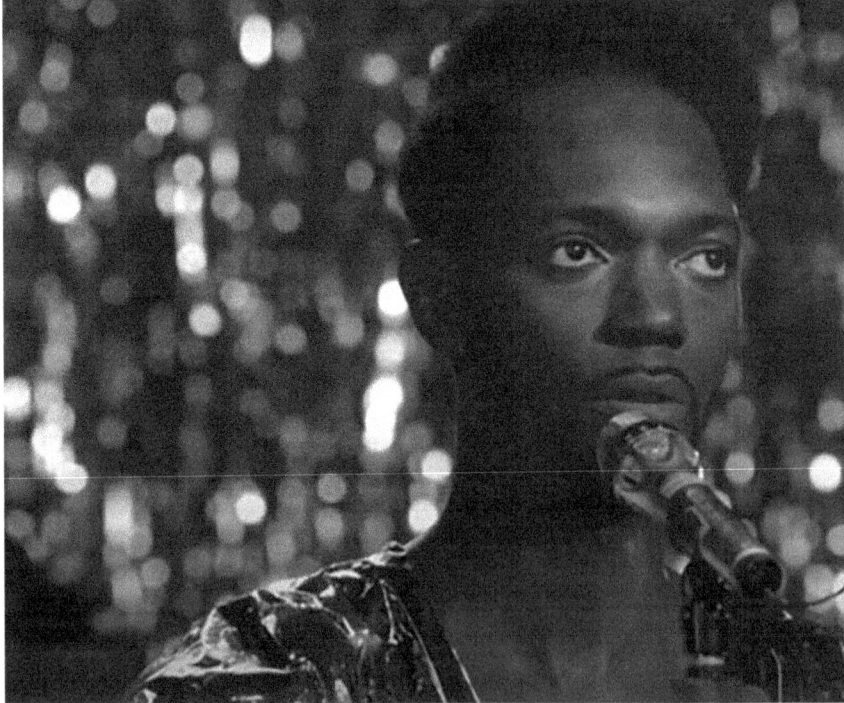

Figure 6.2 *Kaniama Show* (2019), Baloji © Africalia.

in Baloji earning the 2019 Creative of the Year award with the NOWNESS group, positioning the artist alongside Joseph and Nkiru as one of the Black Atlantic's most reputable practitioners operating at the intersections of music and moving images.

The work of award-winning artist Jenn Nkiru likewise echoes Joseph and Baloji's merging of music and moving images across short films, music videos and installations to articulate countercultural forms of Afrodiasporic experiences, frequently focusing on 'music' as a key topic for exploration. Born in London's Peckham area to Ghanaian parents, Nkiru recalls observing during her formative years how the prolific music video director, filmmaker, producer and screenwriter Hype Williams had started 'making videos like [he was] making cinema', offering inspiration for her own experimentations with music and moving images that would likewise subvert strict formal boundaries (Nkiru in conversation with Little 2019). Nkiru studied film at Howard University alongside *Sankofa* director Haile Gerima, describing him as 'the salt' because he offers support and encouragement as 'a source of so much knowledge' yet also recognizing that she has not had 'a career mentor per se' and predominantly 'had to find my own way, following and trusting my intuition and internal compass' (Nkiru in conversation with Hanan 2018).

'Cosmic archaeology' is a concept that Nkiru adopts to describe 'a combination of reclamation and creation' in her personal approach to filmmaking that extends past fixed Western notions of time, moving beyond rigid spatiotemporal boundaries as means of connecting African diasporas in the past, present and future (Nkiru cited by Zonneveld 2020). Citing the influence of her Nigerian grandmother who 'believes I am her mother … [and] calls me Mama' (Nkiru in conversation with Little 2019), the subversion of Western notions of time and space through the cosmic archaeology approach thus stems from Nkiru's understanding of Afrodiasporic experiences and human memory as 'some sort of cosmic energy' connected to the shifting, fluctuating identities of people (from earth and beyond, past, present and future) 'who are forced to migrate, who are made to feel they don't belong' (Nkiru in conversation with Little 2019) which, in turn, attempts 'to bridge the academy, pop culture and art' through audiovisual forms of expression (Nkiru in conversation with Little 2019).

Nkiru's self-explorative *Black Star: Rebirth Is Necessary* (2017) remediates archival footage of pioneering Afrofuturist musician Sun Ra and the revolutionary Black Panther Party, exploring the complexity of Afrodiasporic forms of communication through an amalgamation of past, present and future depictions of black artists and their works. Dizzying montages of diverse visual material are united by frenetic music samples and the voices of Alice Coltrane, Kathleen Cleaver, James Baldwin, Fred Moten, Sun Ra and Steve Reich, detailing Afrodiasporic existences in South Africa, her home city London and many other global destinations. Made in partnership with art magazine Frieze and fashion label Gucci, her media installation piece and short film hybridization *Black to Techno* (2019) delves into techno music's origins in Detroit, exploring how black musicians such as Juan Atkins, Kevin Saunderson and Derrick May shape the works of contemporaries such as James Stinson, Gerald Donald, Jeff Mills and Mike Banks, thereby facilitating the emergence of rave music as well as assisting the establishment of pioneering clubs in the vein of Berlin's Berghain.

Alessandra Raengo and Lauren McLeod Cramer liken Jafa's 'Black Visual Intonations' theory to Nkiru's 'cosmic archaeology' concept because both ideas demonstrate 'a commitment to "Black study" visualized through images that reverberate with the vibrational intensity of the music that inspires them' (Raengo and Cramer 2020: 141). In this case, 'Black study' is drawn from Stefano Harney and Fred Moten's work in *The Undercommons: Fugitive Planning and Black Study* (2013), representing an alternative form of sociality, or resistant way of 'thinking with others' (Halberstam in Harney and Moten 2013: 11), that separates itself from the types of sociality or approaches to thinking that are required – or demanded – within certain institutional contexts, especially as countercultural traditions of critical thought shift and interact across continents (Brar and Sharma 2019). The respective cosmic archaeology and Black Visual Intonation theories – which, in turn, echo the senses of bounded time that the filmmaker aims to evoke through music and moving image amalgamations – therefore allow Nkiru and Jafa to experiment with audiovisual formats unencumbered by systemic expectations while, at the same time, demonstrating a commitment to Afrodiasporic histories and their relationships to the present.

The *liquid blackness* research group at Georgia State University coin the term 'music art video' to recognize 'the situatedness of this type of work, located at the fluid intersection of art installation and experimental film' (Gunn 2020: 163); thus one may draw comparisons between the fluidity of Nkiru's work and the oscillatory nature of Joseph's art as they shift and fluctuate across the Audiovisual Atlantic. As black transmedia artists moving across the rigid boundaries of independent filmmaker, music video director *and* installation artist, the flexible structural parameters of Joseph and Nkiru's works allow the directors to negotiate online platforms *and* physical spaces offline, producing a wide-ranging interdisciplinary, transnational output that fits comfortably in both gallery spaces *and* open-access video-sharing platforms, emphasizing the liberation and freedom imbedded in certain forms of Black Atlantic cultural expression alongside the unbounded senses of time that these modes of communication engender.

Having outlined Joseph's position within the Audiovisual Atlantic's contemporary cultural landscape, I discuss two of his most recent media projects: *Fly Paper* (2017) and *BLKNWS* (2018–Present). I draw from my own experiences of *Fly Paper* at 180 The Strand and footage of *BLKNWS* supplied by my Los Angeles-based contact Nina Sen, as well as her experiences of the installation at the Union Store, exploring how the situatedness or location of a media work affects its encoded (counter)cultural discourses, the (im)balances of its overlapping crossroads.

6.2 (Mis)Remembering Harlem's sounds and spaces: experiences of *Fly Paper* (2017) at 180 The Strand

Joseph's video installation *Fly Paper* premiered at New York's New Museum in 2017 and has been exhibited at 180 The Strand, The Store X Berlin and the Museum of

Contemporary Art. The artwork is in part influenced by the depictions of Harlem's jazz musicians and local black communities in a collaborative book project titled *The Sweet Flypaper of Life* (1984). The book contains a series of connected photographs captured by Roy DeCarava and is accompanied by a short story written by Langston Hughes. While *The Sweet Flypaper of Life* features a variety of intimate images exploring the richness of black people's experiences and 'an intimate rendering of family life' in the neighbourhood of Harlem during the 1940s and 1950s (Godfrey and Whitley 2017: 40), Joseph's blending of nostalgic found footage, contemporary representations of the area and an evocative Afrocentric soundscape frames Harlem 'as musical, *and* as historically black', developing DeCarava and Hughes's lively visual and literary depictions of the area through combinations of music and moving images (my emphasis) (Tobias 2020: 159).

Fly Paper's presence in London was organized and funded by four key collaborators: The Store X, The Vinyl Factory, the New Museum and 180 The Strand. The Store X and The Vinyl Factory often collaborate as one organization under the name The Store X Vinyl Factory. While The Store X originated as a creative company in Berlin offering platforms and networks to develop new ideas and facilitate cultural exchanges across fashion, art and design, The Vinyl Factory specializes in recording music and releasing limited edition materials through their pressing plant.

The symbiotic relationship between The Store X and The Vinyl Factory when organizing exhibitions thus draws from their respective specialisms in order to enhance the experiences of their patrons once an exhibition is completed. After publicizing Joseph's work to The Store X's audiences in London through exhibitions at large venues such as 180 The Strand and the Lisson Gallery, the soundtrack for *Fly Paper* was available to purchase as a limited edition vinyl record released under The Vinyl Factory's imprint. This move in turn lifted certain elements of the installation experience from the confinements of the gallery space while, at the same time, offering Joseph, Blades, The Store X and The Vinyl Factory new opportunities to generate financial profits from the artwork.

Strange Days: Memories of the Future is the name of the free London exhibition set up by The Store X in which *Fly Paper* featured from 2 October to 9 December 2018. The exhibition took place at 180 The Strand, a large arts venue situated near the Thames River in England's capital, and I was able to attend the gallery on two separate occasions because I live and work in the city. 180 The Strand's large exhibition space is situated near Temple Tube Station, opposite the Australian High Commission building in the heart of London's Strand area. The building hosts operations and events for a variety of companies (including: Dazed Media Group, IMG, Charcoal Blue, The Spaces and Fact Magazine) and offers a spacious, multilevel venue for gallery operators. While *Fly Paper* was originally shown at the New Museum's Ground Floor space of their Southern Galleries as part of the exhibition *Kahlil Joseph: Shadow Play* (27 September 2017 to 7 January 2018), the installation's European debut took place at the Store X Berlin before travelling to the UK and subsequently featuring within 180 The Strand's Brutalist building.

The architectural design of the gallery's labyrinthine spaces plays a pivotal role in shaping the ways in which *Fly Paper*'s audial and visual properties interact in *Strange*

Days: Memories of the Future's installations. The New Museum's director Massimiliano Gioni, who co-organized *Fly Paper*'s screening at 180 The Strand, elaborates:

> The Store X always made me think of one of David Cronenberg's first films, *Stereo* (1969), which is set in a Brutalist building in Toronto and imagines a future in which the Canadian Academy for Erotic Inquiry performs brain surgery on a group of volunteers whose power of speech is removed to enhance their telepathic abilities. It is a science fiction movie in which there is no sense of time because all the action is set inside, and the architecture turns into a mirror image of the minds of the patients and of the bizarre theories of the doctor. The movie, just like the architecture of The Store X itself, is a kind of Piranesian fantasy, in which Roman ruins have been substituted by industrial archaeology and 1960s architecture. For this show we [were] using the ground floor of the building and two subterranean levels that seemed particularly appropriate to the crepuscular atmospheres of some of the works in the exhibition. We tried to treat the space as a kind of continuous subjective view, like in those video games where you walk into a tunnel and space seems to develop as you advance: the spaces feel somewhat basic, but they are clean and simple like a digital rendering. You can only walk forward as though the spaces keep growing and repeating themselves.
>
> (Gioni, in conversation with Spice 2018)

In contrast with the spatial design of *Strange Days: Memories of the Future*, Joseph's installation *m.A.A.d.* (2014) had previously featured in 180 The Strand as part of The Store X Vinyl Factory's *The Infinite Mix* exhibition, situated within a series of multimedia works that were presented as distinguishable entities or, in Giono's words, 'closed capsule[s]' that offered little interaction. The art director thus argues that the works featured in *Strange Days: Memories of the Future* differ from *The Infinite Mix* series because they are united by the ways forms of music tie the installations 'like a thread, so you keep progressing in the spaces' (Gioni, in conversation with McLean 2018). The positioning of certain installations within *Strange Days: Memories of the Future* thus creates a sonic 'bleeding' effect whereby the sounds of one artwork are subtly audible while in the immediate vicinity of another installation. However, Joseph's *Fly Paper* stands out in relation to many of the gallery's artworks because the installation is projected onto a screen in a large room of its own, thus the soundproof doors block out significant levels of audio pollution *unless* they are left open at the precise moment when a particularly loud sound resonates from an external source. During both of my experiences of the exhibition at 180 The Strand, attendees passing in and out of the exhibition space provided background noises by opening and closing the doors, drawing attention to *Fly Paper*'s status as an installed component within the broader context of The Store X Vinyl Factory's *Strange Days: Memories of the Future* exhibition rather than maintaining an illusion that the installation was separated from the exhibition's contents.

Joseph argues in 2018 that *Fly Paper*'s 'soundscape is the best expression yet of my explorations into the physicality of sound' (Joseph, cited by Helfet 2018). The project's ghostly soundscape is mixed by music composer, producer and editor James William Blades. Blades is a sound artist who has worked with a range of musicians and filmmakers including Beyoncé, Skepta, Jenn Nkiru and the New York-based directorial group rubber band, as well as partnering with large businesses and corporations such as Google, Harrods, H&M, Mercedes, Nike and Toyota.[2] He and Joseph worked together to shape the sound design for Sampha Sisay's *Process* (2017) and Alice Smith's *Black Mary* (2017), and samples of the latter's music – most notably extracts from her 2015 cover of Nina Simone's *I Put a Spell on You* (1965) – are detectable in the vinyl edition's opening track (that shares the same name as Simone's song) as well the soundtrack's fifth and sixth tracks respectively entitled *Had a Love* and *Moods*.

The sonic aspects of *Fly Paper* play an integral part in the installation's explorations of memory because one 'remembers' Joseph's previous collaborations through audial allusions to these works throughout Blades's meticulously constructed soundscape. The installation's score features samples and original music provided by Alice Smith, Flying Lotus, Kelan Phil Cohran, Kelsey Lu and Thundercat, thereby grounding the sonic aspects of *Fly Paper* within specifically Afrodiasporic cultural contexts in the same way as the artwork's visual content. While DeCarava's photographic representations of Harlem's black citizens are reimagined in *Fly Paper* through a variety of visual forms – including found footage, staged sequences and intimate home videos of Joseph's family – these diverse media forms are united into a cohesive audiovisual whole through the samples and unusual noises which characterize Blades's soundscape. The featured artworks in the *Strange Days: Memories of the Future* exhibition are in turn united thematically by explorations of memory, illustrating how the symbiotic relationships between sight and sound in *Fly Paper* play important roles in terms of generating new meanings *and* representing the 'memory' theme within gallery space that the artwork inhabits.

In the same way that memories of Afrodiasporic music edited through digital software shape the discursive meanings of Joseph and Blades's collaboration, memories of black peoples' experience are a key feature of the short story element of *The Sweet Flypaper of Life* because the collection's photographs are re-contextualized by recollections from a key character, the sick grandmother Sister Mary Bradley (and, in turn, Hughes's fictional narrative charges DeCarava's shots with certain values relating to his literary characters). Written from Sister Mary's perspective, the story is framed by the narrator's rejection of a telegram from the Lord God. God's messenger informs Sister Mary that it is time for her to join the angels in heaven, yet the protagonist declares: 'I'm so tangled up in living, I ain't got time to die' (Hughes and DeCarava [1955] 2018: 3). She then proceeds to list all the characters in her life whose daily activities and affairs compel the narrator to reject the messenger's offer. Each photograph operates in tandem with the text to develop Sister Mary's narration,

---

[2] While Blades and Nkiru's Adidas commercial campaign features Beyoncé promoting her clothing brand Ivy Park, the sound designer's trilogy with rubberband's members Jason Filmore Sondock and Simos Davis was commissioned by the video platform NOWNESS, exploring the ways that colour can extend beyond formal constructions of language to communicate one's thoughts and emotions.

thus one can almost hear 'every horn that ever blowed on every juke-box record in the neighbourhood' through: shots of a capped man sat by a bar's record player, partners locked in a slow dance's embrace and women singing with such passion that their eyes are closed and fingers clenched (ibid. 9–12).

Although it is possible to book tour buses in Harlem and consequently 'see the exterior' of the city in our current epoch, Joseph declares he created *Fly Paper* because he wanted audiences 'to feel like they saw a Harlem that they *can't* see' in the traditional sense (my emphasis) (Joseph, cited by McDermon 2017). The filmmaker's approach to documenting the city through the sonic memories and audial echoes of his collaborators mimics sentiments of DeCarava's Guggenheim Fellowship Application, wherein the photographer confesses he is less interested in composing 'a documentary or sociological statement' centred around Harlem and instead harbours a fascination for establishing 'a creative expression' which foregrounds African-American experiences such as Sister Mary's as a fundamental aspect of the city (DeCarava 1952, cited by Kennedy 2009).

For example, while Mary's first husband passed away many years ago, she acknowledges that she has considered marrying her elderly janitor, whose first wife is also no longer alive. He enjoys playing with children from the block of apartments – especially Sister Mary's granddaughter Ronnie Bell – and has a way of interacting with Sister Mary that the narrator recalls fondly. During an exchange between the pair, the man visits Sister Mary's apartment while she is unwell, declaring as he sees the illness-stricken figure: 'Miss Mary, I hear tell you's down – but with no intentions of going out.' Sister Mary, unwell but resilient, replies emphatically: 'You're right! I done got my feet caught in the sweet flypaper of life – and I'll be dogged if I want to get loose.' Recognizing that Sister Mary's indefatigable spirit is uncharacteristically vulnerable at this moment, the janitor replies: 'It *is* sweet ain't it?' – at once offering hope for Sister Mary and simultaneously pleading with himself that this fragile understanding of 'sweetness' does in fact exist, his consolation for Sister Mary curiously functioning as an indirect method for self-reassurance (Hughes and DeCarava 1955: 92).

During this particular section of *The Sweet Flypaper of Life*, images of an elderly man sitting pensively among ladders and paint tins are imbued with warmth and hopefulness engendered by Hughes's characterization of the janitor. Joseph's family footage of his father Keven Joseph Davis – who moved to Harlem for medical support towards the end of his life – draws from these bittersweet, melancholic moments of intimacy in Hughes and DeCarava's text as entangled sounds from a range of Joseph's collaborators are recalled by the ghostly reverberations of Blades's ambient soundscape. Despite the severity of Keven Joseph Davis's illness, vérité footage of family hospital visits and meandering walks through the city's parks and streets captures the son and father's mutual respect and warmth while, simultaneously, imbuing these moments with subtle tones of sadness thanks to the haunting echoes of Alice Smith's voice as well as Flying Lotus's distorted string and percussion sounds. The contradictory sensations evoked by *Fly Paper*'s combinations of visual, sonic and literary significations suggest that the installation's fragile recollections of Joseph and his father's last moments spent together both yearn for and, at the same time, affirm the existence of the 'sweetness' of life's inescapable flypaper, channelling Joseph's bittersweet awareness of the precarity of his father's being in a manner akin to the janitor's consoling and, paradoxically, pleading words to Sister Mary.

While the sensitive interactions between Joseph and his father – as well as the profound exchanges between Sister Mary and the janitor – illustrate how *Fly Paper* is 'aesthetically inspired by the *soundful* photography of Roy DeCarava … and the equal care he devoted to musicians and everyday people in Harlem', Alessandra Raengo reminds us that, in structural terms, the video installation 'bears the traces of Chris Marker's *Sans Soleil* … with which it shares questions about memory and forgetting, happiness and blackness' (her emphasis) (Raengo 2018). Aspects of DeCarava's photography in *The Sweet Flypaper of Life* which Raengo describes as 'soundful' are thus re-animated in *Fly Paper* by the various personalities who emerge from Hughes's short story as well as the memory-laden filmmaking style of *Sans Soleil*. Catherine Lupton's 2006 book on Marker carries the subtitle 'Memories of the Future' in the same manner as the exhibition 180 The Strand. The phrase aptly reverberates through time and implies that the event's organizers share Raengo's thoughts, generating a creative lineage between certain filmmakers (in the vein of Joseph and Marker) who possess the ability to evoke curious sensations of remembering through filmic events that are: yet to happen, have not happened or, are in the process of happening.

Marker's *Sans Soleil* film moves across diverse national territories in a non-linear, dreamlike fashion, forming an unconventional travel diary for the director whereby *San Soleil*'s film images are 'a kind of tangible memory', abstract concepts and fleeting moments of (unclear) recollection preserved for posterity in a physical format (Rafferty 1990: 5). However, at one moment *Sans Soleil*'s narrator directly poses the question: 'Can anybody remember anything if they don't film, if they don't photograph, if they don't tape?' In turn, the narrator's oversimplification of our memory-making processes is challenged and destabilized in the film when a friend sends Marker footage of a volcano erupting in a provincial Icelandic town. Marker had previously captured an image of three children from this small neighbourhood and described the scene as epitomizing happiness, yet the filmed footage of the volcano feels, for the *Sans Soleil* narrator, 'like the destruction of [his] memory [of the children]' as distinguishable representations of this particular area in Iceland compete, contradict and conflict.

Fly Paper's thematic explorations of memory undercut by flawed processes of (mis) remembering and contested recollections are thus articulated by Joseph's incorporation of illuminating quotes from Marker's documentary. In the English version of *Sans Soleil*, a lone figure stands on the cold shore of an empty beach as actress Alexandra Stewart narrates: 'After so many stories of men who lost their memory, here is the story one who has lost forgetting.' The complexities of recollection are exemplified by *Fly Paper*'s remediation of the very same *Sans Soleil* quote as an elderly man carefully moves through the lobby of his apartment building, his walking stick in hand after traversing Harlem's streets in a slow, careful manner, his suit and panama hat combination reminiscent of the fashion styles of the ageing African-American communities that New York's dance halls of 1950s.

Although *Fly Paper* and *Sans Soleil* both examine memory's complicated relationship with audiovisualization, the countercultural elements of Joseph's Black Atlantic art are articulated through his remediation of the *Sans Soleil* quote 'If they don't see happiness in the picture, at least they'll see the black' just as *Fly Paper* captures a sunset above Harlem's park trees, before cutting to darkness. While both verbally and visually alluding to Marker's film and its thematic explorations through his installation's cut to blackness, Joseph subtly reconfigures Marker's message. Sarah French draws from the philosophical works of Jean-François Lyotard by arguing that Marker refers to the 'Lyotardian sublime' through the manner in which moments of his film exceed 'the limits of language or representation' (French 2010: 65). However, Joseph dissimilarly refers to 'Blackness' in its discursive sense, recognizing the sobering effects of his work's explorations of temporality and morality while nonetheless striving to situate his construction of 'Blackness' and its related discourses at the very heart of such abstract, grand and fundamentally human conversations (Campt 2021: 66–74).

In *Fly Paper*, representations of traditional dress styles and Harlem's elderly African-American dancing community are influenced by a key DeCarava photograph entitled *Dancers* (1956) as well as images from *The Sweet Flypaper of Life*, emphasizing the importance of 'seeing Blackness' across artworks and communicative forms. And yet, the significations of this particular dress style are not clearly delineated. Sister Mary's grandson Rodney, who is frequently depicted wearing a fedora, was abandoned by his parents 'so's they can keep good-timing themselves' and consequently adopted and raised by his grandmother; Sister Mary fears that 'the streets done got Rodney' during his youth due to the lack of parental role models in his life, yet she also proudly acknowledges 'they say in the neighbourhood sometimes Rodney can say things that makes everybody set up and take notice', insinuating that Rodney's stylish attire at once signifies his comportment as a maturing young man *and* his growing distance from his grandmother as street-life gradually draws him in (Decarava and Hughes 1955: 6 and 37).

Although the usage of similar imagery in *Fly Paper* might act as a tribute to Joseph's relationship with his father by fondly harking back to an era of Harlem's cultural and spiritual awakening during its Renaissance period in the 1920s, the 1950s epoch in which DeCarava's photographs are situated were in fact a particularly tumultuous moment for the city, characterized by rent strikes and newly formed pressure groups campaigning for action against racist landlords and unsound living conditions for black people. DeCarava's photograph of a hatted man speaking to a group of men while his face is covered in shadows takes on a variety of meanings in *The Sweet Flypaper of Life*, at once affirming Rodney's oratory skills as well as illustrating the ambivalent, possibly darker side of the literary character's persona whose unknowability concerns Sister Mary. Rodney's lack of clear, stable parental figures thus leaves the man vulnerable to the temptation of 'the streets' as an alternative site of socialization which – for many unguided, marginalized and disempowered black males who were impeded by the racial inequalities marring mainstream American society during the 1950s – offers new possibilities 'to construct masculine identities that place emphasis on toughness, sexual conquest, and street hustling' (Oliver 2006: 921).

While the photographs in *The Sweet Flypaper of Life* never directly capture such characteristics of toxic masculinity, DeCavara's ambiguous representation of the faceless man works in tandem with Hughes's short story to communicate Sister Mary's concern for the hidden parts of her grandson's character which she cannot perceive or understand, illustrating her protective instincts towards and relentless care for Rodney (even in adulthood) alongside the increasing precarity of this relationship's balance as time moves forward and the pair grow further and further apart. The mimicry of these traditional types of clothing and the blurred presentation of the characters' faces in *Fly Paper* thus complicate distinctions between the original sources of the memories (DeCarava's photographs) and the contemporaneous contexts (Joseph's installation and the *Strange Days: Memories of the Future* exhibition) in which these abstract recollections are newly located. Although Joseph represents memories of his father as precious events operating on a spiritual plane beyond the basic spatio-temporal chronology by which human life, or 'the sweet flypaper', is framed, the facelessness of the smartly dressed dancers channels the ambiguity of *The Sweet Flypaper of Life*'s characterization of Rodney. In turn, this undercurrent of unknowability subtly insinuates that even beneath the surface of the most sublime memories an almost indescribable, counterintuitive level of moroseness distorts and undercuts our inability to truly relive the remembered moment. Our incapacity to experience these blissfully recalled moments *in situ* beyond blurred recollections that grow hazier and hazier means that such memories become clouded and foggier – even tinged with sadness – as our minds weaken and the years march forward.

In order to channel DeCarava's spirit of subversion and resistance, *Fly Paper* addresses 'issues of representation and the content of culture', drawing from hidden elements locked away in Blades's soundtrack as well as the vividly displayed qualities in DeCarava's photography and Hughes's writing (Jafa 1992: 253). In turn, the overlapping influences imbuing the installation's moving images and music with its interlocking significations and signs illustrate how 'black consciousness-raising and black experimentation' are in certain contexts deemed 'inseparable' (Crawford 2017: 2). The experimental properties of *Fly Paper*'s aesthetics, therefore, ask us to recall that which unites humanity and, simultaneously, to remember what distinguishes, separates and personalizes human experiences. We are together flypapered flies caught up in something inescapable. However, if audiences fail to recognize that all flies are different – and not all strips of flypaper feel the same – then the memory of Marker's *Sans Soleil* quote, reimagined and transformed by Joseph's artwork, seems all the more prescient. 'At least they'll see the black', it echoes.

6.3 Digital media disruption as new audiovisual aesthetic: disruptive news and countercultural reportage in *BLKNWS* (2018–Present)

BLKNWS (2018 to Present) is a multi-sited installation work dedicated to Afrodiasporic news items. Currently comprised of two channels connected to a remotely controlled newscast system in Joseph's studio, the project was first shown at the Venice Biennale but has since been installed in a range of locations across the world (including: barbershops, clothes stores and the lobby area of hotels) as well as being screened in a range of independent cinemas. One of the most recent versions of *BLKNWS* was co-produced with the Los Angeles Nomadic Division, an organization that coordinates site-specific public arts exhibitions across the city. Between Fall 2020 and Spring 2021, Joseph and the Nomadic Division's co-created project was presented in various black-owned businesses across Los Angeles, including: Patria Coffee Roasters, Hank's Mini Market, Sole Folks, Bloom & Plume Coffee, St. John's Well Child & Family Center Clinic, Natraliart Jamaican Restaurant, Total Luxury Spa, UNION Store, Cedars-Sinai Hospital, Go Get Em Tiger, and Hilltop Coffee + Kitchen. The assortment of coffeeshops, restaurants and health centres here captures its flexibility as a grassroots-orientated, community-driven art project capable of being installed in a plethora of diverse spaces and environments.

Joseph calls the piece 'conceptual journalism', drawing from Marcel Duchamp's understanding of conceptualism and the idea 'anything can be art as long as you give it context' (Joseph in conversation with Solway 2019). In a press release for the project, the Nomadic Division develop the notion of 'conceptual journalism' and offer the term 'conceptual news program', describing *BLKNWS* as 'simultaneously a work of art as well as a media entity … [blurring] the lines between art, reporting, entrepreneurship, and cultural critique', thereby openly emphasizing how the latest iteration of the piece 'aims to bring the work to its largest audience yet, reaching people in their everyday environments' in a fashion that echoes the community-focused ethos that unpinned the Underground Museum (Los Angeles Nomadic Division 2020).[3]

Sean 'Diddy' Combs – the rapper and entrepreneur who has also performed under the names P. Diddy and Puff Daddy – launched a similar project after hosting an online discussion called *State of Emergency: The State of Black America & Coronavirus*. He declared that his channel *REVOLT BLACK NEWS* would aim 'to report the news from our perspective, for our people' since African-American citizens have 'already heard about what we can't do, but this about what we CAN do' (Combs cited by Dinsdale 2020). While writer and curator Kimberly Drew expressed appreciation for Combs's decision to launch a news channel dedicated to reporting on black peoples' issues, she also noted that *BLKNWS* existed before *REVOLT BLACK NEWS*, communicating her disappointment towards the rapper's team for their 'oversight' on the basis that African-American communities 'need a voice right now, but we cannot overwrite the work of our peers' (Drew via her Twitter account @museummammy 2020). Similarly, director Barry Jenkins declared that he was 'SURPRISED then delighted that Kahlil and Diddy came together' before realizing that their projects were separate entities, tweeting:

> Sorry but this ain't right … Kahlil and his family run a community-based organization that brings art to the ground where folks can engage it on THEIR

---

[3] Further installations planned for the Hammer Museum, Hollywood Bureau, Touched by an Angel/SON., and the Joseph-Davis family's Underground Museum (where the project has already been screened) have been put on hold due to county regulations responding to the Covid-19 crisis.

terms. In their space. And for that work and giving THIS is how we salute him? Rather than lifting and sharing his voice, we co-opt and displace it? That ain't right. There just ain't no way that's right. FULL STOP.

(Jenkins via his Twitter account @BarryJenkins 2020)

Both *BLKNWS* and *REVOLT BLACK NEWS* present reports and news features from black peoples' perspectives, seeking to empower members of the African diasporas by centring their experiences and views in a complex mediascape that is institutionally biased towards the underlying 'whiteness' of Euro-American hegemony.[4] Nonetheless, Drew and Jenkins's umbrage towards *REVOLT BLACK NEWS* stems from the absence of acknowledgement of Joseph's influence on the part of Combs. Curator Helen Molesworth – who has worked closely with Joseph: developing the professional links that allowed the Underground Museum to borrow art from the Museum of Contemporary Art, organizing retrospective exhibitions centred on his brother Noah Davis and even featuring in one of *BLKNWS*'s mock news segments – suggests this is a case of plagiarism because *BLKNWS* has 'been circulated widely among Hollywood folks and many music industry people' which in turn makes it difficult to believe that the rapper, 'who owns a Kerry James Marshall [original piece] and professes to be all about the culture, isn't aware of what the director of *Lemonade* is up to' (Molesworth in conversation with Cascone 2020). Neither Joseph nor Combs has openly addressed the issue, yet the similarly Afrocentric and countercultural messages of the two projects suggest that *REVOLT BLACK NEWS* is in part shaped by *BLKNWS*'s alternative framework for modern newscast formats.

Joseph claims that the idea for the project originates from a conversation with filmmaker Ryan Coogler about the biases against – and misrepresentations of – black people on mainstream American news channels. When Joseph 'almost jokingly' suggested that African diasporas should be making their own news, he realized 'in that moment' that such a course of action 'was a very real possibility' (Joseph in conversation with Solway 2019). The pair would continue to talk about the project but Coogler's schedule became too busy following the release of his feature-length superhero film *Black Panther* (2018), so Joseph began developing the idea alone. At first he presented *BLKNWS* as a television show to a range of network executives, who were intrigued by the concept yet ultimately decided against providing monetary support. A day after the opening show of *Fly Paper* in 2017, Joseph was rejected by a TV network over the phone while at a collector's house. The collector who was hosting Joseph noticed his annoyance and, following a three-minute pitch about the project, offered the media artist funding. It was at this point that Joseph 'started thinking about *BLKNWS* potentially as a work of art', generating a conceptualization of the piece as a media installation and eventually leading the 2019 Venice Biennale's director to include a version of the project in the festival (Joseph in conversation with Solway 2019).

---

[4] See also: Williams Greaves's public affairs show *Black Journal* (1968–70).

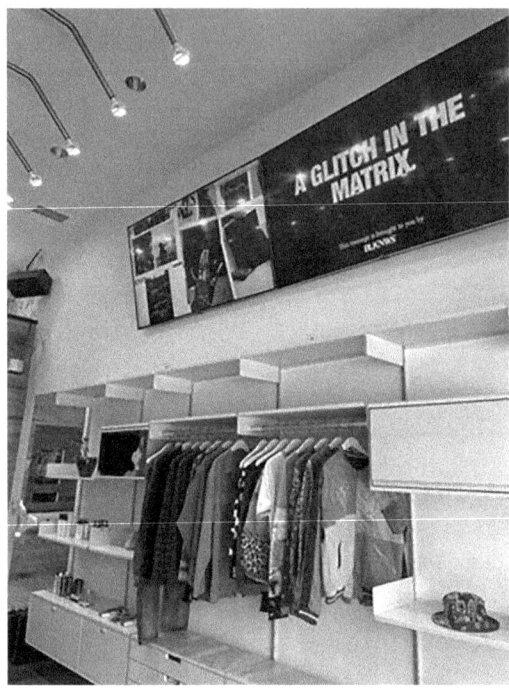

Figure 6.3 Photo of public screening of *BLKNWS* (2018 to Present), Nina Sim © 2021.

ArtNet's Editor-in-Chief Andrew Goldstein observes that Joseph's initial rejections from television networks 'shouldn't come as a surprise' because 'the current media landscape is known to be less than receptive to ideas like this, with surveys finding that writers of color, and in particular black writers, continue to face bias' (Goldstein 2019), citing cultural reporter Cara Buckley's findings to convey the institutional boundaries which initially prevented Joseph's artistic vision from becoming a reality (Buckley 2019). The urgent need to offer countercultural discourses that centre black people's voices is thus captured by Goldstein's pessimistic assessment of the contemporary media landscape, wherein:

> ….the business models for almost all media outlets depend on audience numbers, [so] editors are incentivized to guide their story choice and angling based on what resonates the most reliably with their target demographic. As a (white) editor who pays attention to audience engagement, I can confirm something that won't surprise any close watcher of the news: nothing is more reliable in terms of generating audience engagement than turning out variations on popular narratives that recur, and can be retold, again and again.

Foxnews.com, for instance, loves stories about attractive high-school teachers going to jail for sleeping with their students; People.com loves awful things happening to families, famous and non-famous alike; VanityFair.com loves telling its readers that some infinitesimal new revelation is sure to sink Donald Trump for good. People are crazy for being told stories that, as variations on a well-worn theme, confirm their already-held view of the world. They can tut-tut, ignore any inconvenient detail that doesn't chime with what they believe to be true, and continue contentedly on their way.

> That's why in today's media landscape, you often get a lot of narratives that present stories about black people filtered through a dominantly white perspective – which is immensely pernicious in a country like America where tests have shown that even 'liberal white people', as the anti-racism activist Tim Wise says in a BLKNWS segment, 'internalize biases' to the extent that if they are shown an image of black people for even just 85 milliseconds the 'part of the brain that reacts to fear and anxiety [lights] up like a Christmas tree'. In other words, you get a lot of narratives about black violence and also well-trod leitmotifs like sports excellence, hip-hop excesses and problematic parenting. Anyone, when exposed to such a paucity of story-lines, of depicted modes of identity, runs the risk of, to paraphrase a clip of Maya Angelou from *BLKNWS*, 'believ[ing] their own publicity'.
>
> (Goldstein 2019)

As Goldstein illustrates, the problematic 'default mode' of mainstream news channels centres white perspectives and in turn sustains the underlying forces of white supremacy and anti-Blackness which constitute the neoliberal hegemony. In order to counteract the misrepresentations that ostracize and demonize black people, it is vital for the contemporary wave of Black Atlantic media practitioners such as Joseph to position Afrodiasporic voices at the very centre of their works. However, such an elaborate task – to crystallize the depth and sophistication of Afrodiasporic experiences as a single audiovisual artefact – is by no means an easy feat to execute. Extracted clips and images circulated across social media to promote *BLKNWS* – from Diouana's mask in Ousmane Sembène's *La Noire De ...* (1966) and the work of Los Angeleno painter Henry Taylor, to polaroid photographs of African-American families and headshots of public intellectuals, artists and activists such as Fred Moten, Arthur Jafa and Ilhan Omar – are merged together by a thumping beat and Nina Simone samples from Those Guys and Ras Baraka's song *An American Poem* (2001), thereby capturing the dizzying range of sources which constitute Joseph's project.

However, to complicate matters further, the content of *BLKNWS* is constantly modified and updated because the piece is controlled remotely, thus an announcement detailing the 2021 United States Artist Fellowship award for interdisciplinary movement artist and assistant professor Ni'Ja Whitson was recently positioned alongside rockets launching, chat show hosts and television personalities laughing, and flying cars or 'spinners' from the *Blade Runner* franchise landing. Even snippets from Joseph's own oeuvre – including the 'micro moon' shot from *Black Up* (2011) and a suited man dancing in *Fly Paper* (2017) – briefly appear within BLKNWS's vibrant concoction of media formats, and various hip hop tracks, gospel songs and ambient sounds engender a feeling of cohesion over a captivating (albeit often intense and even overwhelming) array of cultural markers relating to African diasporas and beyond.

While the intensity of the work requires thorough engagement in order to decipher and process the complexity of its various references and news features, *BLKNWS* nonetheless represents an especially promising piece of work within the broader cultural landscape of American news broadcasting channels because it captures the disruptive potential of similar Afrocentric media outlets (including yet also extending past Combs's *REVOLT BLACK NEWS*). Joseph observes: "If we see a story or headline that's good, we will redesign it and make it native to a *BLKNWS* environment. The spectrum of sources that we'll recontextualize will be from the local LA yoga newspaper or magazine to the *New York Times*. So the hierarchy has been completely flattened" (Joseph cited by Dinsdale 2020). By drawing from alternative source materials such as polaroid photos, old films clips and contemporary music videos, Joseph's 'flattening' of preconceived orders and ranks for learning resources offers an attempt to challenge the contemporary mediascape's (mis)representation of black people's experiences.

Many Eurocentric theorizations of taste stem from the controversial proposal of Charles Batteux's *Les Beaux Arts Réduits À Un Même Principe [The Fine Arts Reduced to a Single Principle]* whereby a single theory is adopted to meaningfully encompass all artistic expressions across the world (Batteux [1746] 2015), and Pierre Bourdieu observes that 'the various kinds of cultural competence encountered in a class society derive their social value from the power of social discriminations', meaning that systems for determining the social value of an artwork manifest in ways that are 'always hierarchised' (Bourdieu [1984] 1993: 129). However, *BLKNWS* represents a deliberate effort to create new frameworks of knowledge, drawing from a range of 'unusual' source materials and, in turn, attempting to offer alternative understandings of contemporaneity that encompass yet also surpass the pre-established knowledge frameworks constituting the neoliberal Eurocentric hegemony.

In the original Angelou clip cited by Goldstein, the poet and civil rights activist details the tribulations of being both black and female in a white patriarchal society during the 1970s, exploring the ways in which stereotypes in public discourses shape and influence peoples' private lives. Angelou observes African-American women needed to discover new forms of strength when their spouses – who were supposed to hold dominant positions within the typical American household – struggled to find employment in the aftermath of slavery. During the difficult periods when struggling African-American families relied more and more on the support from their matriarchs, Angelou notes that a black woman would in turn start 'to believe her own publicity ... she sees how strong she is and starts to become a little bit stronger', citing the legacies of the matrilineal relationships which defined West African societies as a key source of inspiration for the period's underappreciated or 'underground' forms of Black femininity (Angelou [1973] 2014). At the same time, however, such moments of strength and assertion which should have been celebrated as triumphs for Black womanhood were twisted by the white mainstream, generating unjust stereotypes in the vein of 'matriarchal ogres', framing Afrocentric matriarchy in a pejorative way.

The filmmaker notes: 'There's this fallacy that news is a linear event ... I can't tell you how many people are grabbed by that little two-minute excerpt with Maya Angelou because they have never seen it. So I recognized the power of stuff that's already out there' (Joseph in conversation with Solway 2019). Angelou speaks eloquently about the complicated situation for black women in the aftermath of the Civil Rights Movement, yet Joseph's recontextualization of her interview within the *BLKNWS* installation allows her countercultural form of femininity to spread into new environments in our contemporary epoch while, simultaneously, emphasizing how misrepresentations of black women in present discourses echo unfair treatment from the past. As well as flattening controversial hierarchies which seek to rank and categorize sources of knowledge, Joseph's achronological approach to newscasting thus communicates the countercultural possibilities imbedded in the *BLKNWS* project, disrupting both the content *and* structure of mainstream news platforms that otherwise sustain modernity's undercurrents of whiteness.

At one point in *BLKNWS*, an interview with Herbie Hancock is juxtaposed against footage of the composer, pianist and multi-instrumentalist on stage, performing an improvised session with one of Joseph's biggest influences, Miles Davis. On one screen Hancock recalls inadvertently playing the wrong chord during a show in Stuttgart, while the other screen portrays Davis stopping mid-performance as he hears a distraction – purportedly coming from Hancock during their time together as the Miles Davis Live Quintet – at a gig in Milan. Hancock explains his immediate reaction was anger and disappointment yet remembers Davis suddenly playing a different set of notes that 'corrected' his original mistake and made the wrong chord 'right'; from the second screen, we see Davis return to his instrument and hear improvised music that appears to react to Hancock's confession and absolve his error. Hancock recalls being astounded by the incident, understanding how to correct one's musical mistakes through improvisation as well as learning on a more broader metaphorical level 'how to make something that was wrong into something that was right' by adapting to the situation and persevering (Hancock 2014). Angelou's interview directly draws attention to the role of Black feminism in undermining hegemonic narratives of whiteness. Hancock's anecdote and Davis's improvisation represent advice to burgeoning musicians and, simultaneously, a malleable form of philosophy that could be applied to the situation of African-American matriarchs in the seventies *as well as* contemporary practitioners of the Black Atlantic's music and moving images, thus capturing the sophistication of *BLKNWS*'s formal parameters as an array of sources merge and interact in new spatiotemporal configurations.

As previously discussed, Paul Gilroy ties the increased visualization of Black Atlantic experiences to the rampant growth of capitalism, lamenting that 'the power of music and sound are receding ... as the relentless power of visual cultures expands' on the basis that the 'antiphonal' ethics which connect 'performer and crowd, participant and community' are eroded by the accelerating proliferation of Afrodiasporic visualizations across new communicative platforms (Gilroy 1993: 203). Caspar Melville understands these concerns, recognizing how Gilroy 'sees the life-enhancing potential and oppositional spirit of Black music subordinated to the process of neoliberal marketization and commodification' (Melville 2020: 9). However, Melville builds on Gilroy's ideas by suggesting that further examination of Black music in our contemporary epoch reveals how its cultures continue to play a pivotal role 'for living with and through difference' *despite* the social conundrums enacted by the dehumanizing effects of the current economic framework (ibid. 11).[5]

Focusing on London's clubbing scenes, Melville draws from Gilroy's arguments that the 'moral economies' and 'convivial post-colonial interactions' which are built around Black music simultaneously 'enrich our cities *and* drive our cultural industries' (my emphasis) (Gilroy 2004b; 2010). Although a London club's existence is automatically tied to commerce as a result of its inescapable position within our current economic framework, Melville argues that these spaces are moral because they are 'driven by the ambition to build a viable future in the midst of de-industrialisation and brutal urban neoliberalisation' and, at the same time, 'bounded by particular social and ethical norms and amount to networks of affiliation and creation which are not reducible to financial exchange' (Melville 2020: 2).

Joseph's *BLKNWS*, then, relies on commercial flows since it exists within the contemporary world order of neoliberal capitalism, yet at the same time the multi-sited installation project nurtures alternative forms of sociality across a range of spaces that cannot be entirely reduced to monetary exchange for its own sake. While *BLKNWS* echoes in part the countercultural energies of the Black music lineages which permeate throughout London's underground clubbing scenes, the installation's merging of Afrodiasporic music with visual modes of communication – whether an interview extract with a prominent activist from several years ago, or an alert parodying the white hysteria of today's mainstream newscasts – can momentarily interrupt the music with a key piece of information, or even merge songs with certain news items to further emphasize their tone, thereby highlighting the didactic possibilities of Black Atlantic audiovisual expression through both verbal *and* non-verbal forms of expression, literal *and* abstract frameworks of knowledge.

Since 'dance is intrinsic' to Black music traditions, its existence across America, Britain and Africa 'carve[s] out performative space for those whose access to other spaces – economic, public, moral – is severely limited', thus reconfiguring spatial relations and, in turn, challenging rigid systemizations and ranked forms of sociality (ibid. 23). Although Afrodiasporic music is globally omnipresent, Melville observes that this form of expression is 'rarely considered a form of art' precisely because its ability to reconfigure spatial arrangements is 'socially useful' for groups across race, class and gender, functioning in a manner deemed irrelevant or unnecessary by classic categorizations of Eurocentric taste (ibid. 22). Black music hence disrupts the ways in which societal hierarchies extract value from discrimination, subverting 'the racialisation of city space ... [unleashing] new spatial imaginaries which materialise

---

[5] See also: David Hesmondhalgh's *The Culture Industries* (2013).

both a diasporic spatiality ... and the imaginative resources for forging new worlds' (ibid. 7).

Drawing from the multicultural 'conviviality' between British citizens from diverse backgrounds as conceptualized by Gilroy in *After Empire: Melancholia or Convivial Culture?* (2004), Melville similarly suggests that the use of digital technologies to produce music for London's warehouse parties, raves and jungle clubs has the capacity to generate new social relations, serving 'as a vital resource to build and sustain multicultural forms of sociality' (Melville 2020: 9). By applying Melville's theorization about digitalization to Joseph's dissemination of remote-controlled countercultural digital content in *BLKNWS*, one may argue that the media artist likewise generates alternative forms of sociality, such as Gilroy's 'convivial' multiculture, as the conceptual news programme's content reaches a range of disparate spaces – from coffee houses and hotel lobbies to barbershops and clothes emporia – engaging with people from a broad variety of social backgrounds and cultural affiliations and, in turn, offering alternative perspectives through which to understand contemporaneity.

It has been rumoured that Joseph is working on transforming *BLKNWS* into a feature-length film. If, as Bourdieu reminds us, the social value of an artwork is consistently hierarchized, then *BLKNWS* in its remote-controlled installation form represents an attempt to challenge the prevalent narratives that reinforce hegemonic understandings of social order and consequently marginalize or mischaracterize Afrodiasporic experiences. Rather than undermining the countercultural qualities of Black music, the merging of the Black Atlantic's audial and visual modes of expression through such multi-sited and interdisciplinary installation artworks as *BLKNWS* gestures towards the subversive potential with which future media forms might challenge Eurocentric formulations of modernity. Fluctuating at the intersections of art and journalism – as well as oscillating at the crossroads of capital, cultural traffic and aesthetics – the volatility and instability of *BLKNWS* represents Joseph's most experimental and pioneering effort in terms of articulating the sheer dynamism and sophistication of black peoples' lives in our contemporary moment through music and moving images. While the sheer range of its content is oftentimes as overwhelming and intense as the contemporary networked environment of digitized neoliberalism, the innovative project offers an invaluable blueprint for future media practitioners who seek to engage Africa, America, Europe and the Caribbean through audiovisual art and, in turn, explore alternative ways of being that ensure accessibility for the community and place Afrodiasporic voices at the heart of our shared cultures.

7

Conclusion(s) and crosscurrents

7.1 Music as the muse: Africa's role in reinventing cinema

As this book on the cross-continental and intercultural movements of a key Black Atlantic audiovisual artist draws to a close, it feels fitting to focus on the inspiration that Joseph, at the helm of Afrodiasporic media's contemporary vanguard, draws from the rebellious, counterculture energies of pioneering Senegalese film-master Djibril Diop Mambéty. Joseph's project *Music Is My Mistress* (2017) – named after Edward K. 'Duke' Ellington's 1976 memoir – is a collaboration with Japanese-French fashion label KENZO. The campaign video is a cultural form interwoven with capitalistic agendas, marketing the luxury fashion house's SS17 (Spring-Summer 2017) collection. In typical Joseph fashion, *Music Is My Mistress* toys with genre configurations as 'a trailer wrapped in a music video inside a short film' (KENZO, cited by Avecedo 2017), subtly backgrounding a variety of alluring looks and clothing styles while using the fashion label's monetary support to employ a high-profile cast, publicizing across the company's social media platforms an intricate exploration of music's significance for Los Angeles's diasporic community.

Ishmael Butler from Shabazz Palaces plays Gamma, an enigmatic recording artist fleeing from a disorientated music manager. With a secretive cellist at his side, Gamma rides and raps through downtown Los Angeles as the manager, portrayed by actor-cum-activist Jesse Williams, scours the rest of the city to no avail. Desperately searching for his music-making quarry, the manager waits in a distant countryside safehouse under the false premise that a singing African Princess will help him find his way. After three wasted days of monotony and frustration, the manager leaves his fool's errand empty-handed; meanwhile, Gamma, the cellist and the African Princess hone their crafts in distant, undisclosed locations, performing to no one in particular yet free to create music without strict restrictions set by record labels and contract expectations.

While marketing an array of KENZO's colourful jumpsuits, dresses and shirts, the advertisement operates as an analogy for the complexity of artistic creation under the conditions of neoliberalism. The manager, consumed by the pressures of capitalistic competition (Srnicek and Williams 2016), reduces music to a purely commercial enterprise. He never encounters Gamma, the cellist or the Princess because his money-driven motives cannot engage with art purely for art's sake: he never appreciates music as an end in itself, therefore he never gains the trust of the triumvirate.

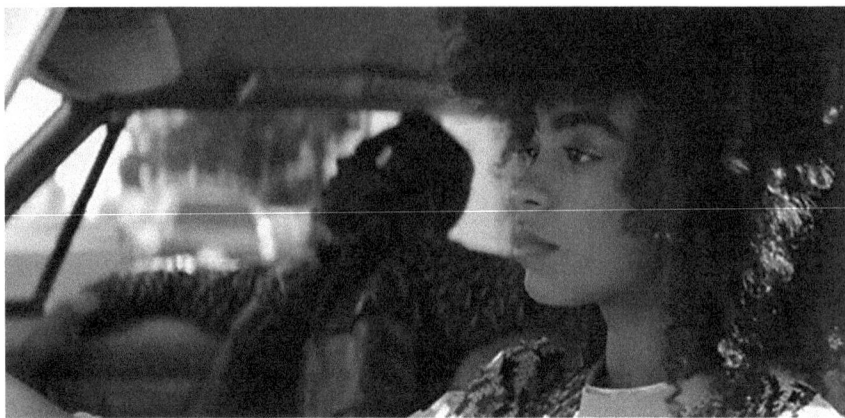

Figure 7.1 *Music Is My Mistress* (2017), Kahlil Joseph © KENZO.

This analogy, in turn, articulates the complexity of Afrodiasporic experiences within the contemporary economic framework. The manager's dogged attempts to sign the triumvirate are fruitless and, at the same time, his understanding of his spiritual past is obfuscated by an obsession with commercial gain. The African Princess – portrayed by *Black-Ish* (2014–Present) actress Tracee Ellis Ross – represents the liberated, unrestricted essence of musical creation and, simultaneously, the spiritual, untamed components of the manager's ancestral heritage that are repressed, quashed and lost in the midst of the contemporary West's hypercompetitive, capitalistic environment.

Although *Music Is My Mistress* casts 'music herself as the central character of an unfolding drama across cultures, space and time' (Kenzo, cited by Aïshti 2017), Joseph amalgamates flows of Black cultural traffic by revealing a quote from Senegalese filmmaker Djibril Diop Mambéty on screen, shimmering beneath the water: 'I believe that Africans, in particular, must reinvent cinema.' Hybridizing advertisements, films and music videos as means of representing diasporic experiences in our contemporary moment, Joseph channels the complexity of existence under neoliberal capitalism to mirror the intricacies of concurrent affiliations to divergent cultural spheres. Indeed, across all of his works, the filmmaker engages with a variety of art forms and geographical spheres across 'cultures, space and time' in order to articulate the complexities of double-consciousness while, simultaneously, reinventing 'traditional' notions of African, American and European cinema by centring Afrodiasporic perspectives.

As the title of *Music Is My Mistress* emphasizes, the centrality of the subversive potential of Black Atlantic music cannot be underplayed in relation to the innovative energies through which Joseph's works attempt to 'reinvent cinema' and indeed a range of other media forms. The merging of Black Atlantic music and moving images, as I have argued throughout this book, is a necessarily collaborative endeavour between filmmakers (in the vein of Joseph and contemporaries such as Baloji and Nkiru) and their creative partners (musicians, business, dancers and myriad other specialists) who wish to challenge the status quo, at once subverting Eurocentric notions of modernity yet, at the same time, offering new ways of understanding and experiencing the contemporary world that emphasize the fragility – and indeed the dangers – of all-encompassing grand narratives such as 'modernism' that attempt to reduce existence to a singular framework or monolithic structure.

Before the turn of the century, critic Graham Fuller relegated the music video form to 'the trash can of popular culture' (Fuller 1996, cited in Reiss and Feineman 1996: 23). However, fears that the music video's 'avowedly commercial agenda … [as] an advertisement for another cultural form' (Railton and Watson 2011: 2) symbolizes the 'eradication of [music's] human element altogether' (Arnold et al 2017: 1) are quashed by the high standard of recent online releases set by exemplars of Black Atlantic audiovisual expression, especially Kahlil Joseph and his brand of film, music video and advertisement hybridizations.

The music video has undergone rapid transformations since MTV's collapse as the mode's primary broadcasting platform. In 1996 – when Fuller voiced his concerns, and MTV audience numbers were starting to decline – television, which had replaced cinema as the 'cultural dominant' of the era (Jameson 1991: 4), was, in turn, challenged by the rising popularity of the internet. Now, the internet's prevalence permits digital access to music videos and other forms of new media through mobile phones, laptop computers, virtual worlds and interactive installations, leading Steven Shaviro to define our historical moment as a 'post-cinematic' epoch wherein small screens supersede 'the big screen' (Shaviro 2010).

In this 'post-cinematic' era, however, one must not consign filmmaking practices to oblivion by falsely assuming that 'cinema is dead' (Greenaway 2007). Chuck Tyron, addressing the ambivalent status of cinema in our age of media convergence, notes the 'very definition of what constitutes a film text is subject to reinterpretation' (Tyron 2009: 4) and Philippe Dubois argues cinema is 'more alive, more multi-faceted, more abundant than ever' as a result of the 'increasingly boundless diversity of its forms and practices' (Dubois 2010: 13). Film and new media both use moving images to 'represent human experience imaginatively' (Mercer 1953: 19), fictionalizing experiences by drawing the universe into a 'circumscribed artificial, yet human, space' (Smith 2001) so that we, the viewership, may better understand the world, our neighbours and ourselves. As well as answering Bogle's call for a 'new black cinema' for Afro-America (Bogle 2016), Joseph's audiovisual work can be situated within frameworks for African filmmaking practices because, as Martin N. Ndlela acknowledges, 'flows and patterns of flows in social media are constantly shaping and reshaping contemporary African film cultures' (Ndlela, cited in Mano et al. 2017: 219).

Amalgamating distinct media qualities in order to articulate the complexity of double-consciousness in this digitalized, neoliberal era, Joseph's works operate as waves of Black cultural traffic 'reconstituting and reenergizing' cultural forms (Elam Jr and Jackson 2005: 5), offering alternative understandings of modernity by exemplifying how African cinema 'deconstructs single identity discourses in both the North *and* South' (my emphasis) (Barlet 2016: 381). However, while the lens of African

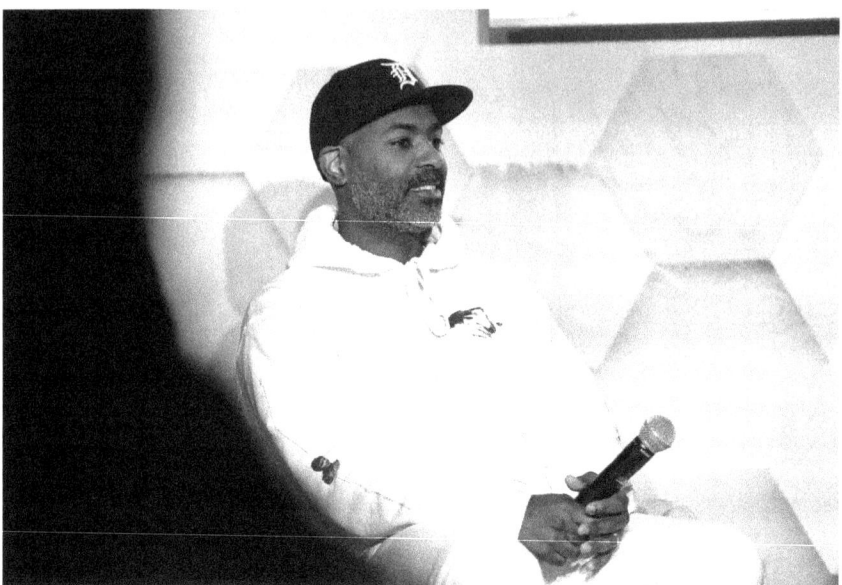

Figure 7.2 Kahlil Joseph speaks during the 2020 Sundance Film Festival – Digital Aerosol and the Re-Imaginarium: A Fireside Chat with Kahlil Joseph and Jesse Williams Panel at the Ray on 26 January 2020 in Park City, Utah. Photo by Morgan Lieberman/Getty Images.

film theory remains a valuable paradigm through which to process and negotiate the director's interdisciplinary and transcontinental collection of art, it is important for future Kahlil Joseph scholars[1] to position his audiovisual works in relation to key African, European *and* American film concepts, thereby enriching cinema's *respective* and, simultaneously, *entwined* theoretical branches.

7.2 Media matters: future pathways for filmmakers and musicians of the Audiovisual Atlantic

So what happens now? Film, Media and Screen Studies – alongside many other subjects captured under the 'humanities' umbrella – are long overdue significant overhauls if

---

[1] While Kinitra D. Brooks and Kameelah L. Martin's foundational *The Lemonade Reader* (2019) thoroughly examines Beyoncé's influence on the project, their collection of essays does not explore Joseph's contributions to the project – or his own unedited, privately unreleased version of *Lemonade* (2016) – at length. Despite the intellectual richness of Joseph's oeuvre, for pedagogical reasons I have not been able to discuss all of his screen texts within this book. Academic discussions that encompass Joseph's underexplored media texts and installations works – including: *The Mirror Between Us* (2012), *You and Gary Oldman* (2012), *Dawn in Luxor* (2014), *Memory Palace* (2015), *Porno* [from *The Reflektor Tapes*] (2015), Joseph's version of *Lemonade* (2016) (on its own and alongside Beyoncé's version), *Wizard of the Upper Amazon* (2016) and *Black Mary* (2017) – would propel Kahlil Joseph scholarship into promising new territories.

we are to move beyond their Western origins towards more globalized futures and new disruptive fields of audio(di)visual research. Meanwhile, outside the academy, sustaining the momentum needed to effectively shift public discussions around politics, art and race remains an increasingly complicated task. Lester K. Spence echoes some of the Black Neoliberal Aesthetic's underlying contradictions by arguing that prominent moments for the #BlackLivesMatter movement have tended to manifest 'in the presence of either a horrific instance of black death or a startling instance of police brutality' which, in turn, implies that graphic forms of suffering inadvertently seem to matter 'rather than black life' in situations where campaigning voices are fighting against powerful institutional forces for precisely the opposite cause (Spence 2015: 145). In the very same breath that he challenges the 'luxury' of defeatism in these difficult times, Paul Gilroy articulates the complexity – and fragility – of action when resisting hostile, all-devouring world systems in the digital age:

> I don't think we can afford the luxury of pessimism. I have been dispirited of late, but when I saw those young people out in the streets in the pandemic, with their masks on, spaced apart, announcing to the world that racism is a bad thing, it was inspiring and uplifting. That banner was taken up very widely and some of the people who took it up were very young. That is hopeful. The question is, can that mobilisation of people be the source of a movement that can carry this forward[?] That's where my own pessimism bites me, because I don't know if the technologies that get people into the streets are so good at keeping them there.
>
> (Gilroy 2020)

The Audiovisual Atlantic's contemporary era of digitalization and enhanced connectivity is rife with both opportunities and obstacles, possibilities and pitfalls. If pessimism is an indulgence, then the paradoxes of these modern times must be scrutinized thoroughly, relentlessly, across the Atlantic, until defeatism retreats and we understand how to use such contradictions to our collective advantage. Strength comes in numbers, after all, for bank balances and protesting crowds alike. And there are some forms of knowledge – of power – that no amount of capital can buy. While the networked present often feels dizzying and overwhelming, it pays to remember we forever move backwards and forwards with friends and foes alike, oscillating like great tides connected by multitudinous undercurrents that move in different directions and at different speeds, forever pushing and pulling with and against contradictory forces and flows.

As a product of our networked environment pushed and pulled in these multiple directions simultaneously, my work is likewise shaped by numerous contradictions and shortcomings that must be navigated and negotiated with care and caution. Since the beginnings of this particular academic journey – stemming back to masters and undergraduate years, when many of the key concerns underpinning this book started to form and coalesce – my mentors championed the importance of crafting academic work meticulously using clear, accessible language. Nonetheless, thanks to formal training in literature and film analysis at UCL (an elitist space that named its lecture theatres after racists and eugenicists; among the first British universities to admit women, teach English and set up a Film Studies programme) and further training across global cinemas, digital media and transcultural discourses at SOAS (once a training centre for colonial administrators and military officers; now a radical, globally minded academic institution that – much like many other universities across the UK – is being worn down by relentless budget cuts and restructuring) certain biases have undoubtedly crept into these pages. In spite of considerable effort to avoid such imbalances, at times I inadvertently overemphasize visual theories in this book when opportunities to draw from their sound-based counterparts have arisen. Geographical biases have slipped into this project too: the book's scope predominantly focuses on the omnidirectional flows between Africa, America and Europe, failing to examine with sufficient depth the Caribbean's relationship to Audiovisual Atlantic culture.

There are strengths and weaknesses, limitations and potential, nuancing all written projects from any given author, hence why I have strived to stress throughout this book the urgent need to apply theories and discourses to the world outside the narrow boundaries of Higher Education. Although my work remains complicated by its own unsolved tensions, I sincerely hope that the book has captured how the contradictions and paradoxes underpinning Kahlil Joseph's transmedia artworks in turn speak volumes about the stuff that matters: that is, you and me, humanity and us. Romain Rolland identifies an 'intimate alliance' between pessimism of intelligence that 'cuts through every delusion' and optimism of the will 'which lives in struggle over and above suffering, doubt, and the blasts of nothingness' (Rolland 1920, cited in Fisher 1988: 292). Developing this line of thought, the imprisoned Antonio Gramsci writes in a letter to his brother that he synthesizes both pessimism and optimism in the face of adversity, consciously arming himself with a patient yet impassioned worldview 'not passive, inert, but animated by perseverance' (Gramsci 2011 [1929]: 299). According to the maxim often attributed to Gramsci, 'the challenge of modernity', then, it seems, 'is to live without illusions and without becoming disillusioned' (Utriainen 2011: 417; Coalter 2013: 62; Slothuus 2021: 343; Beghetto 2022: 62).

The culmination of several years of hard work (some easier than others), *Kahlil Joseph and the Audiovisual Atlantic* represents the study of a key artistic voice operating within today's cultural landscape, an exploration of contemporary audiovisual forms that connect to a tradition of radical humanism as vital and urgent as ever. In an era when political turbulence is rife, where walls threaten to segregate our communities entirely, we cannot afford to forget that the work being done by Joseph and so many others across different parts of the Atlantic will remain at once precious, human and necessary for as long as we – the viewers, listeners, readers, writers, consumers, thinkers, percipients – can strategize ways to support their impact, upholding and sustaining their legacies. In doing so, we ensure that public discourses surrounding audiovisual communication's cultural politics – those underlying values *within* and *beyond* the logic of the marketplace – might continue to expand, evolve and, eventually, thrive in a more equitable manner on local, regional and national levels across our shared planet.

This book thus concludes that Kahlil Joseph's transmedia artworks – fluctuating at the intersections between film, music video and advertisement; the crossroads of capital, cultural traffic and aesthetics; the sights and sounds of the Audiovisual Atlantic's crossflows and crosscurrents – teach important lessons about the experiential dynamics of cultural pluralism in complicated, contradictory times. The 'revolutionary' nature of 'Blackness' in myriad forms inspires millions globally irrespective of the colour of their skin (Akala 2018: 121); and humanity will together share a diverse, networked world 'that is at last recognized in all its complexity' (Barlet 2016: 381) once we embrace the great waves and rhizomatic sub-flows that constitute human culture across Africa, America, Europe, the Caribbean and indeed far beyond the Atlantic Ocean, wherever our shared sun sets. Fast approaching some spectacular destination that swims on the horizon – unfixed yet audible and in sight, moving ever closer as momentum grows – we must and will achieve liberation by sharing our knowledge and experiences until the (dis)illusions that hold us apart dissipate: after everything, expanding our perspectives; at long, long last, decolonizing our minds.

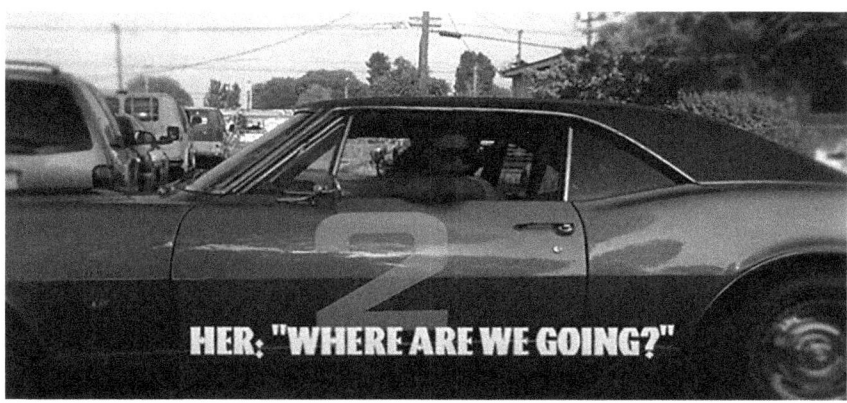

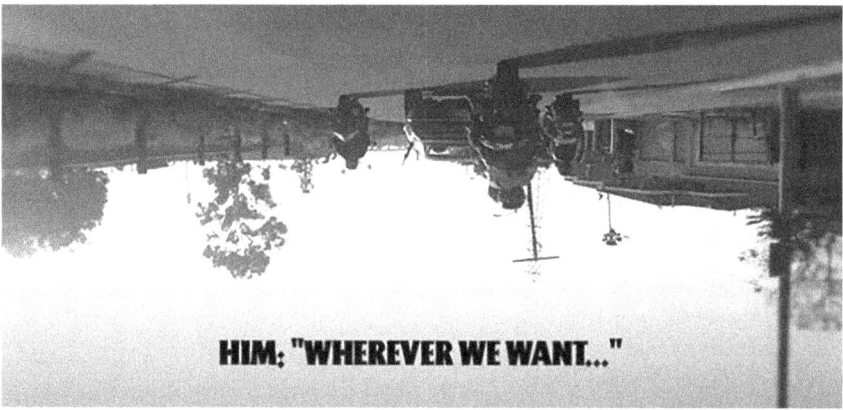

Figures 7.3 and 7.4 *Belhaven Meridian* (2010), Kahlil Joseph and Shabazz Palaces © What Matters Most.

Bibliography

Abernethy, Francis E. (1960), 'The Case for and against Sci-Fi', *The Clearing House*, 34 (8), 474–77.

Adesokan, A. (2011), *Postcolonial Artists and Global Aesthetics*, Bloomington: Indiana University Press, 1–29, 133–55 and 178.

Adichie, C. N. (2009), 'The Dangers of a Single Story', *TED TALKS Youtube*. Available online: https://www.youtube.com/watch?v=D9Ihs241zeg (accessed 3 March 2023).

Africanus, L. (2010), *The History and Description of Africa: And of the Notable Things Therein Contained [1550]. Vol. 2*, Cambridge: Cambridge University Press.

Akala. (2018), *Natives: Race and Class in the Ruins of Empire*, London: Two Roads, 121.

Akomfrah, J. in conversation with S. Sandhu (2012), 'John Akomfrah: Migration and memory', *The Guardian*. Available online: https://www.theguardian.com/film/2012/jan/20/john-akomfrah-migration-memory (accessed 7 November 2023).

Akomfrah, J. (2015), 'Black Independent Filmmaking: A Statement by the Black Audio Film Collective', *Black Camera*, 6 (2), 58–60.

Akomfrah, J. in conversation with J. Canela (2018), 'John Akomfrah "Purple" at Museo Nacional Thyssen-Bornemisza, Madrid', *Mouse Magazine*, February. Available online: http://moussemagazine.it/john-akomfrah-purple-museo-nacional-thyssen-bornemisza-madrid-2018/ (accessed 3 March 2023).

Akudinobi, J. (2006), 'Durable Dreams: Dissent, Critique, and Creativity in Faat Kine and Moolaade', in *Meridians – Feminism, Race, Transnationalism*, Vol. 6, No. 2, London: Duke University Press, 177–94.

Alley-Barnes, M. and J. Danzker (2016), *Young Blood: Noah Davis, Kahlil Joseph, the Underground Museum*, Seattle: Frye Art Museum.

Amatulli, J. (2019), Rare 'Micromoon' Is Gracing Us with Its Presence on Friday the 13th, Huffington Post. Available online: https://www.huffingtonpost.co.uk/entry/micro-moon-friday-the-13th_n_5d766876e4b0752102307612. (accessed 10 January 2024).

Anderson, R. (2016), 'Afrofuturism 2.0 & The Black Speculative Arts Movement: Notes on a Manifesto', *Obsidian*, 42 (1/2), 229.

Anderson, R. and C. Jones (2015), 'Introduction: The Rise of Astro-Blackness', in *Afrofuturism 2.0: The Rise of Astro-Blackness*, Maryland: Lexington Books, vii.

Andrews, I. (2015), *Postmodern Marketing: Is It Dead or Alive?*, Coventry: Warwick University, 1–52. Available online: https://warwick.ac.uk/fac/arts/theatre_s/cp/research/publications/madiss/iain.pdf (accessed 9 September 2018).

Angelou, M. [1973] (2014), 'Maya Angelou on the Noble Story of the Black Woman Hood (1973)', *BillyMoyers.com Vimeo Account*, 29 May. Available online: https://vimeo.com/96833430 (accessed 3 March 2023).

Arayess, S., and D. Geer (2017), 'Social Media Advertising: How to Engage and Comply', *European Food and Feed Law Review*, 12 (6), 529.

Armoo, T. (2017), 'Advertainment – The New Frontier in Marketing to Gen Z', *The Drum*, 24 July. Available online: https://www.thedrum.com/

opinion/2017/07/24/advertainment-the-new-frontier-marketing-gen-z (accessed 3 March 2023).
Arnold, G. et al. (eds.) (2017), *Music/Video: History, Aesthetics, Media*, New York: Bloomsbury, 1.
Aronson, A. B. and M. Kimmel, M. (eds.) (2004), *Men and Masculinities: Volume I: A-J*, Oxford: ABC-CLIO, 30.
Ashe, S., S. Virdee and L. Brown (2016), 'Striking Back against Racist Violence in the East End of London, 1968–1970', *Race and Class*, 58 (1), 34–54.
Astruc, A. (1968), 'The Birth of a New Avant-Garde: La caméra-stylo', in *The New Wave: critical landmarks*, London: Secker/BFI, 17–23.
Austerlitz, S. (2008), *Money for Nothing: A History of the Music Video from the Beatles to the White Stripes*, London: Bloomsbury, 2.
Bakare, L. (2017), '"We Feel Like Aliens": Shabazz Palaces, the Hip-Hop Duo Beamed in from Another Planet', *The Guardian Online*, 9 August. Available online: https://www.theguardian.com/music/2017/aug/09/shabazz-palaces-interview-quazars (accessed 3 March 2023).
Baloji, in conversation with A. Pellerin (2019), 'Baloji's Incredible New Film Confronts Zombie Culture and Shared Isolation', *Dazed Digital*, 14 March. Available online: https://www.dazeddigital.com/music/article/43699/1/baloji-zombie-short-film-watch (accessed 3 March 2023).
Baloji, in conversation with K. Tambini (2019), 'Watch Baloji's Debut Short Film "Kaniama Show"', *OkayAfrica*, 2 May. Available online: https://www.okayafrica.com/baloji-kaniama-show-short-film-watch/?rebelltitem=1#rebelltitem1 (accessed 3 March 2023).
Baloji, cited by A. Reeves (2020), 'A Lesson in the Value of Perspective from Belgian-Congolese Artist and Director Baloji', *Little Black Book*, 23 July. Available online: https://www.lbbonline.com/news/a-lesson-in-the-value-of-perspective-from-belgian-congolese-artist-and-director-baloji (accessed 3 March 2023).
Barlet, O. (2016), *Contemporary African Cinema*, East Lansing: Michigan State University Press, 360–81.
Barnett, M. (2005), 'The Many Faces of Rasta: Doctrinal Diversity within the Rastafari Movement', *Caribbean Quarterly*, 51 (2), 67–78.
Barthes, R. (1957), *Mythologies*, Paris: Les Lettres Nouvelles, 116–18.
Baskin, J. (2010), 'The Perspective of Terrence Malick', *The Point*, Issue 2, 4 April. Available online: https://thepointmag.com/criticism/the-perspective-of-terrence-malick/ (accessed 3 March 2023).
Bastide, R. (1978 [1960]), *The African Religions of Brazil*, Baltimore: John Hopkins, 300 and 329–30.
Batteux, C. [1746] (2015), Young, J. O. (trans.) *The Fine Arts Reduced to a Single Principle*, Oxford: Oxford University Press.
Baudrillard, J. (1988), 'Simulacra and Simulations', in M. Poster (ed.), *Selected Writings*, Stanford: Stanford University Press, 166–84.
Bauman, R. (2008), *Race and the War on Poverty: From Watts to East L.A. (Race and Culture in the American West)*, Norman: University of Oklahoma Press, 22–45.
Bazin, A. (1960), 'The Ontology of the Photographic Image', *Film Quarterly*, 13 (4), 4–9.
Beghetto, R. (2022), *Monstrous Liminality: Or the Uncanny Monsters of Secularized Modernity*, London: Ubiquity Press, 61.

Behlendorf, B. (1993), 'SUBJECT: Can Dumb People Enjoy IDM, Too?', *Way Back Machine*, 3 August. Available online: https://web.archive.org/web/20071118071301/http://elists.resynthesize.com/idm/1993/08/412600/ (accessed 3 March 2023).

Bell, S. et al. (2013), 'Introduction', in S. Bell and J. Paskins (eds.), *Imagining the Future City: London 2062*, London: Ubiquity Press, 1.

Bhattacharyya, G. (2018), *Rethinking Racial Capitalism: Questions of Reproduction and Survival*, London: Rowman and Littlefield.

Bizzo, N. (2007), 'A Video-Iconographical Journey through Queen's Production', *Music in Art*, 32 (1/2), 205.

Björnberg, A. (1994), 'Structural Relationships of Music and Images in Music Video', *Popular Music*, 13 (1), 51.

Blacc, A. interviewed by T. Green (2011), 'Aloe Blacc Interview: "Get rich and share"', The Telegraph, 30 April. Available online: https://www.telegraph.co.uk/culture/music/rockandpopfeatures/8480520/Aloe-Blacc-interview-Get-rich-and-share.html (accessed 3 March 2023).

Bleakley, R. (1978), *African Masks*, North Carolina: Slap-Dash Publishing.

Boehm, L. K. (2009), *Making a Way out of No Way: African American Women and the Second Great Migration*, Mississippi: University Press of Mississippi.

Bogle, D. cited by A. Samuels (2013), 'How 2013 Became the Year of the Slavery Film', *The Daily Beast*, 15 March. Available online: https://www.thedailybeast.com/how-2013-became-the-year-of-the-slavery-film (accessed 3 March 2023).

Bogle, D. (2016), *Toms, Coons, Mulattoes, Mammies, Bucks: An Interpretive History of Blacks in American Film*, New York: Bloomsbury Academic, 477.

Bohn, J. (2002), 'Review: [Untitled]', *Computer Music Journal*, 26 (4), 100.

Bolter, J. D. and R. Grusin (2000), *Remediation: Understanding New Media*, Cambridge: Massachusetts Press.

Bourdieu, P. [1984] (1993), *The Field of Cultural Production*, New York: Columbia University Press, 129.

Bowie, D. in conversation with A. Greene (1983), 'David Criticizes MTV for Not Playing Videos by Black Artists', *MTV News: Flashback*, 11 January 2016. Available online: https://www.youtube.com/watch?v=XZGiVzIr8Qg (accessed 3 March 2023).

Bowie, D. cited by K. A. Maciel (2016), 'Seu Jorge as a Cross-Media Star: Between Local Authenticity and Global Appeal', in T. Bergfelder, L. Shaw and J. L. Vieira (eds.), *Stars and Stardom in Brazilian Cinema*, New York: Berghahn Books, 252.

Bowser, P. and L. Spence (2000), *Writing Himself into History: Oscar Micheaux, His Silent Films and His Audiences*, New Jersey: Rutgers University Press, xii.

Bradshaw, P. (2021), Welcome II the Terrordome Review – Dystopian Drama Offers a Bleak Vision of Britain', *The Guardian*. Available online: https://www.theguardian.com/film/2021/aug/04/welcome-ii-the-terrordome-review-timely-re-release-for-dystopian-drama (accessed 10 November 2023).

Braidotti, R. (2016), 'The Contested Posthumanities', in Braidotti, R. and P. Gilroy (eds.), *Conflicting humanities*, London: Bloomsbury Publishing, 10–11 and 15.

Brar, D. S., and A. Sharma (2019), 'What Is This "Black" in Black Studies? From Black British Cultural Studies to Black Critical Thought in UK Arts and Higher Education', *New Formations*, Vol. 99, 88–109.

Breihan, T. (2014), 'FKA twigs – "Video Girl" Video', *Stereogum*, 29 October. Available online: https://www.stereogum.com/1715105/fka-twigs-video-girl-video/news/ (accessed 3 March 2023).

Briones, M. (2003), 'Call-and-Response: Tracing the Ideological Shifts of Richard Wright through His Correspondence with Friends and Fellow Literati', in *African American Review*, Vol. 37, No. 1, Maryland: Johns Hopkins University Press, 53–64.
Brody, R. (2019), 'When Bad Nazis Happen to Good Directors', *The New Yorker*, 16 December. Available online: https://www.newyorker.com/culture/the-front-row/when-bad-nazis-happen-to-good-directors-terrence-malicks-a-hidden-life (accessed 3 March 2023).
Brooks, D. (2010), "Sister, Can You Line It Out?": Zora Neale Hurston and the Sound of Angular of Black Womanhood', *Amerikastudien/American Studies*, 55 (4), 623.
Brooks, K. D. and K. L. Martin (2019), *The Lemonade Reader*, London: Routledge.
Brown, G. C., J. D. Vigil and E. R. Taylor (2012), 'The Ghettoization of Blacks in Los Angeles: The Emergence of Street Gangs', *Journal of African American Studies*, 16 (2), 209–25.
Brown, J. (2011), 'Lovely Sky Boat: Alice Coltrane and the Metaphysics of Sound', in *Black Utopias: Speculative Life and the Music of Other Worlds*, North Carolina: Duke University Press, 59–60.
Brown, J. (2021), *Black Utopias: Speculative Life and the Music of Other Worlds*, Duke: University Press, 59.
Brunson III, J. (2011), 'Showing, Seeing: Hip-Hop, Visual Culture, and the Show-and-Tell Performance', *Black History Bulletin*, 74 (1), 6–12.
Bryant, C. et al. (1998), *Central Avenue Sounds: Jazz in Los Angeles*, California: University of California Press.
Bryant, T. (2017), 'Sampha's Film Is the Sweetest Type of Love Letter', *Nylon*. Available online: https://www.nylon.com/articles/sampha-process-kahlil-joseph-short-film (accessed 3 March 2023).
Bunch III, L. G. (2019), 'Flies in the Buttermilk: Museums, Diversity, and the Will to Change', in J. Cole and L. Lott (eds.), *Diversity, Equity, Accessibility, and Inclusion in Museums*, Lanham, Maryland: Rowman & Littlefield, 3–9.
Buchsbaum, J. (2015), 'Militant Third World Film Distribution in the United States, 1970–1980', *Revue Canadienne D'Études Cinématographiques/Canadian Journal of Film Studies*, 24 (2), 51–65.
Buckley, C. (2019), 'TV Writers of Color and Others Face Widespread Bias, Survey Finds', *The New York Times*, 14 March. Available online: https://www.nytimes.com/2019/03/14/arts/television/television-writers-harassment.html (accessed 3 March 2023).
Burkart, P. and T. McCourt (2004), 'Infrastructure for the Celestial Jukebox', *Popular Music*, 23 (3), 349–362.
Burke, J. (2017), 'Shabazz Palaces – Quazarz: Born on a Gangster Star/Quazarz VS The Jealous Machines', *Soundblab*, 18 July. Available online: https://soundblab.com/reviews/albums/18721-shabazz-palaces-quazarz-born-on-a-gangster-star-quazarz-vs-the-jealous-machines (accessed 3 March 3023).
Butler, I. in conversation with L. Snoad (2014), 'Telepathic Relations: An Interview with Shabazz Palaces', *The Quietus*, 2 September 2014. Available online: https://thequietus.com/articles/16120-shabazz-palaces-ishmael-butler-interview (accessed 3 March 2023).
Butler, T. and G. Robson (2001), 'Social Capital, Gentrification and Neighbourhood Change in London: A Comparison of Three South London Neighbourhoods', *Urban Studies*, 38 (12), 2145–62.

Busch, A. and M. Annas (eds.) (2008), *Ousmane Sembène Interviews*, Jackson: University of Mississippi, 12.

Byrne, Deirdre C. (2004), 'Science Fiction in South Africa', *PMLA*, 119, (3), 522–5.

Cahan, S. (2016), *Mounting Frustration: The Art Museum in the Age of Black Power*, Durham, NC: Duke University Press.

Caldwell, B. cited A. Field, J. Horak, and J. Stewart (2015), *L.A. Rebellion: Creating a New Black Cinema*, California: University of California Press, 1.

Cameron, E. L. (1998), 'Women=Masks: Initiation Arts in North-Western Province, Zambia', in *African Arts* Vol. 31, No. 2 Cambridge, MA: The MIT Press Spring, 50–61, 93.

Campt, T. (2019), 'The Visual Frequency Black Life: Love, Labor, and the Practice of Refusal', *Social Text*, 140, 37 (3), June 2021, 25–46.

Campt, T. (2021), *A Black Gaze: Artists Changing How We See*, Cambridge, Massachusetts: The MIT Press, 5, 44 and 48–78.

Campt, T., Z. Julius, J. Nkiru and A. Weheliye (2020), 'Frequencies of Blackness: A Listening Session', *The Sojourner Project – Cogut Institute for the Humanities*, 3 December. Available online: https://www.youtube.com/watch?v=wF5dL69w1kU (accessed 3 March 2023).

Cardew, B. (2017), 'Machines of Loving Grace: How Artificial Intelligence Helped Techno Grow Up', *The Guardian Online*, 3 July. Available online: https://www.theguardian.com/music/2017/jul/03/artificial-intelligence-compilation-album-warp-records-idm-intelligent-dance-music (accessed 3 March 2023).

Carmichael, R. (2018), 'Donald Glover Brings His Black Renaissance to Saturday Night Live', *NPR*, 5 June 2018. Available online: https://www.npr.org/sections/therecord/2018/05/06/608874886/donald-glover-brings-his-black-renaissance-to-saturday-night-live (accessed 3 March 2023).

Carus, P. (1905), 'The Conception of the Soul and the Belief in Resurrection among the Egyptians', *The Monist*, 15 (3), 420.

Catlin-Legutko, C. (2019), 'History That Promotes Understanding in a Diverse Society', in J. B. Cole and L. L. Lott (eds.), *Diversity, Equity, Accessibility and Inclusion in Museums*, Lanham, MD: Rowman & Littlefield, 41–8.

Caulfield, K. (2018), 'Post Malone's "Beerbongs & Bentleys" Breaks Streaming Record, Debuts at No. 1 on Billboard 200 Albums Chart', *Billboard*, 5 June. Available online: https://www.billboard.com/articles/columns/chart-beat/8454698/post-malone-beerbongs-and-bentleys-no-1-billboard-200 (accessed 3 March 2023).

Charnley, K. (2017), 'Art on the Brink: Bare Art and the Crisis of Liberal Democracy', in G. Sholette and K. Charnley (eds.), *Delirium and Resistance: Activist Art and the Crisis of Capitalism*, London: Pluto Press, 2.

Chartier, R. (1987), *The Cultural Uses of Print in Early Modern France*, New Jersey: Princeton University Press.

Childs-Davis, F. cited by S. Krishnan (2012), 'Lawyer Keven Davis Was a Mentor to Young Artists', *Seattle Times*, 6 January. Available online: https://www.seattletimes.com/seattle-news/lawyer-keven-davis-was-a-mentor-to-young-artists/ (accessed 3 March 2023).

Chion, M. (1994), *Audiovision: Sound on Screen*, New York: Columbia University Press.

Chion, M. (2013), 'Sensory Aspects of Contemporary Cinema', in J. Richardson, C. Gorbman and C. Vernallis (eds.), *The Oxford Handbook of New Audiovisual Aesthetics*, Oxford: Oxford University Press, 77 and 325.

Ciecko, A. (1999), 'Representing the Spaces of Diaspora in Contemporary British Films by Women Directors', *Cinema Journal*, 38 (3), 67 and 69–71.

Clarke, R. and M. Merlin (2013), *Cannabis: Evolution and Ethnobotany*, California: University of California Press.

Coalter, F. (2013), 'Sport-for-Development: Pessimism of the Intellect, Optimism of the Will', in N. Schulenkorf and D. Adair (eds.), *Global Sport-for-Development: Global Culture and Sport Series*, London: Palgrave Macmillan, 62.

Collin, R. (2017), 'Terrence Malick's Song to Song Plumbs New Boreholes of Crine – Review', *The Telegraph Online*, 3 November. Available online: https://www.telegraph.co.uk/films/2017/03/11/terrence-malicks-song-song-plumbs-new-boreholes-cringe-review/ (accessed 3 March 2023).

Combs, S. cited by E. Dinsdale (2020), 'Artist Kahlil Joseph's BLKNWS project is an antidote to a toxic news cycle', *Dazed Digital*, 18 May. Available online: https://www.dazeddigital.com/art-photography/article/49132/1/artist-kahlil-josephs-blknws-project-is-an-antidote-to-a-toxic-news-cycle (accessed 3 March 2023).

Compton Cowboys Official (2020), *Compton Cowboys Website*. Available online: https://www.comptoncowboys.com/ (accessed 3 March 2023).

Connell, R. W. and J. W. Messerschmidt (2005), 'Hegemonic Masculinity: Rethinking the Concept', *Gender and Society*, 19 (6), 829.

Cook, K. (2013), 'The Vegas Hotspot That Broke All the Rules', *Smithsonian Magazine*, January 2013. Available online: https://www.smithsonianmag.com/history/the-vegas-hotspot-that-broke-all-the-rules-165807434/ (accessed 3 March 2023).

Cook, N. (2001), 'Theorising Music Meaning', *Music Theory Spectrum*, Vol. 23, No. 2 (Fall 2001), Autumn, 170–95.

Cooks, B. (2011), *Exhibiting Blackness: African Americans and the American Art Museum*, Boston: University of Massachusetts Press.

Cook-Wilson, W. (2017), 'Watch Sampha's New Short Film Process, By the Director of Lemonade', *Spin*, 31 March. Available online: https://www.spin.com/2017/03/sampha-short-film-process-watch/ (accessed 3 March 2023).

Coombes, A. E. (1997), *Reinventing Africa: Museums, Material Culture, and Popular Imagination in Late Victorian and Edwardian England*, New Haven, CT: Yale University Press, 2.

Cox, M. (1988), 'Augustine, Jerome, Tyconius and the Lingua Punica', in *Studia Orientalia Electronica*, 64, Helsinki: Finnish Oriental Society, 83–106.

Cramer, L. (2017), 'Icons of Catastrophe: Diagramming Blackness in Until the Quiet Comes', *liquid blackness*, 4 (7), 142–86.

Crawford, M. N. (2017), *Black Post-Blackness: The Black Arts Movement and Twenty-First-Century Aesthetics*, Urbana, IL: University of Illinois Press, 2.

Critchley, S. (2005), 'Calm: On Terrence Malick's The Thin Red Line', in R. Read and J. Goodenough (eds.), *Film as Philosophy: Essays on Cinema after Wittgenstein and Cavell*, Basingstoke: Palgrave Macmillan, 147.

Cullen, M. (2011), 'Shabazz Palaces – Inside Avant Rap's Soul', *The Independent*, 24 June. Available online: https://www.independent.co.uk/arts-entertainment/music/features/shabazz-palaces-inside-avant-raps-soul-2302219.html (accessed 3 March 2023).

Dallas, P. (2017), 'Kahlil Joseph on Sound, Silence and Spirituality', *Extra Extra: Nouveau Magazine Erotique*, Vol. 9, 139–48.

Dams, T. (2020), 'Apple Music Adds Another 52 Countries as Tech Giant Unveils Major Services Expansion', *Variety*, 21 April. Available online: https://variety.com/2020/music/news/apple-music-52-countries-tech-giant-unveils-major-services-expansion-1234585734/ (accessed 3 March 2023).

Davies, W. (2017), *The Limits of Neoliberalism: Authority, Sovereignty and the Logic of Competition*, Los Angeles; London: SAGE Publications Ltd.

Davis, K. in conversation with D. Solway (2017), 'How the Family-Run Underground Museum Became One of L.A.'s Most Vital Cultural Forces', *W Magazine*, 11 August. Available online: https://www.wmagazine.com/story/underground-museum-los-angeles-kahlil-joseph-noah-davis (accessed 3 March 2023).

Davis, K. in conversation with D. Solway (2019), 'Kahlil Joseph Is Challenging Representations of Black Life in America', Surface, 2 December. Available online: https://www.surfacemag.com/articles/kahlil-joseph-challenging-black-life/ (accessed online 3 March 2023).

Davis, K. (2022), Public Announcement on Instagram, 15 March 2022. Available online: https://www.instagram.com/p/CbIQzELL2fR/?igshid=YmMyMTA2M2Y= (accessed 3 March 2023).

DeCarava, R. [1952] Cited By R. Kennedy (2009), 'Roy DeCarava, Harlem Insider Who Photographed Ordinary Life, Dies at 89', *The New York Times*, 28 October. Available online: https://www.nytimes.com/2009/10/29/arts/29decarava.html (accessed 3 March 2023).

DeCarava, R. [1952] Cited By M. Cheers (2009), J. C. Bohrnstedt, *Snapshots of a Century in African American Lives*, Bloomington, IN: Authorhouse.

DeCarava, R. and L. Hughes [1955] (2018), *The Sweet Flypaper of Life*, Oxford: Blackwells, 1–98.

Deleuze, G. and F. Guattari [1972] (1983), R. Hurley, M. Seem and Helen R. Lane (trans.) *Anti-Oedipus: Capitalism and Schizophrenia*, Minneapolis: University of Minnesota Press, 34–5.

Deleuze, G. [1985] (1989), H. Tomlinson and R. Galeta (trans.) *Cinema 2: The Time-Image*, Minneapolis: University of Minnesota Press, xi and 1–125.

Dery, M. (1994), 'Black to the Future: Interviews with Samuel R. Delany, Greg Tate, and Tricia Rose', in M. Dery (ed.), *Flame Wars: The Discourse of Cyberculture*, Durham, NC: Duke University Press, 180 and 221.

De Saussure, F. (1916), *Course in General Linguistics* [Republished 2011], New York: Columbia University Press.

Deterville, D. (2013), 'Kahlil Joseph's Until The Quiet Comes: The Afriscape Ghost Dance on Film [parts i and ii]', *Open Space*, 2 March. Available online: https://openspace.sfmoma.org/2013/03/kahlil-josephs-until-the-quiet-comes-the-afriscape-ghost-dance-on-film/ (accessed 3 March 2023).

DeVeaux, S. (1991), 'Constructing the Jazz Tradition: Jazz Historiography', *Black American Literature Forum*, 25 (3), 525–60.

Diawara, M. (1998), 'Towards a Regional Imaginary in Africa', in F. Jameson and M. Miyoshi (eds.), *The Cultures of Globalization*, Durham, NC: Duke University Press, 103–24.

Diawara, M. in conversation with A. McCluskey (2006), 'Troubling the Waters: A Conversation with Manthia Diawara', *Black Camera*, 21 (1) Spring/Summer, 10.

Dijk, F. (1995), 'Sociological Means: Colonial Reactions to the Radicalization of Rastafari in Jamaica, 1956–1959', *New West Indian Guide/Nieuwe West-Indische Gids*, 69 (1–2), 67–101.

Dima, V. (2012), 'Aural Narrative Plans in Djibril Diop Mambèty's Films', *Journal of Film and Video*, 64 (3), 38–52.

Dima, V. (2014), 'Ousmane Sembène's 'La Noire De..: Melancholia in Photo, Text, and Film', *Journal of African Cultural Studies*, 26 (1), 56.

Diop, M. cited by R. Gilbey, (2018). 'How Beyoncé and Jay-Z Put a Visionary Film Back in the Spotlight', *The Guardian Online*, 7 June. Available online: https://www.theguardian.com/film/2018/jun/17/beyonce-jay-z-put-visionary-film-touki-bouki-africa-spotlight (accessed 3 March 2023).

Dixon, W. W. (1995–6), The Practice of Theory, the Theory of Practice: The Post-Colonial Cinema of Maureen Blackwood and the Sankofa Collective, *Film Criticism*, Fall/Winter 1995–6, 20 (1/2), 132.

Donaldson, J. R. (2012), 'Africobra Manifesto?: "Ten in Search of a Nation"', *Journal of Contemporary African Art*, 30, Spring 2012, 28 and 81.

dos Santos, I. (2001), 'Nesta Cidade Todo Mundo é d'Oxum: In This City Everyone Is Oxum's,' in J. M. Murphy and M. Sanford (eds.), *Osun across the Waters: A Yoruba Goddess in Africa and the Americas*. Bloomington: Indiana University Press, 68–83.

Dougan, N. (2015), 'The Art of FKA twigs' Music Videos Dissected', *The Guardian*, 16 May. Available online: https://www.theguardian.com/culture/2015/may/16/fka-twigs-soundtrack-7-videos-manchester-international-festival-mif (accessed 3 March 2023).

Dovey, L. (2009), *African Film and Literature: Adapting Violence to the Screen*, New York: Columbia University Press, 13–15 and 277.

Drass, R. R. (1986), 'Plains Village Settlements in Central Oklahoma: A Survey Along the Middle Course of the Washita River', *Plains Anthropologist*, 31 (114), 155–66.

Drew, K. (2020), '@museummammy', *Kimberley Drew Twitter Account*, 18 April. Available online: https://twitter.com/museummammy/status/1251593837086232577?s=20 (accessed 3 March 2023).

Du Bois, W. E. B. (1899). *The Philadelphia Negro: A Social Study*, Philadelphia: University of Pennsylvania Press, 325.

Du Bois, W. E. B. (1903), *The Souls of Black Folk*, Chicago: A C McClurg, 1–5.

Du Bois, W. E. B. (1926), 'Criteria of Negro Art', *The Crisis*, October, 296.

Dubois, P. (2010), 'Présentation', in E. Biserna, P. Dubois and F. Monvoisin (eds.), *Extended Cinema/Le cinéma gagne du terrain*, Pasian di Prato: Campanotto Editore, 13.

Ducker, E. (2015), 'Kahlil Joseph's m.A.A.d. Gives New Visual Life to Kendrick Lamar's Breakout Album', *The Verge*, 27 March. Available online: https://www.theverge.com/2015/3/27/8292657/kahlil-joseph-maad-kendrick-lamar-moca (accessed 3 March 2023).

Dyer, R. [1979] (1998), *Stars*, London: Bloomsbury.

Eadington, W. (1999), 'The Economics of Casino Gambling', *The Journal of Economic Perspectives*, 13 (3), 173–92.

Eco, U. (2005), 'Innovation & Repetition: Between Modern & Postmodern Aesthetics', *Daedalus*, 134 (4), 203.

Edmonds, E. (2003), *Rastafari: From Outcasts to Culture Bearers*, Oxford: Oxford University Press.

Edmonds, E. (2012), *Rastafari: A Very Short Introduction*, Oxford: Oxford University Press, 49.

Eferighe, J. (2018), 'Hollywood's Black Renaissance and Why the Glass Ceiling Is Barely Cracked', *Kulture Hub*, 22 February. Available online: https://kulturehub.com/hollywood-black-renaissance/ (accessed 3 March 2023).

Elam Jr., H. and K. Jackson [and American Council of Learned Societies] (eds.) (2005), *Black Cultural Traffic: Crossroads in Global Performance and Popular Culture*, Ann Arbor, MI: University of Michigan, 1–43.

Ellis, T. (1989), 'The New Black Aesthetic', *Callaloo*, Vol. 38, 1989. 233–43.

Eltis, D. and D. Richardson (2010), *Atlas of the Transatlantic Slave Trade*, Connecticut: Yale University Press.

Elwes, C. (2015), *Installation and the Moving Image*, New York: Columbia University Press, 1.

Empire, K. (2018), 'Janelle Monáe: Dirty Computer Review – From Dystopian Android to R&B Party Girl', *The Guardian*. 29 April. Available online: https://www.theguardian.com/music/2018/apr/28/janelle-monae-dirty-computer-observer-review (accessed 3 March 2023).

Enwezor, E. (2007), 'Coalition Building: Black Audio Film Collective and Transnational Postcolonialism', in K. Eshun and A. Sagar (eds.), *The Ghosts of Songs: The Film Art of the Black Audio Film Collective*, Liverpool: Liverpool University Press, 122.

Eshun, K. [1998] (1999), *More Brilliant Than the Sun: Adventures in Sonic Fiction*, London: Quartet Books, 00[-007]–C[215].

Fehrle, J. (2019), 'Introduction: Adaptation in a Convergence Environment', in J. Fehrle and W. Schäfke-Zell (eds.), *Adaptation in the Age of Media Convergence*, Amsterdam: Amsterdam University Press, 8.

Fehrle, J. and W. Schäfke-Zell (eds.) (2019), *Adaptation in the Age of Media Convergence*, Amsterdam: Amsterdam University Press.

Fintoni, L. (2015), 'How Flying Lotus Built Brainfeeder, His Spiritual Little Empire', *The Fader*, 26 August. Available online: https://www.thefader.com/2015/08/26/brainfeeder-flying-lotus-label-interview (accessed 3 March 2023).

Fischer, E. and H. Himmelheber (1984), *The Arts of the Dan in West Africa (No. 1)*, Zurich: Museum Rietberg.

FKA twigs, in conversation with T. Lamont (2014), 'FKA twigs: "I'm Appealing to People Who Want Something Different"', *The Guardian*. Available online: https://www.theguardian.com/music/2014/nov/30/-sp-fka-twigs-interview-lp1-two-weeks-video-girl-robert-pattinson (accessed 3 March 2023).

FKA twigs, in conversation with C. Edwardes (2016), 'FKA twigs on Fame, Spirituality and Robert Pattinson', *Evening Standard*. Available online: https://www.standard.co.uk/lifestyle/esmagazine/fka-twigs-on-fame-spirituality-and-robert-pattinson-a3378536.html (accessed 3 March 2023).

FKA twigs, in conversation with B. Spanos (2019), 'FKA Twigs Strips Off Expectations on Her New Album "Magdalene"', *Rolling Stone*, 11 November. Available online: https://www.rollingstone.com/music/music-features/fka-twigs-magdalene-interview-new-album-909005/ (accessed 3 March 2023).

FKA twigs, cited by Harris, N. (2020), 'FKA twigs Cuts a Striking Figures as She Poses in Quirky Facial Sculptures Made of Recycled Rubbish for Artistic New Collaboration Which Celebrates "Creativity beyond Consumption"', *Mail Online*. Available online: https://www.dailymail.co.uk/tvshowbiz/article-8237387/FKA-twigs-cuts-striking-figure-poses-quirky-facial-sculptures-recycled-rubbish.html (accessed 3 March 2023).

FKA twigs, cited by Hunt, E. (2020), '"Watch FKA twigs" Incredible Performance of Cellophane at the NME Awards 2020', *NME*, 12 Feburary. Available online: https://www.nme.com/nme-awards-2020/watch-fka-twigs-incredible-performance-of-cellophane-at-the-nme-awards-2020-2608176 (accessed 3 March 2023).

FKA twigs, in conversation with C. Shaffer (2019), 'FKA twigs Releases Home with You, Discusses Her Upcoming Album Magdalene', *Rolling Stone*, 7 October. Available online:https://www.rollingstone.com/music/music-news/fka-twigs-home-with-you-magdalene-beats-1-895557/ (accessed 3 March 2023).

Flakierski, H. and T. Sekine (1990), *Socialist Dilemmas: East and West*, New York: M.E. Sharpe, 131.
Forman, M. (2000), '"Represent": Race, Space and Place in Rap Music', *Popular Music*, 19 (1), 65–90.
Foucault, M. (1961), *Folie et déraison: histoire de la folie à l'âge classique*. Vol. 169, Paris: Plon.
French, S. (2010), '"If They Don't See Happiness in the Picture at Least They'll See the Black": Chris Marker's Sans Soleil and the Lyotardian Sublime', *Image and Narrative*, 11 (1), 65.
Freud, S. [1912] (1959), 'The Most Prevalent Form of Degradation in Erotic Life', in J. Riviere (trans.) *Collected Papers*, New York: Basic Books, 4, 204.
Fu-Kiau, K. (2001), 'African Cosmology of the Bântu-Kôngo: Principles of Life and Living', New York: Athelia Henrietta Press.
Fuller, G. (1996) cited in N. Feineman and S. Reiss (2000), *Thirty Frames per Second: The Visionary Art of the Music Video*, New York: Harry N Abrams, 23.
Furstenau, M. and L. MacAvoy (2003), 'Terrence Malick's Heideggerian Cinema', *Vertigo Magazine*, Vol. 2, Issue 5, Summer. Available online: https://www.closeupfilmcentre.com/vertigo_magazine/volume-2-issue-5-summer-2003/terrence-malick-s-heideggerian-cinema/ (accessed 3 March 2023).
Garofalo, R. (1997), *Rockin' Out: Popular Music in the USA*, Boston: Allyn and Bacon, 326.
Gastil, R. D. (1971), '"Selling Out" and the Sociology of Knowledge', *Policy Sciences*, 2 (3), 271–7.
Gaut, B. (1997), 'Film Authorship and Collaboration', in R. Allen and M. Smith (eds.), *Film Theory and Philosophy*, Oxford: Oxford University Press, 22 and 149–72.
Geo, B. (1903), 'The Berbers', *Journal of the Royal African Society*, 2 (6), 161–94.
Gikandi, S. (2014), 'Afterword: Outside the Black Atlantic', *Research in African Literatures*, 45 (3), 241–4.
Giles, J. (2015), 'How Queen's Bohemian Rhapsody Ushered in the Video Age', Ultimate Classic Rock, 10 November. Available online: https://ultimateclassicrock.com/queen-bohemian-rhapsody-video/ (accessed 3 March 2023).
Gill, J. (2012), *Harlem: The Four Hundred Year History from Dutch Village to Capital of Black America*, New York: Open Road+ Grove/Atlantic.
Gilroy, P. (1993), *The Black Atlantic: Modernity and Double Consciousness*, Harvard: Harvard University Press, xi, 4, 15, 36, 40, 89, 91, 124, 123 and 203.
Gilroy, P. (1999), 'Analogues of Mourning, Mourning the Analog', in K. Kelly and E. McDonnell (eds.), *Stars Don't Stand Still in the Sky: Music and Myth*, London: Routledge, 266–7.
Gilroy, P. (2000), *Against Race: Imagining Political Culture beyond the Colour Line*, Harvard: Harvard University Press.
Gilroy, P. ([2000] 2004a), *Between Camps: Nations, Cultures and the Allure of Race beyond the Colour Line*, London: Routledge, 11, 150 and 242.
Gilroy, P. (2004b), 'Melancholia and Multiculture', *Open Democracy*, 2 August. Available online: https://www.opendemocracy.net/en/article_2035jsp/ (accessed 3 March 2023).
Gilroy, P. (2010), *Darker Than Blue: On the Moral Economies of Black Atlantic Culture*, Cambridge, MA: Harvard University Press.
Gilroy, P. (2016), 'Not Yet Humanism or the Non-Jewish Jew Becomes the Non-Humanistic Humanist', in Braidotti, R. and P. Gilroy (eds.), *Conflicting Humanities*, London: Bloomsbury Publishing, 10 and 11.
Gilroy, P. in conversation with L. Henry (2020), 'Prof Lez Henry & Prog Paul Gilroy OUTERVIEW July 2020', *The OUTERVIEW Where Reason Comes First [Prof William*

'Lez' Henry Youtube Channel], July 6. Available online: https://www.youtube.com/watch?v=L7jA3rhEd7o (accessed 3 March 2023).

Gilroy, P. in conversation with S. O'Hagan (2020), 'Paul Gilroy – Interview: 'I Don't Think We Can Afford the Luxury of Pessimism', *The Guardian*, 15 November. Available online: https://www.theguardian.com/culture/2020/nov/15/paul-gilroy-i-dont-think-we-can-afford-the-luxury-of-pessimism (accessed 3 March 2023).

Gioni, M. (2020), 'Kahlil Joseph', *Cura Magazine*, 33, Spring. Available online: https://curamagazine.com/digital/kahlil-joseph/ (accessed 3 March 2023).

Gioni, M. in conversation with M. McLean (2018), 'We Are Strangely Used to Asking Artists to Turn Down Their Sound', *Freize*, 6 October. Available online: https://www.frieze.com/article/we-are-strangely-used-asking-artists-turn-down-their-sound (accessed 12 July 2021).

Gioni, M. in conversation with A. Spice (2018), 'How Sci-fi, Magic Realism and Video Games Inspired New Exhibition Strange Days', *The Vinyl Factory*, 2 October. Available online: https://thevinylfactory.com/features/strange-days-massimiliano-gioni-extract/ (accessed 3 March 2023).

Godfrey, M. and Z. Whitley (eds.) (2017), *Soul of a Nation: Art in the Age of Black Power*, New York: Distributed Arts Publishers, 28, 40 and 118–19.

Golding, V. (2013), 'Museums, Poetics and Affect', *Feminist Review*, Vol. 104, 80–99.

Goldstein, A. (2019), 'Why TV Executives Should Make Artist Kahlil Joseph's "BLKNWS" Network, a Star of the Venice Biennale, into a Reality', *artnet*, 14 May. Available online: https://news.artnet.com/art-world/blknws-kahlil-joseph-vience-biennale-2019-1543222 (accessed 3 March 2023).

Gorton, T. (2014), 'FKA twigs Tells All about Her Google Glass Collab', *Dazed Digital*, 5 December. Available online: https://www.dazeddigital.com/music/article/22835/1/fka-twigs-tells-all-about-her-google-glass-collab (accessed 3 March 2023).

Gottlieb, A. (2013), '"Just Another Word for Jazz": The Signifying Auteur in William Greaves's *Symbiopsychotaxiplasm: Take One*", *Black Camera*, 5 (1), 165.

Goyal, Y. (2014), 'Africa and the Black Atlantic', *Research in African Literatures*, 45 (3), v–xxv.

Gragasin, A. (2018), 'Kahlil Joseph: Shadow Play', *Screen Slate*, 2 January. Available online: https://www.screenslate.com/features/679 (accessed 3 March 2023).

Gramsci, A. (2011) [1929], 'Letter to Carlo: 29 December 1929', in F. Rosengarten (ed.), and R. Rosenthal (trans), *Letters from Prison: Volume 1*, New York: Columbia University Press, 299.

Grandy, E. (2011), 'Review: Shabazz Palaces – Black Up', *Pitchfork*, 27 June. Available online: https://pitchfork.com/reviews/albums/15570-black-up/ (accessed 3 March 2023).

Gray, M. and J. DeFilippis (2015), 'Learning from Las Vegas: Unions and Post-Industrial Urbanisation', *Urban Studies*, 52 (9), 1683–701.

Grayson, G. W. (1988), *A Creek Warrior for Confederacy: The Autobiography of Chief G. W. Grayson*, Oklahoma City: University of Oklahoma.

Greenaway, P. (2007), 'Peter Greenaway, Cinema = Dead', *Westframe Youtube*, 29 June. Available online: https://www.youtube.com/watch?v=-t-9qxqdVm4 (accessed 3 March 2023).

Greenberger, A. (2022), 'Kahlil Joseph to Develop BLKNWS Video Installation into Feature Film', *ARTnews*, 27 January. Available online: https://www.artnews.com/art-news/news/kahlil-joseph-blknws-a24-film-1234616895/ (accessed 3 March 2023).

Greenblatt, S. (1990), 'Culture', in F. Lentricchia and T. McLaughlin (eds.), *Critical Terms for Literary Study*, Chicago: University of Chicago Press 1990, 229.
Griffin, C. (2013), 'Midtown Bowl Closing Its Doors after 52 years', *Our Weekly Los Angeles*, 20 June. Available online: http://ourweekly.com/news/2013/jun/20/midtown-bowl-closing-its-doors-after-52-years/ (accessed 3 March 2023).
Griffin, N. (2010), 'The "Thriller" Diaries', *Vanity Fair*, 24 June. Available online: https://archive.vanityfair.com/article/2010/7/the-thriller-diaries (accessed 3 March 2023).
Grindstaff, L. (2012), 'Reality TV and the Production of "Ordinary Celebrity": Notes from the Field', *Berkeley Journal of Sociology*, 56, 22–40.
Groth, J. C. (1994), 'The Exclusive Value Principle – A Concept for Marketing', *Journal of Product & Brand Management*, Vol. 3, No. 3, Bingley: MCB University Press, 8–18.
Guerrero, E. (1993), 'FRAMING BLACKNESS: The African-American Image in the Cinema of the Nineties', *Cinéaste*, 20 (2), 24.
Gundaker, G. (2011), 'The Kongo Cosmogram in Historical Archaeology and the Moral Compass of Dave the Potter', *Historical Archaeology*, 45 (2), 176–83.
Gunn, J. (2020), 'Intergenerational Pedagogy in Jenn Nkiru's Rebirth Is Necessary', in A. Raengo and L. Cramer (eds.), 'IN FOCUS: Modes of Black Liquidity: Music Video as Black Art', *JCMS: Journal of Cinema and Media Studies*, 59.2, 163–8.
Hagle, W. (2014), 'What Matters Most: An Online Artist and Filmmaking Collective', All My Faves, 27 January. Available online: https://blog.allmyfaves.com/video/what-matters-most-an-online-artist-and-filmmaking-collective/ (accessed 3 March 2023).
Halberstam, J. (2013), 'The Wild Beyond: With and for the Undercommons', in S. Harney and F. Moten, *The Undercommons: Fugitive Planning & Black Study*, Wivenhoe/New York/Port Watson: Minor Compositions, 11.
Hale, L. (2001), 'Reflections of Gender and Sexuality in Brazilian Umbanda', in J. Murphy and M. Sanford, M. (eds.), *Osun Across the Waters: A Yoruba Goddess in Africa and the Americas*, Bloomington, IN: Indiana University Press, 213–30.
Hall, S. (1973), 'Encoding and Decoding in the Television Discourse', Training in the Critical Reading of Televisual Language [Council of Europe Colloquy, Organised by the Council and Centre for Mass Communication Research], Leicester: University of Leicester, 1–19.
Hall, S. (1988), 'New Ethnicities', in K. Mercer (ed.), *Black Film British Cinema*, London: ICA, 28.
Hall, S. (1993a), 'Culture, Community, Nation', *Cultural Studies*, 7 (3), 363 and 375.
Hall, S. (1993b), 'What Is This "Black" in Black Popular Culture?', *Social Justice*, 20 (51–52), 104–14.
Hall, S. (1995), 'Negotiating Caribbean Identities', *New Left Review*, I/209, Jan/Feb, 5.
Hamlet, J. (2011), 'Word! The African American Oral Tradition and Its Rhetorical Impact on American Popular Culture', *Black History Bulletin*, 74 (1), 2011, 27–31.
Hancock, H. (2014), 'Miles Davis According to Herbie Hancock', *SafaJah Youtube Account*, 9 March. Available online: https://www.youtube.com/watch?v=FL4LxrN-iyw (accessed 3 March 2023).
Hanes, R. (1982) 'Cultural Persistence in Nevada: Current Native American Issues', *Journal of California and Great Basin Anthropology*, 4 (2), 203–21.
Hartman, S. (1997), *Scenes of Subjection: Terror, Slavery, and Self-Making in Nineteenth-Century America*, Oxford: Oxford University Press, 7 and 19.
Harvey, D. (2007), *A Brief History of Neoliberalism*, Oxford: Oxford University Press.

Harvie, J. (2013), *Fair Play: Art, Performance and Neoliberalism*, Houndmills, Bakingstoke, Hampshire: Palgrave Macmillian, 193.

Hassler-Forest, D. (2022), *Janelle Monáe's Queer Afrofuturism: Defying Every Label*, New Jersey: Rutgers University Press.

Heinzl, J. (2018), *Feel It All Around: Art Music Video, Art Cinema, and Spectatorship in the Streaming Era*, Doctoral Dissertation, Pittsburgh: University of Pittsburgh, 3.

Hesmondhalgh, D. (2013), *The Culture Industries [Third Edition]*, Thousand Oaks, California: Sage Publications.

Hess, D. J. (1992), 'Umbanda and Quimbanda Magic in Brazil: Rethinking Aspects of Bastide's Work', *Archives de Sciences Sociales Des Religions*, 37 (79), 135–53.

Hilmes, M., C. Huber, D. Jaramillo, A. Martin, D. Milch, A. Nayman, M. Z. Seitz, C. Sharrett, A. Taubin, and B. Willimon, (2014), 'RETHINKING TELEVISION: A Critical Symposium on the New Age of Episodic Narrative Storytelling', *Cinéaste*, 39 (4), 26–38.

Hodge, S. (2016), *Art in Detail: 100 Masterpieces*, London: Thames and Hudson, 6.

Hrabalik, P. (2014), 'History of Czechoslovak Music Video Until 1969', *Bigbit: Internetová encyklopedie rocku*. Available online: http://www.ceskatelevize.cz/specialy/bigbit/ceskoslovensko/clanky/187-historie-ceskoslovenskeho-hudebniho-klipu-do-r-1989/ (accessed 3 March 2023).

Hsu, H. (2017), 'Alice Coltrane's Devotional Music', *The New Yorker*, 17 April. Available online: https://www.newyorker.com/magazine/2017/04/24/alice-coltranes-devotional-music (accessed 3 March 2023).

Huff, Q. (2012), 'A Joy to Experience: Neo-Soul Singer Bilal Oliver', *Pop Matters*, 22 January. Available online: https://www.popmatters.com/152722-featuring-bilal-2495902134.html (accessed 3 March 2023).

Huggins, N. I. (1995), *Voices from the Harlem Renaissance*, Oxford: Oxford University Press, 10.

Husayn, S. (2009), 'Shafiq En'A Free Ka', *Shafiq Husayn Bandcamp*, 6 October. Available online: https://shafiqhusayn.bandcamp.com/album/shafiq-en-a-free-ka (accessed 3 March 2023).

Isoardi, S. (1998), 'Foreword', in Bryant et al. (eds.), *Central Avenue Sounds: Jazz in Los Angeles*, California: University of California Press, xv.

Jackson, K. (2005), 'Introduction', in H. J. Elam and K. Jackson (eds.), *Black Cultural Traffic: Crossroads in Global Performance and Popular Culture*, Ann Arbor, MI: University of Michigan, 1–43.

Jafa, A. (1992), '69', in G. Dent et al., *Black Popular Culture*, Seattle: Bay Press, 249–54.

Jafa, A. in conversation with H. Obrist. (2016), 'Arthur Jafa in conversation with Hans Ulrich Obrist', *Serpentine Galleries Archive 2016*. Available online: https://www.serpentinegalleries.org/whats-on/arthur-jafa-series-utterly-improbable-yet-extraordinary-renditions/#downloads (accessed 3 March 2023).

Jafa, A. in conversation with A. Sargent (2017), 'Arthur Jafa and the Future of Black Cinema', *Interview Magazine*, 11 January. Available online: https://www.interviewmagazine.com/art/arthur-jafa (accessed 3 March 2023).

Jafa, A. in conversation with K. Joseph (2017), 'Kahlil Joseph & Arthur Jafa: In Conversation', *Tate Talks*, 10 August. Available online: https://www.youtube.com/watch?v=otPECh1Q2xQ (accessed 3 March 2023).

Jaji, T. E. (2014), *Stereomodernism: Modernism, Music and Pan-African Solidarity*, Oxford: Oxford University Press, 9–17 and 111.

Jaji, T. E. (2018), 'Meet the Professors: Tsitsi Jaji', *Duke University's Department of African & African American Studies*. Available online: https://www.youtube.com/watch?v=IKFh-0woXHY (accessed 10 November 2023).

James, M. (2020), *Sonic Intimacy: Reggae Sound Systems, Jungle Pirate Radio and Grime Youtube Music Videos*, London: Bloomsbury Academic.

Jameson, F. (1991), *Postmodernism, Or, The Cultural Logic of Late Capitalism*, Durham, NC: Duke University Press 1991, 1–67.

Jameson, F. (2002), *A Singular Modernity: Essay on the Ontology of the Present*, London: Verson, 215.

Jansen, C. (2017), 'Kahlil Joseph's m.A.A.d', *Elephant*, 28 October. Available online: https://elephant.art/kahlil-josephs-m-a-a-d/ (accessed 3 March 2023).

Jarman-Ivens, F. (2007), *Oh Boy!: Masculinities and Popular Music*, London: Routledge, 3.

Jaschik, S. (2019), 'The Shrinking Ph.D. Job Market', *Inside Higher Education 4*. Available online: https://www.insidehighered.com/news/2016/04/04/new-data-show-tightening-phd-job-market-across-disciplines (accessed 3 March 2023).

Jenkins, B. (2020), '@BarryJenkins', *Barry Jenkins Twitter Account*, 21 April. Available online: https://twitter.com/BarryJenkins/status/1252442647886610434?s=20 (accessed 3 March 2023).

Jenkins, H. cited by D. Solway (2017), 'How the Family-Run Underground Museum Became One of L.A.'s Most Vital Cultural Forces', *W Magazine*, 11 August. Available online: https://www.wmagazine.com/story/underground-museum-los-angeles-kahlil-joseph-noah-davis (accessed 3 March 2023).

Jiménez, G. (2011), '"Something 2 Dance 2": Electro Hop in 1980s Los Angeles and Its Afrofuturist Link', *Black Music Research Journal*, 31 (1), 2011, 131–44.

Johnson, B. C. (1986), 'Four Dan Sculptors: Continuity and Change', in *African Arts*, Vol. 20, No. 4, Cambridge, MA: The MIT Press, Aug, 22–4, 26, 82–3.

Jordán, M. (1998), *Art and Initiation among Chokwe and Related Peoples*, New York and Munich: Prestel.

Joseph, K. in conversation with A. Abraham (2017), 'How Artist Kahlil Joseph Restored Faith in the Music Video', *The Guardian Online*, 19 October. Available online: https://www.theguardian.com/artanddesign/2017/oct/19/how-lemonade-director-kahlil-joseph-restored-faith-in-the-music-video (accessed 3 March 2023).

Joseph, K. and What Matters Most (2010), 'Jung at Heart', *NOWNESS*, 10 December. Available online: https://www.nowness.com/story/kahlil-joseph-jung-at-heart (accessed 3 March 2023).

Joseph, K. in conversation with NOWNESS (2013), 'Shorts on Sunday: Wildcat', *Nowness*, 28 April. Available online: https://www.nowness.com/series/shorts-on-sundays/shorts-on-sundays-wildcat (accessed 3 March 2023).

Joseph, K. in conversation with L. Raiss (2014), 'Interview: Kahlil Joseph's Upcoming Film m.A.A.d Will Bring Kendrick Lamar's Debut to Life', *The Fader*, 7 August. Available online: https://www.thefader.com/2014/08/07/interview-kahlil-josephs-upcoming-film-emmaadem-will-bring-kendrick-lamars-debut-to-life (accessed 3 March 2023).

Joseph, K. in conversation with P. Dallas (2017), 'Kahlil Joseph on Sound, Silence and Spirituality', in *Extra Extra: Nouveau Magazine Erotique*, 143–9.

Joseph, K. cited by G. Helfet (2018), 'Kahlil Joseph's Fly Paper Makes European Debut at The Store X Berlin's New Exhibition Space', *The Vinyl Factory*, 26 April. Available online: https://thevinylfactory.com/news/kahlill-joseph-fly-paper-the-store-x-berlin/ (accessed 3 March 2023).

Joseph, K. in conversation with A. Kane (2017), 'The Elusive Director Working with Beyoncé, Kendrick and Sampha', *Dazed Digital* (03.08.17), *Dazed Digital*, 3 August. Available online: http://www.dazeddigital.com/artsandculture/article/36945/1/kahlil-joseph-the-elusive-director-working-with-beyonce-kendrick-sampha (accessed 3 March 2023).

Joseph, K. cited by D. McDermon (2017), 'Kahlil Joseph's New Film Is Steeped in Harlem's History. And His Own', *The New York Times*, 31 October. Available online: https://www.nytimes.com/2017/10/31/arts/design/kahlil-joseph-film-new-museum-fly-paper-roy-de-carava.html (accessed 3 March 2023).

Joseph, K. in conversation with C. Jansen (2018), 'Kahlil Joseph: Caught in a Spell', *Elephant*, 14 October. Available online: https://elephant.art/kahlil-joseph-caught-spell/ (accessed 3 March 2023).

Joseph, K. in conversation with D. Solway (2019), 'Kahlil Joseph Is Challenging Representations of Black Life in America', *Surface Mag*. Available online: https://www.surfacemag.com/articles/kahlil-joseph-challenging-black-life/ (accessed 3 March 2023).

Joseph, K. in conversation with H. Molesworth and K. Davis (2020), 'On Noah Davis: Helen Molesworth, Kahlil Joseph and Karon Davis', *Dialogues: The David Zwirner Podcast*, Episode 18, 1 April. Available online: https://cms.megaphone.fm/channel/dialogues (accessed 3 March 2023).

Joseph, K. in conversation with T. Nance and A. Jafa, Cited By N. Orr (2017), 'It's About the Notes You Don't Play: Friday Evening at the 3rd Annual Blackstar Film Festival', *Shadow and Act*, 20 April. Available online: https://shadowandact.com/its-about-the-notes-you-dont-play-friday-evening-at-the-3rd-annual-blackstar-film-festival (accessed 3 March 2023).

Joseph, K. in conversation with A. Lissoni (2017), 'Kahlil Joseph', *Kaleidoscope* (Fall/Winter 31), Milan: WhiteCirc Distribution. Available online: http://kaleidoscope.media/kahlil-joseph/ (accessed 3 March 2023).

Joseph, K. cited by E. Dinsdale (2020), 'Artist Kahlil Joseph's BLKNWS Project Is an Antidote to a Toxic News Cycle', *Dazed Digital*, 18 May. Available online: https://www.dazeddigital.com/art-photography/article/49132/1/artist-kahlil-josephs-blknws-project-is-an-antidote-to-a-toxic-news-cycle (accessed 3 March 2023).

Josephs, B. (2014), 'Album Review: FKA twigs – LP1', *Consequence*, 11 August. Available online: https://consequence.net/2014/08/album-review-fka-twigs-lp1/ (accessed 3 March 2023).

Julius, Z. (2020), 'Frequencies of Blackness: A Listening Session', in T. Campt, Z. Julius, J. Nkiru and A. Weheliye, *The Sojourner Project – Cogut Institute for the Humanities*, 3 December. Available online: https://www.youtube.com/watch?v=wF5dL69w1kU (accessed 3 March 2023).

Jung, C. G. and A. Jaffé (1961), R. Winston and C. Winston (trans.) *Memories, Dreams and Reflections*, London: Fontana, 178–94.

Jung, C. G. (2009), S. Shamdasani (ed.), M. Kyburz, J. Peck and S. Shamdasani (trans.), *The Red Book: Liber novus*, New York and London: W.W. Norton, 233.

Kane, A. (2017), 'The Elusive Director Working with Beyoncé, Kendrick and Sampha', in *Dazed Digital,* 3 August. Available online: http://www.dazeddigital.com/artsandculture/article/36945/1/kahlil-joseph-the-elusive-director-working-with-beyonce-kendrick-sampha (accessed 10 January 2023).

Kanneh, K. (1998) *African Identities: Race, Nation and Culture in Ethnography, Pan-Africanism and Black Literatures*, London and New York: Routledge, 123.
Kanner, B. (1999), *The 100 Best TV Commercials: And Why They Worked*, New York: Times Books, xviii.
Karenga, R. [1968] (1972), 'Black Cultural Nationalism', in A. Gayle Jr. (ed.), *The Black Aesthetic*, New York: Doubleday Inc., 5.
Keeling, K. (2007), *The Witch's Flight: The Cinematic, the Black Femme, and the Image of Common Sense*, North Carolina: Duke University Press, 62.
KENZO, cited by Y. Avecedo (2018), 'Music Is My Mistress: KENZO Launches Short Film Directed by "Lemonade" Helmer Kahlil Joseph', *Indiewire*, 2 February 2018. Available online: https://www.indiewire.com/2017/02/music-is-my-mistress-lemonade-director-kahlil-joseph-kenzo-jesse-williams-tracee-ellis-ross-1201785617/ (accessed 3 March 2023).
KENZO, cited by Aïshti (2017), 'KENZO Films #4', *A Magazine*, Issue 87, 10 February. Available online: https://issuu.com/aishti/docs/amag87/221 (accessed 3 March 2023).
Keppler, N. (2016), '10 Music Video Milestones', *Mental Floss*, 1 August. Available online: https://www.mentalfloss.com/article/82972/10-music-video-milestones-predated-mtv (accessed 3 March 2023).
Kiersh, E. (1986), 'Run-DMC Is Beating the Rap', *Rolling Stone*, 4 December. Available online: https://www.rollingstone.com/music/music-news/run-d-m-c-is-beating-the-rap-106981/ (accessed 3 March 2023).
Kindem, G. and M. Steele (1991), 'Emitai and Ceddo. Women in Sembène's films', *Jump Cut*, 36, 52–60.
Kirby, J. (2012), 'Ishmael Butler's Shabazz Palaces Is Heavy yet Fleeting Afro-celestial Experience', *Wax Poetics*, Issue 51, Summer. Available online: https://www.waxpoetics.com/blog/features/articles/ishmael-butlers-shabazz-palaces-heavy-yet-fleeting-afro-celestial-experience/ (accessed 3 March 2023).
Kiyaga-Mulindwa, D. (2005), 'Nyabingi Cult and Resistance', in K. Shillington (ed.), *Encyclopedia of African History*, New York: Fitzroy Dearborn.
Knee, A. and K. Musser (1992), 'William Greaves, Documentary Film-Making, and the African-American Experience', *Film Quarterly*, 45 (3), 13–25.
Knight, R. (1985), 'The Harp in India Today', *Ethnomusicology*, 29 (1), 9–28.
Kornhaber, S. (2018), 'Donald Glover Is Watching You Watch Him', *The Atlantic*, 7 May. Available online: https://www.theatlantic.com/entertainment/archive/2018/05/donald-glover-this-is-america-childish-gambino/559805/ (accessed 3 March 2023).
Korsgaard, M. B. (2017), *Music Video after MTV: Audiovisual Studies, New Media, and Popular Music*, London: Routledge, 7.
Krishnan, S. (2012), 'Lawyer Keven Davis Was a Mentor to Young Artists', *Seattle Times*, 6 January. Available online: https://www.seattletimes.com/seattle-news/lawyer-keven-davis-was-a-mentor-to-young-artists/ (accessed 3 March 2023).
Kruger, D. (2011), 'Australian Music Media', *Debbie Kruger Official Website*. Available online: www.debbiekruger.com/broadcaster/ausmusicmedia.html (accessed 3 March 2023).
Ku, R. (2002), 'The Creative Destruction of Copyright: Napster and the New Economics of Digital Technology', *The University of Chicago Law Review*, 69 (1), 264.
Kumar, A. (2012), 'Debates around Authorship and Originality: Hindi during the Colonial Period', *Economic and Political Weekly*, 47 (28), 50–7.
La Follette, L. (2017), 'Looted Antiquities, Art Museums and Restitution in the United States since 1970', *Journal of Contemporary History*, 52 (3), 669–87.

LaGamma, A. (2004), 'Recent Acquisitions, A Selection: 2003–2004', in *The Metropolitan Museum of Art Bulletin*, New Series Vol. 62, No. 2, New York: The Metropolitan Museum of Art, Fall, 46–8.

Lambert, J. (2009), '"Wait for the Next Pictures": Intertextuality and Cliffhanger Continuity in Early Cinema and Comic Strips', *Cinema Journal*, 48 (2), 8.

Landau, J. (1976), 'Otis Redding', in J. Miller (ed.), *The Rolling Stone Illustrated History of Rock & Roll*, New York: Rolling Stone Press, 210–13.

Lee, S. (2010), *Erotic Revolutionaries: Black Women, Sexuality, and Popular Culture*, Lanham, MD: Hamilton Books (Rowman & Littlefield), 128.

Lentin, A. and G. Titley (2011), *The Crisis of Multiculturalism: Racism in a Neoliberal Age*, London: Zed Books.

Lester, P. (2013), 'New Band of the Week [Indie]: FKA twigs (No. 1569)', *The Guardian*, 6 August. Available online: https://www.theguardian.com/music/2013/aug/06/fka-twigs (accessed 3 March 2023).

Lewis, J. (2017), 'The Ecstatic Music of Alice Coltrane Turiyasangitananda', *The Guardian*, 3 May. Available online: https://www.theguardian.com/music/2017/may/03/the-ecstatic-music-of-alice-coltrane-turiyasangitananda-review-truly-numinous-energy (accessed 3 March 2023).

Lewis, S. S. and R. G. Waddy (1969), *Black Artists on Art: Volume 1*, Los Angeles: Contemporary Crafts Publishers.

Lewis, C. T. and C. Short (1879), 'Afer', in *A Latin Dictionary*, Oxford: Clarendon Press.

Linscott, C. (2020), 'Secret Histories and Visual Riffs, or Miles Davis, Alice Coltrane and Flying Lotus Go to the Movies', in A. Raengo and L. Cramer (eds.), *IN FOCUS: Modes of Black Liquidity: Music Video as Black Art*, *JCMS: Journal of Cinema and Media Studies*, 59.2, 150.

Liu, Y. (2019), 'The Entertainment Capital of the World Las Vegas Nevada USA – The Las Vegas Strip Streetscape 2', *360 Cities*. Available online: https://www.360cities.net/image/the-entertainment-capital-of-the-world-las-vegas-nevada-usa-thelas-vegas-stripstreetscape-2-usa (accessed 3 March 2023).

liquid blackness (2016a), 'Kahlil Joseph', *liquidblackness.com*. Available online: https://liquidblackness.com/kahlil-joseph (accessed 3 March 2023).

liquid blackness (2016b), 'HOLDING BLACKNESS IN SUSPENSION: THE FILMS OF KAHLIL JOSEPH', *liquid blackness (www.liquidblackness.com)*. Available online: https://liquidblackness.com/kahlil-joseph-research-project (accessed 3 March 2023).

liquid blackness (2017), 'Holding Blackness: Aesthetics of Suspension', *liquid blackness journal*, Vol. 4, No. 7, October 2017. Available online: https://liquidblackness.com/liquid-blackness-journal-issue-7 (accessed 3 March 2023).

Lloyd, G. (2002), *The Man of Reason: Male and Female in Western Philosophy*, London: Routledge.

Locke, A. (1928), 'Art of Propaganda?', *Harlem*, 1 (1), November, 1.

London, B. (2020), *Video/Art: The First Fifty Years*, London and New York: Phaidon, 10–11 and 250–74.

Lorde, A. [1978] (1984), *Sister Outsider: Essays and Speeches by Audre Lorde*, Freedom, CA: The Cross Press, 54.

Lordi, E. J. (2020), *The Meaning of Soul: Black Music and Resilience since the 1960s*, North Carolina: Duke University Press, 5 and 9.

Los Angeles Nomadic Division (2020), 'Kahlil Joseph BLKNWS', *LAND – Los Angeles Nomadic Division*. Available online: https://nomadicdivision.org/exhibition/blknws/ (accessed 3 March 2023).

Loughrey, C. (2016), 'Spike Lee Was Nearly Kicked Out of NYU for His The Birth of a Nation Short', *The Independent*, 15 August. Available online: https://www.independent.co.uk/arts-entertainment/films/news/spike-lee-was-nearly-kicked-out-nyu-his-birth-nation-short-a7192231.html (accessed 3 March 2023).

Lysloff, R. and L. Gay (2003), *Music and Technoculture*, Middletown, CT: Wesleyan University Press, 185.

Macarthur, K. (2016), 'Las Vegas – The Gambling Capital of the World', *Vegas Mobile Casino*. 31 August. Available online: https://www.vegasmobilecasino.co.uk/las-vegas-gambling-capital-of-the-world/ (accessed 3 March 2023).

MacDonald, S. and J. N. Stewart (2021), 'Preface: William Greaves: Renaissance Man and Race Man', in *William Greaves: Filmmaking as Mission*, New York: Columbia University Press, xvii–xxx.

MacGaffey, W. (1974), 'Oral tradition in central Africa', *The International Journal of African Historical Studies*, 7 (3), 417–26.

Mahon, M. (2004), *Right to Rock: The Black Rock Coalition and the Cultural Politics of Race*, North Carolina: Duke University Press.

Makarah, O. F. (1998), 'Fired Up!', in J. Bobo (ed.), *Black Women Film and Video Artists*, New York: Routledge, 130–1.

Malik, S., C. Chapain, and R. Comunian (2017), 'Rethinking Cultural Diversity in the UK Film Sector: Practices in Community Filmmaking', *Organization*, 24 (3), 308–29.

Mambéty, D. cited by F. Pfaff (1988), *Twenty-five Black African Filmmakers: A Critical Study, with Filmography and Bio-bibliography*, Connecticut: Greenwood Publishing Group, 218.

Marshall, G. (1991), *Spirit of 69: Skinhead Bible*, London: ST Publishing.

Martinez, J. F. (2008), 'Bloods', in L. Kontos and David Brotherton (eds.), *Encyclopedia of Gangs*, Westport, CT: Greenwood Press, 12–13.

Mason, P. (1996), 'Race, Culture, and the Market', *Journal of Black Studies*, 26 (6), 782–808.

Mawere, M. (2015), 'Capturing the Fading Past and Making Nous of the Present-Future of African Museums: An Introduction', in M. Mawere, H. Chiwaura and T. P. Thondhlana (eds.), *African Museums in the Making: Reflections on the Politics of Material and Public Culture in Zimbabwe*, Mankon, Bamenda: Langaa Research and Publishing CIG, 1.

Mawere, M. and T. R. Mubaya (2015), '"A Shadow That Refuses to Leave": The Enduring Legacy of Colonialism in Zimbabwean Museum Governance', in M. Mawere, H. Chiwaura and T. P. Thondhlana (eds.), *African Museums in the Making: Reflections on the Politics of Material and Public Culture in Zimbabwe*, Mankon, Bamenda: Langaa Research and Publishing CIG, 141 and 151.

McCoy, J. (2009), 'Making Violence Ordinary: Radio, Music and the Rwandan Genocide', *African Music*, 8 (3), 85–96.

McQueen, S. in conversation with P. Gilroy (2020), 'Sarah Parker Remond Centre: In Conversation with Steve McQueen [Transcript]', *UCL: Sarah Parker Remond Centre for the Study of Racism and Racialisation*, 26 October. Available online: https://www.ucl.ac.uk/racism-racialisation/transcript-conversation-steve-mcqueen (accessed 3 March 2023).

Mellen, J. (1978), *Big Bad Wolves: Masculinity in American Films*, London: Elm Tree Books, 3.

Melville, C. (2020), *It's a London Thing: How Rare Groove, Acid House and Jungle Remapped the City*, Manchester: Manchester University Press, 1–11, and 20–30.

Menard, D. (2003), 'A Deleuzian Analysis of Tarkovsky's Theory of Time-Pressure, Part 1: Tarkovsky's theory of time-pressure as cine-physics [part ii]', in *Off Screen*, Vol. 7, No. 8, August. Available online: https://offscreen.com/view/tarkovsky (accessed 3 March 2023).

Mercer, J. (1953), 'Two Basic Functions of Cinema', *Journal of the University Film Producers Association*, Vol. 5, No. 3, Champaign, IL: University of Illinois Press, Spring, 17–20.

Merriam-Webster (2002), 'Cheeba', *Merriam Webster: Cheeba*. Available online: https://www.merriam-webster.com/dictionary/cheeba (accessed 3 March 2023).

Metz, A. and C. Benson (2000), *The Madonna Companion*, New York City: Shirmer Books.

Michel, S. (2007), 'MoMA Does a Drive-In', *NY Mag*, 4 January. Available online:https://nymag.com/arts/art/reviews/26286/ (accessed 3 March 2023).

Miller-Young, M. (2008), 'Hip-Hop Honeys and Da Hustlaz: Black Sexualities in the New Hip-Hop Pornography', in *Meridians: Feminism, Race, Transnationalism*, Vol. 8, No. 1, North Carolina: Duke University Press, 261–92.

Millner, S. M. (1985), 'The New South: The New Racism', *Revue Française D'études Américaines*, Vol. 23, 99–113.

Mills, P. (2012), *Media and Popular Music*, Edinburgh: Edinburgh University Press, vii.

Mirowski, P. E. (2016), 'This Is Water (or Is It Neoliberalism?)', *Institute for New Economic Thinking Online*. Available online: https://www.ineteconomics.org/perspectives/blog/this-is-water-or-is-it-neoliberalism (accessed 3 March 2023).

Mirzoeff, N. (2015), *How to see the world*, London: Penguin UK, 12.

Mirzoeff, N. (2023), *White Sight: Visual Politics and Practices of Whiteness*, Massachusetts: The MIT Press, vii.

Mitchell, W. K. (1992), *The Reconfigured Eye: Visual Truth in the Post-photographic Era*, Boston: MIT Press, 51.

Moinzadeh, A. (2016), 'Tendai Maraire on Shabazz Palaces, Musical Prophecies and Bridging American and African Cultures', *Paste Magazine*, 9 September 2016. Available online: https://www.pastemagazine.com/articles/2016/09/tendai-maraire-on-shabazz-palaces-musical-propheci.html (accessed 3 March 2023).

Molesworth, H. (2020), *Noah Davis*, New York, London, Paris and Hong Kong: David Zwirner Books.

Molesworth, H. in conversation with S. Cascone (2020), 'Is Diddy's New Black News Network a Ripoff of Artist Kahlil Joseph's Acclaimed Venice Biennale Project? Some Critics Think So', *artnet*, 21 April. Available online: https://news.artnet.com/art-world/diddy-black-news-kahlil-joseph-1839327 (accessed 3 March 2023).

Monson, I. (1995), 'The Problem with White Hipness: Race, Gender, and Cultural Conceptions in Jazz Historical Discourse', *Journal of the American Musicological Society*, 48 (3), 396–422.

Moore, M. (2020), *The Butterfly Effect: How Kendrick Lamar Ignited the Soul of Black America*, London: Hodder and Stoughton, 47.

Moskowitz, M. (2008), 'The Enduring Importance of Richard Wright', *The Journal of Blacks in Higher Education*, Vol. 59, 58–62.

Moten, F. (2003), *In the Break: The Aesthetics of the Black Radical Tradition*, Minnesota: University of Minnesota Press.

Movshovitz, H. in conversation with Siegel, R. (2007), 'Long-Lost Classic "Killer of Sheep"', Hits Theaters, NPR Transcripts, March 29.

Mudede, C. (2016), 'Touki Bouki Is a Mind-Blowing Afro-Funk Experiment', *The Stranger*, 22 June. Available online: https://www.thestranger.com/film/2016/06/22/24243718/touki-bouki-is-a-mind-blowing-afro-funk-experiment (accessed 3 March 2023).

Mundy, J. (1994), 'Postmodernism and Music Video', *Critical Survey*, 6 (2), 263.
Murphy, J. M. and M. Sanford (eds.) (2001), *Osun Across the Waters: A Yoruba Goddess in Africa and the Americas*, Bloomington, IN: Indiana University Press, 2 and 6.
Munyaradzi, G. and W. Zimidzi (2012), 'Comparison of Western Music and African Music', *Creative Education*, 3 (2), 193–195.
Naftule, A. (2017), Not So Bitter After All: "Killer of Sheep", *Medium*, 19 July 2018. Available online: https://medium.com/@ashleynaftule/not-so-bitter-after-all-killer-of-sheep-c96b9bac6a52#:~:text=In%20a%20film%20full%20of,Master%20of%20Fine%20Arts%20thesis. (accessed 10 January 2024).
Naftule, A. (2018), 'Not So Bitter After All: "Killer of Sheep"', *Medium*, 19 July. Available online: https://medium.com/@ashleynaftule/not-so-bitter-after-all-killer-of-sheep-c96b9bac6a52 (accessed 3 March 2023).
Naremore, J. (2017), *Charles Burnett: A Cinema of Symbolic Knowledge*, Berkeley, NC: University of California Press, 100.
Ndlela, M. N. (2017), 'Social Media and African Films: New Spaces, New Meanings', in W. Mano et al., *African Film Cultures: Contexts of Creation and Circulation*, Cambridge, MA: Cambridge Scholars Publishing, 206–3.
Neal, L. (1968), 'The Black Arts Movements', *The Drama Review: TDR [Black Theatre]*, 12 (4), Summer 28.
Neal, M. A. (2001), *Soul Babies: Black Popular Culture and the Post-Soul Aesthetic*, London: Routledge, 112.
Nero, M. (2019), 'What Is Neo-Soul?', *Liveabout*, 5 March. Available online: https://www.liveabout.com/what-is-neo-soul-2851222 (accessed 3 March 2023).
Ngai, S. (2010), 'Our Aesthetic Categories', *PMLA*, 125 (4), 949.
Niddle, N. K. (2020), 'How MTV Handled Accusations of Racism and Became More Inclusive', *Liveabout*, 14 January. Available online: https://www.liveabout.com/when-mtv-first-aired-black-videos-2834657 (accessed 3 March 2023).
Nkiru, J., in conversation with A. Hanan (2018), 'Director Jenn Nkiru on Greenlighting Projects, Life without a Mentor and Her Love of 35mm', *The Drum*, 23 April. Available online: https://www.thedrum.com/news/2018/04/23/director-jenn-nkiru-greenlighting-projects-life-without-mentor-and-her-love-35mm (accessed 3 March 2023).
Nkiru, J. in conversation with H. F. Little (2019), 'Film-maker Jenn Nkiru's Brain-Bending Vision', *Financial Times*, 7 February. Available online: https://www.ft.com/content/05d2648a-292f-11e9-9222-7024d72222bc (accessed 3 March 2023).
Nkiru, J. in conversation with R. Zonneveld (2020), 'Jenn Nkiru's Art Is an Introduction to Cosmic Archaeology', *i-D*, 31 January. Available online: https://i-d.vice.com/en_uk/article/epgvk7/jenn-nkiru-interview-artist-ummah-chroma (accessed 3 March 2023).
Nkiru, J. (2020), 'Frequencies of Blackness: A Listening Session', in T. Campt, Z. Julius, J. Nkiru and A. Weheliye, *The Sojourner Project – Cogut Institute for the Humanities*, 3 December. Available online: https://www.youtube.com/watch?v=wF5dL69w1kU (accessed 3 March 2023).
Nnaemeka, O. (1998), 'Introduction: Reading the Rainbow', in O. Nnaemeka (ed.), *Sisterhood, Feminisms, and Power: From Africa to the Diaspora*, Trenton, NJ: Africa World Press, 1–35.
Nnaemeka, O. (2004), 'Nego-Feminism: Theorizing, Practicing, and Pruning Africa's Way', *Signs*, 29 (2), 357–85.

Nwonka, C. and S. Malik (2018), 'Cultural Discourses and Practices of Institutionalised Diversity in the UK Film Sector: "Just Get Something Black Made"', *The Sociological Review*, 66 (6), 1111–27.

Nwonka, C. (2020), 'The Black Neoliberal Aesthetic', *European Journal of Cultural Studies*, Vol. 25, Issue 3, 843–62.

O'Brien, S. (2016), 'Why Look at Dead Animals?', *Framework: The Journal of Cinema and Media*, 57 (1), Spring, 32–57.

O'Connor, R. (2018), 'What Did We Do to Deserve Janelle Monáe? Dirty Computer – Review', *Independent*, 27 March. Published 27 March 2018. Accessed 9 September 2018. https://www.independent.co.uk/arts-entertainment/music/reviews/janelle-monae-dirty-computer-review-today-listen-live-prince-tessa-thompson-a8324771.html (accessed 3 March 2023).

O'Dell, L. (2009), 'All-Black Towns', *The Encyclopedia of Oklahoma History and Culture*. Available online: https://www.okhistory.org/publications/enc/entry.php?entry=AL009 (accessed 3 March 2023).

O'Falt, C. (2020), 'Working with Malick: Inside the Dance between Camera, Actor, and Light in "A Hidden Life"', *Indie Wire*, 6 January. Available online: https://www.indiewire.com/2020/01/a-hidden-life-terrence-malick-process-cinematographer-jorg-widmer-valerie-pachner-august-diehl-interview-1202200111/ (accessed 3 March 2023).

Okoth-Obbo, V. (2017), 'Where Neo-Soul Began: 20 Years of Erkyah Badu's Baduizm', *Pitchfork*, 10 February. Available online: https://pitchfork.com/thepitch/1440-where-neo-soul-began-20-years-of-erykah-badus-baduizm/ (accessed 3 March 2023).

Oliver, W. (2006), '"The Streets" – An Alternative Black Male Socialization Institution', *Journal of Black Studies*, 36 (6), 918–37.

Olusoga, D. (2016), *Black and British: A Forgotten History*, London: Pan Macmillan, 504.

Orlando, V. (2017), *New African Cinema*, New Jersey: Rutgers University Press, vii and 1–20.

Osumare, H. (2005), 'Global Hip Hop and the African Diaspora', in H. J. Elam, K. Jackson and American Council of Learned Societies (eds.), *Black Cultural Traffic: Crossroads in Global Performance and Popular Culture*, Michigan: University of Michigan, 266–88.

Pais, N. (2018), 'The house of Bilal', *Gambit*, 7 May 2018. Available online: https://www.theadvocate.com/gambit/new_orleans/music/article_c542388b-72b2-58da-ae51-cb4a8d989e94.html (accessed 3 March 2023).

Palmer, D. in conversation with A. Cornish (2011), 'Found: Very First, or at Least Early, Music Video', NPR: Weekend Edition Sunday, 27 November. Available online: https://www.npr.org/2011/11/27/142821481/found-very-first-or-at-least-very-early-music-video (accessed 3 March 2023).

Palmer, R. (1982), *Deep Blues: A Musical and Cultural History of the Mississippi Delta*, London: Penguin, 146.

Parascandola, L., R. Bone and C. Wade (2010), 'Eric Walrond and the Varying Dynamics of White Patronage during the Harlem Renaissance', *The Langston Hughes Review* 24, 103–11.

Pasquaretta, P. (1994), 'On the "Indianness" of bingo: Gambling and the Native American community', *Critical Inquiry* 20 (4), 694–714.

Pearce, R. (2014), 'Fear and Motels in Las Vegas: Segregation and Celebrity on the Strip', *USSO*, 20 October. Available online: https://usso.uk/fear-and-motels-in-las-vegas-segregation-and-celebrity-on-the-strip/ (accessed 3 March 2023).

Peas, J. (2017), 'In the Spotlight: The Black Media Renaissance Is upon Us', *The Hundreds*, 16 March. Available online: https://thehundreds.com/blogs/content/in-the-spotlight-the-black-media-renaissance-is-upon-us (accessed 3 March 2023).

Peltier, L. (2020), 'Meet the Maker: Melodie McDaniel', *The Journal by Banana Republic*, 21 January. Available online: https://bananarepublic.us/2020/01/21/meet-melodie-mcdaniel/ (accessed 3 March 2023).

Peñalosa, D. (2010), *The Clave Matrix; Afro-Cuban Rhythm: Its Principles and African Origins*. California: Bembe Inc.

Peter, C. and D. Willick (2012), 'Gallery 32 and Los Angeles's African American Arts Community', *NKA: Journal of Contemporary Africa Art*, 30, 16–26.

Pfaff, F. (1988), *Twenty-five Black African Filmmakers: A Critical Study, with Filmography and Bio-Bibliography*, Connecticut: Greenwood Publishing Group.

Phillips, C. (2000), *The Atlantic Sound*, New York: Vintage Books.

Phillips, C. (2001), *A New World Order*, London: Secker & Warburg, 27 and 308.

Pike, D. in conversation with K. Yeoh (2010), 'Interview: Derek Pike', *Juice*, 23 August. Available online: https://juiceonline.com/interview-derek-pike/ (accessed 30 June 2021).

Pogrebin, R. (2020), 'The Larger Costs of Closing a Local Museum during Coronavirus', *The New York Times*, 2 April. Available online: https://www.nytimes.com/2020/03/31/arts/design/underground-museum-los-angeles-coronavirus.html (accessed 3 March 2023).

Poll, R. (2018), 'Can One "Get Out?" The Aesthetics of Afro-Pessimism', *The Journal of the Midwest Modern Language Association*, 51 (2), 72.

Quinn, E. (2004), *Nothing but a 'G' Thang: The Culture and Commerce of Gangsta Rap*, New York: Columbia University Press.

Raengo, A. (2016), 'Suspension, Revisited', *In Media Res*, 14 October 2016. Available online: http://mediacommons.org/imr/2016/10/14/suspension-revisited (accessed 3 March 2023).

Raengo, A. (2018), 'LB ART REVIEWS: KAHLIL JOSEPH'S FLY PAPER', *liquid blackness*. Available online: https://liquidblacknessss.com/curating-for-blackness/arflypaper (accessed 3 March 2023).

Raengo, A. (2023), 'A View from the Music: Anacinema for Other Ends', Media Res, 31 January 2023. Available online: https://mediacommons.org/imr/content/view-music-anacinema-other-ends (accessed 8 March 2023).

Raengo, A. and L. Cramer (2020), 'The Unruly Archives of Black Music Videos', in A. Raengo and L. Cramer (eds.), 'IN FOCUS: Modes of Black Liquidity: Music Video as Black Art,' *JCMS: Journal of Cinema and Media Studies*, 59.2, 138–44.

Rafferty, T. (1990), 'Documentaries', *The Threepenny Review*, Vol. 41, 5.

Railton, D. and P. Watson (2011), *Music Video and the Politics of Representation*, Edinburgh: Edinburgh University Press, 2 and 67.

Ramdeo, J. (2023) '"Who Are You?" Moving from Reflexivity to Self-Reflexivity in Educational Research with Marginalised Groups', *BERA (British Education Research Association)*. Available online: https://www.bera.ac.uk/blog/who-are-you-moving-from-reflexivity-to-self-reflexivity-in-educational-research-with-marginalised-groups (accessed 10 November 2023).

Reckord, V. (1998), 'Back-O-Wall to Hollywood, the Rasta Revolution through the Arts. From Burru Drums to Reggae Riddims: The Evolution of Rasta Warrior', in Nathaniel S. Murrell, William D. Spencer and Adrian A. McFarlane (eds.), *Chanting Down Babylon*, Philadelphia: Temple University Press, 231–52.

Redd, L. N. (1985), 'Rock! It's Still Rhythm and Blues', *The Black Perspective in Music*, 13 (1), 31–47.

Redmond, S. (2018), *Celebrity*, London: Routledge.

Reeves, A. (2020), 'A Lesson in the Value of Perspective from Belgian-Congolese Artist and Director Baloji', *Little Black Book*, 23 July. Available online: https://www.lbbonline.com/news/a-lesson-in-the-value-of-perspective-from-belgian-congolese-artist-and-director-baloji (accessed 3 March 2023).

Reyes, E. A. and A. Jennings (2017), '"It Looks Bad. It's Dangerous." Vacant Lots Dotting South L.A. a Painful Reminder of L.A. Riots', *The Los Angeles Times*, 29 April. Available online: https://www.latimes.com/local/lanow/la-me-ln-vacant-lots-20170423-story.html (accessed 3 March 2023).

Reynolds, S. (1998), *Generation Ecstasy: Into the World of Techno and Rave Culture*, Routledge: New York, 180–205.

Rhoden, W. (2012), 'Keven Davis Helped Venus and Serena Williams Reach Top', *The New York Times*, 8 January. Available online: https://www.nytimes.com/2012/01/09/sports/tennis/keven-davis-helped-venus-and-serena-williams-reach-top.html (accessed 3 March 2023).

Rock, J. in conversation with S. Slovick (2011), 'Inside the Nickerson Gardens Projects with Rapper Jay Rock: "They Can Call Anyone a Terrorist, a Gangbanger, and Put Cameras in Your Neighbourhood"', *LA Weekly*, 17 March. Available online: https://www.laweekly.com/inside-the-nickerson-gardens-projects-with-rapper-jay-rock-they-can-call-anyone-a-terrorist-a-gangbanger-and-put-cameras-in-your-neighborhood/ (accessed 3 March 2023).

Rodriquez, D. (2011), 'Silent Rage and the Politics of Resistance: Countering Seductions of Whiteness and the Road to Politicisation and Empowerment', *Qualitative Inquiry*, 17 (7), 589–90 and 596.

Rolland, R. (1920), 'Review: The Sacrifice of Abraham', in *L'Humanité*, 19 March, Cited By D. J. Fisher (1988), *Romain Rolland and the Politics of Intellectual Engagement*, Berkeley: University of California Press, 292.

Rollock, N. (2013), 'A Political Investment: Revisiting Race and Racism in the Research Process', *Discourse: Studies in the Cultural Politics of Education*, 34 (4), 499 and 507.

Rogers, H. (2010), *Visualising Music: Audio-Visual Relationships in Avant-Garde Film and Video Art*, Berlin: Verlag, 145.

Rogers, H. and J. Barham (eds.) (2017), *The Music and Sound of Experimental Film*, Oxford: Oxford University Press, 19.

Rogers, H. in C. Vernallis, H. Rogers and L. Perrot (2020), *Transmedia Directors: Artistry, Industry, and New Audiovisual Aesthetics*, London: Bloomsbury Academic, 11.

Rubin, V. (1976), *Cannabis and Culture*, Frankfurt: Campus Verlag, 305.

Rush, M. (1997), 'Mighty Silence', *Performing Arts Journal*, 19 (3), 61.

Rush, M. (2007), *Video Art*, London: Thames and Hudson Ltd, 43–56 and 115.

Sampha, in conversation with Music News (2017), 'Sampha Reveals All About His New Film Process', *Music News*, 9 April. Available online: https://www.music-news.com/news/UK/104726/Sampha-reveals-all-about-his-new-film-Process (accessed 3 March 2023).

Sampson, I. (2014), 'FKA twigs's New Google Glass Advert', *The Guardian*, 1 November. Available online: https://www.theguardian.com/tv-and-radio/2014/nov/01/fka-twigs-google-glass-advert (accessed 3 March 2023).

Sanogo, A. (2014), 'Reconsidering the Sembènian Project: Toward an Aesthetics of Change', in Ukadike, N. (ed.), *Critical Approaches to African Cinema Discourse*, Plymouth: Lexington Books, 209–27.

Sarantis, J. (2018), 'Why You Should Know Kahlil Joseph, the Filmmaker Redefining Visuals in Music', *Kulturehub*, 1 October. Available online: https://kulturehub.com/kahlil-joseph-filmmaker-music/ (accessed 30 June 2021).

Schoener, A. (2007), *Harlem on My Mind: Cultural Capital of Black America, 1900–1968*, New York: The New Press.

Sears, D. O. (1969), 'Black Attitudes toward the Political System in the Aftermath of the Watts Insurrection', in *Midwest Journal of Political Science*, Vol. 13, No. 4, Detroit, MI: Wayne State University Press, 515–44.

Segal, D. (2003), 'Rephlexions!: A Braindance Compilation', *Stylus Magazine*, 20 November. Available online: http://stylusmagazine.com/review_ID_1485.html (accessed 9 July 2021).

Sembène, O. cited by A. Busch, and M. Annas (eds.) (2008), *Ousmane Sembène Interviews*, Jackson, MS: University of Mississippi, 12.

Sexton, J. (2017), *Black masculinity and the cinema of policing*, New York: Springer International Publishing, xxvii.

Shaviro, S. (2010), *Post Cinematic Affect*. United Kingdom: Zer0 Books, 1–35.

Shaviro, S. (2017), *Digital Music Videos*. New Jersey: Rutgers University Press.

Shaviro, S. (2023), *The Rhythm Images: Music Videos and New Audiovisual Forms*, London: Bloomsbury Academic.

Shelton, M. D. (1976), 'Fakes, Fakers, and Fakery: Authenticity in African Art', in *African Arts*, Vol. 9, No. 3, Cambridge: The MIT Press, 20–31, 48–74 and 92.

Shin, C.-Y. (2003), '"Reclaiming the Corporeal: The Black Male Body and the "Racial" Mountain in "Looking for Langston"', *Paragraph*, 26 (1/2), 201.

Sidanius, J. and F. Pratto (1993), 'Racism and Support of Free-Market Capitalism: A Cross-Cultural Analysis', *Political Psychology*, 14 (3), 381–401.

Sides, J. (2004), 'Straight into Compton: American Dreams, Urban Nightmares, and the Metamorphosis of a Black Suburb', *American Quarterly*, 56 (3), 583–605.

Siegler, K. (2013), 'After Years of Violence, LA's Watts Sees Crime Subside', *NPR*, 25 July. Available online: https://www.npr.org/sections/codeswitch/2013/07/25/205198028/Once-Crime-Ridden-South-L-A-s-Watts-Sees-Violence-Drop?t=1613491809960 (accessed 3 March 2023).

Silva, T. (2017), 'Welcome to the New Black Renaissance', *Study Breaks*, 27 March. Available online: https://studybreaks.com/culture/black-renaissance/ (accessed 3 March 2023).

Simmonds, F. N. (1988), '"She's Gotta Have It": The Representation of Black Female Sexuality on Film', *Feminist Review*, Vol. 29, 19.

Sinnerbrink, R. (2019), *Terrence Malik: Filmmaker and Philosopher*. London and New York: Bloomsbury.

Slothuus, L. (2021), 'Faith between Reason and Affect: Thinking with Antonio Gramsci', *Distinktion: Journal of Social Theory*, 22 (3), 343.

Sluyter, A. (2020), 'Death of the Middle Passage: A Cartographic Approach to the Transatlantic Slave Trade', *Slaveries and Post-Slaveries [Esclavages & Post-esclavages]*, 3, 27 November 2020. Available online: https://journals.openedition.org/slaveries/3358 (accessed 3 March 2023).

Smith, Z. (2001), 'This Is How It Feels to Me', *The Guardian Online*, 13 October. Available online: https://www.theguardian.com/books/2001/oct/13/fiction.afghanistan (accessed 3 March 2023).

Smith, R. (2007), 'The Museum as Outdoor Movie Screen', *The New York Times*, 18 January. Available online: https://www.nytimes.com/2007/01/18/arts/18moma.html (accessed 3 March 2023).

Smith, S. (2017), 'The Strange World of … Alice Coltrane', *The Quietus*, 3 May. Available online: https://thequietus.com/articles/22328-alice-coltrane-review-john-coltrane (accessed 3 March 2023).

Snead, J. (1994), *White Screens/Black Images: Hollywood from the Dark Side*, London and New York: Routledge, 115–19 and 124.

Solis, G. (2019), 'Soul, Afrofuturism & the Timeliness of Contemporary Jazz Fusions', *Daedelus [American Academy of Arts and Sciences]*, 148 (2), Spring 2019, 23–35.

Solway, D. (2019), 'Kahlil Joseph Is Challenging Representations of Black Life in America', *Surface Mag*. Available online: https://www.surfacemag.com/articles/kahlil-joseph-challenging-black-life/ (accessed 3 March 2023).

Spears, D. (2011), 'Can You Hear Me?', *The New York Times*, 21 July. Available online: https://www.nytimes.com/2011/07/24/arts/design/black-mirror-video-by-doug-aitken-in-greece.html?_r=1&ref=design (accessed 3 March 2023).

Spence, L. K. (2015), *Knocking the Hustle: Against the Neoliberal Turn in Black Politics*, New York: punctumbooks, 145.

Srnicek, A. and A. Williams (2016), *Postcapitalism and a World Without Work*, London: Verso, 2.

Stallings, L. H. (2007), *Mutha' Is a Half Word: Intersections of Folklore, Vernacular, Myth, and Queerness in Black Female Culture*, Columbus: Ohio State University Press, 10–11.

Steiner, C. B. (1994), *African Art in Transit*, Cambridge: Cambridge University Press.

Steingo, G. and J. Sykes (2019), *Remapping Sound Studies*, North Carolina: Duke University Press.

Story, R. (1989), 'Patronage and the Harlem Renaissance: You Get What You Pay For', *CLA Journal*, 32 (3), 284–95.

Stubbs, A. (2019), 'Spike Jonze, Propaganda/Satellite Films, and Music Video Work: Talent Management and the Construction of an Indie-Auteur', in K. Wilkins and W. Moss-Wellington, Wytt (eds.), *ReFocus: The Films of Spike Jonze*, Edinburgh: Edinburgh University Press, 213–30.

Sublette, N. (2008), *The World That Made New Orleans: From Spanish Silver to Congo Square*, Chicago: Chicago Review Press, 124 and 287.

Sullivan, R. (2003), 'Rap and Race: It's Got a Nice Beat, but What About the Message?', *Journal of Black Studies*, 33 (5), 605–22.

Sutton, N. (2020), 'Artist in Focus: Kahlil Joseph', Shades of Noir, 9 July. Available online: https://shadesofnoir.org.uk/artist-in-focus-kahlil-joseph/ (accessed 3 March 2023).

Taborn, K. (2018), *Walking Harlem: The Ultimate Guide to the Cultural Capital of Black America*, New Jersey: Rutgers University Press.

Tafari, I. (1980), 'The Rastafari—Successors of Marcus Garvey', *Caribbean Quarterly*, 26 (4), 1–12.

Tagg, P. (2005), 'Gestural Interconversion and Connotative Precision', *Film International*, 3 (12), January, 20–31.

Tannenbaum, R. and C. Marks (2012*)*, *I Want My MTV: The Uncensored Story of the Music Video Revolution*, New York: New American Library.
Tarasov, A. (2001), 'Offspring of Reforms – Shaven Heads Are Skinheads: The New Fascist Youth Subculture in Russia', *Russian Politics & Law*, 39 (1), 43–89.
Tate, G. (1992), *Flyboy in the Buttermilk: Essays on Contemporary America*, New York: Simon & Schuster, 207.
Taylor, C. (1983), 'New US Black Cinema', *Jump Cut*, Vol. 28, April 1983, 47.
Taylor, M. (2020), 'Rebels with a Cause: The Complex Relationship between Rap and Rock Music', *Afterglow*, 25 August. Available online: https://www.afterglowatx.com/blog/2020/8/25/rebels-with-a-cause-the-complex-relationship-between-rap-and-rock-music (accessed 3 March 2023).
Teshome, G. (1989), 'Third Cinema as Guardian of Popular Memory: Towards a Third Aesthetics', in J. Pines and P. Willemen (eds.), *Questions of Third Cinema*, London: British Film Institute, 53–64.
Tewksbury, D. (2010), 'Roll Bounce: Visionary Producer Shafiq Husayn Debuts New Video', *LA Weekly*, 7 April. Available online: https://www.laweekly.com/roll-bounce-visionary-producer-shafiq-husayn-debuts-new-video/ (accessed 3 March 2023).
Thiong'o, N. W. (1986), *Decolonising the Mind: The Politics of Language in African Literature*, New Hampshire: Heinemann Educational.
Thomas, G. (2013), 'Dragons!: George Jackson in the Cinema with Haile Gerima–from the Watts Films to Teza', *Black Camera*, 4 (2), 55–83.
Thompson-Hernandez, W. (2018), 'For the Compton Cowboys, Horseback Riding Is a Legacy, and Protection', *The New York Times*, 31 March. Available online: https://www.nytimes.com/2018/03/31/us/compton-cowboys-horseback-riding-african-americans.html (accessed 3 March 2023).
Thornton, R. (2005). 'Native American Demographic and Tribal Survival into the Twenty-First Century', *American Studies*, Vol. 46, 23–38.
Thorsen, D. (2020), 'Heaven and Hell', in *What's True about Christianity?: An Introduction to Christain Faith and Practice* Vol. 1, Claremont: Claremont Press, 197–202.
Thuram, L. (2020), *White Thinking: Behind the Mask of Racial Identity*, London: Hero, 196 and 202.
Tillet, S. (2018), 'Spike Lee Takes on the Klan', *The New York Times*, 2 August. Available online: https://www.nytimes.com/2018/08/02/movies/spike-lee-blackkklansman.html (accessed 3 March 2023).
Tobias, J. (2020), 'The Music Film as Essay: Montage as Argument in Kahlil Joseph's Fly Paper and Process', in A. Raengo and L. Cramer (eds.), 'IN FOCUS: Modes of Black Liquidity: Music Video as Black Art', *JCMS: Journal of Cinema and Media Studies*, 59.2, 157–62.
Toeffler, V. cited by C. Hay (2001), 'Video Chat Room Lets Industry Members Network Online', *Billboard*, 17 February, 68.
Tolson, A. L. (1970), 'Black Towns of Oklahoma', *The Black Scholar*, 1 (6), 18–22.
Tomlinson, G. (2002), 'Cultural Dialogics and Jazz: A White Historian Signifies', *Black Music Research Journal*, 22, 71–105.
Torregrossa, M. (2020), '3 Supermoons, an Extra Full Moon, a Blue Moon and a Micro-Moon All to Occur in 2020)', *mlive*, 31 January. Available online: https://www.mlive.com/weather/2020/01/3-supermoons-an-extra-full-moon-a-blue-moon-and-a-micro-moon-all-to-occur-in-2020.html (accessed 3 March 2023).

Tucker, M. in conversation with J. Etter (1983), 'Wildcat Junction No Tame Place', *The Oklahoman*, 11 September. Available online: https://oklahoman.com/article/2038920/wildcat-junction-no-tame-place (accessed 3 March 2023).

Tungate, M. (2007), *Adland: A Global History of Advertising*, London: Kogan Page, 3 and 7.

Turner, D. and M. Kamdibe (2008), 'Haile Gerima: In Search of an Africana Cinema', *Journal of Black Studies*, 38 (6), 969.

Twin, Aphex, in conversation with J. Gross (1997), 'APHEX TWIN', *Perfect Sound Forever [Furious]*, September. Available online: https://www.furious.com/perfect/aphextwin.html (accessed 3 March 2023).

Tyron, C. (2009), *Reinventing Cinema: Movies in the Age of Media Convergence*, New Brunswick; New Jersey; London: Rutgers University Press, 2–4.

Utriainen, T. (2011), 'The Post-Secular Position and Enchanted Bodies', *Scripta Instituti Donneriani Aboensis*, 23, 417.

Vahed, G. (1997), 'Swami Shankeranand and the Consolidation of Hinduism in Natal, 1908–1913', *Journal for the Study of Religion*, 10 (2), 3–33.

Vass, G. (2017), 'Getting inside the Insider Researcher: Does Race-Symmetry Help or Hinder Research?', *International Journal of Research & Method in Education*, 40 (2), 137–8.

Venter, D. J. and E. Neuland (2005), *NEPAD and the African Renaissance*, Johannesburg: Richard Havenga & Associates.

Vernallis, C. (2013), 'Music Video's Second Aesthetic?', in J. Richardson et al (eds.), *The Oxford Handbook of New Audiovisual Aesthetics*, Oxford: Oxford University Press, 437–66.

Vernallis, C. (2013), *Unruly Media: Youtube, Music Video, and the New Digital Cinema*, Oxford: Oxford University Press, 130.

Vernallis, C. (2020), *Transmedia Directors: Artistry, Industry, and New Audiovisual Aesthetics*, C. Vernallis, H. Rogers and L. Perrot (eds.), London: Bloomsbury Academic, 7.

Vernallis, C., H. Rogers, J. Leal and S. Kara (eds.) (2021), *Cybermedia: Explorations in Science, Sound, and Vision*, London: Bloomsbury Academic.

Vernallis, C. (2023), 'Introduction', in *The Media Swirl: Politics, Audiovisuality, and Aesthetics*, North Carolina: Duke University Press, 1–16.

Viator, F. A. (2012), 'Gangster Boogie: Los Angeles and the Rise of Gangsta Rap, 1965–1992', *UC Berkeley*. Available online: https://escholarship.org/uc/item/3hd2d12n (accessed 3 March 2023).

Viator, F. (2020), *To Live and Defy in LA: How Gangsta Rap Changed America*, Massachusetts: Harvard University Press.

Vintges, K. (2017), 'The Battle of Myths', in *A New Dawn for the Second Sex: Women's Freedom Practices in World Perspective*, Amsterdam: Amsterdam University Press, 129–64.

Von Trapp, M. (2020), 'Baloji Signs to Academy Films', *Promonews*, 15 July. Available online: https://www.promonews.tv/news/2020/07/15/baloji-signs-academy-films/65661 (accessed 3 March 2023).

Von Trapp, M. cited by A. Reeves (2020), 'A Lesson in the Value of Perspective from Belgian-Congolese Artist and Director Baloji', *Little Black Book*, 23 July. Available online: https://www.lbbonline.com/news/a-lesson-in-the-value-of-perspective-from-belgian-congolese-artist-and-director-baloji (accessed 3 March 2023).

Wade, B. (1996), 'Performing the Drone in Hindustani Classical Music: What Mughal Paintings Show Us to Hear', *The World of Music*, 38 (2), 41–67.

Wahl, G. (1999), '"I Fought the Law (And I Cold Won!)": Hip-Hop in the Mainstream', *College Literature*, 26 (1), 98–112.

Wald, G. (1997), 'Soul's Revival: White Soul, Nostalgia, and the Culturally Constructed Past', in M. Guillory and R. Green (eds.), *Soul: Black Power, Politics and Pleasure*, New York: New York University Press, 147.

Waldfogel, J. (2017), 'How Digitization Has Created a Golden Age of Music, Movies, Books, and Television', *The Journal of Economic Perspectives*, 31 (3), 195–214.

Walker, K. (2014), 'Ruffneck Constructivists: Press Release', *Alexander Gray Associates*, February 12. Available oline online: https://www.alexandergray.com/other-exhibitions/ruffneck-constructivists (accessed 3 March 2023).

Wallace, D. F. (2009), *This Is Water: Some Thoughts, Delivered on a Significant Occasion, About Living a Compassionate Life*, Boston, MA: Little, Brown.

Warner, T. (2003), *Pop Music Technology and Creativity: Trever Horn and the Digital Revolution*, London: Routledge.

Warp Records (2020), 'About', *Warp Records*. Available online: https://warp.net/about (accessed 3 March 2023).

Washington, K. in conversation with J. Lewis (2016), 'The New Cool: How Kamasi, Kendrick and Co Gave Jazz a New Groove', *The Guardian Online*, 6 October. Available online: https://www.theguardian.com/music/2016/oct/06/new-cool-kamasi-kendrick-gave-jazz-new-groove (accessed 3 March 2023).

Weheliye, A. G. (2003), '"I Am I Be": The Subject of Sonic Afro-modernity', *boundary*, 30 (2), 21 May, 97–114.

Weheliye, A. G. (2005), *Phonographies: Grooves in Sonic Afro-Modernity*, North Carolina: Duke University Press.

Weheliye, A. G. (2014), 'Engendering Phonographies: Sonic Technologies of Blackness', *Small Axe*, 18 (2), 44, 183.

Weier, S. (2014), 'Consider Afro-Pessimism', *Amerikastudien/American Studies*, 59 (3), 419–33.

Weiner, J. (2013), 'The Impossible Body: Storyboard P, the Basquiat of Street Dancing', *The New Yorker*, 30 December. Available online: https://www.newyorker.com/magazine/2014/01/06/the-impossible-body (accessed 3 March 2023).

Wekker, G. in conversation with P. Gilroy (2020), 'Sarah Parker Remond Centre: In Conversation with Gloria Wekker [Transcript]', *UCL: Sarah Parker Remond Centre for the Study of Racism and Racialisation*, 1 October. Available online: https://www.ucl.ac.uk/racism-racialisation/transcript-conversation-gloria-wekker (accessed 3 March 2023).

White, C. (2004), 'The March That Never Happened: Desegregating the Las Vegas Strip', *Nevada Law Journal*, 5 (1), Article 5, 71 and 76.

White, M. (2011), 'Affective Gestures: Hip-Hop Aesthetics, Blackness, and the Literacy of Performance', *From Jim Crow to Jay-Z: Race, Rap, and the Performance of Masculinity*, Champaign: University of Illinois Press, 41.

Wicker, K. (2018), 'It's Official: We Are Experiencing a Black Renaissance', *Think Progress*, 16 March. Available online: https://thinkprogress.org/black-renaissance-2018-93d8b3981e28/ (accessed 3 March 2023).

Wilderson III, F. B. (2016), 'Afro-Pessimism and the End of Redemption', *The Occupied Times*, 30 March. Available online: https://theoccupiedtimes.org/?p=14236 (accessed 3 March 2023).

Williams, P. (2011), 'Fear of a Black Planet', in *Race, Ethnicity and Nuclear War: Representations of Nuclear Weapons and Post-Apocalyptic Worlds*, Liverpool: Liverpool University Press, 105–6.

Willis, W. B. (1998), *The Adinkra Dictionary: A Visual Primer on the Language of Adinkra*. Washington, DC: Pyramid Complex.

Wilmoth, P. (1993), *Glad All Over: The Countdown Years 1975–1987*, Victoria: McPhee Gribble.

Wilson, S. (2010), 'Braindance of the Hikikomori: Towards a Return to Speculative Psychoanalysis', *Paragraph*, 33 (3), 392–409.

Womack, Y. (2013), *Afrofuturism: The World of Black Sci-fi and Fantasy Culture*, Chicago: Chicago Review Press, 9.

Woodhouse, H. (2009), *Selling Out: Academic Freedom and the Corporate Market*, Montreal: McGill-Queen's University Press.

Yanagizawa-Drott, D. (2014), 'Propaganda and Conflict: Evidence from the Rwandan Genocide', *The Quarterly Journal of Economics*, 129 (4), 1947–94.

Young, A. (2011), 'Album Review: Shabazz Palaces – Black Up', *Consequence*, 29 June. Available online: https://consequence.net/2011/06/album-review-shabazz-palaces-black-up/ (accessed 3 March 2023).

Mediography

12 Years a Slave (2013). Dir. Steve McQueen. Produced by Plan B Entertainment, New Regency Productions, River Road Entertainment, Film4, Fox Searchlight Studios and Summit Entertainment.

A Film by Kahlil Joseph and Luke Meier for Vans Syndicate (2010). Dir. Kahlil Joseph. Music by Flying Lotus and Melvin Gibbs. Production by Luke Meier, Chris Gibbs and Omid Fatemi. Available online: https://www.youtube.com/watch?v=PSMVDBdnDY0&t=182s (accessed 3 March 2023).

A Hard Day's Night (1964). Dir. Richard Lester. Music by The Beatles. Produced by United Artists and Proscenium Films.

An Oversimplification of Her Beauty (2012). Dir. Terrence Nance. Produced by MVMT.

Atlanta (2016 to Present). Created by Donald Glover. Produced by FX.

Baloji. *137 Avenue Kaniama* (2018). Bella Union. Available online: https://open.spotify.com/album/4JYfA4WhikxnyDOfCNhCL7?si=xUnbA2IwT0O99kGe4QF6Kw&dl_branch=1 (accessed 3 March 2023).

Bear (1993). Dir. Steve McQueen. Produced by Steve McQueen and Goldsmiths University.

Because I Got High (2000). Dir. Kevin Smith. Music by Afroman. Produced by Universal Records. Available online: https://www.youtube.com/watch?v=WeYsTmIzjkw (accessed 3 March 2023).

Belhaven Meridian (2010). Dir. Kahlil Joseph. Music by Shabazz Palaces. Produced by What Matters Most Collective. Available online: https://www.youtube.com/watch?v=kBefSqSpTEg (accessed 3 March 2023).

Birth of a Nation (2016). Dir. Nate Parker. Produced by Bron Studios.

Black Mary (2017). Dir. Kahlil Joseph. Music by Alice Smith. Produced by Tate. Available online: https://www.youtube.com/watch?v=9sQKkncIKfc (accessed 3 March 2023).

Black Panther (2018). Dir. Ryan Coogler. Produced by Marvel Studios and Walt Disney Pictures.

Black Star: Rebirth Is Necessary (2017). Dir. Jenn Nkiru. Produced by Iconoclast. Available online: https://www.youtube.com/watch?v=vemJFbayDrM (accessed 3 March 2023).

Black to Techno (2019). Dir. Jenn Nkiru. Produced by Frieze Magazine and Iconoclast. Available online: https://www.frieze.com/video/jenn-nkiru-black-techno (accessed 3 March 2023).

Black Up (2011). Dir. Kahlil Joseph. Music by Shabazz Palaces. Produced by What Matters Most Collective. Available online: https://www.youtube.com/watch?v=JUYaa7_Osik (accessed 3 March 2023).

Black-ish (2014 to Present). Created by Kenya Barris. Produced by American Broadcasting Company, FXX and Citytv.

Blade Runner (1982). Dir. Ridley Scott. Produced by The Ladd Company, Shaw Brothers, Blade Runner Partnership.

BLKNWS (2017). Dir. Kahlil Joseph. Music by Miscellaneous Artists.

Bohemian Rhapsody (1975). Dir. Bruce Gowers. Music by Queen. Produced by Hollywood Records and Virgin EMI Records. Available online: https://www.youtube.com/watch?v=fJ9rUzIMcZQ (accessed 3 March 2023).

Boyz N the Hood (1991). Dir. John Singleton. Produced by Columbia Pictures.

Brown Jr., Oscar. *Dime Away from a Hotdog* (1972). Atlantic. Available online: https://www.youtube.com/watch?v=hLpDadFjJnc (accessed 3 March 2023).

Chameleon Street (1989). Dir. Wendell B. Harris Jr. Produced by Gethsemane 84.

Cheeba (2010). Dir. Kahlil Joseph. Music by Shafiq Husayn. Produced by What Matters Most Collective. Available online: https://www.youtube.com/watch?v=IzvWN12ad50 (accessed 3 March 2023).

City of God (2002). Dir. Fernando Meirelles and Kátia Lund. Produced by 02 Filmes, VideoFilmes, Hank Levine Film and Globo Filmes.

Cooke, Sam. *Chain Gang* (1960). RCA Victor. Available online: https://open.spotify.com/track/7v1858htfU0srTDwhxeka8 (accessed 3 March 2023).

Countdown (1974 to 1987). Created by Michael Shrimpton, Robbie Weekes and Ian Meldrum. Produced by the Australian Broadcasting Corporation.

Dáme Si Do Bytu [Let's Get to the Apartment] (1958). Dir. Ladislav Rychman. Music by Kacirkova Bek. Produced by unknown. Available online: https://www.youtube.com/watch?v=lpmAUVchBeg (accessed 3 March 2023).

Daughters of the Dust (1991). Dir. Julie Dash. Produced by Geechee Girls, American Playhouse and WMG Film.

Davis, Miles. *In a Silent Way* (1969). Columbia Records. Available online: https://open.spotify.com/album/0Hs3BomCdwIWRhgT57x22T?si=tnCawgHwR7es-n1NKB8PMA&dl_branch=1 (accessed 3 March 2023).

Dawn in Luxor (2014). Dir. Kahlil Joseph. Music by Shabazz Palaces. Produced by Pulse Films and What Matters Most. Available online: https://www.youtube.com/watch?v=VdXQmhrbuCY (accessed 3 March 2023).

Dear White People (2017 to Present). Created by Justin Simien. Produced by Netflix.

Dirty Computer (2018). Dir. Alan Ferguson, Chuck Lightning and Janelle Monae. Produced by Wondaland. Available online: https://www.youtube.com/watch?v=jdH2Sy-BlNE&t=2001s (accessed 3 March 2023).

Django Unchained (2012). Dir. Quentin Tarantino. Produced by The Weinstein Company and Columbia Pictures.

Do the Right Thing (1989). Dir. Spike Lee. Produced by 40 Acres and a Mule Filmworks.

Dorsey, Lee. *Working in the Coal Mine* (1966). Warner Bros Records Asylum Records. Available online: https://open.spotify.com/track/0mdZ4B9JIUKQKsYkLsoMzu (accessed 3 March 2023).

Dreams Are Colder Than Death (2014). Dir. Arthur Jafa. Produced by Pumpernickel Films and Very Special Projects.

ELEMENT. (2017). Dir. The Little Homies and Jonas Lindstroem. Music by Kendrick Lamar. Produced by Iconoclast and TDE Films. Available online: https://www.youtube.com/watch?v=glaG64Ao7sM (accessed 3 March 2023).

FKA twigs. *LP1* (2014). Young Turks. Available online: https://open.spotify.com/album/25PQxi9SR1OODB5XG6m48J?si=7XJlEqJzSLWzLLtI8TAXyg&dl_branch=1 (accessed 3 March 2023).

Fly Paper (2017). Dir. Kahlil Joseph. Music by James William Blades.

Flying Lotus. *Until the Quiet Comes* (2012). Warp Records. Available online: https://open.spotify.com/album/40aG9ahuLnAv96yoFG75Uy?si=oqPkqbeKSbqK56Dn3d7-Pw&dl_branch=1 (accessed 3 March 2023).

Freedom (2014). Dir. Peter Cousen. Produced by Production One.
Fresh N Clean (2015). Dir. Humans. Music by D Double E. Produced by Riff Raff Films and Electric Theatre Collective. Available online: https://www.youtube.com/watch?v=XCsCJCEjXQY (accessed 3 March 2023).
Friday (1995). Dir. F. Gary Gray. Produced by New Line Cinema and Priority Films.
Get Out (2017). Dir. Jordan Peele. Produced by Blumhouse Productions, Monkeypaw Productions, Universal Pictures and QC Entertainment.
Grandmaster Flash and the Furious Five. *The Message* (1982). Available online: https://open.spotify.com/track/17ZWQORPdH1SSTxkTRxGE3 (accessed 3 March 2023).
Handsworth Songs (1986). Dir. Black Audio Film Collective. Produced by Black Audio Film Colletive (Lina Paul).
Harry Potter and the Goblet of Fire (2005). Dir. Mike Newell. Produced by Warner Bros. Pictures and Heydey Films.
Hathaway, Donny. *Little Ghetto Boy* (1972). Available online: https://open.spotify.com/track/7gqIw0vk5KwMpHYOAT8g1p (accessed 3 March 2023).
Here It Goes Again (2006). Dir. Trish Sie and OK Go. Music by OK Go. Available online: https://www.youtube.com/watch?v=dTAAsCNK7RA (accessed 3 March 2023).
Hip-Hop: Beyond Beats & Rhymes (2006). Dir. Byron Hurt. Massachusetts: Media Education Foundation.
House of Sand (2005). Dir. Andrucha Waddington. Produced by Conspiração Filmes.
House Party! (1990). Dir. Reginald Hudlin. Produced by New Line Cinema.
Hub-Tones (2018). Dir. Jenn Nkiru. Music by Kamasi Washington. Produced by Iconoclast. Available online: https://www.youtube.com/watch?v=u-e6mOTK__Y (accessed 3 March 2023).
Husayn, Shafiq. *En' A-Free Ka* (2009). Rapster Records. Available online: https://open.spotify.com/album/0yFnAm5xzI9TAfhIsAOdk9?si=LTsSJ0WDTjKFLJSHU4-zng&dl_branch=1 (accessed 3 March 2023).
i (2014). Dir. The Little Homies and Alexandre Moor. Music by Kendrick Lamar. Produced by Good Company. Available online: https://www.youtube.com/watch?v=8aShfolR6w8 (accessed 3 March 2023).
I Am Shakespeare: The Henry Green Story (2017). Dir. Stephen Dest. Produced by Stephen Dest and Henry Green.
I Need a Dollar (2010). Dir. Derek Pike. Music by Aloe Blacc. Produced by LRG (Lifted Research Group). Available online: https://www.youtube.com/watch?v=nFZP8zQ5kzk (accessed 3 March 2023).
I Need a Dollar (2010). Dir. Kahlil Joseph. Music by Aloe Blacc. Produced by What Matters Most. Available online: https://vimeo.com/groups/atm/videos/10682667 (accessed 3 March 2023).
I Need a Dollar (teaser) (2010). Dir. Kahlil Joseph. Music by Aloe Blacc. Produced by What Matters Most. Available online: https://www.youtube.com/watch?v=mnf_Rwtdqzk (accessed 3 March 2023).
Ignorance Is Bliss (2010). Dir. The Little Homies. Music by Kendrick Lamar. Produced by Top Dawg Entertainment. Available online: https://www.youtube.com/watch?v=00cr3g6wCG0 (accessed 3 March 2023).
Jackass (2000–2). Created by Johnny Knoxville, Spike Jonze and Jeff Tremaine. Produced by MTV and Dickhouse Productions.
Juice (1992). Dir. Ernest R. Dickerson. Produced by Island World.
Kaniama Show (2019). Dir. Baloji. Produced by Africalia. Available online: https://www.youtube.com/watch?v=7Z7l3_Uos9g (accessed 3 March 2023).

Killer of Sheep. (1977). Dir. Charles Burnett. Produced by UCLA School of Film.

La Noire De … (1966). Dir. Ousmane Sembène. Produced by Filmi Domirev and Les Actualités Françaises.

Lamar, Kendrick. *good kid, m.A.A.d city* (2012). Top Dawg Entertainment, Interscope Records and Aftermath Entertainment. Available online: https://open.spotify.com/album/748dZDqSZy6aPXKcI9H80u?si=vNX4qW7JRIee6Ld9Pzb3qA&dl_branch=1 (accessed 3 March 2023).

Lemonade (2016). Dir. Beyoncé Knowles-Carter, Kahlil Joseph, Dikayl Rimmasch, Todd Tourso, Jonas Åkerlund, Melina Matsoukas and Mark Romanek. Music by Beyoncé Knowles-Carter, Jack White, James Blake, Kendrick Lamar and The Weeknd. Photography: Khalik Allah, Pär M. Ekberg, Santiago Gonzalez, Chayse Irvin, Reed Morano, Dikayl Rimmasch and Malik Hassan Sayeed. Produced by Pepper Carlson, Adam Gambrel, Tracy Keller and Ian Menzies. Available online: https://www.youtube.com/watch?v=gM89Q5Eng_M&list=PLxKHVMqMZqUSPF11Ghs0KqDfOGhB9Vw5E (accessed 3 March 2023).

Looking for Langston (1989). Dir. Isaac Julien. Produced by Sankofa Film & Video Productions.

Love Is the Message, the Message Is Death (2016). Dir. Arthur Jafa. Music by Kanye West. Produced by Arthur Jafa.

Lovecraft Country (2020 to Present). Created by Misha Green. Produced by Monkeypaw Productions, Bad Robot Productions and Warner Bros. Television.

m.A.A.d (2014). Dir. Kahlil Joseph. Music by Kendrick Lamar. Available online: https://www.youtube.com/watch?v=cGkUpjyL7y8 (accessed 29 February 2024).

Memory Palace (2015). Dir. Martine Syms and Kahlil Joseph. Produced by What Matters Most. Available online: https://www.youtube.com/watch?v=3EqAJEgf4vA (accessed 3 March 2023).

Menace II Society (1993). Dir. Albert and Allen Hughes. Produced by New Line Cinema.

Mirror (1975). Dir. Andrei Tarkovsky. Produced by Mosfilm.

Moonlight (2016). Dir. Barry Jenkins. Produced by A24, Plan B Entertainment and Pastel Production.

Music Is My Mistress (2017). Dir. Kahlil Joseph. Produced by KENZO and Annapurna Pictures. Available online: https://fb.watch/7_94mtpxzB/ (accessed 3 March 2023).

Never Look at the Sun (2019). Dir. Baloji. Produced by Cadence Films. Available online: https://vimeo.com/363295829 (accessed 3 March 2023).

Nothing Beats a Londoner (2018). Dir. Megaforce (Riff Raff Films). Created by Wieden+Kennedy London and Nike. Available online: https://www.youtube.com/watch?v=mEB1C59hCvs (accessed 3 March 2023).

Peau de Chagrin/Bleu de Nuit (2018). Dir. Baloji. Produced by Bella Union. Available online: https://www.youtube.com/watch?v=TzHM_JLgqO0 (accessed 3 March 2023).

Process (2017). Dir. Kahlil Joseph. Music by Sampha. Produced by Pulse Films. Available online: https://music.apple.com/us/music-movie/process/1264415035 (accessed 3 March 2023).

Retrograde (2012). Music and Direction by Death Grips. All individual clips available online: https://www.youtube.com/user/mercury00retrograde/videos (accessed 3 March 2023).

REVOLT BLACK NEWS (2020 to Present). Created by Sean Coombes. Produced by Sean Coombes.

Sampha. *Process* (2017). Young Turks. Available online: https://open.spotify.com/albu
m/4fRcYn1zNOHY5LJXuRmJHI?si=OBk4FeWuRQ6qblhfRGl0MA&dl_branch=1
(accessed 3 March 2023).
Sankofa (1993). Dir. Haile Gerima. Produced by Channel 4 and Paramount.
Sans Soleil (1983). Dir. Chris Marker. Produced by Argos Films.
Sarah (1981). Dir. Spike Lee. Produced by New York University.
Scorpio Rising (1964). Dir. Kenneth Anger. Produced by Puck Film Productions.
Available online: https://www.youtube.com/watch?v=GDuu-m0-IjQ (accessed
3 March 2023).
Sedmikrasky (1966). Dir. Věra Chytilov. Produced by Barrandov Studio.
Seu Jorge and Almaz. *Seu Jorge and Almaz* (2010). Stones Throw Records. Available
online: https://open.spotify.com/album/2jWb86KojWDnjz4WHOlclL?si=JjOuCVKhR
H2XmzQ48snbfg&dl_branch=1 (accessed 3 March 2023).
Shabazz Palaces. *Black Up* (2011). Sub Pop. Available online: https://open.spotify.com/albu
m/2dNexssEWbK7rgh0veTjjz?si=Zsp5gkvDTbqI1AA8-5P6jA&dl_branch=1 (accessed
3 March 2023).
Shabazz Palaces. *Of Light* (2009). Sub Pop and Third Man. Available online: https://
open.spotify.com/album/54TkuWdMdAVp3d7rO9epY5?si=fdQ5o6QMRy-
b3wFcLrvS0w&dl_branch=1 (accessed 3 March 2023).
Shaw, Marlena. *Woman of the Ghetto* (1969). Blue Note Records. Available online:
https://open.spotify.com/track/4kfQerxbqsZgi4uWreRjZS (accessed 3 March
2023).
She's Gotta Have It (1986). Dir. Spike Lee. Produced by 40 Acres and a Mule Filmworks.
Silence the Critics (2019). Dir. Tom Kuntz. Music by D Double E. Produced by IKEA and
Mother. Available online: https://www.youtube.com/watch?v=w0EKS2YfLc0 (accessed
3 March 2023).
Sky Captain (1984). Dir. Mary Neema Barnette. Produced by Mary Neema Barnette.
Sorry (2016). Dir. Beyoncé Knowles-Carter and Kahlil Joseph. Produced by Pulse Films.
Available online: https://www.youtube.com/watch?v=QxsmWxxouIM (accessed
3 March 2023).
Soul Train (1971 to 2006). Created by Don Cornelius. Produced by Cornelius-Griffey
Entertainment Inc, Don Cornelius Productions and Tribune Entertainment.
Stachka [Strike] (1925). Dir. Sergei Eisenstein. Produced by Goskino and Mosfilm.
Symbiopsychotaxiplasm: Take One (1968). Dir. William Greaves. Produced by Take One
Productions.
The Answer (1980). Dir. Spike Lee. Produced by Spike Lee and New York University.
The Birth of a Nation (1915). Dir. D. W. Griffith. Produced by David W. Griffith Co.
The Butler (2013). Dir. Lee Daniels. Produced by Lee Daniels Entertainment, Salamander
Pictures and Follow Through Entertainment.
The First World Festival of Negro Arts (1966). Dir. William Greaves. Produced by the
Motion Picture and Television Service of the United States Information Agency.
The Life Aquatic with Steve Zissou (2004). Dir. Wes Anderson. Produced by Touchstone
Pictures and American Empirical Pictures.
The Mirror between Us (2012). Dir. Kahlil Joseph. Produced by Intel. Available online:
https://www.youtube.com/watch?v=5_TDA5AMyVA (accessed 3 March 2023).
The Model – Chapter One: Marcello in Limbo (2010). Music by Seu Jorge.
Produced by What Matters Most. Available online: https://www.youtube.com/
watch?v=m4kgEyYfq_o (accessed 3 March 2023).

The Model – Chapter Two: Oshun and the Dream (2010). Music by Seu Jorge. Produced by What Matters Most. Available online: https://www.youtube.com/watch?v=sx7dv0OL9bU (accessed 3 March 2023).

The North Star (2013). Dir. Thomas K. Philips. Produced by LuckPig Studios, Reel Goode Productions and JRC Productions.

The Osbornes (2002–5). Created Donald Bull, CB Harding, Sarah Pillsbury and Todd Stevens. Produced by Big Head Productions and MTV Networks.

The Reflektor Tapes (2015). Dir. Kahlil Joseph. Music by Arcade Fire. Produced by What Matters Most and Pulse Films.

The Watermelon Woman (1996). Dir. Cheryl Dunye. Produced by Dancing Girl.

This Is America (2018). Dir. Hiro Murai. Music by Childish Gambino. Produced by Doomsday and Wolf + Rothstein. Available online: https://www.youtube.com/watch?v=VYOjWnS4cMY (accessed 3 March 2023).

Those Guys featuring Ras Baraka. *An American Poem* (2001). Basement Boys Music. Available online: https://www.youtube.com/watch?v=6cKxMM6ZxBM (accessed 3 March 2023).

Thriller (1983). Dir. John Landis. Music by Michael Jackson. Produced by MJJ Productions and Optimum Productions. Available online: https://www.youtube.com/watch?v=sOnqjkJTMaA (accessed 3 March 2023).

To Sleep with Anger (1990). Dir. Charles Burnett. Produced by SVS Films.

Touki Bouki (1973). Dir. Djibril Diop Mambéty. Produced by Cinegrit and Studio Kankourama.

Tula: The Revolt (2013). Dir. Jeroen Leinder. Produced by Inspire Pictures and FishEye Feature Films.

Turiyasangitanada, Alice Coltrane. *World Spirituality Classics 1: The Ecstatic Music of Alice Coltrane Turiyasangitanada* (2017). Luaka Bop. Available online: https://open.spotify.com/album/25W9Gqvwa1eWtE7s5SsLsn?si=Gfl7HjvhStu0-w0YUrfLw&dl_branch=1 (accessed 3 March 2023).

Tutu Medley (1986). Dir. Spike Lee. Available online: https://www.youtube.com/watch?v=C2NyIOJHcog (accessed 3 March 2023).

Until the Quiet Comes (2012). Dir. Kahlil Joseph. Music by Flying Lotus. Produced by What Matters Most (Omid Fatemi and Marcus Reposar). Available online: https://www.youtube.com/watch?v=-pVHC1DXQ7U (accessed 3 March 2023).

Up in Smoke (1978). Dir. Lou Adler. Produced by Paramount Pictures.

Video Girl (2014). Dir. Kahlil Joseph. Music by FKA twigs. Produced by Pulse Films. Available online: https://www.youtube.com/watch?v=2jhTiLuGezI (accessed 3 March 2023).

Video Killed the Radio Star (1980). Dir. Russel Mulcahy. Music by The Buggles. Available online: https://www.youtube.com/watch?v=W8r-tXRLazs (accessed 3 March 2023).

Vulnicura VR (2019). Dir. Miscellaneous Artists. Music by Björk. Produced by Analog Studios.

Washington, Dinah. *This Bitter Earth* (1961). Mercury Records. Available online: https://open.spotify.com/track/3MCimW1NfKKOkdqDzNsOXA (accessed 3 March 2023).

Washington, Dinah. *Unforgettable* (1961). Mercury Records. Available online: https://open.spotify.com/track/7anBVIyitaxEZIlMDJPjfb (accessed 3 March 2023).

Watchmen (2019 to Present). Created by Damon Lindelof. Produced by White Rabbit, Paramount Television, DC Entertainment and Warner Bros. Television.

Welcome II the Terrordome (1995). Dir. Ngozi Onwurah. Produced by Channel Four and Non-Aligned Films.

Wildcat (2012). Dir. Kahlil Joseph. Music by Flying Lotus. Produced by What Matters Most. Available online: https://vimeo.com/66703600 (accessed 3 March 2023).

Withers, Bill. *Ain't No Sunshine* (1971). Motown Records. Available online: https://open.spotify.com/track/1k1Bqnv2R0uJXQN4u6LKYt (accessed 3 March 2023).

Within Our Gates (1920). Dir. Oscar Micheaux. Produced by Micheaux Book & Film Company.

Without Me (Vertical Video) (2019). Dir. Colin Tilley. Music by Halsey. Available online: https://www.youtube.com/watch?v=bdPZ2Cu1vNU (accessed 3 March 2023).

Wizard of the Upper Amazon (2016). Dir. Kahlil Joseph. Music by Damian Marley (with additional score by Jeremy Gara and HEALTH).

You and Gary Oldman (2012). Dir. Kahlil Joseph. Produced by 02. Available online: https://www.campaignlive.co.uk/article/o2-you-oldman-vccp/1159632 (accessed 3 March 2023).

Zombies (2019). Dir. Baloji. Production by Baloji BBL and Pieter van Huystee PVH Film. Available online: https://www.youtube.com/watch?v=pJuZ7qhcKho (accessed 3 March 2023).

Index

A
Adesokan, Akinwumi 3, 32–5, 44, 87, 155, 159
advertisement 46, 87, 98, 155
advertisement 5, 8, 20, 24, 44–6, 51–3, 73–4, 77, 86–7, 98–100, 104–5, 110, 129, 154–6, 183–5
Afrofuturism 57, 156–8
Afro-pessimism 22–3, 187–8
Akala 189
Akomfrah, John 137, 142
Anyanwu, Onye 16, 27
Aphex Twin 111–2
Audiovisual Atlantic xviii, 1–6, 44–7, 48–53, 57, 64–6, 79, 87, 97, 101, 105, 110, 120, 129, 141, 161, 166, 186, 188

B
Baloji 163–5, 184
Bantu-Kongo cosmology 2, 12, 37, 75, 115–20
Barthes, Roland 56
Baudrillard, Jean 153–4
Bazin, André 153
Belhaven Meridian 8, 10–1, 45, 50, 53–63, 87, 98, 105, 112, 189
Black Atlantic xvi–xix, 1–4, 19–53, 57, 110, 114–20, 129–32, 137, 141, 155, 159–62, 166–72, 177–80, 183–5
Black Cultural Traffic 3, 18, 30–2, 62, 69, 116, 122, 184, 185
Black Mary 1, 109, 169, 186
Black Neoliberal Aesthetic xvi, xviii, 3, 12–17, 35–7, 40–6, 113–15, 119, 129, 135–7
Black Up 10–1, 46, 87, 97–105, 112, 128, 177
Black Visual Intonations 3, 38, 56, 70–1, 119, 123–9, 137, 142, 166
BLKNWS 47, 161, 166, 173–81

boundless (Black) time 41–2, 64, 71, 122
Bourdieu, Pierre 178, 181
Bowie, David 74, 84

C
Campt, Tina xvi, 39–43, 71, 114–15, 128, 136, 144, 172
Cheeba 45, 63–71
Childs-Davis, Faith 6, 14, 151
Chion, Michel 29, 103–4
Civil Rights 1, 46, 108, 139, 151, 178–9
Coltrane, Alice 92, 111, 121–7, 165
Coltrane, John 39, 111, 121–7
Crossroads of Aesthetics 35, 63, 71, 121–2, 155
Crossroads of Capital 32–4, 43–4, 55–7, 64, 73, 87, 90, 97, 129, 145
Crossroads of Cultural Traffic 30, 44–5, 62, 76, 95, 105, 119, 159

D
Davis, Karon 15–16, 107
Davis, Keven Joseph 6, 13–14, 46, 107, 151, 170
Davis, Noah 6–7, 14–18, 46, 107, 129, 175
De Saussure, Ferdinand 56
DeCarava, Roy 1, 109, 167–72
Deleuze, Gilles 77
Diawara, Manthia 32, 47, 51, 140–1
Dima, Vlad 54, 102–4
Diop Mambéty, Djibril 11, 48–50, 63, 101, 105, 183–4
Dovey, Lindiwe 63, 142
Du Bois, W. E. B. 21, 31–2, 54, 57, 91, 126, 150–1

E
Elam Jr., Harry J. and Kenneth Jackson 3, 30–3, 54, 60–2, 69, 78, 116, 185
Ellis, Trey 151–2
Eshun, Kodwo 124, 142, 158

Index

F
FKA twigs 2, 11, 27, 47, 62, 144–52
Fly Paper 47, 107–9, 117, 131, 161, 166–81
Flying Lotus 2, 12, 27, 53, 62, 105, 111–2, 117–19, 121–4, 153, 162, 169
Foucault, Michel 26

G
Gikandi, Simon 22–4
Gilroy, Paul 17–38, 43–7, 57, 72, 87, 90–1, 118, 144–7, 153, 179–81, 187
Gramsci, Antonio 188

H
Hall, Stuart xvi–xvii, 4–5, 34–6, 56, 113, 132
Hassler-Forest, Dan 163
Higher Education 5, 9, 188
Husayn, Shafiq 53, 63–71

I
Iglooghost 122
installation xvii–xviii, 1, 6, 8, 14, 44–7, 85, 110, 117, 121, 129–30, 136–7, 139–40, 144, 153, 163–8, 171–5, 179–81

J
Jafa, Arthur 10, 27, 38–40, 50, 60–2, 70–1, 110, 122–3, 137, 140–2, 146, 160, 173, 177
Jaji, Tsitsi Ella 3–5, 27–9
Jameson, Fredric 35, 42, 84, 185
Jenkins, Barry 16, 62, 174–5
Julius, Zara and Jenn Nkiru 3, 41–2, 144, 158

K
Korsgaard, Mathias Bonde 29, 46, 85–6

L
La Noire De … 10, 11, 50, 54–62, 177
Lamar, Kendrick 2, 11–14, 27, 46, 53, 62–4, 129–36
Lordi, Emily J. 46, 91–2, 96, 146

M
m.A.A.d. 13–15, 129–37, 168
Malick, Terrence 8–10, 17

marketed time 3, 41–2, 64, 71, 95, 104, 124
McLeod Cramer, Lauren 45, 50, 111, 166
Melville, Caspar 180–1
Mirzoeff, Nicholas 4, 35
The Model: Parts I and II 8, 24, 45, 49, 71–9, 87, 98, 105, 153–6
Molesworth, Helen 7, 18, 175
Moten, Fred 73, 165–6, 177
MTV 29, 82–4, 88, 185
Music Is My Mistress 87, 183–4

N
Neal, Mark Anthony 151
nego-feminism 4, 17, 27–8
neoliberal xvi–xviii, 3–8, 12–17, 30–7, 40–6, 72–4, 77, 83, 87–90, 100, 113–15, 119, 120, 129, 135–7, 155, 158–60, 177–8, 180, 184–8
neoliberalism xvii, 159–60, 181, 183
Nigeria 19, 32, 75
Nkiru, Jenn 3, 41–2, 51, 110, 122–4, 163–6, 169, 184
Nwonka. Clive Chijioke xvi–xix, 12, 35–41, 113–19, 135–7

O
Obioma, Nnaemeka 4–5, 27
Oshun 24, 71–8
Ozu, Yasujirō 9

P
Perrott, Lisa 3, 29, 154, 163
postcolonial 3, 18, 22
Process 8, 16, 24, 47, 74, 77, 86, 144, 152–60

Q
Queen 82, 84
queer 81

R
Raengo, Allessandra 45, 50, 55, 117, 152, 163, 166, 171
Rogers, Holly 18, 29, 131, 154, 163
Rollock, Nicola 4
Ross From Friends 112

S
Sembène, Ousmane 55, 58–9, 63
Senegal 11, 19, 55, 58, 101, 123, 159
Shabazz Palaces 53–62, 97–105, 152, 183
Shaviro, Steven 29, 35, 72, 85, 110, 155–6, 185
Sierra Leone 19, 24, 47, 144, 152–60
Smith, Alice 1–2, 27, 62, 92, 169–70
Smith, Zadie 36, 185
sonic Afro-modernity 3, 25–9
soul (logic) 46, 91–2, 95–7
soul (music) 1, 63–4, 67, 70, 91–2, 94, 97–8, 146, 149
stereomodernism 3, 28–9, 100
still-moving-images 3, 39–43, 56, 71, 114–15, 129, 157

T
Tarkovsky, Andrei 9, 116–17, 120
Tate, Greg 57, 152
Thiong'o, Ngũgĩ wa 69
Touki Bouki 11, 50, 101–5, 128

U
university 6–7, 15, 34, 45, 49, 78, 112, 132, 139, 165–6
Until the Quiet Comes 8, 12, 16, 23, 37, 46, 64, 98, 110, 111–20, 129, 153

V
Vernallis, Carol 3, 18, 29, 55–6, 154, 161–3
Video Girl 16, 47, 144–52

W
Weheliye, Alexander 3, 25–7, 41–2, 144
Wekker, Gloria 22–3
Wildcat 8, 46, 110–1, 121–9, 135

Y
Yoruba 2, 24, 72, 78–9
Young, Bradford 110

Z
Zebu 11, 100–1
Zimbabwe 24, 28, 56, 60